The NatWest Boundary Book

A LORD'S TAVERNERS AUSTRALIA
MISCELLANY OF CRICKET

PREFACE BY HRH THE DUKE OF EDINBURGH, KG.KT.

INTRODUCTION BY SIR DONALD BRADMAN, AC.

Compiled and edited by Leslie Frewin

MACMILLAN
LONDON

♻ NatWest Australia Bank

The Council and Members of The
Lord's Taverners Australia gratefully
acknowledge NatWest Australia Bank's
generous sponsorship and unfailing
support.

First published in the United Kingdom 1988 by
MACMILLAN LONDON LIMITED
4 Little Essex Street London WC2R 3LF
and Basingstoke

Associated companies in Auckland, Delhi, Dublin, Gaborone,
Hamburg, Harare, Hong Kong, Johannesburg, Kuala Lumpur,
Lagos, Manzini, Melbourne, Mexico City, Nairobi, New York,
Singapore and Tokyo.

ISBN 0-333-48420-7

Typeset by Savage Type Pty Ltd, Brisbane.
Printed in Hong Kong.

Contents

His Royal Twelfthmanship, Prince Philip, Duke of Edinburgh,
K.G., K.T. with (left) John Darling, Chairman, The Lord's
Taverners Australia, (right) John Varley, Chief Executive and
Secretary, and Mrs Avril Varley.

Leslie Frewin has a marked talent for putting together entertaining anthologies on the subject of the game of cricket. The Lords Taverners in Britain have already benefitted substantially from the publication of the original "Boundary Book" in 1962 and "Boundary Book: Second Innings" in 1986. I am delighted that he has done the same for the Australian Chapter of the Lords Taverners in Bicentennial Year, and I hope it will be equally successful.

It is sometimes said that Britain and the United States are two countries divided by a single language. I think it might equally be said that Britain and Australia are two countries divided by a single game. Ever since the first encounters between the two sides, the game has a generated a remarkable love/hate relationship between otherwise quite peaceable, and reasonably sober, citizens, who would normally take little interest in any form of sport.

This is in rather sharp contrast to the attitude of those who have proved themselves talented enough to be selected to play against each other in Test Matches. All the evidence suggests that they become firm friends - or most of them, at least.

I hope that this book will give a lot of pleasure to a lot of people, and that it will remind them that there is more to cricket than the results of a few matches. Those are over quite quickly, but the memories, the stories, the friendships and the anticipation of the next encounter go on from generation to generation. Some of the best have been collected in this book.

1987

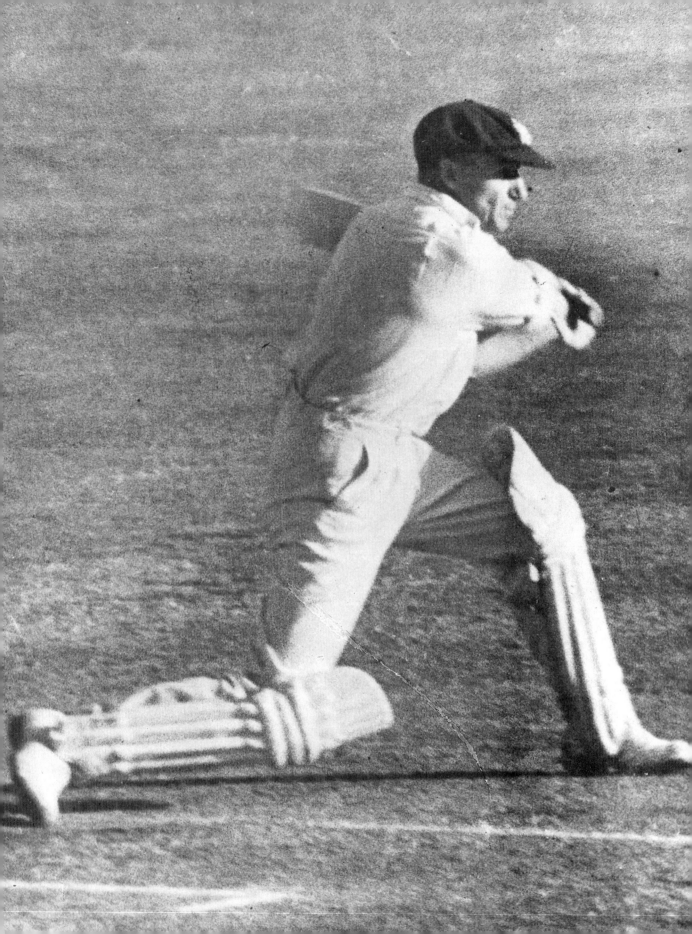

Introduction

Sir Donald Bradman, A.C.

The Lord's Taverners are very much in debt to Leslie Frewin for producing *The Boundary Book*, then later *The Boundary Book: Second Innings* — both of which were highly successful and raised substantial funds for the Lord's Taverners charities in England.

Now Leslie has kindly agreed to burn the midnight oil once again by producing the first Australian *Boundary Book*. Its production is to coincide with Australia's Bicentennial year and this time the profits are to be channelled through the Lord's Taverners Australia to aid disadvantaged Australian children.

If I might be so bold as to speak for all the contributors, I want to express my admiration to Leslie for his quite extraordinary devotion of time and energy to such a worthy cause.

To possess the talent is exceptional and to also possess the will is remarkable. No wonder he finds little difficulty in persuading others to make a modest contribution, top of the list being HRH Prince Philip, Duke of Edinburgh, whose continuing support of The Taverners is a source of pride to us all.

The first of the *Boundary* books was produced in 1962 and I thought I would refresh my memory by reading again some of the articles it contained. Immediately I was filled with a great sadness because the first article was written by the late Sir Neville Cardus (whose writings on cricket gave untold pleasure to so many) and the second was written by one of Australia's greatest sons, the late Rt. Hon. Sir Robert Menzies, former Australian Prime Minister.

They have both taken up permanent residence in the cricketer's Valhalla and without doubt will be debating the wisdom or otherwise of covered wickets or some equally absorbing subject. On second thoughts, it is more likely to be the respective merits of Victor Trumper and Wally Hammond, not so much from the angle of who was the better batsman, but which gave the greater pleasure to those who place a premium on aesthetic qualities. Cardus and Menzies both had a special eye for beauty as distinct from sheer ability.

I knew both men intimately and was enriched by

their friendship. It is sad to think we can no longer pick up a morning newspaper and be charmed by a Cardus description of what happened at Lord's the day before. Nor can we put on a dinner suit with the expectation that this evening we shall be thrilled by an after-dinner speech beyond compare from Sir Robert. I once had the good fortune to hear Lord Birkett and Sir Robert at the same function. The memory will never fade.

I did not dare pursue my quest to ascertain which other contributors to that first book had passed on, though at a glance they were numerous. Better now perhaps to give thanks for those who are still hale and hearty.

Leslie Frewin gave me an idea of who would be featured in his latest production and I was at once excited by the quality as well as the quantity. I'm pleased to say another century is recorded by the latter.

As for the quality, I was so intrigued that I decided to pick an eleven from those included — and challenge any Taverner to beat it. Here is my team in batting order.

> Sir Jack Hobbs
> Sir Leonard Hutton
> Sir Donald Bradman
> Arthur Morris
> Mike Gatting
> Richie Benaud
> Ian Johnson
> Rod Marsh
> Alec Bedser

> Dennis Lillee
> Frank Tyson
> Sam Loxton (12th man)

To ensure impartial decisions, the umpiring will be shared between 'Dickie' Bird (England) and Lou Rowan (Australia) with Steve Randell (Australia) as reserve because the match will be played in Australia in view of the final repository of the funds.

I promise I picked the team impartially, and on merit, and the outcome of five from England and six from Australia is a pure coincidence — though obviously just. I think readers would be hard-pressed to select a better eleven from the first two *Boundary* books.

The proud and successful record of the Lord's Taverners in England undoubtedly inspired the formation of the Australian offshoot. My brief encounters with the Adelaide branch lead me to believe that Australia will prove worthy of its responsibility.

In the hearts and minds of Australians, cricket is preserved just as firmly as in England and my fervent wish is that the two countries will continue to co-operate in fostering cricket and all it stands for. The game has spread its wings in recent years but the fledgling members and/or associate members of the International Cricket Conference will surely continue to seek leadership and assistance from its oldest foundation members and adversaries, England and Australia, to preach the gospel of cricket in other lands.

First knock

Leslie Frewin

I was just beginning to feel less pressurised and rather satisfied with life — always, I should have known, a dangerous condition for a professional writer.

It was early summer 1986 when the publisher collected the manuscript, layouts and illustrations of *The Boundary Book: Second Innings* from the concierge at the Heathrow Sheraton Hotel, where I had left the large parcel just two hours before I boarded a plane bound for Los Angeles. LA was to be the first stop on a lengthy and exhausting tour of American cities for my biography of Dorothy Parker. The publisher of my second cricket anthology for The Lord's Taverners of Great Britain had speeded me on my way to the States with the firm promise that an expert on cricket would stand in for me to comb the page proofs for any slips or 'literals', as they call them, misplaced pictures, captions and so on — the nightmare of all authors and anthologists. Publication of this new *Boundary Book* was to be in the late autumn, a mere few months away.

I never met the promised 'expert' who turned out to be a she! Delightful as I was told she was, I'm sad to say that as it turned out the lady couldn't distinguish a bail from a sightscreen. But I'm nothing if not gallant. *C'est la vie!* In the event, the book did fine — and continues to do so.

And so to America I went; America — the land of that happy ex-actor, Ronald Reagan, who was never so lazily home on the range as when I worked with him on the movie set at Elstree for three debilitating months, day in day out, on a film that my children today have never even heard of. I didn't see Ron this trip, as the Yanks would say, but I could probably have got his autograph if I'd tried, except that I never cared to collect autographs, least of all his, having virtually lived with pretty nearly every well-known actor and actress (yes, Audrey Hepburn, Dietrich, Garland, and the rest,if you *must* know!) through the late '40s and the '50s.

But all that was now a world away. I was feeling rather pleased with myself because the second *Boundary Book* was, then, to all intents finished and my New

York publishers were soon to bring out my new biography about which there was a lot of excitement. I also had a series of appointments lined up in America with learned Doctors of Literature, Philosophy and the rest, all in high eschelons of academe, to help me research what I planned would be a major Churchill book, for publication in 1989. This done, I had returned to my native heath having fulfilled my needs and cleared the decks, so to speak.

Who wouldn't have felt a trifle self-satisfied with life? After all, I had long since thrown off the shackles of the fast life with an apartment in Piccadilly, the centre of London's West End, and the yuppie jetset crowd of those days.

I was now living contentedly in a 16th-century cottage in a lovely Devonshire village, a seat, as they say, which had given birth and life to the celebrated Glyndebourne Opera. I could look out from my windows and see the gently swelling estuary of the River Torridge marry itself into the equally gently swelling Taw with the Atlantic stretching beyond and see from those same windows the overhung waterside, nooks and hideaways where Tarka the Otter had romped and inspired a near neighbour of mine, Henry Williamson, to write his classic tale of that name.

There was, then, nothing now to disturb my days except a modicum of regulated work and a village fete at which it was promised a golden-haired Lady Godiva would mount a honey-coloured cob right in front of my study window. I could, I felt, put up with that particular distraction. That is, until the telephone rang shortly before Christmas.

Well, the ringing telephone is a commonplace enough occurrence but this was a call from Australia, from John Varley, a sterling man and an ex-actor (and, might I say, a very *good* ex-actor) who had shared with me and others those pioneering days (lubricated by countless gallons of ripe English ale) on the forecourt of Lord's Tavern, facing the green, back in the late '50s and early '60s. (Ah, the old Tavern, a second summer home, a shelter from the stormy blast!) John had been,

and still is, Lord's Taverner No. 11 — one short of the appearance of the Twelfth Man, Prince Philip. John had long since declared to me his great affection for the original *Boundary Book* which had, in truth, become a minor classic if not a collector's item in the years since it was first published in 1962. That, too, was the year when I had been honoured with the role of Chairman of the Britain-based Lord's Taverners.

But to get back to the phone call; John fairly pointedly wanted to know if I would do another *Boundary Book!*

'But', I said, '*The Boundary Book: Second Innings* has only been out a month or two and is selling extraordinarily well'.

'No, no', said John, showing slight impatience, 'you're not with me! I mean a Lord's Taverners *Australia* Boundary Book — to be published during the Bicentennial year'.

There was, as Mr Jeffrey Archer would say, a deafening silence on the line. I *think* I caused it.

'I'm really up to my neck at the moment', I said, reminding him that I had many times turned down requests to tackle the *second* book, finally admitting to some high-level pressure which had been applied to nudge me into producing the Mark II version.

'I'm sure the Twelfth Man would give an Australian *Boundary Book* his blessing with a Preface', John went on relentlessly, 'and I'm equally sure The Don would write the opening piece for you. And there's Richie Benaud, Bill O'Reilly, Davo, Frank Tyson and lots of others who'll write for it. Think about it, will you? I'll write . . .'.

I won't go into the whys, wherefores and other machinations that John enlisted to his cause. Only it wasn't long before I was committed to take yet another long flight — this time to Sydney — where I was to carry out research, conduct a series of interviews, talk to possible contributors, meet potential publishers, fly to Canberra for a meeting with Lord's Taverners and the British High Commissioner, attend the Taverners' Aussie Ball at the Regent Hotel, Sydney, stop over for meetings with Air Vice Marshal Hall, Andrew Buckle, Trevor Butler, Mick Letts and other Taverners, and catch another flight for meetings at the Melbourne Cricket Ground with Dr John Lill, Bryce Thomas and Rex Harcourt — all this (and more — *much* more) within the space of two and a half weeks . . .

Jetlag, my limpid accomplice, seldom left me; there were times when I couldn't remember my own name. It is said that if you need a job done speedily and well you must ask a busy man to take it on. I'm not sure whether that maxim applied to me but in between bouts of the lag came a recuperative weekend at John Varley's home at the foot of the Blue Mountains, and the warm good company of his charming wife Avril and their prize-winning dogs.

Somehow I accomplished my many tasks in Australia — preliminary though they were. I even managed to chat over the telephone with a score or more of nice people like Mrs Harold Larwood and her daughter; have lunch with the talented and ever-helpful Mike Coward of the *Sydney Morning Herald*, rummaging through archives, contacting that mine of cricket knowledge, Ken Piesse, as well as making a cursory but illuminating study of the trends of Australian bookselling. (If you want to know, they are *no* different to those that exist in Britain.) There were, too, the libraries — endless pictures and words. . .

And what did I think of it all, this my first trip 'down under'? If I sound like a conventional and boring visiting Hollywood type you must forgive me. I was *truly* bowled over with what little I saw of the country and its people. And the lovely spring days engendered in me a forceful will to work (I couldn't have done much about it if they hadn't — I was hooked!).

I managed, too, to besiege John Varley's Taverners' office in Pitt Street, Sydney, with a barrage of quite specific requests. John had happily done his customary homework and many of my requests were met with the casual rejoinder, 'I thought you might want that (or those)', at which he would walk over to a file and speedily unearth just the data I needed — addresses,

telephone numbers, negatives, positives, papers, lists, documents, *et al.*

Oh, I forgot: the morning I arrived, I had sunk on my bed mentally lagged like an old pipe, hardly knowing, as the English say, whether I was Arthur or Martha, and there was John in my room for a full two hours, talking, informing. . .

I said I needed a bath. As he left, he commanded: 'Now, whatever you do, *don't* go to sleep. There's an important meeting downstairs (at the Union Club) at 1 p.m. — the very day I arrived! The General Manager and the Manager of Corporate Affairs of the NatWest Bank Australia are joining John Darling, our chairman, you and I, along with a potential publisher, for a meeting at which important decisions are to be taken. So, whatever you do, *don't go to sleep!*' The door shut silently behind him. I felt indecently tired, mentally devastated yet, at the same time, exhilarated.

That, roughly, is how it all began.

Back in England once more the hard graft of dealing with a mountain of paperwork started. And, as a result of that, countless telephone calls from cricketers, impresarios, actors, writers, journalists, authors, critics, photographers, while every post — and I mean *every* post — brought a clutch of letters from either New South Wales, the Australian Capital Territory, Queensland, Victoria, South Australia, Tasmania, Western Australia, New Zealand . . . I was sad that it had been quite impossible to visit all those inviting places where cricket and The Lord's Taverners Australia so lustily thrive and to which I was so often and so cordially invited.

And so to the reality of *The NatWest Boundary Book: A Lord's Taverners Australia Miscellany of Cricket*, in the tradition of the two previous books only bigger, and I hope, better. Here, then, it is — with a characteristically wry preface by Prince Philip and a percipient and 'challenging' Introduction by the great Don himself! These, plus a veritable host of international cricket people who have given of their time, expertise and enterprise to make possible the magical line-up of great names which the book boasts. And all have donated their services to help disadvantaged children in Australia to learn to 'play the game'.

Truly, in both content and purpose, an *embarras de richesses!*

Finally, of course, the book is so named because of the extreme generosity of The NatWest Bank Australia who met many of the constructional costs plus the cost of their own ambitious advertising and promotional campaign which will help most effectively to ensure that not only will The Lord's Taverners Australia be the originators and beneficiaries of heightened income through this book but the bank's vigorous publicity campaign will also see to it that there will be few people in the Antipodean and other cricketing territories who will not be aware of the book and the healthy existence of The Lord's Taverners 'down under'.

And its publication will additionally ensure that never again shall I indulge myself by reclining in my favourite armchair wearing a self-satisfied grin on my face! The memory of that Australian phone call will always be there.

I never did trust the telephone. Nor did I, or should I, underestimate the Taverners and their diverting brand of low cunning.

If, as Oscar Wilde said, talent is the infinite capacity for taking pains, be it known to one and all that, in the cause of charity, the Taverners are the most painstaking crowd of talented importuners one is likely to meet. And, I should add, you hardly even recognise their importunism until you are caught up in it and locked in their activities, from which there's no escape.

In short, let the publication of this ambitious book (and not least my total exhaustion!) be a lesson. But what fun it's been!

'I don't think I ever saw a bowler beat the bat as much as Davidson and this is probably because there are more right- than left-handers in the world . . .'

'Davo'

Richie Benaud

They called him 'Al Pal', or the 'Mayor of Gosford', and he was one of the finest all-round cricketers the world has seen. Few bowlers could match his late swing and awkward movement off the pitch and there weren't many better fieldsmen in any position in the world. As a batsman he more often than not turned the tide for Australia after the early batsmen had failed.

I first struck him in 1945 when he was playing for Gosford High School and represented Northern High Schools against Combined Metropolitan High Schools in a match at the end of the school season. In those days he was a hard-hitting left-hand batsman and, as always, a brilliant fieldsman, but he bowled left-arm unorthodox over the wrist deliveries rather than the ones that later made him famous. We went on our first tour together to England in 1953 and thereafter Davidson never missed a match other than through injury, nor an overseas tour. I played against him for a couple of years in this Combined School cricket and then suddenly he came from Gosford to play with Northern Districts and was an immediate success. So much so that he played his first Sheffield Shield match in 1949, only three years after leaving school cricket.

There are great cricketers in every era and Davidson was one of the greatest Australia has produced, particularly in the period from 1957 to 1963. This was after Miller and Lindwall had left the scene — Lindwall temporarily — thus allowing Davidson full scope with the new ball rather than condemning him to come on when the shine had all but disappeared. He was injury prone but never left the field or stopped bowling for any other than a very real reason. I caught Johnny Waite off him one day in Cape Town in one of those dismissals where fieldsmen and captain work on a certain plan and it happens to come off. Alan had been limping back to bowl and then boring in at the batsmen and moving the ball late, either into or away from them. Then he would limp back and Ian Craig would ask him if he were all right — he would say 'no' and get a sympathetic pat on the shoulder and then bore in again and produce yet another magnificent delivery.

The Cape Town pitch was very slow and I asked Craig if I could come up three yards at gully, for the one that flew off the thick edge and wouldn't normally carry. Davo limped back for the next ball and Waite square drove it like a bullet. I caught the red blur, body parallel to the ground, and was just rolling over for the second time when Davo arrived alongside me, saying excitedly, 'It was the old trap, you know. The old trap'. It had taken him just two seconds to get to me and the boys thought it was the quickest he had moved all day. This was the match where he was on the massage table so much that we had a copper plaque engraved and nailed on the table; it was inscribed 'The A. K. Davidson Autograph Massage Table'.

I saw Waite in South Africa some time later and he recalled this particular incident in the context of Davidson's Test performances and bowling skill. Waite contended that Alan was at his best when not feeling 100 per cent fit. He said the real danger time was when you could see him limping back or looking sorry for himself.

I have never played with or against a more penetrative opening bowler, possibly because of the particular angle in which he came at the batsman, bowling from wide of the return crease to a point just outside the off-stump and then swinging late to round about middle stump or middle and leg. He wasn't a big swinger of the ball but he certainly moved it as late as anyone I have seen, and this was one of the prime reasons that he was so successful. He only needed to hold the ball across the seam for variety, and deliver it with the same action as for the in-swinger, and I will defy any batsman in the world to pick the fact that the ball will continue straight on instead of swinging in.

He used to do this sometimes and at other times he would cut the ball away from the right-hander in a fashion that made him the joy of wicket-keeper Wally Grout and his slip fieldsmen. He and Grout used to refer jocularly to the fact that they had 'made' one another, each pointing out that the other would never have done as well without the benefit of either the bowling or wicket-keeping of the other. There was a lot in this, for Grout took some magnificent catches off Davidson, both on the off- and leg-side, and developed a great understanding with him, as well as the ability to pick the way the ball was going to slant.

I think Grout was one of the finest wicket-keepers of all time, fit to be ranked level with Tallon and Langley in my time, but in many ways he was lucky that he played in the same era as a great fast bowler who could find the edge of the bat as often as did Davidson.

I don't think I ever saw a bowler beat the bat as much as Davidson and this was probably because there are more right- than left-handers in the world and once the shine had gone from the ball he was constantly coming at them from such an angle that even if they played straight it was still possible to be beaten. Some said that he didn't like bowling against left-handers but this was a fallacy and they were really great players.

For the five years after 1957–58, whenever the side was in trouble, the captain, whether it was Craig, Harvey, or myself, always looked to Davidson and rarely did he fail. There was always the thought that at some stage he might break down but the times when he left the field could be counted on the fingers of one hand and he bowled a lot of overs for Australia and New South Wales. In the fourth Test in Adelaide in 1962–63 he badly tore a hamstring muscle but still played in the fifth, and in the first Test I ever captained in high temperature in Brisbane he left the field with heat exhaustion in the first session. There were one or two other occasions when he wasn't feeling too well but it was no wonder considering the amount of work he was given.

I used him unmercifully because he was the best bowler I had and, in fact, the best bowler in the world at that time, constantly worrying the batsmen and thinking them out even if the pitch was unsympathetic to his type of bowling. He bowled well all over the world, irrespective of conditions, sometimes concentrating on bowling as fast as he could in the initial overs and then bowling within himself with the occasional

Alan 'Davo' Davidson (right) and Neil Harvey walk on to the field for their last Test match, Australia versus MCC, February 1963.

quick delivery to unsettle the batsmen. And he could be quick, too!

He is always listed as a fast-medium bowler and indeed I think of him as such, but he could be really slippery at times and his bumper lifted at the batsman from a spot on the pitch further up than most. He rarely wasted a bouncer and generally had it about shoulder height at the batsman, and there were few bowlers who provided more difficulty with this ball than Davidson. One day in Melbourne, in the second Test in which I captained him, he had three for none in his second over — Richardson caught by Grout, Graveney lbw and Watson bowled — in an astonishing display of swing bowling. Graveney played no stroke at the ball that dismissed him and it came back so late and so quickly that he had only just begun to shuffle across when it hit him.

In England in 1961 he was uncertain of being fit for the second Test at Lord's the day before the match, when Harvey, McDonald and I were settling down to choose the side. He called me across to the massage table and said that he didn't think he'd be able to play, a statement that was a crushing blow in view of the fact that I had just declared myself unavailable to the co-selectors. I said to him that he would have to play as Neil was captaining the side and he'd need every bit of support he could get. Davidson has a great regard for Harvey and immediately said that he'd try for 'the little bloke', and he went out the next day and took five for 42, a magnificent display of fast bowling.

Marvellous character, Davo! Two of the things I'll always remember him for are when I took the fluke catch off him at Western Province that day — and how he changed from an invalid to an athletic broad jumper in two seconds to pump my hand and clap me on the back — and the day I felled him with a 'clever' throw. Wes Hall was the batsman at the SCG and he had been playing his shot and running a few yards up the pitch to try and force a throw. I was at mid-wicket and decided to pick the ball up with my back to Wes and throw the stumps down at the batting end next time he

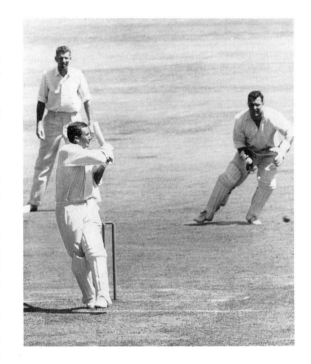

Richie Benaud pulls a ball to fine leg, Australia versus South Africa, 1964.

tried it. Unfortunately I forgot to tell Davo. The ball hit him in the throat and he went down like a felled steer — gave a final convulsive twitch and we thought he had left us. Up and about 50 seconds later, he bored in at Wes and the next delivery was just about the quickest he bowled all day.

Those two performances live in the memory but they were just two of many that set him apart from the ordinary run-of-the-mill fast bowler. In Sydney in 1962–63 he took five for 25 in England's second innings, routing them with an almost unplayable series of in-swingers and away cutters. But I suppose my fondest memory of him is at Manchester in 1961 when he and McKenzie added 98 priceless runs for the last wicket and then Davo shattered Statham's stumps to win the match late on the last day.

'. . . In desperation Blackham put forward a compromise. "If you ask me, I know a better man than either Deane or Harry, and that is Percy Lewis; but as you won't take Percy Lewis then I go straight for Kenny Burn of Tasmania". . .'

Cricket's greatest blunder

Rick Smith

Mainland Australians tend to regard Tasmanians as a race apart, the holders of peculiar ideas and often subject to strange behaviour. When a mainland Australian is introduced to a Tasmanian the response is usually to look you up and down, raise an eyebrow, and say, 'Really!', as if they don't quite believe you.

It would not come as a surprise to most Australians, then, to discover that a Tasmanian, although a somewhat innocent party, was at the bottom of this country's strangest cricket selection. It was a mistake so extraordinary that it taxes the mind to wonder how it could have occurred, even back in 1890 when communication breakdowns could have been excused. The normally staid *Wisden* went so far as to call it 'a ludicrous blunder' and 'a serious mistake'.

In those far off days, Australian cricket tours were private enterprises with the players dividing the profits at the end of the tour. The sums were, in some cases, quite impressive. Way back in 1878 George Bailey received £750, a considerable amount in those days.

When the selectors sat down to choose the 1890 team they were faced with a problem concerning wicket-keepers. First choice was John McCarthy Blackham. He had kept in the very first Test in 1877 and had held a mortgage on the job ever since. Obviously Blackham was essential to the campaign, but discussion broke down when attempting to select his deputy. The choice fluctuated between Sid Deane of New South Wales and Victoria's Jack Harry. As both had plenty of hometown support, an apparently insoluble deadlock was reached.

In desperation Blackham put forward a compromise: 'If you ask me, I know a better man than either Deane or Harry, and that is Percy Lewis; but as you won't take Percy Lewis then I go straight for Kenny Burn of Tasmania.' As most at the meeting knew little about Burn and were happy to break the deadlock, they deferred to Blackham's opinion and sent Burn an invitation to join the tour. In doing so they selected as reserve 'keeper a man who had never kept wicket in his life!

Edwin James Kenneth Burn was born near Richmond, Tasmania, on 17 September 1862. Of Scottish parentage, he showed early cricketing ability and made his debut for the island on a tour of New Zealand's South Island in 1883–84. He was relatively unsuccessful there, as were most of the batsmen, but he soon developed into a sound and consistent right-hand bat. Prior to the 1890 tour Burn's best effort was an innings of 99 against G. F. Vernon's Englishmen in 1888. As a result of that innings he was invited to appear in two of the trial matches to help select the team to tour England later that year. However he produced nothing extraordinary and missed the tour.

Kenny Burn in 1890 was a sound and talented batsman, a useful medium-pace bowler, but definitely not a wicketkeeper.

The reasons for making such an incredible selection remain unclear. Why did Blackham say what he did? Where did he get his information from? It seems that Harry Trott had praised Burn's keeping and this prompted Blackham's comments. When one asks where Trott secured this information there appears to be no obvious answer.

So the blunder was committed and the invitation duly sent. It reached Burn as he was playing in a North v South game in Launceston. As it required him to leave at very short notice he was reluctant to accept, but eventually his team mates persuaded him to go.

Arrangements were hurriedly made and Burn caught the steamer to Melbourne. Unfortunately, as his boat made its way into Port Phillip Bay it passed the ship carrying the Australians to England, via Adelaide. Burn had literally missed the boat.

However all was not lost. He caught the train to Adelaide where he would arrive before his team mates. J. J. Lyons, the South Australian big hitter, was sent to meet him and Kenny Burn made it to the Adelaide wharf to meet the boat. He had all his luggage with him: one small, black bag, which reputedly contained a change of clothes and some toiletries. What is it they say about Scots and extravagance?

When the team had digested his travelling requirements, Kenny Burn had an even greater shock for them. 'I'm here, but I've never kept wicket in my life!' One can only imagine the stunned looks as the statement was delivered — and the questions Blackham received that evening.

So the Australian team toured England in 1890 with just one wicket-keeper. From time to time others spelled Blackham behind the stumps, with skipper Billy Murdoch usually filling the role, but Kenny Burn was not one of them. His absolute refusal to do the job could not have endeared him to the team and he was selected in only five of the 17 matches before the first Test. In those games he made just 38 runs, but fate conspired to get him into the Test team. Fate certainly seemed to be on his side. S. P. Jones was seriously ill and F. Walters wasn't considered worthy, so in went Burn. He made only a handful of runs in the two Tests, the third was abandoned without a ball being bowled, and tour figures of just 355 runs at 10.14 seemed to condemn him to cricketing oblivion.

However, the Kenny Burn story did not end in 1890. He was Tasmania's first choice captain for the next 20 years as he carved out an impressive record. At the age of 46 he made a superb century against A. O. Jones's Englishmen and, in his very last game, two years later, he top scored in both innings. He had maintained an astonishing consistency which included making more than 500 runs in 15 consecutive seasons. The first Tasmanian to score 1000 runs in a season, Burn once scored seven hundreds in seven innings and on another occasion scored triple centuries in successive weeks!

There were certainly times in those 20 years when he should have played for Australia again, but he never did. The 1890 fiasco must have told against him.

The little Scotsman was a tough competitor and he did have one last laugh. He outlived all his colleagues and at the time of his death, on 20 July 1956 at the age of 93, he was the oldest living Test cricketer. Perhaps it should also be pointed out that not once in all those years did Kenny Burn ever deign to keep wicket.

Kenny Burn.

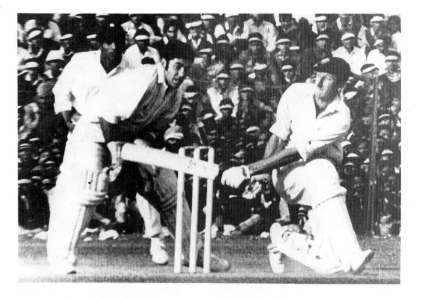

'The Phantom' strikes: Australian skipper Bill Lawry pulls Prasanna of India for four during the Australian second innings in the third Test, India versus Australia, November 1969. Lawry was born at Thornbury, Victoria. After playing club cricket he made his debut for Victoria just before his 19th birthday. In his Test debut he made 57 at Edgbaston. He won his place in the Australian Test team touring England in 1961 under Richie Benaud's leadership.

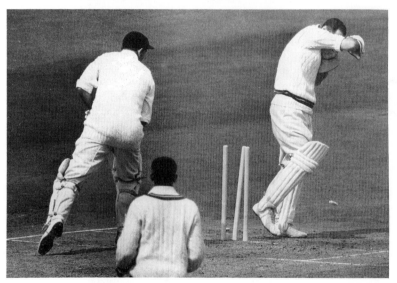

Fourth Test, England versus West Indies, fourth day, England batting, second innings, August 1966. Tom Graveney (England) is clean bowled by Lance Gibbs for 19. West Indies wicket-keeper J. Hendriks protects his face.

'So immense are Botham's energies, however, that a cricket field cannot contain them.'

The face of a champion — Ian Botham

A. W. Riter

Ian Botham aged eight.

As England tottered towards their umpteenth defeat in the West Indies, in 1986, one of their cricketers continued to enjoy life on the boundary at Port of Spain. When the crowd offered him a bottle of rum, he took a swig. When his captain called him to account for drinking, the large beefy fellow bent over for his backside to be beaten, thus providing the Trinidad crowd with the only entertainment England could offer that Easter Monday.

In many establishment eyes, this behaviour was all too typical of a person who has always tried to hit rules and conventions for six. Such larrikin antics, so the case against him goes, are unworthy of any 30-year-old sporting the England colours, and particularly of the best all-rounder England has had in its Test history, who has not only scored match-winning, spine-tingling centuries but is a handful of wickets away from the world Test record.

Ian Terence Botham may be England's lion, his critics feel, but that is no reason why he should wear a mane, and one streaked with highlights at that. The rumours of wild carousing, his conviction in February 1986 for possession of cannabis leave an impression that he is an over-confident, overweight lout. (It is not a new impression to all members of the MCC, some of whom still recall how he would fling down bad bouncers at them in the nets while he was still a teenage member of the Lord's ground staff.)

But Botham in actuality is a fellow of infinite zest. He has many 'pros' and almost as many 'cons'. He is compassionate, generous, a chivalrous opponent and, by the standards of super-stars, far from egocentric; he can be offensive, ill-disciplined, and inconsiderate of others. Yet whatever he does — batting, bowling, walking the length of Britain — he does with an energy that is rather wonderful in our tired age; and the people, if not the authorities, admire him for it.

In most people's eyes, Botham is installed as a great British sporting hero, notwithstanding his failures in the West Indies. He does not claim that status on the basis that he is the first cricketer since W. G. Grace to

Jubilant England captain David Gower holds a replica of the Ashes trophy aloft with team-mate Ian Botham at the Oval, after their triumphant win against Australia on 2 September 1985. England clinched the Ashes by an innings and 94 runs before lunch.

Hughes reaches to catch Botham off Higgs at the Sydney Cricket Ground.

Ian Botham is about to be caught by Allan Border during the Queensland versus England match at the 'Gabba, October 1986.

Umpire Alan Whitehead warning Botham for intimidatory bowling during the third Test at Trent Bridge, Nottingham, 1985.

be displayed in the National Portrait Gallery. It is a status that would be accorded him by anyone who saw the public acclaiming Botham as he walked through the streets of Britain in November 1985, as if he were not so much a Pied Piper as a latter-day prophet.

The cricket, however, had to come first. And he was a kind of miracle worker on the field from his Test debut in 1977 until April 1980. Everything he touched turned to gold man-of-the-match awards. Then he damaged his back, lost his bowling and his nerve while batting, became England captain at the age of 24, and his luck ran dry — until, in the middle of 1981, he resigned moments before he was due to be sacked.

It was, therefore, against an immediate background of human fallibility that he performed heroics of which English cricket has never seen the like. His hitting against Australia at Headingley; his batting in the next Test at Old Trafford, which *The Times* saluted on its front page as the finest Test innings; his beserk burst of bowling at Edgbaston which took five wickets for one run. So long as cricket is played, nobody is going to have three such Test matches as Botham did.

He has done more, too, than bat and bowl energeti-

cally. Cricket had liked to call itself the national game; but in pre-Botham days it had become far from that. It was, except perhaps in Yorkshire and Lancashire, the game of the middle class. It was predominantly the game of middle class, middle-aged men — and not only those who watched it, but those who played it. In the year before Botham entered the England team, more than half its players were well into their 30s, one (Brian Close) was 45.

More than anyone or anything, although it is an unquantifiable matter, Botham has popularised cricket in the last decade to make it a truly national game. He has given cricket a virile image to replace the old one of two men with plastic macs, sandwiches and a dog. Thereby he has attracted the football supporter to go along and see the summer game; he has attracted both sexes, most classes and all ages. Love him or hate him, he has generated huge publicity for cricket.

Not that everyone has welcomed this development. It is not so long since a patrician voice was heard to murmur in the Lord's Long Room: 'I warned you, you know, that we should never have let that chap out of the corporals' mess.'

So immense are Botham's energies, however, that a cricket field cannot contain them and they have spilt over into a variety of activities, one of them illegal. In February 1985 he was fined £100, with £25 in costs, for the possession of cannabis, following a police raid on his former Humberside home (he has since moved to North Yorkshire with his wife Kathy and three children). But it cost him much more, including his contract with Saab and free car.

He goes salmon fishing every September. He owns a couple of racehorses. He has had a go at motor racing (sometimes on the M5) and at flying. He has hit a golf ball at the Belfry as far as Ballesteros. In the United States he has attempted baseball and an acting career, since his former Walter Mitty manager, Tim Hudson, believed Botham could give Hollywood another facelift. But he spent three weeks unnoticed in Malibu, to Botham's considerable but bravely disguised disgust. Then, Botham decided that walking from John o' Groats to Land's End would be a suitable challenge for his energies, and in accomplishing that walk in aid of a charity, the Leukaemia Research Fund, he graduated from cricket to national hero. He may also have sapped his fabled constitution.

The better to appreciate what those 874 miles entailed, take the day that began at Molineux, the football ground of Wolverhampton Wanderers. Soon after eight o'clock it grew light and a few schoolchildren assembled. At 8.30 Botham and his three fellow walkers arrived, the town crier rang his bell and everyone set off.

At first the procession comprised no more than 50 but a lot of police were around to clear the traffic, while the late Ted Moult with a stick led the way. The two oldest of the four main walkers were shuffling along by this stage on sore shins, bad ankles, strained backs and rickety knee-joints. Botham and John Border, brother of Allan the Australian captain, kept them going with ribald urgings, and by the time they left Wolverhampton their number had swollen to 150.

Kidderminster at lunchtime provided a tremendous reception, wide-eyed schoolkids waving flags, bands playing, money thrown into the buckets carried by volunteers. From factory floors they came to shout 'Good on yer, Ian!'. There was an immense rapport, as if he had been drinking with everyone the night before. And everyone can identify with Botham, since he does not represent any particular region or social group (his father works for Westland, his younger brother is a farm worker). And there, now and again, were the victims of leukaemia whom he would either touch or carry along the road for a while. 'It was not quite palm fronds and donkeys in Jerusalem,' said one observer, 'but he does have this simple tug on people.'

The afternoon was a question of supporting the stragglers, Botham dropping back to rally the troops. In the last five miles the psychological games began: 'It's just over the hill', when the end was still another hour away. But Botham and Border jigged and jogged, turning a cartwheel or two, until his wife appeared with their five-day-old daughter Rebecca, whom in turn he carried along.

Once the stage was over, his feet made an appalling sight: not just blisters but four large, open sores bigger than ten-pence pieces. And there were still another 10 days to go. But more than £800,000 has been raised for leukaemia research.

So why do so many newspapers try to do him down? The answer, partly, is that Botham is a man of his times, but more particularly of the English *Sun* newspaper. He has a contract with them worth £37,500 a year, and out of circulation rivalry some of the other tabloids try to make him into an anti-hero.

The prime reason, though, why the media have been attacking Botham is that, for once in his career, he failed to single-handedly rescue England in the summer of 1986. The West Indian fast bowlers were mowing down all the batsmen and not even the man of infinite zest was able to stop them. But he remains an entertainer who constantly entertains, and stands up to the scrutiny of newspapers and television no worse than most folk heroes.

A fine action shot of Dirk Wellham, former NSW and Australian player, taken during the NSW v Queensland match at Sydney Cricket Ground in January 1986.

Dr Cashman, a leading cricket historian, has produced much valuable work not least on crowds in both India and Australia. His 'Ave a Go, Yer Mug: Australian Cricket Crowds from Larrikin to Ocker won the Literary Award of the Australian Cricket Society for 1984–85. His biography of Spofforth is soon to be published.

27 May 1878

Richard Cashman

No less authority than Lord Hawke contended that the game played at Lord's on Monday 27 May 1878, when Australia (41 and 1–12) beat the MCC (33 and 19) by nine wickets, 'marked the commencement of the modern era of cricket'.

What is regarded as the first official Australian tour started inauspiciously. There was not much enthusiasm for what fast bowler Fred Spofforth later referred to as 'our somewhat experimental tour' in cricket circles, nor was there much press coverage when the team left Australia. At least one local paper, the *Argus*, was not all that sanguine about the future of Australian tours to England: it predicted, on 4 October 1877, that visits of this kind were not likely to be of frequent occurrence. When the team sailed out of Sydney for Brisbane on the first leg of their Australasian tour on 3 November 1877, the demonstration on the wharf was of the 'mildest description'. The tour was organised as a private venture, the leading associations, the New South Wales Cricket Association and the Victorian Cricketers' Association not only withheld their patronage but played no role whatsoever in the organisation of the tour, the selection of the team or the financing of the venture. The team had no blazers — though they did have blue and white caps — and no baggage master; two took it in turns to drag an immense canvas bag until it was lost in London early in the tour. With the team performing well in its initial tour of the Australian colonies, there was a little more public enthusiasm when the team finally departed Sydney on 29 March bound for San Francisco.

English officialdom, too, was rather dubious about the colonials: influential Surrey secretary Charles Alcock commented later that 'the idea of a visit from an Australian team . . . was at first treated as something of a joke by our English cricketers . . . we were slow to accredit the Colonials with the extraordinary advance they had in reality made in the development of the sport which they had learned from English professors'. There was no certainty that the tour would be a financial success and the players, who had each contributed £50 on the basis of a joint stock company, stood to lose money.

Conditions, too, favoured the strong MCC side playing on its home ground. The Australians had only arrived in England two weeks prior on 13 May and, after a few days' practice at Trent Bridge in what *Wisden* referred to as 'boisterous ungenial cricketing weather', had played just one match against the powerful Notts side where they were easily defeated (by an innings and 14 runs) in trying conditions on a very sloppy wicket. Spofforth, who found it difficult to hold a swollen and soft ball and to obtain a foothold on the slippery turf, was 'innocuous' and relatively expensive (1/39) in a low-scoring game in which the English champion, Alfred Shaw, returned 11/55. The Australians, inadequately clothed in light silk shirts and no under-vests 'shivered in the cold wind'. So it was a difficult assignment to take on the cream of the English players so soon in the tour before the visitors had run into any real form.

The match had an added dimension in that it was regarded as of more significance, and a much greater test for the Australians, than what are now recognised as the first two Tests which were played in Australia in March 1878. Australia had the distinction of winning the very first Test by 45 runs (although it lost the second) but the victory, while very significant to Australians, did not loom as large in the eyes of the English *cognoscenti* as it was not achieved against a representative English team: the Australians were pitted against a team of professionals which did not include many of the leading batsmen, such as the amateurs W. G. Grace and A. N. Hornby.

So when the MCC picked a side which included most of the leading amateurs and professionals and, in the opinion of one English paper, *Globe*, 'was as good a one as could be found to represent London and England, and probably nearly as good as the Club had ever turned out', it was assumed as a matter of course that the MCC would win. After all, the MCC attack was shouldered by Shaw and Morley, who had bested the

The famous cartoon of 'the Demon' Spofforth. 'A tall, lean, wiry athlete inly lit / With mind, and saturnine control of it.'

Australian batsmen at Nottingham, just seven days before, and most commentators believed that the English batsmen were a class above their colonial counterparts.

The Illustrated Sporting and Dramatic News, commenting on 1 June, after the game was played and lost, thought that the MCC XI 'had a blemish or two in strength' but had to admit that the side was 'a decidedly good one'.

Conditions at Lord's on 27 May — the weather was cold and unsettled and the pitch was very sodden — should have favoured the home team but it was the

Australian bowlers Spofforth (10/20) and Boyle (9/17) who humbled the MCC twice in a day. The home club had started badly, losing W. G. off the second ball and declining to 2/5 when Boyle bowled Booth for no score. Grace, who was dismissed by Frank Allan — who never quite lived up to his extravagant nickname 'Bowler of the Century' — may well have been guilty of overconfidence as he hit the first ball to the square leg boundary and was caught, off the next, at square leg. Hornby and Ridley then added 20 runs against Allan and Boyle to take the score to 2/25. The introduction of Spofforth, as first-change bowler, altered the situation dramatically: he took six wickets for just four runs off 23 balls including a hat-trick, the first of three in first-class cricket. It was an unusual hat-trick: after Hearne was bowled for 0, the next two batsmen, Shaw and Vernon, were both stumped by Murdoch, also for no score. It was also the first of two first-class hat-tricks in just seven months, Spofforth took the first hat-trick in Test cricket, at Melbourne on 2 January 1879. From this point on the MCC lost another 18 wickets for just 27 runs. All told Spofforth bowled 59 balls for 20 runs and 10 wickets; in today's terms, a wicket every over.

Many of the spectators who rushed to the ground after the first innings collapse of the MCC — the crowd is said to have swelled from one to five thousand during the day — must have anticipated that the MCC would make amends in the second innings, particularly after Shaw and Morley had hit back to dismiss the Australians for just 41 runs with Shaw taking 5/10 off 134 balls. This was not the case, the second innings of the MCC began and ended even more disastrously than the first. W. G. Grace was dropped by Murdoch off Spofforth's very first ball only to be bowled by the next, 'a beautiful breakback'. A. J. Webbe was bowled by the very next ball. Boyle's first over was equally sensational: he bowled Booth on the second and Ridley on the fourth ball. When Spofforth hit Hornby in the following over, and he was forced to retire for one, five MCC batsmen were back in the pavilion, and four were out, for just one run!

Hornby returned later in the innings, with W. G. as his runner, but soon fell to Boyle. The MCC never recovered and were dismissed for just 19 runs. The Australians easily hit up the runs required for victory for the loss of just one wicket. It was Harry Boyle who took the bowling honours in the second innings returning the impressive figures of 6/3 off 33 balls. Although Spofforth's figures in this innings were less impressive (he took 4/16 off 36 balls), he made the initial critical breakthrough in that he accounted for the champion, Grace, and took the sting out of Hornby's batting. (W. G. had a relatively poor season against the Australians: just 56 in five innings at an average of 11.2.)

The match was all over in four and a half hours. The news spread like wildfire and created a sensation in London and throughout England. *Punch* acclaimed the victory with a poem which included a celebrated pun:

The Australian came down like a wolf on the fold,
The Mary'bone Cracks for a trifle were bowled;
Our Grace before dinner was very soon done,
And our Grace after dinner did not get a run.

Chastened by the experience, the MCC challenged the Australians to a return fixture on the following day but the visitors declined on the grounds that a rest day would be welcome given the arduous tour timetable. Perhaps, too, they sensed that they had nothing to gain from a second encounter with the MCC.

The English press was at a loss to explain the defeat of the MCC: the Australians, claimed the *Pall Mall Gazette*, had no 'consummate an all-rounder' of the stature of Grace, nor did they have 'such [a] master of the [bowling] craft' as Alfred Shaw. This is an interesting comment, which appeared the day after the match, because the writer still believed that the MCC had the better batting and bowling. So explanations of defeat drew on the 'element of luck', the 'strangeness' of the Australian bowling and the 'contemptible' batting of the MCC who presumably underestimated their opponents: the same newspaper was scathing of the home bats: 'men who are so nervous or so out of practice that they cannot keep half-volleys out of their wickets have no right to appear in a first-class match.'

The one point that the English press were prepared to concede was that the Australians were a fine fielding side and superior to the English team. During the tour it was noted that the Australians pioneered the practice of more attacking and aggressive fielding rather than bowling to set fields: dispensing with long-leg and long-slip, popularising the silly mid-on position, which became known as Boyley's Mid-on (because he became a specialist there) and returning the ball to the 'keeper on the full from the deep whereas the English practice had always been to return it on the first bounce. Six of the eleven, Spofforth later claimed, could throw a cricket ball more than 100 yards and the Australian throwing was more accurate than the English. The Australians also had a number of very fast movers, including Tommy Horan and Alec Bannerman. Jack Blackham, who was an exceptional wicket-keeper of pioneering technique and who had introduced the practice of 'keeping without a long stop — thereby providing an extra fieldsman in an attacking position — was the focal point of the fielding 'attack'. Much of the credit for the imaginative field placements and changes of bowling must go to the tour captain, Dave Gregory. On 27 May 1878 the Australian field, while not flawless, was much admired.

The importance of the victory cannot be overestimated because it proved that the Australians could be worthy opposition to the leading English teams and, as the *Sporting Life* correctly predicted on 29 May, 'the Australians are sure to draw wherever they go'. The victory assured that the 1878 tour would be a profitable venture and helped establish tours as an attractive and money-generating proposition. The victory also created the suspicion, which was proven to be a reality as the tour progressed, that while England might still have an edge in batting, the tourists' bowling, in addition to the fielding, was superior to the English.

Spofforth himself later reflected on the significance of this victory:

I well remember that, when we left Lord's and returned to our hotel, we could scarcely realise our victory, and all the evening callers kept pouring in with congratulations. It is impossible to over-estimate the importance of this victory in its effect on the future matches and the destiny of Australian cricket, for another defeat like that at Nottingham might have made us lose heart, besides giving the English public a far lower idea of our merits than we deserved.

It is interesting to note that, while Spofforth and Boyle were equal partners in the destruction of the MCC (their figures were almost identical — Spofforth (10/20) took one more wicket but Boyle (9/17) had the slightly better average), it was Spofforth who dominated the media limelight. Tom Horan later recalled that whenever their train stopped on the way to future engagements, a crowd would gather round the carriage enquiring: 'which be Spoffen?' Spofforth and Boyle are not remembered as a pair in the same way that Turner and Ferris, Gregory and McDonald, Lindwall and Miller were.

There are a number of reasons for this. Over the 1878 tour, as a whole, and on subsequent tours Spofforth proved that he was a far better bowler than medium-paced Boyle whose outstanding feature was his 'unerring accuracy', his ability to tie up one end, so that the strike bowler, Spofforth, could operate from the other end. It was Spofforth who created uncertainty and fear in the mind of England's star batsman, W. G. Grace. Most critics of the time did not rate Boyle as a top-class bowler.

Spofforth's star status was enhanced by his much-admired spirit, his combative personality and his striking physical presence. Tall, gaunt, eminently recognisable, with a prominent nose, Spofforth seemed to reflect the popular physical notions of what the Devil looked like, hence the nickname 'The Demon'. Physically he was the perfect foil for his arch rival, the ebullient, overpowering and, in today's terms, overweight batsman W. G. Grace, the archetypal John Bull, whose ever-expanding girth and luxuriant facial growth reflected the expansionary mood of the Victorian era; a time when a thickening girth and a spreading empire were not frowned upon. Spofforth represented the antithesis of this image.

27 May 1878 was an important day in the life of Fred Spofforth; it was the day when he first really staked his claim to be a world-class bowler. When the team left Australia the *Sydney Morning Herald* published pen portraits of the tourists. Among them was 'F. Spofforth — The fastest bowler in the world, perhaps; varies his pace with great success; pretty fair batsman and excellent field'. By the time the tour ended, some 15 months later, Spofforth was generally regarded not only as the quickest but as the best bowler in the world by some leading authorities. 'His bowling', stated the editor of *John Lillywhite's Cricketers' Companion for 1879*, 'I consider second to none in the world.'

The Lord's cricket match was also the day in which Spofforth's nickname, 'The Demon' became more widely and universally recognised. 'The Demon' from this day superseded all other nicknames including 'The Windjammer', a Sydney term for a yorker, 'Loup' and a delightful schoolboy invention, 'Legs and wings'.

It wasn't the day, however, when Spofforth was first called a demon because the 'demon' association was around well before 27 May 1878. There are Australian and even English references which establish this. It was from this day, however, that 'The Demon' nickname became more widely, even universally, recognised simply because it was on this day that Spofforth's claim to international stardom was established.

There is another rather fanciful story about how 'The Demon' acquired his name which suggests that an excited Spofforth could not contain himself after his 10-wicket haul and jumped around the dressing room exclaiming: 'I'm a Demon.' This alleged happening doesn't ring true with the Spofforth personality. Fred Spofforth could be volatile at times but was not particularly demonstrative on or off the field.

It was Spofforth, too, who achieved many accolades outside cricket circles. He was only the second crick-

eter to appear in a 'Spy' cartoon in the *Vanity Fair* series. W. G. Grace was the first cricketer in the series; his cartoon, which appeared on 9 June 1877, was simply captioned 'Cricket'. Spofforth's caricature appeared on 13 July 1878 and was labelled 'The Demon' and became one of the most famous and much reproduced cartoons in the *Vanity Fair* series. The original sold for £2200 in 1985. Spofforth was the first Australian so honoured and only another two appeared in the series of 47 prints produced between 1877 and 1913: George Bonnor in 1884 and Sammy Woods, who was Australian-born but who played all his senior cricket in England, in 1892.

Buoyed by their success at Lord's, the Australians more than held their own with many of the best elevens in the country. They won 10 (drew four and lost five) of the eleven-a-side games. When the Australian team steamed into Sydney on 25 November 1878 they were met by an enormous flotilla on the harbour and a crowd of 20,000 gathered at Circular Quay, about one-tenth of the city, to meet the team. They were, as Spofforth later recalled, the 'heroes of the hour':

I shall never forget the reception — an immense contrast to our cool 'send off'. Innumerable steamers and rowing boats came down to Port Jackson to meet us, and all the principal streets of the city were decorated with flags and flowers, while the old motto, 'Advance Australia' seemed to span every corner. We were driven through the town by Mr Want, in a four-horse coach, and at the Town Hall the Mayor met us and presented an address of congratulation. At Melbourne and Adelaide the same thing was repeated.

The match at Lord's on 27 May 1878 did in fact usher in the modern era of cricket. Before that time the English domestic cricket occupied the centre stage and tours to other countries, while profitable, were of peripheral interest. By proving themselves competitive, the 1878 Australians gave international cricket a great boost and altered forever the landscape of English and overseas cricket.

'After a week's gentle cricket in Hobart in Tasmania — where at the Wrest Point Casino I made my customary annual donation to the croupier's benevolent fund . . .'

'Blowers' Down Under

Henry Blofeld

Australia has become a second home for me and when I landed in Sydney on Sunday 16 October 1983, it was my eleventh visit to the country. It was all gloriously familiar, especially when my all-Australian taxi driver — unusual these days for they are mostly new Australians, usually from Greece — turned to me at a traffic light and said in ringing tones, 'What have you lot gone and done to Geoff Boycott then?'. The Sunday papers proclaimed loudly on the battle for the Australian captaincy between Kim Hughes and Rod Marsh. I knew I was back.

The first-ever five-Test series against Pakistan was unlikely to set Australian pulses racing too fast, but, when it was over, the beloved West Indies were to fly in to make up the third side for the one-day Benson & Hedges World Series Cup competition. It was a season for which the Packer-owned marketing arm of the Australian Cricket Board had found the disarming catch-phrase of 'Thunder Downunder'.

It looked like being muted thunder, for Pakistan's leading player and captain, Imran Khan, was unlikely to be fit. The stress fracture to his left shin had not healed properly and there was the likelihood that he would only be able to play as a batsman (as indeed happened).

While Australia won the series more easily than their 2–0 margin of victory suggested and the cricket as a contest was at times rather less than interesting, a great deal happened to make an amusing, intriguing and memorable summer. The domestic political problems which govern Pakistan cricket were seen at their most absurd and were a constant background to the action in Australia.

Abdul Qadir's leg-breaks had their moments; little Qasim Omar revealed himself as a potential winner of the Victoria Cross when it came to taking on Australia's fast bowlers; and finally, Greg Chappell, Dennis Lillee and Rod Marsh all played their last Test match for Australia, with Lillee keeping one last blazing row with the authorities going right to the end of his career.

I am still not sure that I fully understood the machinations of Pakistan's politicians or the exact course of all that happened in Lahore and Karachi, which succeeded only in undermining the team in Australia. It all began some time before the players left home when the selectors chose as captain Zaheer Abbas who had taken Pakistan to India in September, where by all accounts he had not done much of a job.

The Chairman of the Board of Control for Cricket in Pakistan, Air Marshal Nur Khan, immediately replaced Zaheer with Imran who had presumably assured the Air Marshal of his fitness, but apparently without producing any medical evidence in support. Imran then insisted on making some changes to the party, and one of those who had originally been chosen and was now left out was Shoaib Mohammad, the son of the 'Little Master', Hanif. Unwittingly, Shoaib had become a political hot potato because the chairman of the selectors, Haseeb Asan, who had picked the side for Australia, was a permanent house guest of Shoaib's father.

When Pakistan arrived in Brisbane for the first match of the tour, Imran saw a specialist who immediately prescribed a complete rest and no cricket for at least 15 days. This news brought howls of anguish from Karachi which supports Zaheer, the local boy — Imran's home is in Lahore — and petitions were sent to General Zia, the President of Pakistan, demanding that Nur Khan be sacked. It was hardly the ideal start for Pakistan and not a ball had been bowled.

The tempo was maintained when a satisfying piece of scandal erupted in Australia. News came winging through from the west that Dennis Lillee had been offered the vice-captaincy of Western Australia which he had graciously accepted. Later that day, he was interviewed by Bob Maumill on Perth radio station 6PR — the great man was not currently talking to the newspapers in Perth — and was asked if his acceptance meant that he had made it up with the State captain, Kim Hughes.

'Just because I have a drink with a bloke in the bar, it doesn't mean I am showing my sexual preferences,' came the illuminating reply.

Pakistan politics did not sit on the sidelines for long — it soon became clear that without Imran's bowling Pakistan badly needed the services of Sarfraz Nawaz. Sarfraz had not been selected for the recent tour of India and had dared openly to criticise the selectors for failing to do so.

For his pains he was banned from international cricket for six months by the Pakistan board. While we were in Adelaide for the South Australian game, news came through that Sarfraz had been officially reprieved and that his arrival was imminent.

The first Test in Perth was played on a green pitch: Pakistan's batsmen were overwhelmed by Australia's four fast bowlers and Australia won by an innings. Wayne Phillips, lucky to play his first Test innings against such a poor attack, made 159 for Australia, but it was Qasim Omar's bravery that really stole the show. In the first innings he batted 150 minutes for 48 and never flinched once, although he was hit all over the body. When he was finally out, he lay on the massage table in the pavilion while the Pakistan physio applied ice-packs to the worst of the bruises. Five were in place and as he approached with a sixth, Omar smiled up at him and said, 'Wouldn't it be better if I got into the fridge?'.

At the Sydney Cricket Ground in the New South Wales game I saw the magnificent new electronic scoreboard in action for the first time. In the pavilion I came across Channel 9's newest commentator, actress Kate Fitzpatrick, interviewing Imran and brushing up on her leg-breaks and googlies. Then, on the Saturday evening, I found myself with Imran at David Bowie's party at the Sebel Town House after a concert at the Showground. I am afraid I gave the hero a dreadful ear-bashing.

It was Pakistan politics again in Brisbane. It had become clear in Sydney after more medical advice that Imran was not going to be able to play until the fourth Test and then only as a batsman. Just before the second Test at the Gabba, word had come through from Pakistan that Zaheer had been appointed over Imran as the official tour captain. Zaheer's immediate reaction was to summon Sarfraz and batsman Salim Malik from Pakistan. According to information at the time, the much-harassed manager, Intikhab Alam, spent most of the night trying to track down Air Marshal Nur Khan for confirmation. He eventually ran him to ground in London and, by all accounts, Nur Khan instantly re-appointed Imran in between the pips.

When I arrived in Pakistan with the England side the following March, I was told that Zaheer had indeed been appointed, but that his most influential supporters in Karachi had got on to him in Brisbane and told him on no account to accept, for he was on a hiding to nothing. Their view was that this was Imran's side, it was going to be a disastrous tour in any event and Zaheer should keep his distance and allow Imran to take the blame. Accordingly, Imran was re-appointed. Rain prevented another Australian victory and when the Pakistanis flew into Melbourne they were met by the redoubtable Sarfraz whom the Pakistan authorities at home had located in Bombay.

Tennis was the game uppermost in many people's minds in Melbourne, for the Australian Open was being played at Kooyong where I spent a happy if rather wet day. At the Melbourne Cricket Ground, two 100s by Mudassar and one by Javed Miandad brought Pakistan a splendid victory after Victoria had batted for most of the first two days. It was my first glimpse of the splendid new MCG press box, which is both warm and comfortable. In Melbourne I joined Radio 3UZ's commentary team with former Victoria players Ian Meckiff, Ray Jordan and Jack Potter in addition to John Mackinnon — and we all had a lot of fun in a jokey TMS sort of way.

Then it was Adelaide for the third Test where the Pakistanis were joined by Salim Malik, to the surprise of some, since it was thought that, when Imran had returned to the captaincy in Brisbane, he had endorsed Sarfraz's invitation but had rescinded Salim's — I could never understand why Salim was not originally selected, for he is one of the outstanding young batsmen in

the world. It was Sarfraz more than anyone who lifted Pakistan's performance in this match after a disastrous first day. He enabled them to draw the match after taking them to a position from which they just might have won, but Abdul Qadir still insisted on bowling round the wicket to Australia's phalanx of left-handers. Qasim Omar made 100. Mohsin Khan made 150 and Lillee took 6 for 171 and gave a press conference to wave two fingers at those who had been writing him off.

After a week's gentle cricket at Hobart in Tasmania — where at the Wrest Point Casino I made my customary annual donation to the croupier's benevolent fund — it was on to Melbourne for Christmas and the fourth Test. Mohsin Khan made another big 100, Imran batted well and again Pakistan batted themselves into a position which could have brought victory. But Graham Yallop then made 200 and the straight bat and cool nerve of Imran steered Pakistan through to an anxious draw on the last day.

Remarkably, the series was therefore still undecided when the sides foregathered in Sydney for the fifth Test. As it happened, the game was very one-sided with Australia winning by 10 wickets, but by the end it had become a truly momentous occasion.

The first incident of note came on the first day when Greg Chappell caught Mudassar at second slip off Lawson and equalled Colin Cowdrey's record of 120 catches in Test cricket. Then, late on the second day, Sarfraz played forward to Lillee and was lbw giving Lillee his 350th Test wicket. Moments later Rod Marsh caught Azeem Hafeez off Lillee and took his tally of Test dismissals to 350.

During the day, rumours of Greg Chappell's impending retirement had been circulating round the ground and now as he left the field he confirmed the news when interviewed by his brother Ian in front of the Channel 9 television cameras. I don't know whether Lillee's nose had been put out of joint by this news, but inside the pavilion he now decided that he too was going to call it a day.

By now, Lillee was quite expert at giving press conferences and he gave another with considerable aplomb the next morning in the Noble Stand. He told us he was going to retire to a farm in the depths of Western Australia and enjoy the simple things of life. Greg Chappell then signed off with a magnificent innings of 182, which took him past Sir Donald Bradman's Australian record of 6996 runs. Lillee and Marsh took the number of dismissals to 355. It was a fairytale ending for all of them.

One of the most historic photographs ever taken of a touring Australian Test party. With King George V and Queen Mary at Windsor Castle, 1934, are (left to right) Grimmett, Bromley, Brown, Darling, Kippax, Ponsford, Barnett, Bull, O'Reilly, Woodfull, Fleetwood-Smith, Chipperfield, Wall, Bushby, Oldfield, Ebeling and McCabe. Bradman was not present due to illness.

*The Australian team celebrate
victory led by captain Allan Border
(second from right), England
versus Australia, second Test,
Lord's, July 1985.*

Master of University House and recently retired as Emeritus Professor of English at Australian National University, Canberra, and a Member of the Australian Academy of Humanities, Professor Elliott delivered the following speech at the ACT branch of The Lord's Taverners Australia in 1987.

A touch of the crics

Ralph Elliott

Professor Ralph Elliott.

After I had accepted your kind invitation to propose a toast to a tavernful of cricketers, I realised that as I knew practically nothing about cricket, I needed to do some homework on this esoteric subject, despite Lord Snow's off-putting comment: 'Try explaining cricket to an intelligent foreigner. It is harder than explaining Chomsky's generational grammar.' Well, I did once have a go at Chomsky, so I persevered with cricket.

There are in fact several crickets, I discovered; indeed, there are some 2400 species of them, all belonging to the orthopterous family of *Gryllidae*, which is the Latin name for grasshoppers, also known as W. G. Gracehoppers. They are omnivorous, which in plain English means that they eat up their opponents, usually on large grassy plots or village greens.

The word 'cricket' itself appears to derive from the French verb *criquer*, which means 'to creak', and it is said that the males of the species produce a strange sound, technically known as 'stridulation', by rubbing together their leathery forewings. Whether this sound is of an amorous or belligerent nature I have not been able to ascertain; it probably signifies both.

So far so good. Being a lifelong student of English letters, I next turned to some of my favourite authors — Shakespeare, Milton, Dickens — for further enlightenment. It was John Milton who coined the phrase 'cricket on the hearth', which was probably a misprint for 'cricket on the heath', which the poet failed to notice because he was, after all, blind. Cricket or crickets, I imagine, were more probably to be encountered on a heath, even in Milton's time, than on a hearth, although the later association with ashes no doubt derives from this unfortunate typographical error.

Charles Dickens, unaware of the misprint, adopted Milton's phrase as the title of one of his Christmas stories. I suspect that Dickens was not at all sure what he was talking about when in this story he makes the improbable Mrs Dorothy Peerybingle exclaim: 'To have a cricket on the hearth is the luckiest thing in all

'A Kind of Cricket and Bowls'. From the border of The Romance of Alexander, *a manuscript in the Bodleian Library, Oxford, written and illuminated circa 1340.*

the world.' She and her husband, the equally improbable John Peerybingle, were a blessed pair, well matched, whose affections had stood the test of time — you could almost call it a Test match — hence it is not surprising that John should think of his wife, in Dicken's inimitable phrase, as 'his cricket in chief', or captain, as we would now say. No doubt, he stridulated vigorously, happily rubbing his leathery forewings together, while thus addressing his beloved.

But other activities besides stridulation, I discovered, are associated with cricket. It is, I understand, a sport. And here we do well to remember the classic definition of sport by that great French sportsman Jean-Marie Brohm: 'Sport,' explained Monsieur Brohm in 1975 with admirable succinctness, 'is an armoured apparatus for coercion, an instrument of bourgeois hegemony in a Gramscian sense, dominated by a phallocratic and fascistoid idea of virility. It is mechanisation of the body conceived on a robot, ruled by the principle of productivity.'

Virility, conception, productivity — I seemed to be getting closer to the secrets of sport in general and of cricket in particular. Was the Earl of Gloucester in the opening scene of Shakespeare's *King Lear* thinking of cricket when he referred to the begetting of his bastard son Edmund as 'there was good sport at his making'? Was Milton thinking yet again of cricket on the hearth or on the heath when he wrote about 'sporting with Amaryllis in the shade'?

Be that as it may; there must have been rivals for the umbrageous favours of Amaryllis, because we next hear of the use of a small staff or crutch, known as a 'cric', with which lovers of the sport armed themselves against their opponents who were in the habit of lobbing small, hard, round objects at them. We have graphic illustration of such confrontation from an ecclesiastical source, which adds a religious dimension to our subject. After all, the Lord's Taverners are indeed 'the *Lord's* Taverners', *tabernarii Domini* in the language of the Church. There is evidence that the confrontation I mentioned occurred in medieval monasteries (which in a curiously duplicated spelling have come to be known in South Australia as 'Chappells'), as we know from a fourteenth-century illumination in a Bodleian Library manuscript in Oxford. This pictures a monk of the Benedictine, or as some would have it the Benaudictine, Order brandishing a 'cric' at another monk about to lob a small, hard, round object at him. Meanwhile other monks appear to be lolling about the pasture, probably stridulating, and occasionally exclaiming 'qui est?', which in modern colloquial English could be rendered as 'how's that?'.

There is another curious thing about these monastic pastimes. As they were clearly a bit short of leathery forewings to be rubbed together, these clerics apparently used to rub those small, hard, round objects vigorously along their cassocks, leaving conspicuous leathery marks, a peculiar custom which appears to have survived to this day among those who subscribe to the doctrines of the *tabernarii Domini*.

The round object is still with us, a small, very hard ball, which caused the well-known British actor Robert Morley to declare with justifiable conviction that 'the ball is man's most disastrous invention, not excluding the wheel'. This surely is a judgement which anyone would heartily endorse who has ever been struck by a ball whether on safari through the Bobby Simpson Desert, or promenading along the edge of Rodney Marsh, or, for that matter, while quietly sporting with Amaryllis on the village green to the shouts of 'how's that?'.

Certain conclusions emerge from these lexical, literary, zoological, and historical observations which, if you will permit me, I will now share with you.

Of the two major species of cricket, the stridulating and the sporting, it seems to me that the Lord's Taverners are primarily connected with the latter. The sport or game of cricket is sometimes thought of as a leisurely, peaceful, Sunday afternoon pastime, with sunhats, and deck chairs, and cool drinks, the chirpings of 2400 *Gryllidae* punctuated by the sound of ball on bat and occasionally drowned by applause as another ball splashes into the Dennis Lillee Pond on the boundary. The very antithesis, in other words, to cruel bloodsports like rugby or Australian Rules, or for that matter boxing, which has been aptly described as 'the only sport in the world where two guys get paid for something they'd be arrested for if they got drunk and did it for nothing'.

But even cricketers can be bloodthirsty, as I discovered to my dismay. Did not the great Jeff Thomson say, not long ago, that 'it won't take much work to get me psyched up to hating anyone'? Is it humanly possible to hurl a small, hard, round object, not unlike a bullet, at a fellow human being without aggressive intent? Is it humanly possible to wield a 'cric' in self-defence without hitting back at your adversary with all possible violence? Is it to be wondered at that Rod Marsh referred in his book *The Inside Edge* to one Test as 'A cricket field? It looked like a bloody battlefield'?

The survival rate is high, however, higher than in the other sports I have mentioned. I ascribe this, among other factors, to the religious connotations of a sport once practised by monks, to the relatively innocuous lifestyles of grasshoppers, and not least to the preference of discretion over valour, so well exemplified by the distinguished company of The Lord's Taverners here assembled. Who would not willingly exchange the 'cric' for the cup, the bat for the beaker, the Test for the Tavern? Where better to dream or converse in hushed tones of the Great Constantine, of the Allan Border country, of the legendary Don flowing quietly through Australian cricket history, of the wondrous pleasure dome of Imran Khan, the Lion of Pakistan, once acclaimed as the sexiest and most glamorous cricketer in the world, of whom Samuel Taylor Coleridge would have sung had he not confused him with Kubla Khan, — where indeed than among your fellow *tabernarii*, for whom 'stridulation' rhymes with 'adulation' and for whom the chirping of the cricket on hearth or oval brings back some of the happiest memories of their lives?

Your Excellencies, Mr Chairman, Sir John, Taverners, Ladies and Gentlemen, I give you the toast to 'The Lord's Taverners Australia'.

'Indeed, the law of Australian cricket is replete with stirring and romantic stories of the dizzy progress of adolescence . . .'

The young lions

Mike Coward

Mike Coward.

Australians have regarded precocious cricketers as a rich natural resource and a national treasure since 18-year-old Tom Garrett opened the bowling in the first Test match. For more than 100 years their flowering has been considered inevitable; as profitable and as satisfying as the ritual harvesting of wheat and wool.

The passage of time, however, has wrought great changes. By and large, nowadays, the country's economic health is determined by what lies beneath and not atop the wide brown land. Much the same can be said of Australian cricket. Its future prosperity depends on a wealth which is still to be unearthed. In summers gone, only rarely was there cause to question the existence of untapped stocks. Indeed, was there not an inexhaustible supply, even an embarrassment of riches?

Those sunny, heady days are now but a faded memory. The gods have turned their backs; the green baggy cap has lost its form. Despite the unprecedented popular appeal of the one truly national sporting passion, Australian cricket approaches the 1990s in convulsions; in the throes of a commodity crisis.

To the discomfort of a people historically obsessed with sports, no longer can it be presumed that a Garrett, an Archie Jackson, a Neil Harvey or a Doug Walters is waiting in the wings.

Such was the plight of Australian Test cricket at the time of the country's bicentennial celebrations that the game's hierarchy were compelled to take initiatives hitherto unthinkable. First, there was the formal appointment of the indefatigable Bob Simpson as national coach. Second was the establishment, in Adelaide, of the Australian Institute of Sport's cricket academy.

Jointly funded by the Federal Government, the South Australian Government, the SA Cricket Association, the Australian Cricket Board and a corporate sponsor, the academy provides a stage for the elite young cricketers of tomorrow to strut their stuff before chief coach Jack Potter, the erstwhile Victorian captain and peripheral Test batsman.

Other than being bold and imaginative, such enterprise can be interpreted as a tacit admission by the overlords of the utter collapse of the traditional education processes which once ensured a lofty standing for Australia throughout the international cricket community. The disintegration of the infrastructure is a consequence of the most turbulent and painful period in the history of Australian cricket — 1977 to 1987.

As strong and imposing as it seemed, the framework was unable to withstand the strain of the great divide of 1977–79 and, barely six years later, the herding of opportunities and mercenaries by South African cricket authorities.

Australian cricket, which once stood so tall, approached the 1990s on its knees. Its plight, and the complex question of its future, was debated with characteristic animation. Indeed, within the fraternity, the inquisition was deemed to be more important than the extravagant salutes to self-esteem that were the bicentennial celebrations.

Ian Chappell, whose jousts with authority have been lavishly documented for more than 20 years, made some particularly pertinent and acerbic observations as a journalist and commentator. And, as ever, he was prepared to apportion blame. Chappell, who remains a demigod to the *hoi polloi* and the enfant terrible or agent provacateur to the establishment, charged the game's most influential administrators with culpable neglect of duty.

While he has been party to revolution and, at times, an unabashed confrontationist, Chappell is of pure stock and, at heart, a concerned cricket traditionalist.

'There is a lack of cricket knowledge at the top level of Australian cricket. It has not been recognised that the traditional education process has broken down,' he says. 'If we are saying now [in May 1987] that the Australian cricket team is ordinary and Australian cricket is ordinary, then if something isn't done very quickly it could be a hell of a lot worse in five years time.

'In the past we've always said another Lillee or Walters or Harvey will come along and, sure, they

have. But I'm not sure whether we now have the system to produce them. I think we have to work out ways of producing them.' And not one cry of 'heretic' was heard throughout the land.

Potter, either oblivious to or unconcerned at the politicised nature of his new office, was also forthright. 'I don't think the Australian Cricket Board had thought about the need for it [the academy] because Australia was being carried through by Lillee, the Chappells, Marsh, Walters, Thomson and the rest. There should have been a nurturing, a nursery of talent but I don't think they [the ACB] ever thought these guys would break down or get old.'

Simpson, who surely now has returned more often to centre stage than did Melba, is not so dispirited. While with great reluctance he concedes that Bowral is unlikely to provide an unsuspecting world with another Don Bradman, Simpson retains faith in the system. He is optimistic that somewhere, be it in an urban ghetto or in the mulga, a prodigy is bound to emerge.

As coach of the Test team, Simpson is devoting all his energies to the re-establishment of the powerful peer-group procedure, once the strength of Australian cricket. He is convinced that much of the cancer is benign and can be eradicated if this and subsequent generations of cricketers again care for and coach each other and leave a worthwhile legacy by taking a legitimate interest in the welfare of the Australian game.

While the cynical consider Simpson to be a timeworn altruist, his devotees, predominantly those who have grown weary of the selfishness which pervades contemporary cricket, point to the fact that he successfully turned back the clock in 1977.

It is not, of course, as though Australia has been utterly bereft of youthful players of daring and promise in recent years. Indeed, Craig McDermott was aged 19 and about to make an impression in England when he won high praise from Clive Lloyd, and Stephen Waugh was just six months into his 21st year when his abundant all-round skills were formally recognised by despairing selectors.

From the formative days of Australian cricket, a healthy regard has always been paid to the special gifts and ambitions of the young. On countless occasions selectors have hurried the rarely talented into the international arena, safe in the knowledge that they will be taught the lessons of cricket and life by wise old hands.

Indeed, the lore of Australian cricket is replete with stirring and romantic stories of the dizzy progress of adolescents; of the debut for Victoria by Len Junor at the age of 15 and 265 days, of Jack Badcock's graduation to the first-class ranks at 15 and 313 days and of the grand entrance to the South Australian XI by the incomparable Clem Hill at 16 and nine days after he had scored 360 in an inter-collegiate match. Ian Craig played the first of 11 Tests at the age of 17 and 239 days — indeed, he was at the helm at 22 — and Archie Jackson, Neil Harvey and Doug Walters scored their first Test hundreds at 19.

So, what of the future? Will Australian cricket continue to place such store in the might of the young? Is there a band of brave young warriors intent on restoring lustre to the image of Australian cricket before the turn of the century? While the likes of Graeme Hick and Mohammad Azharuddin remain well concealed there is a group of fledglings whose potential has aroused considerable attention and interest.

Perhaps inspired by the deeds of Allan Border, a modern master, and Dean Jones, who at the age of 25 presented his credentials in Madras, they have a priceless opportunity to lead a renaissance movement. It is, of course, fraught with danger to nominate those who will comprise the vanguard. Indeed, the current state of Australian cricket is such that the pundits, along with those who divine, tend to shy away from the tasks they once so relished.

Be that as it may, let it not be said that the indigenous scribbler has lost his sense of intrepidity. In halcyon days, incomparable fast bowlers were synonymous with the Australian game. From Spofforth to Lillee they served with true grit. Unquestionably, the paucity of quality pacemen since Lillee has had much to do with the decline; the abject loss of power, pride and influence.

It could be that a young man of European descent, Andris (Andrew) Zesers, has the capacity to relieve this suffering. A strapping son of a Latvian couple who immigrated in 1948, Zesers is possessed of boundless energy and a wicked, quicker short delivery and is intent on developing a wider range of pace. Others of his ilk whose cards can be marked are Chris Killen, Paul Stepto, Paul Carew, a left-armer, and Allister de Winter, who is being encouraged to approach front-line duty with greater intensity.

Western Australia, which since the days of Tony Lock and John Inverarity has nurtured so many capable players, is now offering for assessment the talents of Tom Moody, a tall, aggressive batsman who confesses to a penchant for the limited-over game and Mark Palmer, a wicket-keeper who is said to have turned the head of Rodney Marsh.

To the east reside Mark Taylor, a left-handed opening batsman more intent on occupation than improvisation, Ian Stenhouse, a powerful left-handed number three, Geoff Parker, an upper-order batsman of special skills and Joe Scuderi who first produced his all-round wares in the tropical north of Queensland.

Cometh the moment . . . Go forth young men: a country awaits, pregnant in anticipation of the rebirth of Australian cricket.

'The only time I played cricket was at school when I was forced to, otherwise it was the whip.'

State of play

**Jimmy Edwards DFC, MA
(and don't you forget it!)**

'The Prof' Jimmy Edwards holds forth.

I've been a little bit what the Americans call 'uptight' about writing this piece because (a) I'm not getting paid for it and (b) It cost me a hundred bucks to attend a recent Taverners' Ball in Sydney. I would also like to correct our revered announcer at the ball that I was *not* a past Chairman of the Lord's Taverners but a past President — if I may say so. There is of course a fine distinction — and I am the only past President in England who has never been to Lord's and doesn't intend to go!

Inherently and basically, I am not a keen cricketer — well, *'chacun a son gout'* as the French say. I have other leanings or proclivities. The only time I played cricket was at school when I was forced to, otherwise it was the whip. And in my school magazine it was said at the end of my first term in the school eleven — it is eleven, isn't it? — 'Edwards Minor — a player of great *bonhomie*, always convulsed with laughter when bowled, usually for a duck' — and that's about as far as my cricketing career has gone.

I play other games, of course. Our Twelfth Man and I have literally brushed shoulders in the sport we both shared for some years — what the Cockneys called 'Orse 'Ockey' — 'Ockey on 'Orseback'. Some people call it polo. I've always said it was a very dangerous game, but at least you get knocked about by posh people! I remember riding off the ground and saying to Prince Philip, 'Why don't you ride close to me, Your Royal Highness, and you'll get your picture in the papers.' And suddenly there it was in the *Daily Mirror*. And underneath it the caption read 'Jim and friend'.

There have been more serious occasions when I was playing against His Royal Highness. On one such occasion it was his birthday — I don't remember which one and it would be indelicate of me to mention it. As we were coming off the ground I said to him, 'I wonder if it would be an appropriate moment for me to wish you many happy returns?' He said to me very kindly, 'Why don't you bring your team up to the tent for a drink?' Like an idiot I said, 'Which tent?' He said, 'The one with the Royal Standard on it, of course!'.

I must say the last Taverners' Ball was more loaded with protocol than I was prepared for. I wasn't expecting a band who had failed to tune up. I was prepared for the National Anthem. But I wasn't prepared for what followed it. A tune invented by Gough Whitlam, if I remember — the words of which have mercifully eluded me. But a lot of people ask me — and of course there's a simple answer — why I am in the third *Boundary Book*? One thing is to get a bit of publicity — and the other thing, of course, is that I have now lived in Australia for two years.

I live in a place called Perth which is at the end of the great country. There I have become a ratepayer which is a little embarrassing. But I am now thinking of standing as Mayor of Cottesloe. Well, I mean, if Clint Eastwood can do it, so can I.

There are so many things that I love about Australia. As it happens, before moving here, I had been to Australia more than 25 times. In fact, to slightly misquote an immigration officer when I came through on my tenth visit: 'Jeez Jim, not you again!' You can imagine if you like what he really did say! But like a good Briton, I have been to all the Australian States. I can remember a delicious occasion in Brisbane when I was eating oysters with my dear friend Eric Sykes, who is *not* a polo player — he has one or two other things in his favour. We had the oysters and the waiter turned out to be one of those extraordinary ethnic gentlemen from the extraordinarily immense country called Ethnia, which is entirely stuffed with incipient taxi drivers. This fellow was, in fact, a head waiter. He said (and I will effect the accent if I may): ' 'Ow did you like the oysters, Mr Jimmy?'

I said, 'They were very nice in their way but I would rather have had Whitstables'. So he said, 'Have some Whitstables with your steak. Any Whitstables you like, carrots, peas?' Yes, I love the sort of abandoned things people say in Australia. I've learnt to face up to the country and its habits now. You say to a chap 'How far is it from Sydney to Melbourne?' and he says, 'four vodkas'.

There was once a wonderful moment in Tasmania — I dare say some of you have suffered Hobart. I was there on a rather wet Friday evening and a gentleman showed me to my bedroom which was in a pub. Outside there was a ghastly sort of concrete freize, no light coming in. He said, 'You might like to know, Mr Edwards, this is the very room that Tony Hancock slept in the week before he committed suicide'. And I said, 'I can well see how the idea came into his head'.

One is never entirely alone in Australia. I am now fixed up in Perth and what I love — and I must pay tribute to the ABC which purveys classical music 24 hours a day — is that they do have some wonderful announcers who effect the Pommy accent better than I. There was one the other day who said: 'Now we have the sports news from England. The Grand National was run at Aintree, and was won by . . .' whatever it was and 'in the semi-final of the football cup, Everton beat Sheffield 2–1 on Wednesday.' Ah, well, never mind.

At the risk of pushing my luck, I will tell you an actual joke as I am meant to be a comedian — but, remember, I am doing it for nothing. This is about an Irishman — most of the jokes are about Irishmen — who was told by his doctor that he should put a fresh pair of socks on every day. By Sunday he couldn't get his boots on. The same Irishman was told by a friend that oysters improved your sexual urge, drive and success. He went down to the shop and bought a dozen. The next morning he went back to the shop and said, 'I want some of my money back. Three of them didn't work'.

I don't know whether any of you have done any motor car driving in Australia. It's hair-raising. In England, I was driving along the M1 — it's been open for 12 years and under repair for 10. I was motoring up it some time last year when I saw a police car in my mirror. I knew it was a police car because on the roof it said ECILOP. So I pulled into the side and as he came towards me I said, 'Officer, I was not exceeding the speed limit'. He said, 'It's nothing to do with that, Sir, but I think you should know that about a mile back your door opened and your wife fell out'. I said, 'Thank heavens you told me, I thought I had gone deaf for a minute'.

One more police joke: A policeman went out on night duty and came back a little earlier than expected and found his wife in bed with three other gentlemen. He stood at the door of the bedroom and said 'Ullo, Ullo, Ullo'. And she said, 'What's the matter, darling? Aren't you talking to me?'

Finally, two policemen were standing in Piccadilly Circus late at night. One turned to the other and said, 'Ere, I can't wait to get home and tear the wife's knick-ers off'. The other one said, 'Why's that?' And he said, 'They're killing me'.

As I said, I have visited Australia many times and one of the things which disturbs me is that it is such a diffuse country, so many warring elements, so many people don't like the other part of Australia: in Perth they call Sydney and it environs 'The Eastern States' and in Sydney they call Perth, 'The Other End'. I do hope that one day, through the good offices of the Lord's Taverners, we might start some sort of . . . unification.

And that's enough for now.

'Who knows what the outcome of the 1932–33 rubber would have been if that one delivery from a bush bowler had been a fraction to the right!'

Australian and English cricket — *vive la difference!*

Frank Tyson

I could see that my mate Alan was having a bit of trouble with the opening bowlers. As the new 'Pommie' medico, he had been roped into playing in the first game of the season for Sale-Maffra in the Australian bush in Gippsland. My college recollections of his batting was that he was the archetypal player, raised on a diet of all that was best in the Golden Age of the game. He was tall, fair-haired and addicted to the easeful front-foot drive which automatically stamped him as a product of the English public school system. He used to be renowned at university for his 'not a man move' off-side strokes which kept the spectators on that side of the wicket busier than the opposing fieldsmen.

Now here he was, placed in the front line of responsibility, embarrassed by the untoward bounce of an unfamiliar concrete pitch, and definitely struggling

Frank 'The Typhoon' Tyson.

against Antipodean bush bowlers. After the first hour's play 'the Doc' was exactly 1 not out. His drives had been placed to perfection and sped over the cropped infield only to be pulled up dead by the no-man's land of foot-high grass which flourished uncut only 20 metres from the pitch! Finally Alan's skipper could stand the inaction no longer. He rested his can of Fosters on a tree stump and rose from his seat beneath a shady gum tree to advance halfway to the wicket to deliver spenetic advice: 'Stop poncing around Doc, and hit the bloody ball in the air! That's the only way you'll score runs in this bloody comp!'

Aussie country cricketers are pragmatic, competitive, crafty to a degree and bonny fighters to boot. One of the favourite run-making ploys of Alan's Maffra team-mates was to steer the ball into a clump of bushes and long grass at square leg and advise the opposing fieldsmen against pursuit because of the brown snakes which lurked there! Once a hostile fast bowler from the Gippsland area all but averted the calamity of the 1932–33 bodyline Test series between England and Australia. Just before the first Test in Sydney, the provocative English skipper, Douglas Jardine, took a few days sabbatical leave 'huntin' and shootin'' with the Gilder family in Gippsland. The son of the Gilder's had attended Oxford University with Jardine.

A Saturday afternoon tour of the local cricket scene brought Jardine and his hosts face to face with a game in which a certain bowler of electrifying speed called Lonegan was playing. Jardine was persuaded to 'have a hit' against Lonegan. The latter bowled only one delivery, which reared from just short of a length and missed Jardine's patrician brow by a millimetre before thudding into the 'keeper's gloves. Discretion being the better part of valour, Jardine withdrew. But who knows what the outcome of the 1932–33 rubber would have been if that one delivery from a bush bowler had been a fraction to the right!

There have been demon bowlers from the outback whose self-esteem transcended their true ability. One such individual once interrupted an evening talk given by the Australian fast bowler Ernie McCormick to a cricket club in the Dandenong hills near Melbourne. Ernie had spent the afternoon coaching youngsters and finished the session with a demonstration of fast bowling which splintered the orange box targets specially provided for this spectacular display. An interested spectactor of the day's events was a black spade-bearded giant who in the Australian vernacular was built like a country dunny.

This individual now interrupted Ernie's talk with the remark: 'McCormick, you're no quick bowler. I'm two yards faster than you. My run-up is so long that I have to run into the ground to bowl. It's only when I get to the oval itself, that the batsmen stand up!' So saying, the bearded one slammed out of the room, mounted his horse tethered outside and rode off into the darkness and the hills!

'Mac' was still remembered by the Australian public even at the time of the Centenary Test in 1977, by which stage he was 70. The septuagenarian was entering the Melbourne Cricket Ground to attend a cocktail party when he was accosted by a youngster, obviously an obituary writer in the making, who asked him with pertinent impertinence: 'Excuse me mister, didn't you use to be Ernie McCormick?'

It was only by sheer chance that McCormick became a quickie. When he first arrived at the Richmond Cricket Club in the early 1920s he was a tall, gangly wicket-keeper, who seemed to spend most of his time at practice bowling at an embarrassingly live pace in the junior nets. One evening he was invited to test the skills of the club senior players; when one of his first deliveries hit the first eleven skipper, Les Keating, on the head, Ernie's future as a Test fast bowler was sealed.

By the common consensus of his contemporary batsmen, Ernie was one of the speediest of pre-Second World War bowlers. And it was not just international batsmen who vouched for the fact. On one occasion the big paceman opened the attack for Richmond in a preseason practice match up-country. His first delivery hit the opposing batsman full-toss on the toe and the stricken unfortunate was carried off the field to take no further part in the game. 'Mac' forgot the incident until he met the victim of his 'toe-crusher' at a football match the following winter. Ernie was on his way to a convivial lunch in the Richmond clubrooms before the game when he spotted his former opponent on the terrace below. He threw him a wave, but the man was not willing to allow the opportunity to pass of showing the fast bowler the result of his handiwork. He followed him and arrived in front of Ernie's table just as he was about to tuck into an enormous steak.

'Do you remember hitting me on the toe in Richmond's practice match?' he began. 'Look what you did!' So saying, he peeled off his left shoe and sock and plonked his foot on the table alongside Ernie's plate. His misshapen big toe was still a horrible sight; it looked like a brown onion. 'Mac' expressed his regret politely and honour having been satisfied, his victim replaced his sock and shoe and departed leaving behind him a table sitting in stunned, amused silence.

After a few moments, George, one of the lunchers, spoke up: 'I can only say Ernie, that I am glad that you did not hit him in the box!'

Ernie had that most precious possession of any cricketer and the *sine qua non* of any fast bowler: a sense of humour. During the 1938 Australian tour of England, he was having a lot of trouble with his run-up and began the opening match of the season at Worcester with one of the longest overs ever seen in first-class cricket. As the number of balls extended well into double figures, a team-mate approached him at the end of his run and asked him if he was okay.

'I'm alright,' replied Ernie, 'I'm just a bit deaf from the umpire shouting in my ear. And I think that he's getting a bit hoarse too!'

My mate Alan could take consolation from Ernie's Worcester experience. Apparently Australian cricketers sometimes have as much difficulty with English conditions as he had with the demon bowlers from the bush and the Gippsland outfields!

Australian fast bowler Ernie McCormick.

First Test, England versus New Zealand, Lord's, July 1969. R. C. Motz is bowled by Derek Underwood for 15.

O W Z A T

'Lord Ted' Dexter of England is bowled by McKenzie for 10 during the fourth Test, England versus Australia at Headingley, July 1968.

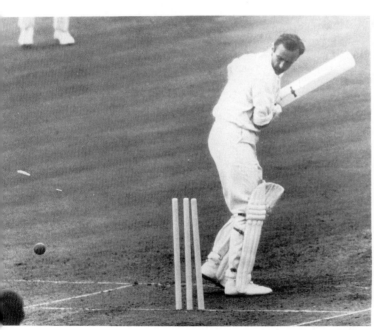

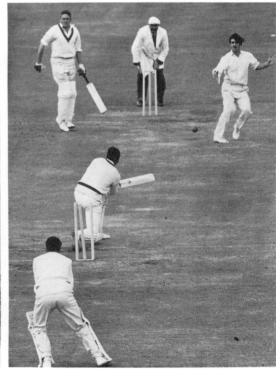

Left: Aussie captain Greg Chappell is bowled by Alan Jones for 21 at Lord's, MCC versus Australia, May 1977.

43

Freddie Trueman bowls Australian captain Richie Benaud for a duck in the third Test between Australia and England at Leeds, July 1961. England won by eight wickets.

Bill O'Reilly gets Compton, the young England player, after he had scored 14 during the first Test (first day) England versus Australia, July 1938.

Bedser is bowled by Johnston for a duck during the final day of the final Test, England versus Australia, at the Oval, Kennington, August 1949.

England opener Graham Gooch is bowled for 115 during the one-day international versus Australia at Edgbaston, June 1985.

This unique photograph is of famed cricket writer E. W. ('Jim') Swanton holding the Wisden of 1940, which he had with him throughout the war and during his incarceration as a prisoner of the Japanese. The book is bound in old gas-caping and was read by more people than any other single copy of Wisden — it went in and out of innumerable POW libraries as Swanton and his fellow prisoners were moved up river. Desmond Jackson, whom the editor brought together with Jim Swanton through the following article, declares that the 1940 Wisden was, indeed, the most sought-after book in Tarso. To join the library there, it was necessary to contribute a book which was recovered on leaving the camp. Jackson had two books — both of good 'swop' value — Green Rushes by Maurice Walsh and Captain Blood by Sabatini. To borrow the Wisden it was necessary to have your name on a waiting list. When your turn arrived you could only keep it for 24 hours. Desmond Jackson waited two months and, by illegally using a peanut oil light, read it for about 20 of his 24 hours.

'Good evening. This is the Allied Broadcasting Corporation transmitting from Tarso and tonight Radio Newsreel brings you a cricketing feature about the world's greatest batsman . . .'

Radio newsreel — POW style

Desmond H. Jackson

Desmond H. Jackson.

I was having an afternoon rest, still suffering from the effects of a severe bout of malaria, when I heard someone speaking to me from the foot of my uncomfortable bunk.

'What did you say?' I muttered as I recognised Reg McWilliams, a fellow Tasmanian, grinning down at me.

'I said, are you going to Radio Newsreel tonight? It's ''The Life of Bradman'',' answered Reg, who offered no apology for breaking into my siesta.

'Of course I am. Nothing could make me miss that,' I replied. 'Will we go together?'

'Right, I'll pick you up at a quarter to seven.'

I nodded and Reg ambled out of the long hospital hut in which I had been a patient for several weeks.

It was January 1944 and the place was Tarso, a grim prisoner-of-war base camp in the jungle on the Burma-Siam Railway, 130 kilometres from its starting point in Thailand. Comprising a large number of bamboo huts, roofed with matted palm fronds called atap, it was built close to the east bank of the River Kwa Noi and its inmates were mainly seriously ill survivors of railway construction gangs.

As in all Japanese POW camps, food rations were extremely inadequate and discipline was harsh. Immediate physical punishment was inflicted on a prisoner who committed even a slight breach of the strict code of conduct to which everyone was subject and guards, with bayonets fixed, constantly patrolled the camp area.

Death was an ever-present spectre in the dank atmosphere of Tarso and funerals of dead prisoners were daily occurrences, despite the great skill and dedication of the camp's Allied medical officers, who worked tirelessly under primitive conditions, with virtually no drugs or equipment.

Tarso was a sinister hell-hole of suffering and despair: a place where the sick either died or recovered some degree of health, only to be sent away to perform more slave labour for their captors.

But there was one bright aspect — the Japanese permitted the prisoners to have limited entertainment and one of the important weekly events was Tuesday night's 'Radio Newsreel', a show which was usually produced by Major E. W. (Jim) Swanton, known throughout the cricketing world as an outstanding commentator. Like Reg McWilliams and me, Swanton was recovering from a long and terrible ordeal on the railway and soon after his arrival at Tarso he joined the camp entertainment committee.

With the authority of the Japanese, the committee had created an open air theatre, utilising a small concave hill which rose steeply from a flat area at its foot. A stage of bamboo and covered with matting was built on the flat land and the POW audience simply sat on the slopes of the hill.

On Tuesdays, a structure shaped like a huge radio set was placed in the centre of the stage. Also made of bamboo and matting, it was about nine feet tall by seven feet wide. Some two feet from its top, a rectangular section had been cut away and crude lamps burning peanut oil were placed on a ledge behind and below the aperture to give the impression of a lighted dial. Under that, there was a 'speaker' — a large round hole covered with hessian — while wings of high bamboo matting extended from each side of the radio set to the edges of the stage, effectively screening actors and assistants from the audience on the hill.

The weekly 'Radio Newsreel' programs were entertaining documentaries, read by performers who stood behind the 'speaker' of the radio and 'The Life of Bradman' promised to be of particular interest, especially to the Australians and the British.

When Reg and I sat down on the hill, it was already crowded and there was a loud hum of excited conversation. Not so different to a theatre at home I thought. It was a cool night but the sky was cloudless with no wind and most had brought something to sit on as a defence against the early dew. At 7 o'clock, all fell silent and the well modulated voice of an invisible announcer opened the show.

'Good evening. This is the Allied Broadcasting Corporation transmitting from Tarso and tonight Radio Newsreel brings you a cricketing feature about the world's greatest batsman. Our programme is "The Life of Bradman" and will be presented by the well-known sporting personality, E. W. (Jim) Swanton.'

After some warm applause, Major Swanton's pleasing English voice came clearly through the speaker.

'Donald George Bradman was born at Cootamundra in New South Wales on the 27th August, 1908. He was the youngest of five children and in 1911, the family moved to Bowral, about 85 miles south-west of Sydney.'

Already, the audience was warming to the subject. 'In his early childhood, he enjoyed music and showed promise at a number of games — tennis, rugby, athletics and, of course, cricket.'

Swanton then described how Bradman gradually developed his batting talents by throwing a golf ball against a curved, brick tank-stand and hitting the rebounding ball with a cricket stump and by employing a similar method to sharpen his fielding. By this time, each man present was so engrossed in the performance that he had quite forgotten his problems and his unhappy lot.

'While he was still a schoolboy, he was making high scores for the Bowral town club in the Berrima District Association and by the time he was 17, the competition was dominated by Bradman and a young bowler who played for Wingello — none other than W. J. (Bill) O'Reilly.

'In the summer of 1926, Bradman joined St George, the Sydney grade club, and in December 1927 he was selected in the New South Wales team for its Sheffield Shield match against South Australia at Adelaide. He scored a century in his very first innings and so, his illustrious first-class career began on a high note.'

The men on the hill, now completely lost in the enthralling subject, stirred in anticipation. Many, including me, had seen Bradman bat and most knew the basic facts of his story but we all listened as though we were hearing about him for the first time.

'He scored 134 not out against Victoria at the end of

his first year and his good form continued into the 1928-29 season when England, led by A. P. F. Chapman, toured Australia. Bradman was an automatic choice for the first Test at Brisbane and the Australian public simmered with anticipation. But, alas, he failed, his scores being only 18 and 1.'

A quiet groan escaped from the audience and I was glad to note that this depressing information was received with dismay by the English as well as the Australians.

'Worse still, Australia, caught on a sticky wicket, was beaten by a record 675 runs and for the second Test, which England won by eight wickets, Bradman was dropped to 12th man.'

From the hill came a spontaneous murmur of disapproval.

'But he really launched his international career in the third Test at Melbourne where he scored 79 and 112. Australia lost that match and also the next — both by narrow margins — but they won the fifth Test by 5 wickets, largely due to Bradman's 123 and 37 not out.'

A cheer went up from the Australians and the Major was quick to put things in proper perspective by referring to the remarkable achievements in that series of W. R. Hammond who amassed 905 runs at an average of 113.

'Just the same,' continued Swanton, 'the outstanding innings of that season came from Bradman who gave notice of his true potential by hitting his first mammoth score — 340 not out against Victoria. And the 1690 first-class runs he made in 1928-29 still remains an Australian record. In the following year, he went from strength to strength and in January 1930, on the Sydney Cricket Ground, he broke Bill Ponsford's world record score of 437 by hitting an incredible 452 not out in 415 minutes. Both these innings were against unfortunate Queensland. That [domestic] season, Bradman scored 1586 runs in 16 visits to the wicket at an average of 113.'

The listening cricket lovers in the audience lapped up the impressive statistics and secretly yearned for more. Swanton did not let them down. He went on to describe the impact which this cricketing prodigy had on the English public when the Australian team led by Woodfull, arrived in England for the 1930 season. Immediately, Bradman gave a taste of his genius — 236 in the opening match at Worcester and 185 not out in the next at Leicester. Many triumphs followed, including a marvellous 254 in the second Test at Lords and then came the third Test at Headingley, Leeds.

'Australia batted first and when Archie Jackson was out for 1 Bradman came in, virtually as an opener. By late afternoon, he had reached 283, four short of the previous highest Test innings, made by R. E. Foster of England in 1903. The excitement of Bradman passing Foster's score was captured vividly by this historic recording.'

There was a short pause during which a murmur of puzzled curiosity ran through the audience. Then, out of the speaker came the noise of a large excited crowd, over which the raised voice of a commentator could be heard.

'This is an amazing performance,' the voice said, 'no bowler has caused Bradman the slightest trouble and he thoroughly deserves to break Foster's record. Tate has reached his mark and he turns.'

By then the crowd noise had died away and the only sound coming from the speaker was the commentator's voice. On the hill, we were all spellbound.

'Tate is running in and he reaches the crease.'

A split second later we heard the unmistakably sweet noise of a cricket bat meeting a cricket ball, followed by a great burst of applause.

'Good ball,' cried the commentator, 'right on the stumps. But Bradman, using his feet beautifully, has driven it straight to the fence. A wonderful shot for four to bring him to 287, equal to the record. The ball has been returned to Tate and he is walking back with a pensive look on his face.'

The crowd noise subsided but it was very evident that the listening prisoners were greatly affected by the vividly realistic and quite unexpected simulated broadcast. It made us feel that we were at home, sitting by the radio, listening to a ball by ball description of a match actually in progress, even though we knew that it had been played more than 13 years before.

'Tate runs in; he bowls and Bradman pushes the ball to leg.'

For several seconds the commentator's voice was drowned by a roar from the 'spectators' but it quickly emerged again.

'Only one run but that's enough and Foster's record is broken. Bradman is smiling broadly and the England players are all round him, shaking his hand. Now he waves his bat to the crowd.'

The noise of applause increased and as it slowly died away the prisoners began to clap in spontaneous appreciation of the exciting commentary and sound effects which Swanton and his small band of helpers had so cleverly and unexpectedly produced.

The Major went on to describe the remainder of the 1930 tour and pointed out that Australia regained the Ashes by winning the series 2-1 mainly because of the predominance of Bradman, who made 2960 first-class runs during that summer at an average of 98. In Tests, he totalled 974 runs at 139, figures which clearly demonstrated his formidable influence.

After summarising The Don's great success against West Indies in 1930-31 and South Africa in 1931-32, Swanton added a romantic touch by mentioning Bradman's courtship of a lovely Sydney girl, Jessie Menzies, whom he married in April 1932.

Then, with great tact, because the audience was about half English and half Australian, he dealt with the notorious England tour of Australia in 1932-33.

'That series caused a great deal of controversy and bitterness and I don't propose to say much about it. England won back the Ashes by 4 matches to 1 largely because Bradman's average was reduced to that of a very good batsman. Some said he failed: yet in 8 innings, he scored 396 runs for an average of 56. It would have been an excellent result for anyone other than The Don. He was unable to play in the first Test

through illness but listen to this recording of his performances in the second at Melbourne, which Australia won by 111 runs.'

Again we heard some excellently simulated ball by ball description, complete with striking sound effects. We listened to Fingleton and O'Brien batting in the opening innings and O'Brien being run out for 10, making the score 2 for 67. The roar of applause coming from the speaker heralded the arrival of Bradman at the wicket, followed by an expectant hush as Bowes ran in to bowl and then a suppressed groan of agonised disbelief as the delivery smacked into the stumps. Bradman was out first ball and we were as shocked as the Melbourne crowd.

But next came a far more satisfying description because the commentary switched to Australia's second innings with the score at 9 for 222, The Don on 98 and Ironmonger, arguably the least accomplished batsman in international cricket, coming in to bat.

I was tingling with excitement for, on that day, at the age of 12, I was at the Melbourne Cricket Ground with my father, watching my first Test match and more importantly, watching Bradman for the first time.

The vivid word-picture coming through the speaker enabled me to recall very clearly how Ironmonger survived two vicious deliveries from Hammond to complete the over — each time without moving his bat at all. That he was not dismissed was a miracle. And then came the next over with Bradman hitting the fifth ball from Voce for three to reach his hundred.

The approval of the partisan Melbourne crowd thundered through the speaker and was echoed by the men on the hill. The description continued and Ironmonger had just been run out for a duck, leaving The Don on 103 not out, when suddenly there was silence.

Immediately, I saw two guards standing beside the stage. We were back to reality and all knew that if the show was to continue, normal formalities would have to be observed and quickly at that.

The Allied Camp Commander, Colonel Harvey, was sitting close to the stage and rising to his feet, he gave the order 'kiotske'. The audience stood and came to attention.

'Keray,' called the Colonel. All bowed and the guards acknowledged the salute by inclining their heads slightly.

'Nowray,' called Harvey. It was the order to come back to attention. The guards went behind the screen and we hoped that they would not find something to cause them annoyance. They didn't and shortly afterwards, they reappeared, called 'OK' to the Colonel and stomped away. Protocol had been satisfied and amidst a buzz of conversation, consisting mainly of rude comments about the Japanese, we sat down.

Major Swanton resumed his absorbing story as though nothing had occurred to interrupt it.

'After a phenomenally successful 1933-34 home season, Bradman was back in England with Woodfull's 1934 Australian team. Again, he began with a double century against Worcester but soon afterwards he had an unaccountable lapse of form when he hit only one century in 19 innings. But this unusual situation ended with a vengeance for in his last seven knocks, he scored five hundreds, including 304 in the fourth Test at Headingley and 244 in the fifth at The Oval. At Leeds, Ponsford and Bradman put on 388 for the 4th wicket but England saved the game with the help of some bad weather. At The Oval, Ponsford and Bradman did even better, scoring 451 for the 2nd wicket to enable Australia to win easily and to regain the Ashes by 2 matches to 1. Despite some great bowling by O'Reilly and Grimmett and some fine batting by Ponsford, Woodfull, Brown and McCabe, Bradman was once more the difference between the two sides.'

The Major drew some gasps of dismay from the hill when he described how The Don became seriously ill in England at the end of that tour and nearly died. The audience was visibly moved by this segment because all were involved in a struggle against sickness and disease and we had a strong sense of fellow feeling for Bradman in his ordeal.

Swanton described his slow recovery and how, after

missing the 1934-35 home season because of the illness, he resumed playing late in 1935 as captain of South Australia, to where he had moved from New South Wales. We thrilled to a brief description of his dazzling form for his new State — 1173 runs in nine innings, including two triple centuries, one of which hurt me a little because it was made against my island State of Tasmania — 369 in 253 minutes.

'Then came England's 1936-37 Australian visit, by which time Bradman had been appointed a Test selector and captain of Australia. His early form that season was well below his usual high standard and England won the first two Tests. But in the third, the Bradman supremacy asserted itself. In Australia's second innings, Fingleton and Bradman put on 346 for the sixth wicket and Australia won easily. Let us go over to Melbourne and listen to a little of what happened.'

Again, a simulated broadcast enraptured the prisoners, who were treated to descriptions of several highlights of that partnership, in particular an over describing a tense contest between Bradman and Verity, the only English bowler who was able to subdue the great batsman during his long innings of 270.

'Australia also won the next two Tests to retain the Ashes 3-2',' Swanton went on. 'And once more Bradman was the dominating factor with 212 in the fourth match and 169 in the fifth.'

I hoped there would be a ball by ball description of part of the innings of 169 because I watched that match, which was played at Melbourne. But I hoped in vain and the Major quickly moved through the 1937-38 Australian season to Australia's tour of England in 1938.

'And so we come to the last pre-war series. Bradman was again captain and needless to say, he commenced with a third double century, against Worcester — 258. His record against that hapless country was three innings, 700 runs, average 233.'

Gasps of amazement came from the hill.

'Once more he had a great tour and he scored freely against the counties. Hutton and Compton made their debits in the first Test, each hitting centuries. England had the better of the first two games but both were drawn, largely because of knocks of 144 not out by Bradman in the second innings of the first Test and 102 not out in the second innings of the second. Both were great match-saving performances.

'At Headingley, Australia won by five wickets and The Don's contributions were 103 and 16. His 103 virtually won the match, although O'Reilly and Fleetwood-Smith bowled magnificently. And we come to the fourth and last pre-war Test, played at The Oval. It was a plumb wicket and when he won the toss, Hammond had no hesitation in batting.'

Most of the Australians on the hill stirred uneasily, knowing that for them, an unhappy part of the story was about to unfold.

'Against a weakened Australian attack because McCormick could not play, England batted for almost three days and amassed 903 for 7 declared.'

From the hill, groans of Australian disgust mingled with polite English applause.

'And worse still for Australia, Hutton broke Bradman's record by making 364 in 13 hours of intense concentration. We will replay a recording of him passing Bradman's 334.'

Again, the simulated broadcast captured our imagination and the whole audience joined in applauding the English batsman's achievement. The Australians felt a sense of pride when they heard that the first to congratulate Hutton was Bradman himself.

'Shortly afterwards, when The Don was taking a turn with the ball, he tripped and broke a bone in his ankle. He was carried off the ground and that was the end of his cricket for that tour. Fingleton could not bat through injury and Australia was beaten by an innings and 579 runs. Thus, the series was squared but as holder, Australia retained the Ashes.

'Bradman's record for the tour was 2429 runs with 13 centuries, average 115. His greatness is illustrated by the fact that the next best batsman was Brown with 1854 runs at 58.'

The Major then briefly referred to The Don's subsequent two Australian seasons when in 22 innings he hit 11 centuries, six of which were in succession.

'By now the war had come. In 1940, Bradman enlisted in the RAAF but was seconded to the Army in which he was commissioned. Shortly after, he was again stricken with a serious illness. Despite this, he played in two patriotic matches but scored only 18 runs in four innings. In the last one he was bowled by O'Reilly for 12. We in Thailand are prevented from having news of him and we can only hope that he has recovered. What we do know is that he is by far the greatest batsman the world has known and I doubt that there will ever be a better one. He is also a great captain and a fine man.

'He has already made 92 centuries — about one in every three innings — and about 23,000 runs at an average of 95. Incredible figures. Let us hope that before long, when the war is over, we will all have the profound pleasure of again seeing or hearing Donald George Bradman at the crease in Test matches, displaying once more his extraordinary skills.'

After a short pause, the announcer's voice came through the speaker. 'The Allied Broadcasting Corporation at Tarso thanks you all for tuning in tonight and I hope you have enjoyed the programme. This station is now closing down but first a reminder that the next Radio Newsreel will be presented at the same time next Tuesday night. Make sure that you are listening.'

Well before the end of the announcement, the whole audience was on its feet, applauding with great warmth. Everyone appreciated the excellence of the performance which, by stirring so many exciting and nostalgic memories, had enabled each man to forget for a brief period the awful conditions under which he was being forced to exist.

While Reg and I were walking back to our huts I said, 'Great show, wasn't it?' 'Wonderful,' replied Reg.

We said no more for our minds were strangely at peace and we knew that we had just experienced something that we would always remember.

Happiness is eight million words at 80-odd

Michael Davie

Michael Davie.

How pleasant to be Mr Swanton! He is proof that it is possible to lead a happy life.

He is 82, though he looks 10 years younger and behaves as if he were 20 years younger. Signing himself E. W. Swanton, and invariably called Jim, he is the doyen of cricket writers. Not only is he 82 this year; 1987 was also his 60th year as a journalist. He joined the *London Evening Standard* in 1927.

He has solved the problem of the English winter by dodging it. He used to go on cricket tours to hot countries, paid for by someone else. Now he goes to the West Indies.

Wherever he goes, in cricket circles, he is known, recognised and, for the most part, honoured. Outside cricket circles, nobody has heard of him. But cricket circles are wide. Swanton and the Prime Minister of Australia ('a very good fielder') are on 'Bob' and 'Jim' terms. Also on first name terms are Swanton and Lord Home. So were Swanton and Menzies.

He has solved the problem of retirement by not retiring. He started drawing his pension from the *London Daily Telegraph*, where he had been cricket correspondent since 1946, 41 years ago. But when I visited him at his rambling and snug old house in the middle of Sandwich, Kent, just before he left for Barbados I found him, on a Sunday afternoon, at his desk. That week, he had had three pieces in the *Telegraph*; about a county cricketer who has taken more wickets than he has scored runs; about benefit matches; and an obituary. He had just finished editing the latest version of the monumental *Barclay's World of Cricket* (described by Sir Donald Bradman as the best book on cricket ever produced). He was hurrying to get another book to the publishers. And when I arrived he was writing his monthly notes for *The Cricketer* magazine, on whose board he sits.

Since then, I have been doing some sums. Before he joined the *Evening Standard*, he wrote as a youthful freelance two interviews with two famous players, Frank Woolley and W. R. Hammond. At the *Standard* he was prolific. Afternoon papers before the war gave

53

yards of space to cricket reports. During the Second World War, he had the grim experience of being a Japanese prisoner of war on the Burma Road. Somehow surviving, he was soon back at the cricket.

He always wrote longer stories for the *Telegraph* than any of his rivals wrote for any other paper. Sometimes, to the incredulity of the rest of the press box, he was accompanied and assisted by a secretary. The words poured out. In winters, if he was not reporting a tour, there were the books. He has always had some book or another on the stocks. So: say he has averaged 3000 words a week for 48 weeks of the year for 60 years minus the six years of the war. It follows that he has written at least 7 776 000 words about cricket — so far. Has anyone ever written more on a single subject?

When I put my sums to him, he thought a bit and said he supposed I must be about right, adding that he had written a fair amount on rugby football, too, in his time. Nor should one forget that for 40-odd years he was a cricket commentator for the BBC, starting in 1934. Add the publicly spoken words to the published words, and the mind reels. On non-sporting subjects, he has restricted himself to autobiography and a series of essays on the main Australian cities.

Yet the last thing he looks or behaves like is a writer of any kind. He is large, of almost W. G. Grace proportions, often wears a Free Forester tie, and is always well turned out, with the gentlemanly air even in a press box of having dropped in to enjoy a day's cricket, not to do a job. Perhaps the secret of his benevolent serenity is that it has never been a job. His long-timer colleague Michael Melford once remarked: 'Cricket is not a game. It's a way of life.'

The gentlemanly air has been resented by some. They have put Swanton down as a snob. Nothing could be further from the truth. He sees others not in terms of social class, but in terms of whether or not they are good for cricket. His two cricketing heroes, he told me, are the late Frank Woolley and Sir Garfield Sobers (of Barbados) — Sobers not only because of his skill but because of his unselfishness.

Most cricketers are conservative in politics. So, in general, is Swanton. But he has taken a firm pro-black line in opposing sporting links with South Africa, a policy 'not quite on the *Daily Telegraph* wavelength'. He was a church warden for 10 years in Sandwich. Was he against apartheid on Christian grounds, I asked? He seemed startled by the mention of religion, but conceded that that was the case.

One man not embraced by Swanton's general benevolence is Mr Kerry Packer, the Australian tycoon who tore the cricket world apart in 1977. Swanton spoke about him so sharply that I asked if he was talking for publication. 'You can say what you like about Packer,' he said. Swanton thinks that the damage done to cricket by Packer's invention of World Series Cricket — the one-day games played in pyjamas — persists, and is the cause of the decline of Australia's playing standards.

'Nobody,' he says, 'damn well knows' the terms of the secret deal that Packer struck with the Australian Cricket Board in 1979, when the split between Packer's rebels and traditional cricket was patched up. Alone among the national boards of the cricket-playing countries, the ACB publishes no financial accounts. Swanton believes that Packer still gets most of the profits flowing in from one-day internationals in Australia, such as those shown on BBC2 in the 'highlights' brought from Packer.

Swanton sent up a 'quiet hallelujah' when he read that Packer had sold his TV interests to Alan Bond, the beer and real estate tycoon from Western Australia. He assumed that Bond would be easier for traditional cricket to deal with. His optimism waned when I said I wouldn't bet on it.

Swanton is a slice of cricket history himself. He has been told that he saw W. G. Grace in action but cannot remember it. He can however rattle off the names and initials of every player in the first match he does remember seeing, which was Yorkshire v. Surrey just after the First World War. One of them was D. J. Knight, who went in first with Jack Hobbs and made a hundred in each innings; Knight's over-possessive father pulled strings to keep him away from the war, and so many friends of his were killed that he felt 'diminished' and eventually took his own life.

I asked Swanton who had most surprised him by showing an interest in cricket. 'One person who was potty about cricket was Charlie Chaplin.' But it was not so surprising when you remembered that Chaplin grew up in Kennington, near the Oval. He told Swanton that Bobby Abel and Hobbs were boyhood heroes. Why are cricketing peers such rare birds now? Swanton agreed that there used to be more of them about. He said he opened the batting for MCC against the Lords at Lord's in 1937, expecting easy pickings; but it had been Swanton c Remnant b Dunglass 0. Lord Dunglass became Lord Home.

What is his most treasured memento? He picked up from his desk a large silver paper-knife inscribed to F. E. Woolley from the Kent committee in 1913. 'A more useless thing to give a professional cricketer you can scarcely imagine.' said Swanton. Woolley died 13 years ago, aged 91. Swanton has a photograph of him sitting in the Swanton garden aged 89. When Woolley watched Sobers, 'his eyes glowed'. Swanton said: 'There was no better chap in my view than the old professional cricketer.'

Swanton is still a power at Lord's. He had much to do with the construction of the indoor cricket school there, which is open to all-comers the year round, and the new library, also open to the public, provided they are serious cricket researchers and make an appointment.

He has never wanted cricket or Lord's to be exclusive. He showed typical devotion to the cause on 13 January 1987, the date of a MCC Arts and Library Committee meeting, when, although Sandwich was virtually cut off by snow, he spent seven hours struggling in vain to reach the meeting. No sane 80-year-old would have ventured out of doors.

Nor has he yet run out of ideas. He told me that he and Tim Rice form a two-man working party to start an MCC publishing imprint, in alliance with Collins the publishers. Its first publication is to be a 'Treasures of Lord's' by a director of Christie's.

Before I left he showed me a joke he has just discovered. For his new book, he had been looking at an *Evening Standard* of 1937 with the headline 'Wellard hits 50 in 11 minutes'. On the same page, he suddenly noticed another story saying that because Hampshire had turned up one short to play a county match, a local policeman had been pressed into service and had had to borrow a pair of white flannels.

The policeman was named, said the *Standard*, 'P. C. Harlott': the first mention in print of John Arlott, Swanton reckoned.

For his birthday, one imagines an all-night multiracial celebration with steel bands. On the other hand, he may be busy typing a piece about new young Barbadian batsmen, heading for his eight-millionth word.

*The England and Australian teams photographed at Lord's during the
second Test match, June 1948. Picture shows (back row) G. Evans,
R. Lindwall, D. Ring, S. Loxton, R. Hamence, C. McCool, G. Emmett,
D. Tallon. (centre row) N. Harvey, W. Brown, H. Dollery, R. Saggers,
W. Johnston, A. Bedser, K. Miller, A. Coxon, E. Toshack, J. Laker,
D. Wright, S. Barnes. (front row) D. Compton, I. Johnson, L. Hutton,
A. L. Hassett, N. Yardley, D. Bradman, W. Edrich, A. Morris,
C. Washbrook, K. Johnston. (J. Young, England, is absent).*

'It was the greatest thrill I ever had in cricket. Even more so than when I was first selected for Australia.'

On bowling at Bradman (and taking his wicket!)

Ian Johnson

Bowling at Don Bradman, although somewhat frightening, was nevertheless a tremendous thrill. Yet it wasn't as awe-inspiring as one might expect. The reason, of course, was that he reduced all bowlers (with the possible exception of Bill O'Reilly) to a common level.

One bowler might well be much more accomplished than another when bowling to a normally good batsman. But, when bowling to Bradman, the difference in their abilities was nullified because of his supreme skill. All were the same to him, such was his genius. Consequently you felt as good as anybody else.

The thought of getting him out rarely entered your mind. Few people ever did that in normal conditions although there was the occasion during the 1946–47 series when Alec Bedser became one of that select few. He sent one down in line with off stump. It dipped in to land leg then cut back to take off. Don claims it was the best ball ever bowled to him.

Then there were the two famous balls Eric Hollies sent down to Don in his final Test innings at the Oval in 1948. Don had received a magnificent reception from the crowd when he went to the wicket. On reaching there the England team gathered round and gave him three cheers. The whole scene brought a lump to many throats.

Don took guard, looked around the field then shaped up as Eric moved in. It was a leg break. Don played forward but it beat the outside edge. The next ball he played forward again. This time it was the wrong'un and beat the inside edge to take the stumps. They were probably the best two balls Hollies ever sent down. Don returned to the dressing room and lay down on the rubbing down table without saying a word, obviously bitterly disappointed at the ending to his Test career. We all felt for him and with him. After a time, I walked across and said:. 'Bad luck Don, the reception must have affected you.' 'No, Ian,' he replied, 'they were two beautiful balls and would have beaten me if I'd been a hundred.'

Surely one of sport's most gracious salutes.

Yes, they were two very rare exceptions. Normally you bowled at him to the best of your ability knowing that you were just as likely to be bowling as anybody else when he got out. So you approached the task with a certain resignation.

Two things you knew were certain: He would not succumb to fatigue. He was much too fit for that. Nor would he fall to lack of concentration. He liked making runs too much for that. In any case he did not need to concentrate as intensely as most. Batting came much easier to him such was his superiority over bowlers.

I recall on one occasion I had been batting well in what were difficult conditions for me. It had been quite a struggle but I had survived until I had a sudden rush of blood to the head. On my return to the dressing room Don said: 'What did you do that for? You were going excellently but just threw it away.' I snapped back: 'It's all very well for you to say that, but I found it damned hard work out there and I had to concentrate like hell. You can't understand how tough it is for us mere mortals.' To which he replied: 'No. I guess you're right. I didn't think of that.'

Countless stories have been told of his batting prowess. All stress his incomparability. Two occasions that stand out in my mind took place at the Melbourne Cricket Ground before the war. The matches were Victoria v. South Australia. In one, Victoria batted first and were dismissed late on the first day for just over 200. South Australia started its innings and it soon became obvious that Don wanted to bat late into the third day to set Victoria a formidable total on a wearing pitch. So, when he came in at number three there were no fireworks and we rather felt, although we were not really troubling him, at least we were controlling the situation. He reached 86 when the new ball came due (it was every 200 runs in those days). We thought our tearaway fast bowler, Barry Scott, might just trouble him.

An attacking field was set. In the slips we waited in nervous anticipation as Scott came thundering in with the new ball. Bradman took 15 off the over to pass his

century. He then settled back to play along sedately until he reached 189. Doug Ring was bowling beautifully and seemed to have Don in control, occasionally troubling him. So we thought. Doug came in to bowl with Don on that 189 and he promptly took 13 off the over to pass his 200. Again he settled back to unhurried cricket. That was the point with Bradman. You never had him. He dictated the play and set the tempo for his side.

Then there was that other time. It was earlier, during the 1935–36 season. The Australian team was in South Africa but Bradman, for some reason or another, missed the tour. I wasn't playing in the match but was told the story by the Victorian wicket-keeper, Stan Quinn. He said that when Don came to the wicket he (Quinn) waited for the ball to get past the bat, preferably after being snicked. He concentrated his whole attention on not fumbling when it did happen. He waited in vain.

Don made something over 300 and Quinn swears that he did not take one ball when Don was on strike. None beat the bat nor did he allow any to pass. He played every ball delivered to him in scoring those 300 runs. Unbelievable.

Yes. That was the incredible Bradman. Those incidents alone show that, when bowling to him you were at the mercy of his moods and fancies. Anything that happened was outside your control. That is why bowling at him was not the ordeal one would imagine. He really did reduce all bowlers to a common level.

I did not bowl at him a great deal pre-war. I was more a batsman who bowled in those days. But I did bowl at him quite a bit after the war. And I always had a feeling of futility but always with the knowledge that even he had to get out sometime, and it was as likely to happen with me bowling as with anybody else. Then came that magical day: he did get out when I was bowling.

It was the greatest thrill I ever had in cricket. Even more so than when I was first selected for Australia. More so, too, than when I was made Australian cap-

58

tain. You see, those selections and appointments, thrills though they are, were not entirely unexpected. There is newspaper discussion on the team and/or captaincy so you can fairly accurately assess your chances. But taking Bradman's wicket for the first time! That was totally unexpected. (I say the first time as it gives the impression that it happened often in later games. Alas, this is not quite correct. I did it once more and the thrill was still great. But no. Not like that first time!) This is how it happened. It was in Adelaide in the 1946–47 season. Don was 48 and sighting the ball. I was bowling well — to the other batsmen. I was troubling them with a four five field. A slip, cover, extra cover and mid-off with a big gap between cover and slip. On the leg side there was a man behind square, one in front of square, a shortish mid-wicket, a mid-on and deep square leg. I was attacking off stump, turning in.

As I said, I was worrying the other batsmen but Don was just moving down the wicket, pushing the ball between mid-wicket and mid-on. I'd move mid-wicket straighter. Then he'd push the ball between mid-wicket and the man in front of square, sometimes for a single, other times for twos. But he scored off every ball. It was typical of the frustration you had when bowling to him; the sense of futility.

I had not bowled my cutter to him, being conscious of the gaps on the off-side, but the continuing frustration caused me to think: 'What the hell!' So I ran in, delivered the cutter in line with off stump.

Don moved down the wicket and my eyes were about to wander to the off expecting to see the ball scurrying to the fence. But, wonder of wonders, Don was shaping again to push to the on-side. He hadn't picked it.

He played to the on-side for spin that wasn't there. The ball turned from the leg and missed his bat by inches. He was stranded.

Now in these moments a million thoughts can flash through your mind in an instant. They did through mine. The ball took an eternity to reach Bill Baker, the 'keeper. He's sure to fumble it, I thought. He didn't, he took it cleanly. He'll miss the stumps when he strikes for them. He took the bails. The umpire is sure to say not out. He nodded his head and raised the finger. The Don grinned and headed for the pavilion.

I was dumbfounded, dazed. I walked round the stumps at the bowler's end. I plucked a blade of grass and chewed it. I had taken *his* wicket. It was unreal. I walked round the stumps again. Ah, yes. I must admit it, I was in a state of stunned euphoria!

Ray Jordan (centre, standing with glass) with his Victorian teammates celebrate winning the 1962–63 Sheffield Shield.

Nine for Australia

Ray Jordan

I came into the Victorian side for the 1959–60 season, replacing Len Maddocks, who toured New Zealand in Australia's second eleven, as was done in those days.

It was the last Shield game for the season against West Australia. Coming back from the Indian tour were Colin McDonald and Ian Meckiff, as well as Lindsay Kline, who couldn't play due to hepatitis.

I never played with or against Ian Meckiff during my grade cricket, so I was oblivious to how fast or inaccur-ate he was. He opened the bowling to left-hander Laurie Sawle, now chairman of selectors for the Aus-tralian cricket team. His first ball strayed down the leg-side and left me for dead — four byes resulted!

I went back further, around 20 yards, only to see his next ball fly down the leg-side for another four byes. I went back to 24 yards and the same thing happened.

I dropped my first catch off Alan Connolly, given by Laurie Sawle, and when I went into bat Victoria was six wickets for more than 300 runs. I lasted one ball, caught in first slip for a golden duck!

I missed the next season when Len Maddocks came back; that was the year the West Indies toured for the tied Test match.

When I returned to the Victoria side in 1961–62, Bill Lawry was captain, Cowper and Connolly were getting established, Stackpole and Redpath were coming into the team with me and we were classed by the great 'Nugget' Miller as the worst Shield side ever from Victoria.

The next season, Meckiff, Connolly and Colin Guest totalled more than 50 wickets for us to win the Shield — my greatest thrill in sport.

'Stay at the wicket. I'm taking the others, plus the 12th man, leaving one chap to double as 12th man and scorer.

A bail had never travelled that distance before

G. B. Martin

Australia's indomitable Ray
Lindwall taking Len Hutton's
wicket to dismiss the former
England captain for a duck during
a charity match in England, April
1956.

One of the joys of cricket lies in its universal acceptance in so many areas of our world; areas where beliefs, customs and languages are no barriers to the enjoyment of the game. Many countries exchange visits, and lasting friendships are made because people are fascinated by the subtleties of a game whose history spreads through the development of their social fabric. The sophisticated game we watch had its origins in more bucolic arenas than the old-world charm of Lord's or the massive concrete pillars and stands of Melbourne.

In Tasmania, as in many parts of the world, summer days are spent in weekly tussles for supremacy. Especially is this so in country centres of the island. Players engage in battle royal with enthusiasm and an astonishing degree of expertise. I recall vividly one such 'Test' played in the Tamar Valley some years ago. The visiting team compiled a sizeable total and seemed proud of their efforts. As the home side was about to embark on the chase for the necessary runs, an urgent call came for assistance to quell a fire which was threatening the local caravan park. As most of the batting side were voluntary members of the local fire brigade, the visitors felt confident victory was theirs. The local skipper sized up the situation, strode grimly to the wicket and issued the following orders to guardians of the crease: 'Stay at the wicket. I'm taking the others, plus the 12th man, leaving one chap to double as 12th man and scorer.'

About an hour later several dishevelled figures were seen galloping back to the ground with feverish enquiries about the state of the game. Satisfied with assurances that all was well at the crease, they then set about the more serious business of scoring the required runs to win.

Umpires, the arbiters of the fate of many a struggling batsman and flagging bowler, often display a very human side to their natures. In one match I appealed for what I really considered to be a very doubtful lbw decision. Without hesitation the finger of doom dispatched the offender to the gloom of the pavilion. At the afternoon tea break I chatted with the same umpire about the closeness of decisions. Imagine my surprise when he told me that had I appealed two deliveries earlier, the result would have been the same. He added that as the batsman had been dropped twice already, it was high time he was given out!

Tasmania, the smallest Australian State, was admitted to the Sheffield Shield competition in the 1977–78 season. It was led by the famous Lancashire spinner, Jack Simmons, who is remembered with special affection on the island. With his lads he captured the Gillette Cup by defeating Western Australia and he then led the State to its first Shield victory in 1979 at Devonport.

The magnificent playing surface at this oval has been admired by many local and overseas players. However, in the early days of TV coverage it was necessary for the commentators to climb a 10-metre tower to arrive at the microphone. By mid-afternoon a strong sea-breeze would blow from Bass Strait, about 200 metres away, and the life of the commentator would be endangered, as the bitter wind lifted the tarpaulin covers, threatening to decant everybody several kilometres inland.

As I looked on the balmy scene below, where thousands of Tasmanians were engrossed in the struggle, I noticed they were clad in shorts and bathers, while I was wishing for an extra layer or two of wool. It seemed so strange that there were two extremes of temperature at the same place.

Between the two world wars Tasmania was visited by the MCC at four-yearly intervals. My late father had made a score of 121 in only 126 minutes against Gilligan's side in Launceston. When the next MCC side came to Launceston they were led by A. P. F. Chapman, and everybody was anxious to see if my father, an attacking batsman, could repeat his previous century. He began in a somewhat subdued manner, but after reaching his half-century, began to hit out freely and rapidly went to the late eighties. His rate was so good that sections of the crowd began to call on Chapman to bring back Harold Larwood.

Chapman at last relented and the Notts express took the ball. The batsman had taken two boundaries and reached 92 when the great 'Lol' walked back a few extra paces and delivered a terrifying ball which clipped the wicket and knocked the bail an incredible 60 metres (66 yards) away behind the 'keeper. Patsy Hendren wouldn't let anyone touch the bail until a measuring device was procured and it was established that a world record had been created — a bail had never travelled that distance before. The feat was recorded in *Wisden* for all to see.

The sporting world is full of the performances of heroes who have become larger-than-life figures. They represent guidelines for everybody to admire and emulate. Young lads try to hit the ball out of the ground because they feel the spirit of Botham stirring in them. I remember the elegance of Worrall, the majesty of Hammond and the barely-controlled power of Sobers. My mind is filled with nostalgia as I look back over my years in the game, both as player and commentator, and I am grateful for the experience I have enjoyed.

G. B. Martin.

The 'Honorary Pom'

Michael Melford

Jack Fingleton will be remembered for many things: for the runs he made as a successful opening batsman for Australia in the 1930s; for his courage in the bodyline series; for his shrewd and entertaining writing on cricket, more appreciated perhaps in England than in Australia; for his career as a lobby correspondent in Canberra; and, throughout a life which ended in November 1981, as a devoted Australian.

If this last quality suggests that he viewed non-Australians warily, that is not wholly inaccurate, but many in England who remember him with affection may feel that it needs qualification.

Certainly he was suspicious of many things English and of many Englishmen but there were a lot of aspects of English life, and, of course, Scottish, Welsh and Irish, which he appreciated. He loved the English countryside — he talked about his visits to places such as Castle Combe for weeks afterwards. In his last years he would stay on for some time after the tour was over as if reluctant to say goodbye.

He respected English traditions. The English stuffpot was not for him but he could be very well disposed to unconventional Englishmen, even if one could never guess which one it would be. He was known for his touchiness but he was easy to get on with if you touched the right note. Then it was that his humour came out to the extent that he would even accept a measure of leg-pulling, which may have amazed those who knew only his more abrasive side.

He often stayed with John Woodcock at Longparish, beside the Test ground in Hampshire, and was in his element there. His entry into village life was not an immediate success. Having been persuaded to play in a match at the neighbouring village of Hurstbourne Priors — this in the late 1950s — he received a monstrous decision from a local umpire. Nobody was left in any doubt of his displeasure and when he mislaid the New South Wales cap in which he had been batting, his main concern for its recovery was loudly expressed. 'I wouldn't like it to fall into the hands of that umpire,' he said.

Jack Fingleton in his playing heyday makes a classic drive through cover.

He did not easily forget. At Christmas he sent a card of good wishes to all at Longparish, 'except that umpire who gave me out'. Years later, when he and I were staying at Longparish, there was a minor break-in. The police were called and were joined in their investigations by an indignant Fingleton — Fingo of the Yard, as Woodcock called him. 'I didn't know you had any crime in these parts', he told the local CID, 'though I would have believed anything of that umpire who gave me out at Hurstbourne Priors.'

There was one England tour of New Zealand on which the press party had the pleasure of Fingo's company. If there was one set of people of whom he was more suspicious than Englishmen, it was New Zealanders and he embraced England's cause in the Test series with almost embarrassing enthusiasm.

New Zealand cricket at the time had some fine players but not enough of them and it was badly in need of encouragement. Or so it seemed to us. At the end of a long tour of Australia the English party was inevitably looking forward keenly to getting home and passions were not running high. It was certainly not the end of the world if New Zealand did well. Fingo, with his true Australian love of winning, could not understand this anaemic attitude.

His concern for England's performance was such that we invested him with the title of 'Honorary Pom'. He was delighted. It appealed to his sense of humour and I think he was also rather touched. In later years he would sometimes sign himself to selected friends, J. H. Fingleton, Hon. Pom.

Somehow it reflected not only his mixed feelings for the mother country but the blend of humour and irascibility, of kindness and criticism, which made him such good value as a companion — and which has made him much missed.

Jack Fingleton's here — can you pick the other all-time greats? Test cricket celebrities were in force for Perth's first Test match, December 1970. Here is the line-up of Australian and English internationals. On handrail, from top: John Rutherford, Norm O'Neill, Bob Simpson, Lindsay Hassett, Barry Jarman, Tony Lock, Gordon Becker and Sir Donald Bradman. Second row, from top: Peter Loader, Jim Hubble, Frank Tyson, Bill O'Reilly, Ken Meuleman, Jack Ryder, Keith Slater, Fingleton, Syd Barnes and Denis Compton. Photo by John Campbell (Daily News).

Coloured clothing and dirty sneakers?

Arthur Morris

I often wonder whether one-dayers will be the cricket of the future and Test matches go the way of the Sheffield Shield.

It's got to the stage with Shield games that the players swap team lists with the spectators and when someone phones to ask when the game starts, the answer is, when can you get here?

Colour television and great promotion (the promoters could fill the SCG for a chess match) have attracted a new breed of spectators who crave instant action. And it all points to coloured clothing and dirty sneakers from hereon in.

I can take the one dayers — or leave them. To me, it's like taking All-Bran — you know it's good for the system but at the same time it does produce a lot of rubbish. And those dreadful exercises before play commences. No wonder the players are pooped at the end of the day.

A few years ago, it is said, Sir Donald Bradman, when dropping in to Adelaide Oval to watch an England team practice, found no one in the nets but players doing their group exercises. 'What are they doing?' Sir Donald is reported to have asked. 'Getting fit, Sir Donald. How did you keep fit?' 'By batting,' was the reply.

Well, what would the Bradmans, Huttons, Hassetts, O'Reillys, Lindwalls and all of us old-timers do if we were playing today? Would we go in for all that prancing, cuddling, diving, hamming, posing, all dressed up in those pretty trousers and shirts?

Would we? If the price was right, of couse we would! Any rich sponsors about for a geriatrics' pyjama game?

From left, Ray Lindwall, Arthur Morris and Keith Miller in jovial mood.

Australian Test opener David Boon hooking.

Australia's new-ball speedster Craig McDermott.

*Pakistan's tall, right-handed batsman Mohsin Hasan Khan cuts one
through the off side as Australian 'keeper Wayne Phillips watches.*

Indian captain Kapil Dev, one of the great all-rounders of the decade.

The 'wild card' of England cricket,
Ian Terence Botham.

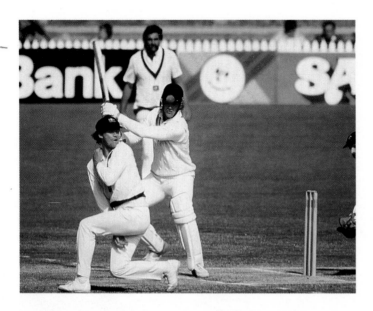

England opener Chris Broad gets one past a flinching Dean Jones watched by Australian 'keeper Greg Dyer and Merv Hughes.

West Indies master batsman Viv Richards clubs a ball to leg during the Melbourne Test of season 1984–85. 'Keeper Steve Rixon, slip Greg Ritchie and non-striker Joel Garner watch.

*New Zealand's greatest bowler
Richard Hadlee in his delivery
stride, versus Australia in
Melbourne, 1980.*

*Former Australian 'keeper Rod Marsh hoiks a ball on the leg side
watched by his England counterpart Bob Taylor.*

India's 'little master' Sunil Gavaskar.

Towering chest, head and shoulders above umpire Tony Crafter, West Indian 'Big Bird' Joel Garner winds up for another big delivery versus Australia, December 1984.

New Zealand's prolific run-scorer, Martin Crowe, in action versus Australia in December 1985.

England's elegant David Gower, a left-handed batsman of rare brilliance.

One of the bright young hopes of
Australian cricket, right-arm
seamer and stroke-player Simon
O'Donnell walks back to his
mark.

*England captain Mike Gatting heads for the dressing room after making
a duck in the fifth Test versus Australia in January 1987. This Test win
ended Australia's record barren run of 14 matches but Gatting and his
men had a wonderful summer, retaining the Ashes and winning both
limited over contests.*

Wessels flinches, Phillips watches as New Zealand opener John Wright gets one away during the Brisbane Test versus Australia in 1985.

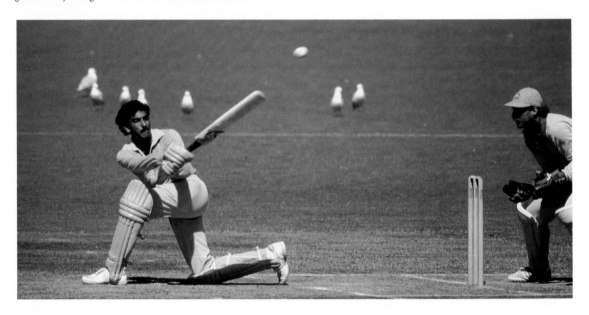

Big-hitting Indian Ravi Shastri, who equalled Sobers's six sixes off one over in season 1984–85, leaves Phillips watching during the triangular World Series Cup in Australia in 1985–86.

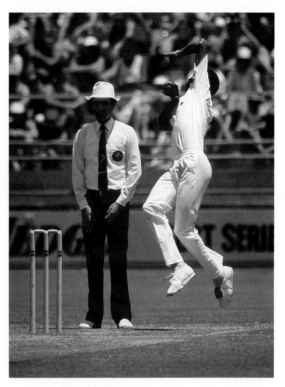

England's main strike bowler, Graham Dilley, charges in during the fifth Test versus Australia, January 1987.

England fast bowler Phillip DeFreitas bounds into his delivery stride during his debut Test, versus Australia in November 1986.

New Zealand's one-day seam specialist Martin Snedden celebrates another scalp during the limited overs tournament in Australia during season 1982–83.

*Australian opener Geoff Marsh plays a ball to leg watched by Indian
'keeper Syed Kirmani during the 1985–86 Test series.*

'Can it bat as well?' asked the amazed captain.

The tale of a horse

Derek Nimmo

Derek Nimmo.

When visiting Melbourne shortly before a first Tuesday in November, I was told a story concerning a local cricket team located near Bendigo. It seems they were one player short for a frightfully important match and they were at a loss how to make up their side. Good fortune smiled — a local grazier offered the services of his horse.

'Can the horse bowl?' the captain asked.

'Bowl? You're looking at the next Dennis Lillee. Just you try and put the ball on his hoof.'

The horse was accordingly selected for the important match. The local team, winning the toss, put their opponents in. To the amazement of the crowds, the horse bowled the opposition out for no runs whatsoever.

'Can it bat as well?' asked the amazed captain.

'Bat?' echoed the farmer. 'You're looking at the next Don Bradman. Just you put him in to open the innings.'

The horse was duly padded up. The first ball came down and the horse hit it towards the boundary. 'Run, run,' shouted the team.

'Don't be bloody silly,' shouted the farmer. 'If he could run, he'd be at Flemington.'*

---

* All Australians will know the significance of the first Tuesday in November — the day of the Melbourne Cup — Flemington, indeed, is the racecourse at which this, the most famous meeting in the Southern Hemisphere, takes place.

'But I'll tell thi' what, I wish that buggar Lindwall had been born in Leeds.'

'Yon Laads are Reet Cobbers'

Michael Parkinson

Michael Parkinson.

In an ever-changing world there are but two tribes remaining with the traditional view that life is centred round strong beer, docile women and good cricket — not necessarily in that order. They are called Australians and Yorkshiremen. It is my firm conviction that, when Britain severed relations with its colonies and joined the Common Market in the mistaken belief that we could find anything in common with wogs who don't play cricket, Yorkshire should immediately have declared UDI, appointed Fred Trueman Prime Minister and signed a Treaty of Alignment with Australia.

When I was a kid I was brought up to respect and hate the Australians. I was told that they would rob, cheat and go to any lengths to win at cricket. 'Just like us,' said my old man, 'us' meaning Yorkshire and not England. My lasting memories of cricket in my childhood are to do with being taken by my father to see the Australians at Bramall Lane or Headingley. There was then, as there is now, a special look about an Australian and a Yorkshire side as it takes the field. Others look rag, tag and bobtail as they come down the pavilion steps, but the Aussies and the Tykes, no matter whether they are a great side or a poor one, always resemble a powerful and intimidating body of men.

The first time I saw the Australians was just after the war and we went to Bramall Lane, rising with the birds so that we could get there three hours before start of play to ensure admittance. Even then we had to sit on the grass. If memory serves me, Hutton and Lowson opened for Yorkshire and certainly it was Lindwall who bowled the first over for Australia. His first ball was wide down the leg side and went into the crowd for four byes. The fielder at fine leg waited for the ball to come out of the crowd and became increasingly restive when it didn't appear. Finally it was handed to him, whereupon he started laughing and called over the umpire.

The ball, shining red and new only minutes before, was now as dirty and scuffed as a small boy's toe-cap. Some Yorkshireman sitting in the crowd had rubbed it in the dirt and removed all vestige of shine. A new ball was ordered. 'Silly bugger,' said my old man, 'he ought to have just rubbed a bit off so they didn't notice.'

That day I couldn't take my eyes off Lindwall. It was my first look at a great fast bowler and from that day on, whenever he played in the county, I went to see him. Once I cycled the 30 miles [48 km] to Bradford to see him bowl at Hutton. I would have walked twice that distance if needs be to see the connoisseur's delight, the master bowler attacking the complete batsman.

Yorkshire batted and I shall never forget the Australians taking the field with fifteen thousand pairs of Yorkshire eyes on Lindwall as he went through his limbering-up routine, every man in the crowd wishing he'd do himself a serious injury. Then the roar as Hutton came to the wicket, pale faced under the blue cap, the man whose wicket the Australians prized the most, the player to whom Lindwall paid the supreme compliment of never bowling badly to him.

Hutton took guard and complete silence fell upon the ground. I swear that, as Lindwall began his approach to the wicket, one of cricket's most menacing and thrilling sights, you could hear his footsteps on the turf. He bowled the perfect ball, an inswinging yorker, and Hutton's stumps rocked in their sockets like drunken sailors. The Australians rejoiced like only they can and the Yorkshire crowd reacted to bitter, numbing disappointment with an uncanny stillness. Crestfallen, Hutton walked back to the pavilion and the crowd was so hushed you could hear him take his gloves off.

'What's tha' reckon to that then?' asked the man behind me to his neighbour as Hutton disappeared into the pavilion. 'Not much,' said his friend. 'But I'll tell thi' what, I wish that buggar Lindwall had been born in Leeds.' Raymond Russell Lindwall, for all he is assured of his place among the immortals of cricket, never knew higher praise than that.

Any comparison of cricketing stories, apocryphal or otherwise, about Australian and Yorkshire cricketers, underlines the similarities between the two tribes. By which I mean that a story summing up the York-shireman's attitude to the game would be equally accurate and authentic-sounding if copied word for word with 'Australian' substituted for 'Yorkshire'.

It is no matter of chance that one of the best stories on cricket was written by an Australian about playing in Yorkshire. I am referring to Jack Fingleton's magnificent account of playing at Bramall Lane with Bradman's team in 1938 when Yorkshire came within an inch of winning. What sets the piece apart from others is Fingleton's perception of the affinities between the two teams, the matching of a supreme pair of gamecocks.

He summed it up precisely with this passage about the team's arrival at Bramall Lane:

It is easy to mistake the atmosphere that receives rather than greets you on this ground. It seems to bristle with belligerence. The looks bore through you in cold analysis as you go to the nets before the game. At Lord's going to the nets, one is greeted with cheery nods and smiles and often a call of 'good luck'. There's none of that at Bramall Lane. . . . The grim look of the spectators, the postures and the gestures of the eleven robust Yorkshiremen with the white rose on their caps all issue a challenge to the Australians and it runs something like this: 'We are Yorkshire. Tha's playin' wi' cricket fire laad when tha' cooms here. We're noo abaht to show tha' laad, tha's noot sa good as tha' thinks.'

One can argue with the accent but not with the article's real authenticity of mood and attitude.

It was at Bramall Lane, alas a cricket ground no more, that I saw the final starburst from the sublime player and entertainer Fred Trueman. Like the actor he was, Fred chose the setting and the occasion carefully. Bramall Lane was where he started as a young, raw tearaway and it was on the same ground 20 seasons later in 1968 that he gave us the last look of a great fast bowler and old sweat in action.

He skippered the Yorkshire side that day and, after winning the toss and contributing a typically swashbuckling and humorous innings, declared at 355 for nine. He opened the bowling himself off his long run and for the last time we were privileged to see this man being what he always claimed he was, 't'best fast bowler that ever drew breath'.

In this, his last match at Bramall Lane, he showed the entire repertoire of his talents, not just his bowling and his batting but his fielding too, reminding us that he was one of the best close fielders in the world when he dived far to his right at second slip to catch Doug Walters off Richard Hutton.

Directed by Trueman, who ran the entire operation with the panache of a theatrical impresario, Yorkshire beat the Australians by an innings and 69 runs, the first time they had beaten the tourists since 1902. It was Trueman's swansong and it was fitting he should have achieved it against a team he regarded as the dearest of enemies.

One story sums up completely Fred Trueman's attitude towards the Australians. It was on his last tour down under and Fred was becoming increasingly impatient with being told that everything in Australia was newer and superior in comparison to anything else. This, he reckoned, was the prerogative of the Yorkshireman and not the upstart Aussie. His patience broke when he was shown the Sydney Harbour Bridge.

'What do you think of our bridge?' asked his host as they surveyed the majestic structure. 'Your bridge? *Our* bloody bridge, you should say. Buggar me, a Yorkshire firm, Dorman & Long, built it . . . and you bastards still haven't paid for it.'

Tempus fugit

I'm growing fonder of the pitch,
Though growing dimmer of the eyes
I'm never sure the ball is there which
Causes echoes of surprise.

I tend to swipe or cuff the thing
Or forward play when ball is gone,
My late cut's late for everything —
A matter I don't dwell upon.

The same with bowling, time was when
I'd swing it in to leg stump fast,
Or rampantly ball-rub, and then
Tear into off. But that is past.

I'd measure wickets, lean and trim
So green and rolled, with studied eye:
I never lost the will to win —
('I say, old chap, was that a bye?')

There's much in the pavilion missed,
My pads seem eaten up with mould,
But I've been by the angels kiss'd —
Although it's true I'm growing old.

If there's tomorrow — (field of sun!)
I'll play again with brittle bones askew,
And snatch a catch, or contemplate a run
In mem'ry, like I used to do.

And when time bowls me out — as time bowls all
(The canny lob you thought you might have seen),
I'll seek Valhalla's field of bat and ball;
I'll seek Valhalla's verdant village green.

— *Leslie Frewin*

A bit quick

Lord Chalfont

Lord Chalfont.

In 1943 the cricket ground of the Poona club was a place of sheer enchantment — especially to a young infantry officer on leave from the jungles of north Burma. The wicket was hard and true, the outfield was of that intense emerald green which makes even Lord's look comparatively greyish; and around the boundary was a riot of jacaranda, flame of the forest and crimson bougainvillea.

The pavilion was the Poona clubhouse itself — a jewel of the Raj with silent Indian waiters wearing snow-white *pagris* and cheerfully carrying cold glasses of gin *piaz* to their colonial oppressors. Even as I write these words I can smell the first evening fragrance of night-scented jasmine as we sat on the verandah after a match, earnestly discussing the eyesight of one of the umpires and the marital status of the parents of the other. It was in this matchless setting that Captain Smylie of the King's Shropshire Light Infantry achieved glory on the cricket field — in a manner of speaking; but I am getting ahead of myself. It happened, as some of the old story-tellers used to say, in this wise.

During a brief leave from the jungle war, Captain Smylie (which is not his real name, nor was he really in the King's Shropshire Light Infantry) returned to his regimental base near Poona to find that a great match of cricket had been arranged there between an Army Command XI and a visiting team from the Royal Australian Air Force. He was, at that time, a reasonably competent opening bat, of about the standard which, had he been a bowler, would have been described as 'military medium'. If I say that in much later years he went in at number seven for the Gentlemen of Shropshire, some idea may be gained of his proficiency, as well as of the somewhat liberal Salopian interpretation of the word gentleman.

Anyway, as a result of one or two rather airy shots through the extra cover area in a club match just before the arrival of the Australians, Smylie was selected to open for the Command XI, a fairly motley collection of servicemen and Indian civil servants — the services providing one or two English county professionals bearing the rank of quartermaster Sergeant Instructor (Physical Training). They looked like Patsy Hendren and they wore very tight dark blue cricket caps with long peaks.

The captain of the home team was an immensely languid Colonel of the Greenjacket mafia, who habitually wore a Free Foresters cap and kept up his yellowish cream trousers with an I Zingari tie. He fielded at deepish mid-off, batted number eight and did not bowl. His sole contribution was that indefinable quality known as leadership, which he demonstrated by moving his field about irrationally at frequent intervals, wearing his silk shirt buttoned at the wrist and swearing inventively at anyone who dropped a catch or otherwise disgraced himself in the field. He actually got the Command XI together for a net before the match (an unheard-of exercise in keenness) and gave them a 'team talk', the main gist of which was that if they couldn't beat a collection of antipodean Air Force pansies they should all give up cricket and soldiering and find a job as a light orchestra in a brothel.

The great day, to coin a phrase, dawned. The RAAF party appeared at the clubhouse, looking more like Australians than would have seemed humanly possible. Some resembled Paul Hogan, there was one who had hair like Richie Benaud and another who looked like Don Bradman but who fortunately turned out to be called Fred and to be in charge of the baggage. They were all the colour of pickled walnuts and they had thirsts of continental proportions.

The Command XI's captain, who actually *liked* to be called 'Skipper', having strolled out to the wicket in his Douglas Jardine gear, won the toss and malevolently elected to bat. This meant that Captain Smylie had to pad up at once and go out to open the innings, passing through a small group of the opposition who were discussing in ringingly clear Oz accents how they proposed to dismantle the Poms. He swore later that as he reached the crease and prepared to take guard, he heard the wicket-keeper pass to first slip one of those nuggets of philosophical wisdom for which our former

dominions have become famous: 'Once you've got them by the goolies, mate,' came the stage whisper, 'their hearts and minds'll follow.'

Now the next part of this story may strike the reader as somewhat surprising, since history relates that Captain Smylie was, as Brian Johnston might say, in pretty good nick. A couple of hours later, he was still there, having accumulated, if that is not too patronising a word, 84 runs, mainly by exploiting one of his favourite shots, a Compton-like sweep down to long leg, often executed, to the fury of the bowler, from a ball pitching on or even just outside the off-stump.

Meanwhile, around him, wickets were falling with depressing regularity until he began to understand the feelings of the boy who stood on the burning deck. Eventually, he was joined by his 'skipper', who did a lot of bat-twirling, gazed around the ground in a minatory fashion as though suspecting that the perfidious Australians were fielding 15 men, and faced up to his first ball. It was a docile half-volley which he struck magisterially into the covers and set off, crying archaically 'Come one!'. Although it was clearly the striker's call, it seemed to Smylie that extra cover was moving in much too fast and he had already taken note that he had an arm like Colin Bland. He therefore sent his astonished 'skipper' back. The Colonel was, not surprisingly, run out by yards and he departed into the middle distance leaving behind, like an invisible vapour-trail, a string of highly original profanity.

At this stage it occurred to Smylie that if he was to have any chance of reaching a hundred, he would have to get a move on. This evidently occurred to the Australian captain too; at the beginning of the next over he threw the ball to a tall, powerfully athletic figure with a mane of shiny black hair, who had hitherto taken no more energetic part in the proceedings than to pick up two nonchalant catches in the slips. To say that the events which followed were traumatic would be to understate the case; apocalyptic would be nearer the mark.

The big man came in off a fairly short run and the

first ball pitched on the off-stump, went away a little and fizzed past Smylie's chin like a grenade fragment. There was no real danger that he might have been caught off it, as he was still halfway through his back lift when it hit the wicketkeeper's gloves with a sound like the crack of doom. Realising that this fellow was, as they say, 'a bit quick', Smylie managed to get his bat to the next delivery and it went between first and second slip — the bat, that is; history does not relate where the ball went.

It was the third ball which was Smylie's nemesis. Bowled off a slightly longer run, it was a swinging yorker and it struck him a thunderous blow on the left ankle. As he had clearly been totally incapacitated, not to say rendered unconscious with pain, the opposition was thoughtful enough not to appeal for lbw, although it would have been, as Trevor Bailey would say, 'fairly adjacent'. There was, in any case, no need to trouble the umpire, as there was no possibility that Smylie would take any further part in the proceedings.

Looking appropriately heroic, he was taken off on a stretcher to the Poona Base Military Hospital. There he learned from an RAMC doctor wearing suede shoes that he had sustained a depressed fracture of the lateral malleolus, a piece of dubious skeletal intelligence which did nothing to mitigate either the agony or the humiliation. After a plaster cast had been applied Smylie returned to take part in the post-mortem around the bar. The Australian captain told him over a comradely *burra-peg* or two, that he had not really intended to let the big fellow bowl against a crowd of weedy Poms in the Indian outback, but he was damned if anybody was going to get a hundred against his lot. The Command XI had, it seemed, made 183 all out; the

RAAF had beaten them by several wickets — how many, it would be uncouth to specify. The 'skipper' was of the opinion that if Smylie had not deliberately run him out they might have given them a run for their money; furthermore, he pointed out unfeelingly, Smylie probably would not now be hobbling about like an old woman.

For the gallant Captain Smylie, however, nothing could dim the glory of that most memorable day which has been captured forever by an entry in the club scorebook, unorthodox perhaps, but entered by an Indian scorer who had no wish to deprive him of his moment of fame. At the top of the page for the Australian game is inscribed quite simply the legend 'Captain D. J. R. Smylie, retired hurt, b. Miller K. 84'. Since then Captain Smylie has risen to a measure of fame and fortune; but that, beyond any shadow of a doubt, was his finest hour.

The Prince of Wales is seen in this historic photograph seated, with the I Zingari team, with cigar in hand, in the chair on the left.

Cricket in 1866, or when King Edward, then Prince of Wales, was bowled for a duck

This photograph of the historic cricket match at Sandringham in which King Edward went in first and made a 'duck' hangs in the pavilion at Lord's Cricket Ground in London.

King Edward, then Prince of Wales, was 24 and was playing for I Zingari against the Gentlemen of Norfolk. The score was I Zingari 277 (R. A. Fitzgerald 101); Gentlemen of Norfolk 119 and 60. The teams were 12-a-side and the match lasted two days — 17 and 18 July, 1866.

As the Prince was not adept at the game, it was hoped that Wright, the Norfolk Gentlemen's fast bowler, who had a round-arm delivery level with the shoulder, would favour the Prince with one or two easy balls. Everyone in the big crowd wanted to see the Prince make a few runs. To the general annoyance of the onlookers, Wright shattered the royal stumps second ball!

The scorebook recording King Edward's only known appearance in a cricket match was found by the present Prince of Wales, Prince Charles, in a cupboard at St James's Palace. He has presented it to the Norfolk County Cricket Club. The historic entry in the scorebook of that day reads: HRH P. of Wales b. Wright 0.

'During this session Milburn hit 28 fours and four sixes.

A scorer looks back

Robert Spence

In twenty-five years as an official scorer for the Queensland Cricket Association it has been my privilege to witness some great innings played at the Brisbane Cricket Ground. As all official scorers know only too well, their duties these days go far beyond the normal recording of details in the conventional scorebook. The concentration required to record and have available as required by the press a great deal of statistical data, leaves a scorer little time to reflect on the great deeds as they unfold before him or her. Thus it is that on reflection I am recalling just three of the great innings which it has been my privilege to record at the 'Gabba ground.

The three batsmen involved in these innings are Grahame Thomas for New South Wales, Colin Milburn for Western Australia and Greg Chappell for Queensland.

The first involved Thomas in a match against Queensland early in the 1965–66 season. As usual Queensland was involved in an early game at home against New South Wales in a season which was to be highlighted later by a Test series against England. Shortly after lunch on the Saturday, thanks to fine bowling by Allan and Duncan, New South Wales had been dismissed for 108 in reply to the home side's first innings total of 307. Queensland captain Peter Burge enforced the follow on and at 2 p.m. Simpson and Thomas opened for New South Wales. The visitors were soon in trouble when Simpson retired with a broken left forearm from Allan's third delivery. From the fourth, O'Neill was out to a gully catch by Burge leaving New South Wales virtually two down for no score as Booth joined Thomas.

Some hint of what was to come came in the sixth over of the innings when 15 runs were taken from Duncan's third over, 14 of these to Thomas with three fours and a two. He reached 50 shortly before tea from 70 balls with nine fours. At tea, after batting for 90 minutes, he was 59 from 74 balls with 11 fours. He had reached 74 from 102 balls when Allan, who had 1 for 24 from seven overs, bowled the 27th over of the innings (Allan's eighth). Thomas turned the full force of his attack on Allan, taking 21 from the over, one six, three fours and one three to take his score to 95 from 110 deliveries. He proceeded quietly from there, reaching his century from 118 deliveries with 16 fours and one six. He continued his dominance of the Queensland bowlers, nine runs (two fours and a single) coming from Duncan. A few overs later he took 16 from Duncan's 12th over (four fours) during the course of which he reached 150 from 162 balls with 27 fours and one six. Then after taking 12 (three fours) from medium-pacer John Mackay, he was out caught at the wicket off Veivers for 182 from 188 balls with 33 fours and one six. The partnership for the second wicket had realised 236 of which Booth scored 53 from 139 deliveries.

Looking back, I recall that during most of this brilliant innings of some 182 minutes, the press covering the match were naturally pre-occupied with the extent of Simpson's injury, in view of the approaching Test series against England. An innings which to me was so memorable enabled New South Wales to fight back and eventually win the match by 27 runs.

Another day, another match: This time Colin Milburn is out middle stump at the hands of Lance Gibbs. Milburn scored 42 in this, the second innings of the fourth Test match, England versus West Indies, fourth day at Headingley, August 1966.

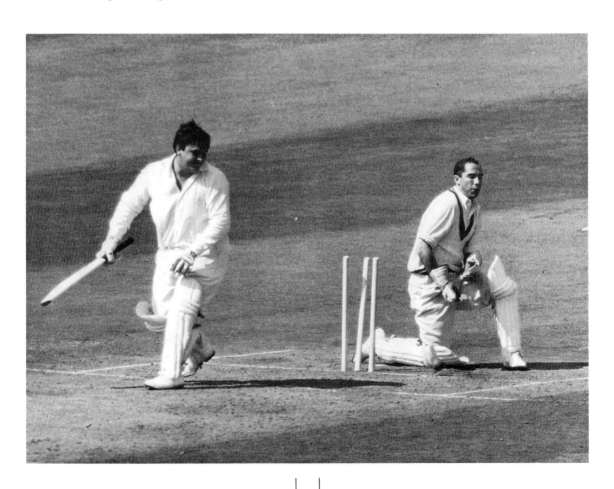

The second of these memorable innings came from the England batsman Colin Milburn playing in season 1968–69 for Western Australia. It was a hot November day in Brisbane and the Western Australia innings was opened by Milburn and Derek Chadwick. Peter Allan captained Queensland in the absence of Sam Trimble, who had been injured in the opening match against New South Wales. Allan recalls that the wicket was very true and no swing could be obtained by the Queensland pace bowlers in the hot conditions. Allan recalls that during his second over with the new ball he decided to bowl well up to the batsmen and in doing this bowled a maiden over to Milburn. He continued these tactics in his next over but Milburn, from a ball right up on the batting crease, back cut the delivery for four. Allan thought to himself 'what do I do?' and indeed this was to be in the minds of all Queensland players — especially the bowlers.

At lunch Western Australia were 93 without loss, the pre-lunch session of 110 minutes having yielded 22 overs for this total of which Milburn had contributed 61 from 92 balls. During this session Duncan's fifth over yielded 13 runs of which Milburn took 9 (two fours and a single) from the six balls of the over he faced. Duncan's next over yielded 16 runs (four fours) all to Milburn.

Between lunch and tea, a session of 120 minutes, the Western Australia openers took the score from 93 to 322 from 28 eight-ball overs. Of these Milburn scored 181 from 134 balls faced. During this session Milburn hit 28 fours, and four sixes. The Queensland bowlers whose deliveries were dispatched over the 'Gabba fence were Paulsen (1), Surti (1) and Allan (2). Milburn at tea was 242 having batted for 230 minutes. He scored hs runs from 226 deliveries and his tally included 38 fours and four sixes. He was dismissed caught and bowled from Morgan's sixth delivery after tea. His brilliant innings ended at 243, these runs being scored off a record opening stand with Chadwick of 328 runs.

Usually to other than statisticians, cricket statistics do not make for interesting reading. On this occasion however I think I might be pardoned for quoting Colin Milburn's sectional figures when he set the 'Gabba alight on that November day back in 1968.

Total	Time	Fours	Sixes	Balls
50 runs	88 mins	9	—	79
100 runs	143 mins	17	—	128
150 runs	176 mins	24	1	166
200 runs	209 mins	32	2	202
243 runs	234 mins	38	4	228

Tony Lock was able to close the Western Australian innings at a record score of 5 declared for 615. His bowlers dismissed Queensland twice to win the match by an innings and 75 runs. It was after Milburn's innings that Peter Burge in congratulating Milburn on his innings said, 'Thank you, Ollie, for helping the cause of the big men'.

The scenario for the third innings I am recalling was set at the 'Gabba in late October of 1975. No play had been possible on the Friday, the first of the four scheduled days of the match in season 1975–76 against New South Wales in Brisbane. Damp conditions also halted play for 45 minutes on the Saturday and Greg Chappell, on winning the toss, asked New South Wales to bat first. The points system used in Sheffield Shield matches that season provided for batting and bowling bonus points for first innings and as a result there were declarations in each first innings. New South Wales closed at 7 for 250 and Queensland at 9 for 227. New South Wales were dismissed for 141 soon after 3.30 p.m. on the last day leaving Queensland to score 165 for the outright win in 17 minutes plus 15 overs to be bowled in the last hour. Chappell elected to open the innings with Trimble who took strike to left-arm pace bowler Gilmour. Chappell faced Colley in the second over and took 7 runs (a four and a three) from the four deliveries he faced in that over. He then proceeded to cut loose on Gilmour in that bowler's second over taking 22 runs (five fours and a two) from the 10 deliveries bowled (two no balls). He then had scored 29 runs from 14 deliveries. The next six deliveries yielded seven runs (no boundaries), and then a boundary and a single from four deliveries from Colley were followed by similar scores from four deliveries off Gilmour's fourth over. Chappell then was 46 from 28 deliveries while Trimble had picked up 21 from the 33 deliveries he had faced. Walters had meanwhile relieved Colley at the Southern end and from his second over 18 runs were taken 11 (one six, two twos and a single) to Chappell and seven (a four, a two and a single) to Trimble. Pascoe had relieved Gilmour at the Northern end and 15 runs came from his third over, 10 to Chappell and five to Trimble.

Chappell was caught by Colley off Walters in the next over having scored 86 from 55 deliveries in 72 minutes with 11 fours and a six. The opening stand with Trimble was worth 146 and set Queensland well on the way to a win by eight wickets with nine balls remaining. Trimble made a valuable contribution to the victory scoring 66 not out in 90 minutes from 72 balls.

During the course of Chappell's short though brilliant innings, Brisbane policeman Tom Warwick, umpiring this match with Ray Doxey, narrowly escaped serious injury when a fierce drive by Chappell struck him on the left shoulder as he ducked to avoid the Queensland captain in full cry. Tom had a large bruise on his left shoulder to show at work next day.

There have of course been many memorable displays by batsmen, bowlers and fieldsmen during the time I have been scoring at the 'Gabba. The three I have recalled stand out in my memory. I trust I shall be privileged to share in more pleasant experiences as seen from the scorers' box at Brisbane.

'Langi Kal Kal is a youth training centre for young male offenders aged between 16 and 21.'

The boys from Kal Kal

Martin J. Tobin

Martin J. ('Tobs') Tobin.

For one who was brought up with cricket and the household names of cricket like 'The Don', Richie Benaud, Alan Davidson and later, through my playing days, the Lawrys, Stackpoles, Chappells and the like, I now sit to write about the heroes and the household names of Langi Kal Kal, the names that have made the Balyarta Bombers famous.

Names like 'Sony', 'U-Bolt', 'Eddie the Mouth' and 'The Boy' are folk heroes at Langi and have brought the Bombers fame in the shape of two premierships and several other finals performances. But before I tell some of the tales surrounding these folk heroes, I should at least shed some light upon where and how the Balyarta Bombers from Langi Kal Kal came into being.

Langi Kal Kal is a youth training centre for young male offenders aged between 16 and 21, sentenced to a period of detention for offences committed against society. Those classified to Langi Kal Kal are not the hardened, sophisticated young adolescents who have committed numerous or extremely serious offences. More often they are young people who have originated from inadequate or deprived family environments, these disadvantages usually leaving the individual inadequate in social skills and healthy personality development.

Langi is situated some 45 kilometres west of Ballarat in Victoria's central highlands. It is set on nearly 3000 acres and is a community within a community. At Langi there is an experience-based social learning program with a token economy that endeavours to set the young offender upon the right track to take his place within the community on release or parole.

For many years Langi played traditional cricket in the Ballarat Cricket Association, but during the early '80s it was becoming obvious to many that this type of cricket was no longer the 'real thing' for the Langi lads. Less and less we were getting lads who had had any training in cricket, yet there were often those who wanted to play and, as with all levels of cricket, there were always those who were better than others. The usual situation arose: too few did too much and those that did too little got 'cheesed off' and then there were too few to play the games.

In September 1984, after a discussion with Frank Tyson, director of coaching in Victoria, Lord's Taverner, TV commentator and 'Pom', I made an approach to Andrew Buckle, then secretary of the Victorian Branch of the Lord's Taverners and by the Christmas of '84 Langi Kal Kal Y.T.C. had played its first game of *indoor* cricket. The team was playing in competition 'D1' and unlike the traditional Saturday competition cricket, a new enthusiasm, a new era, was underway at Langi. Initially we tried to confine this indoor cricket to one section (Balyarta Max 19 trainees), but the popularity was so overwhelming that it had to become centre-wide.

We had a name, the Balyarta Bombers, and we had players, the first season saw 22 individuals play this eight-a-side game, and there were more and more wanting to play. (This game seemed to get all the trainees interested. Well, why not? Each player has to bowl two overs and bat for four overs. In the traditional game you could field in the hot sun for five hours and not get a touch of the ball.)

Since those early days in 1984–85, the Balyarta Bombers have played 11 seasons of indoor cricket and, thanks totally to the continued sponsorship of the Lord's Taverners, we have used about 25 players per season with a maximum of 33 in the one just completed. In all we have used 290 individual players, 90 per cent of whom were introduced to cricket via the Balyarta Bombers.

Besides myself, the captain/coach and sole selector, the next player on our team list can only total 19 games. This is shared by four Balyarta Bombers: 'Sony', 'The Mouth', 'U-Bolt' and 'Glen'.

In the early days there was always an individual who had played cricket at school but few who had ever gone any further. On one occasion this young lad, Glen, came to me and asked about indoor cricket. He showed particular interest in the ball, what it was made of and how hard it was. I asked if he had ever played outdoor cricket. 'Yeah, but only when they use a tennis ball,' came the reply. After telling this story to the manager of the Ballarat Indoor Cricket Association, Ernie Pascoe, he gave me a couple of balls and on showing them to Glen, the young offender asked if he could have a go. He got his chance and for the remainder of his time at Langi was a regular member of the side. He contacted me several times after his release and to my knowledge is still playing indoor cricket in Shepparton, and hasn't been in trouble since his release. Hopefully some of the credit for this can go to the Lord's Taverners and the influence of the Balyarta Bombers.

On another occasion — in fact the start of our second season — I did the usual rounds of Langi and listed all those interested in playing. I picked the side, five of whom were first gamers. Batting pairs sorted out and ready to go, one of the lads came up to me holding a bat and said, 'How do you hold this thing?' I must have looked somewhat surprised. He continued, 'I've never seen a real one before and I don't want to look too stupid out there!' The situation resolved, he, too, turned out to be a fair player. There are lots of stories about the Balyarta Bombers and its players over the seasons, however I did promise to tell some of those that belong to the folk heroes of the Balyarta Bombers.

Eddie 'The Mouth' arrived at Langi during the final season of outdoor cricket and was soon involved in this activity and, as his nickname suggests, he wasn't backward at telling people about his prowess and on several occasions proved it. Eddie was still there when the Balyarta Bombers started.

Eddie took to indoor cricket like a duck to water. His bowling was adequate and he had the knack of getting wickets, but his batting was excellent and his fielding brilliant. After several games he had shown enough for Ernie Pascoe to ask if Eddie could play 'superleague' with the Ballarat centre. Arrangements were made for Eddie to be taken to Ballarat on Saturdays and travel with the team to Melbourne. No problems — Eddie fulfilled his agreement.

However, the fourth game of the season saw the end to Eddie's superleague career with Ballarat. The team was to play at Campbellfield and Eddie was at home that weekend on leave. Ernie had taken Eddie through travel details from his home near Dandenong to Campbellfield. However, come the day, Eddie failed to show. Eddie, before coming to Langi, had a very heavy drug problem. He had again been tempted into old habits. He did, however, attempt to get to the game and followed all instructions — except getting off the train. He had fallen asleep and travelled the Melbourne rail system for some six hours before waking and going home!

Eddie might not have ever again played superleague, but he did return to Langi on two more visits, caused through his drug habits, and was lucky enough to play in both of our premiership sides. On the sad side, Eddie had only ever played sport while in institutions. He first played cricket at the age of 14 at Bayswater Y.T.C. Then he missed a couple of years till his first visit to Langi. He continued with his sport on each stay at Langi and soon after his release from Langi was again sentenced, but this time to prison. His whereabouts today are unknown. A tremendous amount of natural ability never used to its fullest potential — that's Eddie 'The Mouth'.

'U-Bolt' — a nickname earned by virtue of a hard to pronounce surname — is a success story by the standards placed upon us by society. 'U-Bolt' never did anything during his first stay with us at Langi. He was lazy (well, it appeared that way), he wouldn't have a go at anything and became stuck in a rut similar to his lifestyle outside, without the alcohol. 'U-Bolt' left us and returned to his old lifestyle and somehow found the energy to reoffend. He returned to Langi and was this time forced to move and work. He was asked if he'd like to try indoor cricket and it took some time but he eventually said yes. He wasn't an instant success but with his own motivation, having found something he liked and enjoyed, and through determination and help from 'Sony', he improved and became a very

important cog in our first premiership win. 'U-Bolt' had improved from just a player who made up numbers to one who was more than handy in the field, a good solid opener with partner 'Sony' and an excellent medium-pacer who has the knack of being able to cut the ball off the pitch. All these skills were honed through his own determination and the help of one of the most talented young players it has been my pleasure to play with —'Sony'.

'U-Bolt' was paroled a week prior to the grand final but was living in Ballarat upon his release and was thus able to take part. We won due to a big effort from 'U-Bolt' and only a truly magnificent effort from 'Sony' cost 'U-Bolt' the best on ground in the grand final award. After this, 'U-Bolt' took up playing with several sides in Ballarat and also took on umpiring at the Ballarat ICA. He is still doing both and has successfully completed his parole, due mainly to the opportunity to be part of the Balyarta Bombers.

I've already mentioned 'Sony', and it must be stated that he would have to be one of the most gifted young players I've seen. An Aborigine with all the skills of a veteran, he also has the ability to develop the skills of others. 'Sony' could inspire anyone and was the main reason during the spring season of '85 that we had such a successful time. 'Sony' played 12 of the 14 games that season plus the two finals games. Coincidentally, we lost only two games, even though we had played 21 individuals during the season. 'Sony's' ability was so admired that 'A1' sides were asking about him. Ernie Pascoe again was able to arrange the draw so that we could play several games just prior to the A grade games and 'Sony' was able to show some of his many skills at a level which should have seen more of this very talented lad.

'Sony' played some very spectacular games with great diving catches, totally deceiving batsmen with sheer bowling speed and being able to destroy the best bowling with his technically correct, aggressive batting. He was a player who could literally win a game by himself.

But none of his top performances can rival the ones from 'The Boy' — Tony. Although a good all-round performer, he put up one of the best individual performances seen by any Balyarta Bomber during one match. Although the game was close, we were never going to lose, particularly when he came on to bowl. The first four balls removed the bails and the batsman was getting frustrated at not being able to get bat to ball. 'The Boy' came in with the fifth ball. There was a great yell from the batsman as he hit one. The yell of excitement turned to a howl of disappointment when he saw the ball go straight back to the bowler for a safe catch. All smiles, 'The Boy' started in for the sixth ball and the bails came off again. Everyone was getting carried away by the excitement. The batsman played forward at the seventh ball but missed it. It just missed the stumps, to a big groan. Batsman happy! The last ball and 'The Boy' comes in with a full toss. The batsman goes crack, straight into the ground and takes off for a run, only to be run out. Seven wickets in one over and minus 35 runs. We really were easy winners due to 'The Boy's' big over.

These are just a few of the stories of the folk heroes of the Balyarta Bombers. One could add lots of others, some very humorous and others of sheer skill or guts and determination. But there is one more story I must relate. During our third season it was arranged for Frank Tyson to come to a game and watch the Balyarta Bombers and then travel to Langi Kal Kal and speak to the boys at our best and fairest night.

All was arranged and publicised throughout the centre. It was going to be a big night but the reaction wasn't as expected. For days before the big event trainees were saying, 'Who wants to listen to that "Pommie", he knows nothing about cricket!' Panic started to set in with thoughts of 'only the players will turn up'. The big night arrived. Andrew Buckle and Frank Tyson arrived at Ballarat and were introduced to the players. The game began; it should have been an easy game and an easy win was expected. However, that was not to be; all the lads could seem to do was look to see if 'Typhoon' Tyson was watching them. Many silly mistakes were made and somehow the game was lost.

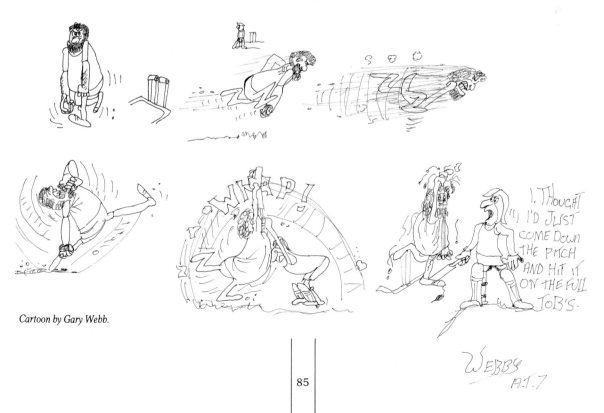

Cartoon by Gary Webb.

Now back to Langi Kal Kal. The players returned and all was ready; food was out, trainees from both sections, about 40 including staff, had come to see Mr Tyson, but still the same mood prevailed. Andrew Buckle and Mr Tyson arrived and immediately he was 'King of the Kal'. Trainees surrounded him like bees round a honey pot. Andrew Buckle and staff were deserted while Frank attempted to get some nourishment, surrounded by trainees asking some very intelligent questions on cricket.

The vote-counting came and went and Mr Tyson was asked to award the trophies. He spoke to each of the players and offered some advice for improvement in the individual's game. 'The Pommie' who 'knew nothing' had won over the lads of Langi. It turned out to be a very successful night and one that was talked about for many months afterwards.

The Balyarta Bombers exist today only thanks to the patronage and sponsorship of the Lord's Taverners and I must thank them for their continued support in making this activity possible for the lads at Langi. It has been most successful in giving the lads an opportunity to try a community-based activity which is not only fun and played at the individual's own level but also socially acceptable.

Origins of the Sheffield Shield

Jack Pollard

Jack Pollard, cricket historian.

Henry North Holroyd was a cricket buff. He was never an outstanding player although he was considered good enough in 1856, as Viscount Pevensey, to play for the Gentlemen of Sussex against the Gentlemen of Kent.

He surrounded himself with cricket memorabilia and although he dabbled in politics — he was Member of Parliament for East Sussex from 1857 to 1865 — he was most at home in the company of cricketers. When he became the third Earl of Sheffield and took over the titles Baron Sheffield of Dunsmore, Meath, Baron Sheffield of Rosscommon in Ireland and Baron Sheffield of Sheffield in Yorkshire, he became renowned for his patronage of cricket. He built in the estate of his family home at Sheffield Park, Sussex, a splendid ground, which was opened in 1846. No charge was ever made for admittance.

Lord Sheffield's staff of gardeners, butlers and groundsmen included many noted for their cricket skills. Five Australian teams opened their England tours at Sheffield Park and so did the 1894 South African team.

His Lordship became president of the Sussex County Club in 1879 and over the next 18 years sustained the county's playing strength with his purse, bringing in the famous professionals Alfred Shaw and William Mycroft to coach promising young Sussex players.

Shaw became his permanent adviser on cricket and managed several teams on tours sponsored by his Lordship, including one to the Arctic Circle where they played cricket on ice around midnight.

In 1891, when many of Lord Sheffield's friends were worried about their investments in Australia, he decided to take a first-hand look at developments in the colony and at the same time play a bit of cricket. He wrote to Arthur Shrewsbury, the 'Geoffrey Boycott' of the period, who had made four tours to Australia, seeking advice on the financial pitfalls of an Australian tour.

Shrewsbury had made both profits and losses from Australian tours and he went to great trouble to set down an income and expenditure account for a proposed Australian trip. This balance sheet, reprinted in full in Peter Wynne-Thomas's marvellous book *Give Me Arthur*, included advice on how much to tip ships' stewards, the cost of sleeping cars on Australian trains and even the charge for bands at big matches.

Shrewsbury strongly advised Lord Sheffield to include W. G. Grace in his touring team, adding that Grace would probably charge 1500 pounds to go, but that Grace's presence would add at least 2000 to the tour takings.

Shrewsbury at the time was conducting an intensive sales drive in Australia and New Zealand, where there was great interest in the bats and other cricket gear produced at Shrewsbury's Nottingham headquarters. He used Frank Illingworth, of Melbourne, as his Australian agent with the special task of forcing money out of those who incurred bad debts. On Shrewsbury's recommendation, Lord Sheffield appointed Illingworth his advance agent and sent a retainer to seal the deal.

Grace at first refused Lord Sheffield's invitation to make the tour. His Lordship responded by inviting Grace to Sheffield Park for tea, after which Grace announced his intention of touring and taking his wife and children along, too. Later it emerged that Lord Sheffield had paid Grace, ostensibly an amateur, 3000 pounds plus all expenses for his wife and family. Shrewsbury declined to tour as his business was then at a crucial stage in its development.

Lord Sheffield's team, captained by Grace and managed by Shaw, arrived in Australia with cricket popularity at a low ebb. The previous two Australian teams to England had been soundly beaten, and squabbles between Melbourne and Sydney had brought such a decline in standards that nobody in Australia was prepared to finance an England tour.

They ran into immediate snags. Lord Sheffield's agent, Frank Illingworth, having been paid in advance and with nothing to receive, absconded. Fortunately, Ben Wardill, secretary of the Melbourne Cricket Club, who had visited Sheffield Park as manager of the 1886 Australian team, had gone to Adelaide to watch the

start of the tour and was able to fill in for Illingworth.

His Lordship was deeply moved by the warmth of Australians' welcome for his team but aghast at the extent of the hospitality arranged for them around the States. Most of all he hated the speech-making his Australian hosts expected of him and he promptly handed over this chore to Grace.

Grace was never short of a few words but even he was shaken by the incessant speeches, both as a listener and an exponent. 'If I'd known I was going to be saddled with all this gasbagging I'd have asked for more money,' he said. At the grounds bands paid by his Lordship struck up 'See The Conquering Hero Comes', every time the heavily overweight Grace waddled out to bat. But he was still good enough to bat right through England's innings in the second match of the tour against Victoria in Melbourne, finishing with 159 not out.

When the team arrived in Sydney, New South Wales Cricket Association officials somehow got the dates mixed and failed to turn up to welcome his Lordship, who had to find a hotel on his own. When the embarrassed official finally showed up and confronted him with another packed schedule of speeches, Lord Sheffield called a halt and went off to Tasmania, claiming he could not stand the heat on Australia's mainland.

Unhappily, Lord Sheffield's brief stay in Sydney was long enough for a reporter from the *Bulletin* magazine to take a close look at him. This resulted in the following report appearing on 5 December, 1891:

Critically considered, Lord Sheffield is merely a non-aggressive representation of deplorable social and political systems, and better deserves to be wept and groaned over than cheered at. But, regarded as a simple-minded old fellow who runs a wholesome show for its own glory and with an amiable desire to amuse more people than himself, Lord Sheffield is not so displeasing . . . as long as he keeps his coronet in the pocket of his baggy pants, we don't mind.

Lord Sheffield's reaction to this kind of treatment

A rare photograph of Lord Sheffield, benefactor of Sussex and Australian cricket.

was not recorded by reporters who found him occupying the most expensive suite in a Hobart hotel and spending his days talking with derelicts in nearby parks, ever ready with handouts.

He was in fact a surprisingly earthy figure far removed from Australian ideas of wealthy noblemen. He was fat and roughly shaven, with hair that needed cutting and combing and a little fringe of beard under his chin. His shoes were scuffed and worn, his trousers unpressed and his pockets appeared to bulge with spikey objects. The *Bulletin* said he was averse to women, but was a shrewd man whose good nature would have made him the ideal landlord for a country pub.

In Lord Sheffield's absence, Grace came under increasing attack from the *Bulletin* and other Australian journals and began to show the accuracy of Shrewsbury's forecast that he could 'drink enough wine to sink a ship'. The stirring continued throughout the tour with the *Bulletin* reporting that Grace insulted Australian left-hander Billy Bruce, that Lord Sheffield threatened to cancel his deal with Grace unless he apologised to Bruce, and finally that Grace and his team-mate Andrew Stoddart had exchanged blows.

Understandably, Grace complained in his memoirs that he had been badly treated by the Australian press. Lord Sheffield returned to the mainland ready to accept cricket officials' apologies for all the jibes. In Adelaide before he left he instructed Shaw to provide him with a list of leading charities to which he sent cheques.

On the way home aboard the *Valetta*, his team defeated by two Tests to one, Lord Sheffield found time to write out a cheque for Ben Wardill, which he sent back to Australia with a request that it be used for the development of Australian cricket as a gesture for the warm welcome his side had received. In view of the vicious attacks his players had received from the *Bulletin* and other journals, it was a classic piece of cricket diplomacy.

The tour had cost his Lordship 16,000 pounds and his losses amounted to 2000 pounds, but it had revived Australian cricket. Not long afterwards the Sussex county team, for years without a regular captain, received a wonderful bonus when the appointment of Australia's Billy Murdoch as a full-time county skipper was announced. Murdoch spent six happy years as captain of Sussex, handing over to Ranjitsinhji in 1899 an immensely powerful batting side that had had the benefit of skilful leadership.

Lord Sheffield continued as Sussex president until 1897 when he went to work in Istanbul as a diplomat, a strange posting for a man who had objected to Australia's mainland heat. He resumed the Sussex presidency in 1904, when he made a special donation of 1000 pounds to county funds.

He died in 1909, thankful that his 150-pound gift to Australian cricket had been spent on what became our most important domestic trophy, but still the most unphotographed character cricket has known. Even his ancestors at Sheffield Park are unable to provide a photograph of him. The Australian Cricket Board has a bust of him, but the public has to make do with a few indistinct and blurred images from the turn of the century.

A premier game

It seems that those in the higher echelons of diplomacy, Prime Ministers in particular, have traditionally been lovers of cricket. Sir James Callaghan, a Labour Prime Minister, confessed to the editor that he only ever hit one four at school and was an indifferent bowler. He made up for his lack of prowess by following Hampshire with fanaticism in the 1920s, worshipping Lionel Tennyson, Phil Mead, Kennedy and Brown. He claims that among the greatest moments of his life was sitting next to Neil Harvey and Stan McCabe at a House of Commons dinner. It is incidental, perhaps, that when Ted Dexter stood against him in the General Election of 1964, Sir James triumphed. He claims, too, with some pride, that he attended the Sydney Cricket Ground with Bert Evatt, the former Leader of the Australian Labor Party, 31 years ago.

Some of those Prime Ministers who have been or are *aficionados* of the game are gathered together in the following photo-feature which ends with a 'striking shot' of Australian Prime Minister Bob Hawke.

A sort of sartorial splendour! Major C. R. Attlee (later Prime Minister of Britain) goes out to bat with Sir Edwin Stockton (right) for the North during the North versus South match at the Oval, 14 June 1923.

Prime Minister Ted Heath (centre) shares a joke with Billy Griffiths (left), a redoubtable secretary of MCC and Colin Cowdrey.

The West Indies fast bowler Lance Gibbs shows Australian Prime Minister Sir Robert Menzies how to handle the ball. Sir Robert was addicted to cricket.

The Rt. Hon. Margaret Thatcher shares enjoyment of the game with her husband, Denis, who is a tireless worker for The Lord's Taverners' cause. Mrs Thatcher gives fund-raising dinners for the Taverners at 10 Downing Street, London.

Prime Minister Sir Alec Douglas-Home, now Lord Home of the Hirsel, shown at the centenary dinner of the Middlesex County Cricket Club, July 1964. With him at the London soiree (left to right) are P. J. Burge, B. C. Booth, W. A. Lawry and R. M. Cowper of the visiting Australian Test team.

During a match at Kingston Oval, Canberra, on 14 October 1984, between the Prime Minister's XI and the Parliamentary Press Gallery, the Australian Prime Minister, Mr Bob Hawke, played a short ball onto his face. The Canberra Times photographer, Peter Wells, was on hand to record the shattered glass flying over the Prime Minister's left shoulder. The PM retired hurt, but apart from a black eye suffered no permanent damage. The photo won the Australian Press Photograph of the Year Award. (Picture courtesy of the Canberra Times).

The son of the peerless Bill Woodfull looks back and reminds us of the purpose and pleasures of cricket.

Thanks for the memory

W. J. Woodfull

Today we have seen a great game and perhaps the result was never in doubt since 'The Con' took the first over. Did we lose an early wicket? I don't remember, and it doesn't really matter. Cricket will always be the winner for it is indeed a great game, standing head and shoulders above all others for its enduring team spirit and honesty above all. The spirit of the game has always been synonymous with fair play in all walks of life. If any action falls short of the ideal, it has, for generations, been referred to as 'not being cricket'. What higher praise could one give to our great game?

The game has certainly come a long way since its inception with two stumps at either end and a 'bail' on top at either end, underarm and lob bowling, or even more recently in the 1920s, with uncovered wickets open to the elements and a time limit of three days for Test matches between those two arch-rivals, England and Australia. Even more recently, of course, we have seen the introduction of one-day cricket, almost a completely different game, and perhaps not one for the purists.

Throughout the history of civilisation as we know it today, change has always been regarded with, at least suspicion, if not disdain, but it is amazing to me that those changes, almost without exception, achieve the desired results. So let us not be too critical of these changes. Those who make such decisions are highly respected followers and ex-international players and they surely do not take their responsibilities lightly.

I can look back on the years 1920 to 1938 with awe and wonderment, and I can go further back if I look up the records, or I can be much more up-to-date if I wish, once more with the help of records and statistics. But the game is not about those things. It is about 11 men combining to form a team and where individual thoughts and aspirations take second place.

But what about the personalities? The names of Grace, Gregory, Hobbs, Trumper, Bardsley, McCarthy Ranji and oh so many more conjure up vivid pictures of the masters in action.

And what about the '30s? — Ponsford, McCabe,

The two captains, D. R. Jardine (left) and W. M. Woodfull toss before the start of the third Test, England versus Australia, 1932, in Adelaide.

Bradman, Jackson, Oldfield, Grimmett and O'Reilly for starters (who would need 11 players with those seven in your side?). Or, once again, Hobbs, Sutcliffe, Tate, Larwood, Hammond, Chapman and Verity. It must have been hard to get a game in those days!

Is it any wonder that we look back on those days with loving memories. Those and so many others were household names, almost members of the family. But, alas, today, there are so many Test matches being played around the world that the cricketing public are being offered more than they can comfortably digest. But now I start to sound like one of the 'old-timers' (which I am!). Shouldn't every player aspire to represent his country? And if there are more countries playing our great game at international level, then that must be good.

The days of the great blood matches between Victoria and New South Wales are gone forever. These were great matches in their day, but the public want (and have every right to see), the best in the world.

This great game will continue to be one of the greatest of all time. But as we think about the game today, perhaps we should not lose sight of that old adage:

> And when the one Great Scorer
> comes to write against your name
> He writes — not that you won or lost,
> But how you played the game.

This is what cricket is surely all about and this is what our daily lives should be all about. In closing the innings, may I say what a joy it has been to be a spectator, a participant and a commentator of and for our great game. We have a wonderful team up here and thank goodness I'm not a selector.

Village cricket

Gerald Bullett

Flowing together by devious channels
From farm and brickyard, forest and dene,
Thirteen men in glittering flannels
Move to their stations out on the green.

Long-limbed Waggoner, stern, unbudging,
Stands like a rock behind the bails.
Dairyman umpire, gravely judging,
Spares no thought for his milking-pails.

Bricklayer bowls, a perfect length.
Grocery snicks and sneaks a run.
Law, wiping with all his strength,
Is caught by Chemist at mid-on.

Two to the boundary, a four and a six,
Put the spectators in fear of their lives:
Shepherd the slogger is up to his tricks,
Blithely unwary of weans and wives.

Lord of the manor makes thirty-four.
Parson contributes, smooth and trim,
A cautious twelve to the mounting score:
Leg-before wicket disposes of him.

Patient, dramatic, serious, genial,
From over to over the game goes on,
Weaving a pattern of hardy perennial,
Civilization under the sun.

'It was cricket at its best with everyone properly dressed.'

Under the spreading chestnut tree

Greg Burns

The Blues Cricket Club of 15 to 20 members was based in Guildford, Surrey, and was largely made up of people who worked in the 'City'. These were London stockbrokers, bankers and the like and some were former public school boys. Our blue tie had a yellow duck as a motif.

Guildford is a 'dormitory' area about 35 minutes south of London on the fast line to Portsmouth. We lived there. I was invited to play with the Blues as a rather different Oz diplomat from Australia House in London. My cricketing role was that of a medium paced, off-spin bowler and given a turning wicket I could occasionally be a problem.

The Blues were keen cricketers and had a full fixture list against local Surrey villages over each summer weekend; all we lacked was proper net practice. As is the case in most English village cricket, one played oneself into form and fitness as the season progressed. I never knew the Blues to have a net.

It was cricket at its best with everyone properly dressed. Played seriously, the white-coated umpires, scorers, scoreboard and wives, kids, arvo tea and spreading oaks and chestnut trees were all part of it.

Greg Burns.

Stumps were drawn at 7 p.m. as a reluctant sun departed and we repaired to the local inn for a few pints of bitter with the opposition.

The matches were played on Sundays from 2 p.m. to 7 and all sorts of people turned out for the village teams. A regular opponent here and there was Tony Lock who loved his Surrey village cricket. We had Peter May play with us in his first match after recovering from a back ailment — he was a friend of our 'keeper.

One memorable match was against Byfleet, who were really well above village cricket standards, but we had an annual 'slaughter' fixture with them. On this occasion they had two Surrey colts fast bowlers playing with them. They were after the practice and a slew of wickets.

The Blues, with a sprinkling of 'old boys' from British public schools, had some superbly trained batsmen. Eyes on the ball, raised left elbow, beautiful footwork, bat down the line, etc. One only had to look at them to see their classic styles and potential but they only fired very occasionally.

These classic styles would sometimes give us a glorious 50 full of stroke-play which you would travel far

to see. Not always, however, as it took weeks for our chaps to start to see the ball properly with only match practice.

Meanwhile, the less gifted plodders (including me) would seek to hold the side together and avoid defeat while hoping one of our more gifted players would fire. This was the situation on our famous day against Byfleet, who routinely won every year. The young Surrey colts fast bowlers set about us with gusto. I don't think any of us had experienced such genuine fast bowling for years, if indeed at all.

In an earlier typical Blues 'they shall not pass' effort, I had been required at number 10 to hold up an end to prevent defeat and surprised even myself how well I could play a defensive straight bat and we lasted. This led to me being nurtured as a steady but boring left-handed opening bat instead of a wild, slashing late-order hitter who rarely scored anything much.

So here was a tight situation against Byfleet with two Surrey colts (anxious for blood) glaring at us down the pitch and a depressing feeling of being outclassed even before the match started. I doubt if I have ever faced fast bowling of the scorching quality now involved and what saved the day for the Blues was that this applied also to the Byfleet eleven.

My opening partner George and I tried to play straight and of course we snicked as the ball was moving a yard at blinding speed from either end. However, the Byfleet team was also mesmerised by the sheer speed of these colts and the snicked ball sped through to the boundary over and over again. Occasionally they got a hand to it, but not enough to hold.

In no time we were 50, nearly all from snicks. George went for 25 and in came Morley-Clark, one of our ex-public schoolboys. Well, it was his day to howl and he had his eye in. We were treated to a scintillating display of square cuts and cavalier driving such as only can come from being properly trained. He rapidly compiled a memorable half-century. I went for 35 and there we were in a lordly position in village cricket (especially for the Blues) of being 2 for 110 and we went on to make a highly respectable 6 for 190 or so at our time limit.

This was unprecedented against the much stronger Byfleet eleven and it inspired the Blues to great heights in the field. The bowlers kept on line and length, the team held the catches and we won outright for the first time ever. Never before had we even looked like winning. The aim had always been not to disgrace ourselves and so lose the next year's fixture.

The Blues' win was a triumph of village cricket and never will I forget the village blacksmiths, the older spin bowlers, the trained public school boy cuts and drives, the former and current Test cricketers who turned out occasionally and above all, the seriousness and the fun of English village cricket. In its way a quintessence of cricket — played hard and followed by the conviviality of a beer at the local. Many of these hostelries were located literally under the old chestnut tree on the edge of the village green.

I had three wonderful years of it and 20 years later when making our valedictory call on London as we headed home for retirement, 17 members and wives of the old Blues attended Sunday drinks in a Guildford pub to say God speed.

Names of villages and towns like Shere, Haslemere, Byfleet (of course), Abinger Hammer, Albury, Witley, Dunsfold, Godalming, Farnham, will live forever with cricket.

In my own case, vale came in Iran, of all places, where teams from the diplomatic cricketing nations played on Fridays on a hockey field in the huge Shah's Olympic Stadium complex — 6000 ft up with the glorious snowy backdrop of 13,000 ft Mt Towchal. The altitude proved a bit much for the old knees.

My last posting was in New York and early on my wife and I became well and truly lost trying to work our way north up the Hudson Valley. We finally located Broadway which is the W9 and runs from Battery Point on Manhattan away north to Montreal. Miles along we entered some open park areas and all we could see were cricket matches being played in all directions. Closer inspection revealed numerous West Indian and Caribbean-based teams locked in fierce combat on the 'village' cricket pitches. It did my heart good and restored my faith in human nature to see what cricket can bring about, even in the home of baseball.

Greg Burns is a retired Australian Senior Trade Commissioner who served in London, Kuala Lumpur, Tehran, Beijing and New York. He is honorary treasurer of the Lord's Taverners, Canberra branch.

A tour of the auld country

Ken Piesse

Ken Piesse in fine bowling action.

Life can be tough, terribly tough, even for a holidaying cricket writer, enjoying the luxury of some hot English sun and a few social fixtures with some midweek cricket mates, thousands of miles from home.

Instead of shivering through the coldest part of Melbourne's traditionally bleak winter, we basked in 26 degree sunshine enjoying Lord's, the British Open and some pick-up games at some of England's prettiest cricket grounds.

We had a strongish contingent, enhanced for one match by Test legend Rodney Marsh, and by first-class Australians Paul Jackson, Michael Dimattina and Peter King, who substituted when their own professional commitments allowed — and when some of our old timers broke down.

The locals treated us fabulously, invariably insisting on us sharing pints of bitter, Pimms and port and anything else alcoholic at luncheon and tea interval. It's a different way of playing cricket but to refuse would be an insult and anyway, we weren't over to play against Test cricketers — or so I thought.

We beat the Village XI at Eastcote and won in the last over at Amersham before taking on the Thames Valley Gents at Teddington, a couple of mighty swipes from historic Hampton Court, the imposing palace home for so many British monarchs.

On arrival at the ground and having had huge glasses of Pimms thrust into our hands, we recognised a couple of the opposing team. They bore an uncanny resemblance to two Aussie Test players, all-rounder Steve Waugh and fast bowler David Gilbert, and on closer examination and after several 'G'days' we realised we could be in for quite an afternoon.

Few seemed worried about the prospect of suddenly playing against them, except our openers who hurriedly retreated to the dressing room to check to see if they had brought their helmets!

I'd taken four wickets and been hit for three sixes in the opening fixture of the tour, just reward I thought for some rather erratic wrist spinning which the local village XI treated in death or glory fashion.

Our much-travelled skipper, wicket-keeper Mark Foster, laughed as we trekked onto the field. 'It could be Waugh or Piesse today!' he exclaimed. The Gents scored freely, especially to the short end-to-end boundaries on the straight drive. 'Fossie' told me to warm-up. Suddenly a wicket fell and we sighted Waugh, S. emerging from the pavilion, swinging his Symonds and looking rather too keen for our liking.

I'm just a club standard trundler and had rarely ever bowled in such august company, but took my turn at the crease as planned, and in two pre-lunch overs, didn't do too badly. Waugh hit one over the top of mid-on for four, but it was just out of reach and according to my mates, 'could have gone anywhere'.

We all sat down to roast spatchcock, exotic salads, English blueberry pie, French wines, more Pimms and port and coffee. I wondered if Waugh and his not out partner would be partaking fully. Afterall, he was only on a day-off from his Lancashire League duties with Nelson and it was still weeks before he was due to play at Somerset.

I bypassed the red but had several glasses of white wine. Lunch went for an hour and 40 minutes. We had little choice but to partake! Several of our party were so impressed by the hospitality that they asked for reserves to field for them upon resumption.

As a bowler, in the middle of a spell, I marched straight out and watched from first slip as Victorian left-arm tweaker Jackson almost deceived Waugh with a quicker one which found the edge and splayed to fine leg. Jacko had also 'gone easy' at lunch.

Now Waugh was at my end for the new over and I hesitated, throwing my mid-off back two-thirds of the way to the boundary, realising I was bowling into a slight breeze and the ball could balloon. I wasn't sure what to expect but fortified by Jackson's success in tossing one faster into the block hole, I aimed a quicker, flatter leggie as close as I could to Waugh's middle stump.

It felt good out of the hand but a moment later, it was volleyed high over my head, straight over my mid-off for six. A big one. Nice shot, I thought. Okay, slower this time, really try and spin it, high and twisty. You might get a stumping. Here we go. Waugh advanced. One, two and whack! Away it went, one bounce into the sight screen.

He appeared in extremely good nick. 'Don't worry, keep tossing them up,' said my skipper, reassuring me. I tried again. Higher in trajectory but with more top spin. It didn't work. This time he really middled the ball and if he had been playing on the expansive Adelaide Oval, where the fittest run five on the straight drive, I'm sure it still would have been six. At Teddington it deserved a 12.

Waugh grinned slightly. The silence from my teammates was deafening. I waited for my field, which had now scattered, to resume their positions and away I went. Again up, on middle and off, flattish. He waited, took one step and back it came, hurtling over my head, one bounce into the sightscreen. Four more.

Twenty runs off four balls. I could feel myself flushing a little. I said to Waugh: 'I thought you wanted some good write-ups this season!' He was fiddling with his pad and just smiled. I went around the wicket, thinking a change of angle can often confuse. I went for the wrong 'un. It was dangerous but what choice did I have?

He waited for it to bounce and repeating his fierce straight hitting, planted it over long on, halfway across the adjoining oval. Twenty-six runs off five balls. Thank goodness for six-ball overs, I thought.

I was in a daze as I wheeled in for the last delivery. I don't remember what I tried to do, but away it went again straight, high and handsome, over the top. Six more.

'Over!' said the umpire, handing me my jumper, realising I'd had enough. I'd been hit for 6, 4, 6, 4, 6, 6 (32). There was muffled laughter from some of our blokes. 'I've never seen 32 hit off an over before!' said Nigel Murch, our ex-Victorian fast bowler.

I glanced at Waugh, thinking I needed a bit of sympathy. 'Sorry,' was all he said. 'Ever done that before?'

I asked as calmly as I could. 'No, never,' he said.

He made 90 in 45 minutes and was out lofting the competitive Jackson into the wind where Melbourne club player Warren Ayres took an old-fashioned Australian Rules high mark, right on the line at long off. He walked off to thunderous applause. 'Nothing you could do about that,' said several sympathetic teammates who walked my way after congratulating Ayres.

I noticed that Waugh accepted one of the long, tall coolers from the chief gent of the Thames Valley XI as he walked into the pavilion. I wish he had been as eager to please his hosts at lunchtime. I certainly will be — and won't make the mistake again of bowling immediately after the break.

We didn't have a return fixture at Teddington on this trip but further battle is planned for 1989. I think I might conveniently pull a hamstring on the morning of the match and take in some culture when we're drawn against the Gents.

Buckingham Palace, the National Portrait Gallery, Trafalgar Square. I don't mind a good ol' dose of London foot. I might even join the queues reading the newspapers at Australia House. Anything would be better than going in with the Thames Valley gents and one S. Waugh again!

Steve Waugh.

Ken Piesse, 32, has edited the Australian *Cricketer* magazine since 1978. Like all cricket-mad lads, he said he once had an ambition to play for Australia. 'Nothing is now further from my mind,' he says, 'even if another leggie, Bob Holland, did play Test cricket at 40.'

'Anthony Trollope . . . may at first seem an unlikely contender for a place in cricket anthology.'

Trollope's Test match

Dennis Castle

Dennis Castle.

Once, in the now-fast dimming past, cricket anthologies revived golden oldies and quotable quotes. Among them would be Dickens's send-up in *Pickwick Papers*, Mary Russell Mitford's amazing analysis of the 19th century game at all levels, Thomas Moult, Neville Cardus, Robertson-Glasgow, A. G. Macdonnell — even Sir Henry Newbolt's *Vitai Lampada* . . . *'There's a breathless hush in the Close tonight — Ten to make and the match to win'* . . . These and many more cropped up periodically in potpourri form for cricketophile bookshelves. Now the one-day game appears to have bred a generation of more ruthless ravers to whom *'Play up, play up and play the game'* is no longer acceptable. Literary gems have become mothball mementoes of good losers. Winning is paramount simply because being mere runners-up is headlined by the media as a disgrace of almost criminal proportions. Who wants to read the poetry of the game when the spectator majority build up a bull ring atmosphere? Yet, for the record, there is one fantastic cricket episode which could appeal to today's high-tensioned audiences even though it was written more than a hundred years ago.

Anthony Trollope, famed for his Barchester sagas, recently adapted successfully for television, may at first seem an unlikely contender for a place in cricket anthology. However, in an uncharacteristic novel *The Fixed Period*, published 1882, he included a semi-science fiction account of a Test match he envisaged taking place a century later, that is, in the 1980s. Gerald Brodribb did refer to it briefly in his excellent *English Game* but that was published in 1948 when Trollope's seemingly absurd prophecies still had 32 years to run. In 1948 man had not yet set foot on the moon, the Beatles were still infants and Denis Compton ruled OK — so anything could happen. Now Trollope's century has passed, his predictions for our time deserve a new look. While he was mostly wildly off-target, some minor details do bear scrutiny. Certainly they were perhaps not so outlandish as his vitriolic critics averred in 1882.

Unlike Trollope's contemporaries — Dickens, Thackeray, George Elliot (pen name of Marion Evans, a close friend of Trollope) — he was more weighty, less subtle in his attacks on the social behavioural patterns of his time. He lacked humour, was blunt, forthright and intolerant yet possessed a most telling simplistic style. While often slated by reviewers he remained a consistent best-seller. Even by modern standards few authors were more prolific. Many of his 66 published works ran into three volumes per title and great artists like Sir John Millais illustrated his chapters.

Born 1815, Anthony Trollope was the fourth child in a family of seven. His mother, Fanny, was already a successful writer, famed for her book *Domestic Manners of the Americans*, written after the Trollope family visited the United States in 1831. She became a literary celebrity on both sides of the Atlantic and from her Anthony obviously inherited the ability to write of foreign lands without displeasing their inhabitants, as Dickens had done in *Martin Chuzzlewit*, anticipating American males' desire to be John Wayne.

Fanny was also a country vicar's daughter. This background provided Anthony with first-hand knowledge of clerical life which he was to portray so vividly in novels, much to the Church of England's disquiet. His father, sadly, was a briefless barrister, a dire failure. He later turned to farming only once more to run into debt. A born loser, he died insane in 1835 when Anthony was 20. When only seven Anthony had been sent to Harrow; at 11, his father failing to pay his bills, the boy was transferred to a private school at Sunbury. An upsurge in his mother's royalties switched him to Marlborough but, like Dickens, W. S. Gilbert and other 19th century writers, Fanny's works were ruthlessly pirated in America before copyright laws were legalised. With the family income again reduced, Anthony returned to Harrow as a cheap fee day-boy.

As one destined to conceive the craziest Test match ever in print, the boy saw good cricket at his two prestigious public schools, both of which produced several famous international players. Anthony's father, however, could never adequately equip him for the classroom, let alone sport. Unlike Lord Byron in 1805, Anthony never qualified for the Harrow XI to play Eton

Anthony Trollope as seen by the famous cartoonist Spy (Leslie Ward) in Vanity Fair, *April 1873, under the heading 'Men Of The Day'. Spy also sketched many cricketers including 'The Demon' bowler of Australia F. R. Spofforth. To appear as a Spy cartoon was a form of 19th century Oscar award. It meant that Trollope was a star author despite the unflattering image.*

at Lord's. Byron, of course, conned his way into the team. Pulling his noble rank to oust a better man ensured his lifelong boast of playing at Lord's. Yet he was lame, gave away runs in the field and had to bat with a runner in both innings for dismal low scores. Such autocracy was beyond young Anthony Trollope; he never played the game at all.

Oddly enough, like Byron, he did possess a remote 'blue blood' background of which he was inordinately proud. His great-grandfather, Sir Thomas Trollope, was descended from a baronetcy created in 1641 during the Cromwellian Civil War although the earlier knighthood had been bestowed on a Sir Andrew Trollope 200 years earlier in the Wars of the Roses. The Trollopes seem to thrive on civil wars! To this day cricket reporters still headline 'The Roses War' when Yorkshire's white rose emblem meets the red of Lancashire at Headingley and Old Trafford in often rather uncivil war on those two unpredictable pitches, as many Australians will agree.

A distant cousin of young Anthony became the 7th baronet, later Lord Kesteven, a Lincolnshire title, but always remained entirely aloof from the impecunious branch of the family. Doubtless he was appalled at his barrister relative's blundering blots on the family escutcheon but Fanny valiantly maintained an outward show of keeping up with the gentry. Anthony was enthralled by the family name's derivation. The Trollopes obdurately insisted that a knight called Tallyhosier landed with William of Normandy. When king of England, William watched a hunt at which Tallyhosier slew three wolves single-handed to be dubbed by his majesty 'Troisloups'. French names became bastardised by Anglo-Saxon less-cultured phonetics and the name became 'Trollope'. A pity really. As all male Trollopes were to enjoy following the hounds, Tallyhosier had a hunt rallying call ring to it!

Young Anthony made the tragic mistake of quoting his 'lineage' at Harrow. He possessed no Byronic good looks nor Regency buck gamesmanship. His classmates ridiculed his birthright claim. 'Trollope' was equated with a whore. Anthony stood no chance. In his autobi-ography he described his schoolboy self as 'skulking about . . . ill-dressed and dirty . . . lonely and forsaken. I had no friends and was despised by all'. This was no abject whine. He cited this distress to prove just how much penury he had to overcome before being acclaimed a best-selling author.

And who can blame him? Of the seven Trollope children, five died of tuberculosis in very early years and only Anthony survived to live past age 30. His upbringing was hardly conducive to success. An Irish writer who had sat next to Anthony during studies at Harrow, William Gregory, later described him as . . . 'filthy to look upon . . . his exercises a mass of blots and smudges . . . yet he was no sneak . . . his faults were external and gave no sign of promise . . .' and that his teachers regarded him as 'an incorrigible dunce'. Significantly, while Trollope became a 19th century household name, 'Gregory' survives only in Australian cricket circles! Certainly after such a horrendous start in life, Trollope's literary success is nothing short of a miracle. He could absorb punishment, was never self-pitying but turned his personal facts of life into saleable fiction of the highest class.

Trollope spent the majority of his life employed by the British Post Office. At first in London as a mere underpaid clerk, shabby but industrious, he rose to become an Official Surveyor, despite much resentment from his seniors. Many of his innovations are still practised in the Royal Mail service today, albeit in modernised forms. His duties took him all over Britain, Ireland, Europe, West Indies, New Zealand, Australia and the United States where he personally organised the Anglo-American Postal Treaty. Yet, despite this highly onerous job, almost half his novels and travelogues were written during those duties to Queen Victoria's Mail. He remained ever a rebel constantly falling foul of authority who tried to blame his public writing success as being 'done in the Company's time'. Yet they could never fault him for lack of diligence, poor attendance or slipshod work. Although his superiors took credit for the invention of the pillar box, the first being sited in Jersey, Trollope always insisted that it was solely his idea.

His approach to writing might seem mechanical but he was no hack. Rising at 5.30 every morning he would pen 500 words per half hour, with his watch at his elbow. Even this strict scheduled discipline never impaired his amazing inspiration. To maintain thought continuity, he transported a self-designed desk containing powdered ink, quills and paper into railway compartments, ships cabins or drab hotel bedrooms. However much his surroundings varied he always had his familiar tools of trade before him. He wrote hard-hitting stuff knocking uninspired bishops, avaricious landed gentry and boastful, self-made merchants. He laid bare their fallibility knowing just where to hit pomposity in its overweight belly. In spite of such social and moral attacks he also handled love stories tenderly and with utter sincerity.

Rose, his wife, understood him completely. She fair-copied many of his later manuscripts as did his elder son, Henry, who eventually joined Chapman & Hall, publishers of several Trollope books. One hopes that the 'blots and smudges' of his schooldays had been overcome by then, for he was now part of the 19th century *literati*. From his earliest work he appears to have bypassed youthful experimentation straight into sound middle-aged experience.

His marriage was ideal. Although obviously conventionally Victorian in her subservience to the man of the house, Rose was an integral partner in his work. With the example of her mother-in-law Fanny, when sole earner in a disintegrating home, Rose quietly played her part. That Trollope should find a wife who could contain his irascibility, defiance and completely workaholic style of living was a stroke of good fortune his talent deserved after such a miserable childhood.

On a visit to America, Trollope became enamoured with an early trend-setting women's liberator, Kate Field. She was almost a female counterpart of Trollope — save in her head-turning beauty. Whether she was his mistress in the full sexual sense is open to question.

Her outspokenness was a rarity in the 19th century even in America. Trollope certainly saw her as 'copy'. She influenced several of his fictional heroines who stood up for marital rights hitherto not accepted by the Victorian dominant male. Steadfast in the background, Rose tactfully turned a blind eye to her husband's infatuation. She befriended Kate who stayed with them in London and in Italy. Doubtless sensible to the fact that the girl was an adjunct of her husband's literary output, Rose could be said, in Victorian cliche, to know which side her bread was buttered.

Trollope tried to marry Kate Field off to several eligible bachelors during their travels, as if devising a plot for a novel, but she would have none of them. She remained a life-long spinster friend of the family, speaking her mind, which Trollope must have translated into eternal triangle romances.

In 1867, Trollope was 52 and still a much-travelled Post Office Surveyor. The position of Assistant Post Master General fell vacant and he was next in line but, having been constantly at odds with Sir Rowland Hill, the top man, a junior official was promoted over Trollope's head. He could not accept this and resigned in high dudgeon, thereby giving up a good state pension. What cannot be determined today is whether he actually needed a salaried job. He was a highly-paid writer, his two sons had been well educated and Rose kept their various homes in spotless order. Perhaps he still feared the poverty of his own childhood and saw the Post Office as a buffer against a falling-off in book sales. Another factor could have been the daily stimulus of meeting people.

Immediately he stood as a Liberal candidate in a by-election at Beverley. He was not deeply political and his motive may have been to get a seat in the House of Commons so that he could qualify as Post Master General after all! His campaign however was more as an umpire for the Empire than deeply aware of that Yorkshire town's real needs. He lost badly but still seemed bent on avoiding a freelance life by becoming editor of St Paul's Magazine, a job almost as short-lived as his parliamentary aspirations. His views were better expressed through his fictional characters than in belligerant editorials. Quarrelling with influential people was highly dangerous in the 19th century. He had few real friends although W. M. Thackeray remained a staunch admirer of his work. Trollope could be likened to a strong reliable shire horse consumed with the urge to enter steeplechases! Trollope obviously inherited his father's inner apprehensions regarding money and, above all, lacked social tact.

The Fixed Period, written in 1882, was far removed from any of his previous novels. Indeed it went almost absurdly 'over the top', a mad escapade which he must have known would create controversy of the worst kind — bad publicity. The story concerned a fictional Pacific Island British 'colony', Britannula, as he envisaged its government and social culture in a hundred years time — 1980. Trollope illustrated that century's progress with inventions such as a steam tricycle travelling at 25 m.p.h and carrying electrical headlights, a machine which recorded and replayed speech, and a direct telephone line between England and Australia. All such prophecies were derivative. Phones were non-existent in Trollope's world but they were already in American inventors' pipelines as was the gramophone. Electricity was in use in a minor degree in London theatres by then so Trollope was only improvising upon known 'progress'. However it was not these advancements that so offended the English reading public. Trollope had forecast legal euthanasia on his 1980s island — mandatory death for all subjects beyond the age of 67!

He must have realised this subject would horrify the status quo of all God-fearing people — it was taboo, evil, anti-Christian. Only murderers could be so sentenced by hanging judges otherwise 'thou shalt not kill'. So a British battleship sails into Gladstone, the capital of Britannula, to put a stop to this barbaric practice — and the British press men o' war fired broadsides castigating Trollope for such an unsavoury, disgraceful concept. 'Essentially ghastly!' boomed *The Times*. 'An elephantine joke', trumpeted *The Nation*, 'by a person without a sense of humour'. Reviewers ran out of adjectives condemning this blasphemy, all aimed to allay the superstitious fears indoctrinated by hell and brimstone clergy. A deacon who personally rebuked Trollope for 'this somewhat grim jest' received the reply: 'No, it is all true. I mean every word of it.'

Did he? Could he really imagine that such compulsory 'deadlines' could be enforced by the 1980s? In any event, by then the death sentence for killing had been rescinded in Britain. In modern context, Trollope's prediction conjures up a Lady Macbeth chairperson of a Doomwatch council checking birth certificates in the town hall to polish off uneconomic pensioners. *The Fixed Period* certainly created a furore but both the press and the clergy saw to it that its impact was as restricted as the Britannula population. Yet into this gruesome theme Trollope introduced a Test match.

The motivation behind this heavy-handed attempt at light relief with a cricket match is incomprehensible. Trollope must have imagined some portly Victorian John Bull of a prime minister writing to placate H.E. the Governor of Britannula: 'We cannot condone you making your pensioners walk the plank at 67. They are entitled to their normal span. However, if you find financing almshouses a drain on resources, tell you what, we will play you fellars at cricket on your Gladstone ground. We'd attract bigger 'gates' than the early pearly ones you deemed necessary for your pensioners . . .'

Trollope should have included another Kate Field in this novel. By the 1980s Britain had a woman prime minister. Not even George Orwell in his famous book *1984* had forseen 'Big Sister'.

Having successfully scotched euthanasia with gunboat diplomacy, England sends its 1980 team to Britannula captained by Sir Kennington Oval! As a subplot to such a macabre drama, this incongruous cricket interlude cannot be taken seriously. Yet Trollope vowed 'it was true'. England have a month's practice at Gladstone. This was obviously a skit on Melbourne, also named after a British prime minister. Trollope visited the city many times during two long Australian tours. He writes that the Gladstone ground 'has been extended by an acre or so' so that 'sixteen fielders are needed'. This prediction could perhaps be equated with the use today of 12th, 13th, 14th and 15th men being brought on when bowlers 'limp off', after completing their stint, for a cold shower and a cooling beer.

Trollope mentions that Gladstone spectators needed binoculars. Again not an innovation today. As far back as 1846 W. J. Corey advocated use of a telescope: 'I saw the play of the batter perfectly with the bowling and wicket-keeping. I wonder why I had not been told to get one before?' Today's grounds are ringed with zoom lenses and soon umpires will make their decisions from pocket videos. Incidentally, to clear up a point made by my nephew, 19th century cricket was seen in colour, not black and white, even through telescopes.

England bat first, opening with Sir Kennington Oval and Sir Lord's Longstop. The latter 'is completely enveloped in india-rubber guards with a machine on his head by which his brain and features are protected'. Trollope undoubtedly saw the *Punch* cartoon of 1854 but the machine 'helmet' seems his own idea — spot on the 1980s. Human bowling was apparently on the wane. England had brought over a catapult ball projector but Britannula had gone a stage further. They had invented a steam pump bowling machine 'ridden into place by attendant engineers' — quite a job for the ground staff in 1980! Adjusting it for the right trajectory takes 15 minutes, a record some strolling, long-distance fast bowlers seem intent upon breaking today.

While catapult machines are still advertised in cricket journals today, they were well in vogue in the 19th century. Nicholas Wanostrocht, who in order to avoid scorers' spelling mistakes had played under the name of Felix, had built such a rig. This he practised against, also wearing a forearm pad, now in use today. Felix then faced the great Kent all-rounder, Alfred Mynn, in a single-wicket match at Lord's — and lost.

*'New cricketing dress, to protect
All-England against the present
swift bowling.'* Punch, *1854.*

Mynn's level-with-the-shoulder fast bowling proved more destructive than the catapult.

Trollope was doubtless aware of this contraption being a contributor to the magazine *Once A Week* which, in 1861 published an article by N. Silver deploring such a practice. 'Science is entering the game. She has invented a machine called, classically, a catapult . . . made to supersede the art of bowling. I am haunted by hideous dreams that the days of cricketers are numbered and that, 'ere long, matches will be played by steam . . .' Yet as Felix proved to his cost bowling machines did not reproduce the grunts of power, the thundering footfalls and grimacing venom of Dennis Lillee, Fred Trueman or any West Indian quartet.

It seems credible that Trollope used N. Silver's 'nightmare dream' in *The Fixed Period*. The first ball of the Gladstone Test is finally triggered off from the steam machine: 'Suddenly there comes a sharp snap . . . a little smoke and lo, Sir Kennington Oval is out. Bowled without a stroke!' (Getting out in this way is bang up to date). 'Sir Oval's dismissal is greeted by the sound of kettle drums, trumpets, fifes and clarinets — and a huge gun is let off. This crescendo occurs every time a wicket is taken . . .' Here Trollope is almost exactly right for the 1980s. Only omitted are rattling coins in empty beer cans, booing on the bowlers run-up to put batsmen off and the Mexico wave. Even diehard veteran spectators might also have preferred euthanasia if Trollope had dared to introduce a nude streaker!

England are all out in three days for a mere 1100. Who received the scorebook credit for taking Sir Oval's wicket is not mentioned. Probably the three engineers must have had the task of appealing for lbws. Not an easy responsibility as the umpires would have to wear ear-plugs to avoid early deafness with the ball being trench-mortared six times an over. And did either a steam machine or catapult bowl no-balls? Trollope does not elucidate.

Britannula, more used to their own steam device, do not play the tourists' catapult too well and England's second innings is dominated by Sir K. Oval's 300 which sets the home side 1500 to win. After a poor start the rot is stopped by Britannula's captain, Jack Neverbend, who sends every ball 'away into infinite space' — certainly a prophetic term for the 1980s. Jack bats on into the final day — the match has taken a week — when Britannula, with only three wickets in hand, still require 560 to win. The first ball is driven by Jack 'with such velocity that the bowler's wicket is smashed to atoms . . .' a word with deeper significance than mere fragmentation in the 20th century.

England, up against it, suddenly dispense with the catapult — obviously the elastic was by now overstretched — and revert to old-fashioned hand bowling. This traditional do-it-yourself delivery is left to Sir K. Oval: 'at one moment flinging the ball with tremendous impetus and then just rolling it up with most provoking langour' a foretaste perhaps of Botham's middle-aged act today. While the scorers were no doubt in a quandary sorting out the bowling analyses between 'steam', 'catapult' and 'live' overs, Jack Neverbend remains undismayed.

With the last man at the other end he hits 39 in one over. In 1980 this would have meant a spate of no-balls, wides and overthrows although, on Trollope's envisaged huge ground with at least nine all run to third man, fielders would need the combined stamina of Tarzan and King Kong plus the throwing arm of the Incredible Hulk to keep the runs down. Deftly Jack farms the bowling. As the pavilion clock [steam-driven?] strikes six Jack sent the ball flying into the air perfectly regardless of whether it might be caught or not, knowing that the one run needed to win would be scored before it came down from the heavens into the hands of any Englishman. It was caught by Stumps but by that time Britannula had won her victory.' Jack Neverbend remained undefeated with 1275, in Victorian parlance, 'the hero of the hour'.

Did Trollope foresee a change in Law 32 in 1980 or were both he and his publishers, Blackwoods, ignorant of 'The Striker being caught no runs shall be scored'?

My guess is the latter — no one bothered to check. As for Mr Stumps, he could have been the suitably armoured wicket-keeper or, with 19th century penchant for puns, merely 'short leg'. Trollope's prediction of a week-long game in the 1980s was already dated by 1939. The timeless Test in Durban was left drawn, the England team just making the boat home after 10 days. By 1980 that could never happen again. Like the Britannula government the controllers of international cricket have set a five-day deadline!

Obviously Trollope had a less than sketchy idea of the game's rules. The match is absurd, yet within the context of dire drama did he intend any irony, innuendo or symbolism in the amalgam of sporting farce and ritual murder? As a glimpse of cricket a hundred years on there are but few similarities. Certainly there is a slender link between euthanasia and cryonic suspension as practised in America today. In his biography *Anthony Trollope*, James Pope Hennessy states that his subject was no H. G. Wells or George Orwell in the prediction class nor, may I add, did he possess the extraordinary skill of Jules Verne who was much nearer the mark for the 20th century.

Trollope's was a careless shot in the dark writing in a *milieu* for which his style was entirely unsuited. Yet in the character of Jack Neverbend we can match him today with tacklers of missions impossible, Superman, Wonderwoman and, dare I say it, Batman! I feel it safe to assume that Trollope moulded Neverbend's innings on Charles Bannerman's great innings of 165, retired hurt, in the first-ever Test against England at Melbourne in 1877. Trollope's younger son Fred emigrated to Australia and married Susan Farrand. His parents made the long voyage to Australia twice, the first to attend the wedding in 1871. On both visits they stayed at Fred's sheep station at Mortray. Trollope wrote several books there on his travelling desk, despite boredom with eating mutton — even for tea! He was there again in 1875 and doubtless Fred eventually sent him Melbourne *Argus* cuttings of Bannerman's knock and Australia's victory.

Fred Trollope owed much to his father both financially and in family loyalty. Twice he saved the Mortray station from bankruptcy. Fred and Susan eventually produced six sons and two daughters, the majority of whom Anthony and Rose never saw but they entered into the rougher lifestyle down under with great fortitude. In England, as did his ancestors, Trollope enjoyed hunting. Indeed, the family crest, a rearing stag, was embossed on Trollope's notepaper despite the link with the baronetcy being, relatively speaking, well out of his reach. Despite his sardonic characterisations of the 'upper crust' dignitaries in his novels, Trollope must have nursed a secret longing to join the Sir Kennington Ovals and Sir Lord's Longstops he so lampooned in print.

In England he regularly rode to hounds. Later in Australia he tried stag hunting. Two hundred and fifty people gathered at a Melbourne heath for the hunt breakfast. Trollope, overweight and poor-sighted, fell at the first fence. He later wrote of kangaroo hunts at which four horsemen with a dog each risked their necks against this agile animal who could turn and savage their pursuers with great ferocity. Trollope described one 'roo who suddenly swept up a yapping terrier and carrying it 10 miles before setting it down unharmed, a chase after Trollope's own heart.

Australia provided several settings for later books. He studied the Gulong and Gympie gold mines for his novel *James Caldigate* and also compiled a vast travelogue *Australia & New Zealand*, a thousand pages long and, by his own admission, 'very dull'. *The American Senator* was written almost entirely in Australia proving he did not require immediate environmental stimulus for his plots. Voyages overseas were never rest cures for him, just workaholic exercises in experience. His memories of the lands he visited were always needle-sharp. That rough and ready exterior covered a meticulous mind. He understood commerce, the law and the church. With first-hand experience of genteel poverty he caught the moods of his time but, ironically, he was unable to transcribe into the future.

The Fixed Period was a complete fiasco — both volumes. His affronted critics ignored his poor cricket knowledge under the shock waves of euthanasia. Ignominiously the book was hastily swept under the carpet of castigation. There was a brief comparison made with Charles Darwin, whose *Origin of Species* in 1859 had caused the biggest upset in 19th century print. The theory that ape had fathered man and then used clubs to beat each other had fascinated Trollope, especially as it offended the church against which he also campaigned. But Darwin's 'sacrilege' against Adam and Eve had stood the test of scientific time. Trollope's brash attempt to breach staid 19th century peace of mind was a damp squib stamped out after smouldering only briefly. What bizarre rush of blood prompted the book is forever a mystery.

Trollope knew his craft well. Senility cannot be blamed for the lapse. Certainly *The Fixed Period* was the last of his books he saw in print but, by then, he had written four more, including his autobiography, all published in 1883–84 after his death. These proved popular, running, in all, to nine volumes. He did how-ever reveal that he favoured euthanasia when, in a letter, he wrote: 'Men should arrange for their own departure.' No place for umpires in that statement!

Tragedy clouded his last days. In November 1882, the year Darwin also died, Trollope suffered a stroke which left him paralysed and speechless. During such misery he must have prayed for euthanasia. He died in late December. By uncanny coincidence he was 67, the exact age Britannula had decreed life should end. That however was never mentioned in his otherwise ful-some obituaries.

Long after his burial in London, a freak turn of fortune in the family tree made Fred's third son in Australia the 14th Trollope baronet. This would have pleased old Anthony immensely. While weak on cricket he was nevertheless a great all-rounder, a truculent stonewaller, a cunning wicket-taker of pomposity and a sure catcher of cant, especially among the clergy. No doubt the MCC with Dr W. G. Grace then at the helm hated Britannula beating England — by steam. Today it would be by 'seam' . . . to be fair Trollope was, after all, only one letter out.

'But Mailey liked that full toss best. He said it was as good as a Saturday afternoon.'

He bowled like a millionaire

R. C. Robertson-Glasgow

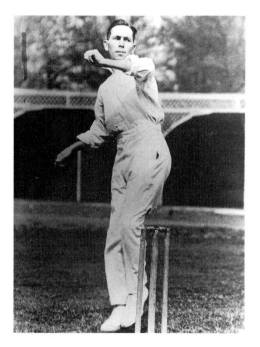

One of the great leg-spin and googly bowlers, Arthur Mailey was a member of the triumphant Australian teams of the 1920s. His bowling was characterised by his exceptional power to spin the ball. Mailey played 21 times for Australia and took 99 wickets. He was also a cartoonist and writer of considerable talent as his autobiography, Ten For 66 And All That, *proved.*

In his last Test match for Australia against England, at the Oval in 1926, Arthur Mailey bowled Jack Hobbs with a full toss. In the same innings, but with more propriety, he also bowled Sutcliffe and Woolley, had A. P. F. Chapman stumped, and G. T. S. Stevens and Wilfred Rhodes caught. But Mailey liked that full toss best. He said it was as good as a Saturday afternoon.

As a bowler of slow leg-breaks and googlies, Mailey was imaginative and experimental. He would invite a batsman's contempt with a wide, lull him with long-hops, then send him witlessly pondering to the pavilion with one that struck venomously from leg-stump to the top of the off. Like P. G. H. Fender, he was never devoted to precision for its own dull sake, but to the supreme art of conquering a batsman according to arrangement. 'Sometimes,' he once remarked, 'I am attacked by waves of accuracy; and I don't trust them.'

Such a bowler needs rich support from his own batsmen and fellow bowlers, and for most of his Test career Mailey had it. Unsolicited help, too, came in his first series, 1920–21, from those of our own batsmen who, in a manner always surprising to the Australian, regarded leg-breaks as a form of voodoo, and awaited execution with hypnotised acquiescence.

In the following summer, in England, Mailey was equally great. The extent of his work was diminished, but its performance made easier, by the preceding attack of Gregory and McDonald. The batsmen who survived those masters of pace seldom retained the freshness of mind and body needed to combat Mailey's guile. In the same season Mailey took all 10 Gloucestershire wickets in an innings at Cheltenham.

But many will remember him rather by the wickets that he didn't take, in those matches which rarely escape into print. In these, working on foreknowledge or a whispered suggestion, he would dispense tactful full-pitchers and self-starting boundaries, and, in the long intervals, gladden autograph books with quaint pictures. Yet he was never just the famous fellow, relaxing.

To him all occasions were equally great, or small. He

went into a Test match, as Joe Coyne used to go on to the stage, apparently because he happened to be walking that way. He gave of his wonderful best, and, if it failed, well, there was a conversation to renew with that comical gate-keeper, or an exceptional moustache to be sketched down there behind square-leg.

When he had retired from playing Test cricket he used to come over to England to report and depict it with a sort of casual exactitude entirely his own. He was exquisitely tickled by the solemnity that often overwhelms the press, and once, while dozens of pencils were immortalising some maiden over or no-ball, he leant over and whispered: 'Will you join me in hymn number 403?'

Mailey and Grimmett fail to be compared for excellence, and it could be a long argument; but, whatever be the answer on their performances in England, Mailey, with his severer spin, was the man in Australia. Both, in their own line and time, were better than anything of that kind in English cricket.

Arthur Mailey was number one pick for New South Wales and Australia for a decade after the First World War. Born at Waterloo, New South Wales, on 3 January 1886, he did not make his Test debut until 34, but took 99 wickets at 33.91 in 21 Tests from 1920–26 with a best performance of 9/121. He died on New Year's Eve, 1967, aged 81.

DRAWN BY
ARTHUR MAILEY

AUSTRALIA'S GREATEST BATSMAN

A glance to leg

*Women's cricket —
past and present*

"Marry me and do the teas for the club on Saturdays."

Women's cricket — the Australian view

Ann Mitchell, Australian team manager

Australian women's cricket came of age in 1987 when its national team beat England in a one-day and a Test series in England. This marked the first loss at home for England since international games for women began in 1934.

The Australians were thrilled with the results. Previous to this tour they had begun to assert their supremacy — they beat England in the final of the World Cup in India in 1978, and again in the final of the World Cup in New Zealand in 1982, then in the five-Test series in Australia in 1984–85. To defeat England on their own home ground was the ultimate dream come true for 1987 Aussies.

I have been involved with Australian teams for a long while, first as a player in 1975 and then from 1977 onwards as manager for most of the long series. In that time standards have improved and the whole sport has been organised along more professional lines. Having a coach, physiotherapist and scorer to support the team on tour, as we had in 1987, makes for a more efficient unit.

The Australian and England women's cricket teams before the one-day international at Lord's, July 1987.

Not content to win games on tour, our 1987 team also set about remaking the record book. In the second Test played at Collingham, Yorkshire, Denise Annetts (193) and Lindsay Reeler (110) put together the highest partnership in first-class cricket — 309. Denise showed real class and her 193 makes her the highest scorer ever in women's international cricket. Such performances by our batters won the admiration of cricket lovers in England. Our bowling and fielding departments did almost as well, with spinners Jenny Owens and Lyn Fullston regularly claiming four or five wickets in an innings.

So the Australians at the moment feel quite justified in calling themselves world champions. The only people to dispute this title are the New Zealanders who beat Australia 2–1 in the Shell Cup one-day series in Australia in January of 1987. We will justify the claim to the title and avenge that loss to New Zealand when we play all countries in the World Cup to be held in Australia in November–December 1988. Teams from England, India, Ireland, New Zealand and The Netherlands will come to do battle with us in this one-day competition. Unfortunately it does not seem likely that the West Indies will participate due to lack of finances.

The improvement in our standards is the result of a combination of factors. There has been an upsurge of interest in the sport in the 1970s and '80s as administrators have tried to promote the game for women through all avenues. Today young women have the opportunity to play the sport at both primary and high schools. There is more coaching available for them as people realise that women are serious about playing the sport. Sponsors, pleased with the success of the national side and the growing exposure in the media, are prepared to back the game. Federal and State Governments have given financial assistance which has permitted a more professional approach.

The highlight of each season in Australia is the national championships, currently sponsored by the Commonwealth Bank. States compete at three levels: open, under-21 and under-18 and they form the springboard to success on the international scene.

At the open championships in January 1988, held in Canberra for the first time, an Australian team was chosen to go to New Zealand for the Shell Cup. From the under-21 and under-18 championships (in Adelaide and Melbourne respectively), the best young players were selected to form development squads for specialist coaching.

The competition is great and there is good incentive. Our players can make it if they've got the talent and dedication. From our tour of England and Ireland in 1987, I sensed that English standards have dropped because they do not appear to offer the same incentive to their players and the game is not being developed in the schools. Meanwhile, Ireland is pushing ahead, following Australia's example, and is determined to become a force on the international scene.

Whatever happens, 1988 will be an interesting year for women's cricket, culminating with the World Cup final in Melbourne on 18 December. Naturally, I expect Australia to remain world champions — but it is not going to be easy.

Twenty-five-year-old Lindsay Reeler on her way to an impressive 69 in the one-day international at Lord's in July 1987. Lindsay, born and brought up in Zambia, emigrated to Australia 15 years ago and could have played hockey for Australia but opted for cricket.

Gels at play in the 1890s

Nancy Joyce

Regency rompings had to give place, in the fullness of time, to the sobriety of the Victorians, and if the girls played cricket at all, they did it in the discreet obscurity of the home circle, or more rarely still, at some advanced seminary for young ladies.

But before this temporary eclipse, a noteworthy occurrence must be recorded. The very structure and substance of the game, in the early years of the century, was undergoing transformation with the introduction of round-arm bowling, and this metamorphosis, the historians agree, was in the first instance due to a woman.

Christina Willes was sister to John Willes, Kentish squire and patron of all manly sports, and now of immortal memory, since his tombstone stands engraved for all to see — 'He was the first to introduce round-arm bowling in cricket'. It appears that while Mr Willes, keen cricketer that he was, was convalescing from an illness, he used to induce his sister to throw a ball at him in the barn of his home at Tonford, near Canterbury. She did so with a round-arm action that avoided entanglement in the voluminous skirts of the period. He was so struck by her success that he forthwith adopted the style himself, and devoted the remainder of his cricketing days to securing its recognition. But it was an uphill battle: the effort cost him his patience, and cricket one of its most devoted adherents. In a famous match at Lord's in 1822, playing for Kent against MCC — the story has often been told — he was no-balled by Noah Mann for bowling his new-fangled stuff. He threw down the ball, jumped on his horse and rode away, out of Lord's, declaring he would never play again. Nor did he, though his sister's invention was made law six years later.

In the period of which we are now speaking, when the art of playing was almost universally eclipsed by the art of watching, pride of place must be given to Mrs Grace. Here was the supreme exponent of the indirect influence, the power behind the throne. Or was it, in her case, on the throne? For Mrs Martha Grace (1812–1884) mother of W. G., his four brothers and his three sisters, was a woman of commanding presence. Exactly to what extent she took part in the family games in the orchard does indeed appear open to question. The old lady herself, when aged more than 70, declared that she used to bowl to her sons; and George Anderson stated that she was an even better player than her husband, and could throw a cricket ball, properly, as far as 70 yards; but W. G. denied this. She understood the game though, there is no doubt of that, and in Richard Daft's opinion, knew 10 times more about it than any lady he ever knew. One story goes that in 1866, W. G. then 17, having made very few runs, was caught at square leg off a half-cock stroke and on his return to the private tent, his mother was heard to chide him sorrowfully: 'Willie, Willie, haven't I told you over and over again how to play that ball?' It must, too, have been about that time that she wrote to George Parr, asking him to include her son (E. M.) in his England XI, but adding that she had a younger son (W. G.) who would in time be better still, 'because his back play was sounder' and 'he always played with a straight bat'.

In fact she became a legend in her lifetime. As an elderly lady, her hair in ringlets, she held her levees at the Gloucestershire matches, her sons hovering attentively about her as she criticised their form, vented her distaste for left-handed batsmen or commented unfavourably on a fieldsman who threw in underarm. If she was unable to be present on an important occasion, they posted the score-sheet to her night by night, or sent her a telegram if there was anything special.

There have been other famous mothers: C. J. T. Pool, of Northants, D. C. Collins, the old Cambridge Blue and J. W. Greenstock, the old Oxford Blue, have all owned to being coached by their mothers while Henry Bagshaw, of Derbyshire, remembered being bowled to by his grandmother. There is a pleasing story about Greenstock. His mother was absolutely determined that her first-born son should become a cricket Blue and a family council was held while the child was in his cradle. It was decided that the surest way to achieve his Blue for him was to bring him up left-handed, and this was done. From left-handed rattle he graduated, in easy stages, to the left-handed tossing up of cricket balls and, sure enough, he eventually tossed them for Malvern and Oxford. But heredity, perhaps, had something to do with it, for who was this sanguine mother? None other than 'Jackie' Foster, herself no mean performer, and sister to the famous brothers of Worcestershire, 'Fostershire', as it was called in the palmy days of H. K., W. L., R. E., and the others.

Then came the 1880s and '90s when cricket for women arrived again, and with what a flourish! Cricket in the great country houses, professional women cricketers on tour, cricket in the schools, the colleges, the villages, the colonies. Cricket in *Punch* and in the pages of J. M. Barrie.

It is easy to see what happened in the country houses. The young men had their cricket weeks, exclusive sash encircling aristocratic middle, with champagne to restore them and a bevy of young ladies to score and applaud, and dance until the small hours of each cricketing day. It was natural — what more so? — that the ladies should demand their little game. So the gentlemen umpired and the ladies did their playing, quite charming and delightful, and that was that — away they tripped in boater and bustle, to the next week. No constitution, no continuity, until White Heather burst upon the scene.

This celebrated club, founded in 1887 and still eating dinners to this day, is without doubt the oldest of the ladies' clubs in England. It was started, according to the copper-plate inscription prefacing the great leather score-book, 'by 8 ladies, Hon. M. Brassey, Hon. B. Brassey, Lady Milner, Lady Idina Nevill, Lady Henry Nevill, Hon. M. Lawrence, Miss Chandos Pole, and Miss Street', and the reason? — 'it was thought advisable to start a club in consequence of the large amount of 'Cricket at Normanhurst, Glynde and Eridge'. (Eridge being the country seat of the Nevill family: Normanhurst that of the Brasseys.) It flourished: from eight members in 1887 it had increased to 50 in 1891.

Of the cricket, it is hard to appraise the standard of the early days: the majority of White Heather's opponents appeared as transient, disembodied beings who figured with a fine impartiality, now on one side, now on the other, and the evenly contested games against boys' preparatory schools belong to a later period. But of its members' prominence in the social and political life of the day, there was certainly no question. One founder member, in due course Marchioness of Willingham, was to achieve fame as Vicereine of India, whose impact on her surroundings, expressed in a favourite colour scheme, earned her the soubriquet *Mauve qui peut*. Lady Milner was responsible for another viceroy's wife, for her daughter, in the fullness of time, was to become Marchioness of Linlithgow.

Lady Idina Nevill, founder member and eventually Countess Brassey, started life as opening bowler of 'undeniable chisellers' in 1887, and graduated inevitably to President, which office she adorned in uncompromising felt hat, pink, white, and green club tie, and jaunty sprig of the appropriate emblem pinned to left shoulder. As the years went on, the signature of Lady de la Warr masked another founder in Hon. M. Brassey: that of Lady Abergavenny, Lady Henry Nevill. And from founders to founders' kin, for the Duchess of Richmond, Mrs Leveson-Gower, and Mrs B. Stacey, secretary of White Heather for many years, were all members of the Brassey family; Lady Camden was a Nevill, and Lady Cantelupe and her sisters connected by marriage. The club harboured many other good cricketers, the four Miss Lofts, Mrs Cattley, Miss Hornby, Miss Le Fleming among them: Miss Georgie Waters, a fine player, was secretary from 1911 until her death in 1950.

But the most celebrated of all, of course, was Miss Lucy Ridsdale, elder daughter of Colonel Ridsdale, of Rottingdean, Sussex, and subsequently Countess Baldwin. It was she who entertained a general meeting at No. 10 Downing Street at the height of the General Strike in 1926 (at election times the club had difficulty in raising a side). It was she who electrified Mr H. L. Collins, captain of an Australian touring team, by confiding to him her one time batting average of 62, and her recipe for curing nerves in young women. 'One strange thing [sic] about my batting was that I was frightfully nervous when I went in. But when I became engaged to Mr Baldwin I lost all my nervousness, and it was the year that I was married that I made by best batting average, 62 runs for the season.' History, what there is of it, is on Lady Baldwin's side. Opening for White Heather against Lady E. Somerset's XI at Westonbirt, 22 July 1892, we find Miss Ridsdale made 76.

From White Heather to the Original English Lady Cricketers is a far cry indeed in spirit and intention, although contemporary in time. The latter comprised a troupe of two professional teams organised in 1890 to stump the country, and spread the game abroad. The 'colonial tour' remained a pious hope, and no record exists of matches played against 'Lady Amateurs'. But the exhibition matches were stage-managed, not with invariable success: W. G.'s comment was that if they expected to popularise the game among women, they failed dismally. Mr Rockley Wilson saw them play at Llandudno when he was 10 years old, and even at that age thought nothing of them. It was said at the time that they might be Original and English, but they were neither Ladies nor Cricketers.

During the 1890s, though the game could not fairly be described as popular, a number of clubs did achieve a brief existence, not so grand as White Heather, nor so business-like as the professionals. There were the 'Dragonflies', or Derbyshire Ladies, to whom White Heather lost a close two-day match in 1896, Mrs Baldwin's younger sister scoring 53 for White Heather and a Miss Fitzherbert the same number for the victorious 'Dragonflies', whose star bowler Miss Thornewill came out with a match analysis of 12 wickets for 69 in a by no means low-scoring game. Clifton Ladies was captained by Miss Ethel Lomas (afterwards Lady

BELSKY . . .

'Oh, quite the prettiest l.b.w. I've ever seen!'

Since this book is the best of the past and present in cricket, the editor makes no excuse for reproducing this Belsky cartoon from his earlier Cricket Bag.

Carpenter) and Miss Bessie Grace, daughter of W. G., was renowned as a great hitter. Severn Valley, led by Miss Maud Matthews (now Mrs Hesketh Pritchard) and Miss Edith May, of Piercebridge, was another force to be reckoned with, and indeed, finally deposed the all-conquering Dragonflies.

From time to time, though not often, dark hints of the ladies' prowess leaked out to a waiting world. It was another Miss Grace, no relation to W. G. and Bessie, who in 1887 made 217 at Burton Joyce, Nottinghamshire, 'against the really good bowling of four men': Wootton Courntenay C. C., incidentally, numbered a regular member in a Mrs May Brown, and to glance back to the 1830s, George Parr's neighbouring rival village of Bingham always included in their ranks a Miss D. 'who was able to hold her own with the best of them'. Back again to all-ladies cricket, Miss Wright in 1899 hit up 106 out of 142 at Sidmouth, and Miss Leslie Crawford, sister to a famous trio of brothers, got 107 for the Ladies of Caterham while her faster-scoring brother, on a neighbouring ground, was running up *his* century in 19 minutes! It was Miss Mabel Bryant, however, who really hit the headlines. Playing in 1901 for the Visitors to Eastbourne against the Residents, she scored 224 not out in two and a quarter hours. 'I saw her make five consecutive fours to the boundary,' wrote a male onlooker, 'three cuts between point and slip, an off-drive and a leg hit. She also obtained five wickets in each innings. On one occasion, in bowling down a wicket, she smashed a stump, and carried away a portion of it as a memento!'

And what of the Empire all this time? There were stirrings. By 1888 it was worthwhile for an English XI to visit Cork; a photographer, all bustles and boaters, gives the names of the players — three Miss Townsends, two Miss Meades, two Miss Eyres — quite a family party, but who raised the team, and with what success they executed their Irish pilgrimage are details lost to the historian.

The account of the first match in Australia 'played quite on the principle adopted in England', was printed in *Cricket* for May 1886, and must be of abiding historical interest:

'There were considerably over a thousand persons at the [Sydney] Association Cricket Ground on Monday afternoon, the majority of those present being ladies . . . The two elevens were called the Siroccos and Fernleas respectively, the former wearing a cardinal and blue costume, while the latter were attired in black and gold. Play began at 2 p.m. and continued until half past six o'clock. The Burwood band played selections during the afternoon. Miss L. Gregory captained the wearers of the yellow and black, while her sister Miss Nellie led on the amazons of the scarlet and blue . . .

'The palm for all-round cricket must be awarded to Miss R. Deane, who displayed such excellence in all departments of the game that many players in our senior clubs would envy. The Misses Gregory and Englestoff also shone to great advantage, evincing a thorough knowledge of the intricacies of the game. The wicket-keepers Miss L. Gregory and Miss Jeffreys were very smart behind the sticks, and at times fairly brought the house down with dexterity. The fielding was generally good, but the ladies with several exceptions could not throw. Their bowling was mostly round-arm, the obsolete grubber being resorted to only by one bowler.'

Miss Rosalie Deane was to achieve lasting fame as the first scorer of a century in each innings, which feat she accomplished at Sydney in 1891, making 195 and 104 for the Intercolonial Ladies Club v. the Sydney Club.

The New Zealand entry for this date carried a more amateurish ring. On 28 October 1886, eleven Marahua girls challenged eleven of the Riwaka cricketers to a match 'any time they like. Dinner and Dance provided. All welcome'. A sporting invitation.

Woman's place in the ranks of literature was, however, tenuous. There was Sir James Barrie, of course: any aspiring reporter could well do worse than turn up *The Greenwood Hat*, and read therein Anon's (J. M. B.'s) superb ball-by-ball commentary, in 'Ladies at Cricket', on the match between school and neighbourhood dominated by a young woman called 'Mary Dear', the great catcher of the side, who was shouted for by all her team-mates to catch each catch that offered, no matter whither it was hit. Indeed, this capable fielder caused the only little cloud on an otherwise carefree horizon — 'for the gaiety of them was a new delight on cricket field. The Marechal Niel captain came out to complain that Mary was catching too many, and had no right to catch balls hit in the direction of another fielder.' But mercifully, 'after consultation between the umpires, the decision was given in Mary's favour'.

Womanly influence was shed, albeit indirectly, on Barrie's famous cricket club for authors, the 'Allahakbarries' — A. E. W. Mason, Bernard Partridge, J. C. Squire, Augustine Birrell and the rest, for their captain has divulged his method of selection. The married ones he chose because he liked their wives, the bachelors for their peculiarities of countenance. This explains, then, the editor of *Punch*'s apostrophe to himself after Making the Winning Hit:

Virgin, and chosen for your facial oddity
In you your captain found a rare commodity
Omitting not what other men omitted.
You went to make the winning hit, and hit it!

But the 'dear enemy' of the Allahakbarries, the lovely actress Mary Anderson, was, despite her titular leadership of the opposition, a non-player. She 'never (such is the glory of woman) could follow the game despite deep study, and always called it "crickets".' What need had she of drab detail, who commanded weapons so much more effective? For she had 'a powerful way of wandering round the field with the Allahakbarries' top scorer, who when he came back would tell Anon sheepishly that he had promised to play for her in the second innings . . .'

Beside J. M. B., other literary mentions pale into triviality. Andrew Lang's stanzas 'To Helen after seeing her bowl with her usual success' appear astonishingly laboured: Helen Mather's forgotten tale wherein the heroine attired in knickerbockers tied at the ankle, clouts the German Fraulein wicket-keeper on the nose — appears quite amazingly puerile: and the political satire in *Punch* of 1892, in which the Lady Cricketers are all mixed up with enfranchisement and the Women's Liberal Federation, and W. G. with W. E. G., well, it sends us back to our history books for elucidation. 'A team of our own', says the Fair One in the caption, flashing dark glances at a tremulous Grand Old Man. 'I should think so. If we're good enough to scout for you, why shouldn't we take a turn with the bat?'

All in all, however, the whole thing was not taken too seriously, and opinion was frankly sceptical about cricket ever proving a summer game for women. But Richard Daft, courteous though doubtful, was on the right tack when he advocated a shorter pitch, a smaller bat, and a lighter ball, when 'the game might be played by ladies to advantage', and 'more wrist and elbow work would be seen in their batting if they had a lighter bat to play with'.

The smaller bat and the lighter ball were in fact adopted after many years had passed, though it has been considered wiser not to tamper with the length of the pitch. In connection with the ball, a curious piece of history may be related. Mr Alfred Reader, proprietor of the cricket ball works at Teston, was asked by Gamages in 1897 to make a special ball suitable for ladies. After experiment, he produced a five ounce model of exquisite pellucid blue, and this was supplied to Gamages in half-gross lots. The size was right, but alas, the colour not surprisingly proved quite invisible against a background of grass and sky. One ball only, of beautiful leather and first-class workmanship, has been preserved as a memento of this curious episode.

My Ode to Cricket

Sheila Scotter

Cut lunches, champagne, camaraderie
Runs, risks and rain
Innings and outings and Indians
Catches, champions and Chappells by three
Kent v Hampshire matches as a child
England the enemy now I am an Aussie
Taverners, Tests and all-night television.

*Sheila Scotter, Lord's Taverners'
founder member number 79, with
Greg Chappell at the annual
Taverners match at Red Hill,
Victoria.*

*Marlene Matthews, the Olympic
and Commonwealth Games
sprinter, replying to 'Our Guests'
at The Lord's Taverners' national
dinner, Regent Hotel, Sydney,
27 May 1986.*

'Where in the Southern Hemisphere could one play cricket where the spectators partook of strawberries and cream? . . .'

A Colonial view of the sward

(Reflections from 1978)

Paul Sheahan

Paul Sheahan neatly turns a ball round the corner in a Minor Counties match at Stoke-on-Trent, England.

'Come one' is what I have learned the refined Englishman says in preference to a raucous 'Yeah'. However refined it may be, it almost brought about my downfall in the first game of this season. I had taken what is euphemistically called a 'plunger' in my initial sortie into the world of English social cricket last season and was desperate to get off the mark in 1978.

A colleague here at Winchester took me aside to ask whether I would play for the Common Room in their annual clash with the Winchester Doctors. I readily agreed but was rather taken aback when told that the toss would take place at 6.25 pm! The great day arrived, we won the toss and batted; fortunately we did bat first because by the time the doctors batted it was a case of 'Deep into the darkness peering, long I stood there, wondering, fearing . . .' After a short while I found myself at the crease — 'Come one' as I pushed to mid-on. To my horror, the doctor at mid-wicket appeared like a bolt from the blue and threw down the stumps at my end. A sonorous appeal; a studied rejection; none-too-mild surprise in the opposition camp, as it was a 'needle' game. At the conclusion of the over, one of the doctors said to the umpire, a certain Arthur Kingsbury, a man of fine mettle, 'That must have been close'. With a faintly familiar statement Arthur replied, 'Close! He was out by a mile but I'd come to see him bat!'

The same Arthur Kingsbury exacted his revenge later in the season when the Common Room played the Winchester Staff. I found myself batting with carefree abandon against an attack that was not likely to force the England selectors to reconsider the touring party, on a pitch, let me hasten to add, that was very close to the road and, therefore, within range of a terrace of the staff houses. Circumstances allowed some indiscriminate hitting. Slog number one caused dismay in some quarters: it went through the upstairs bedroom window of the end house. The owner's wife returned home a minute or so later, quite fortuitously, to find a score of grimy little faces — you must pardon the Dickensian allusion, they really do wash well at Winchester College — peering over the fence, shrieking with laughter. She was not amused, understandably, as she had to clear up a myriad of glass slivers in the room.

On the other hand, it brought innumerable benefits to her husband: the recounting of the story has been worth many a pint in the Queen Inn! Slog number two broke a couple of tiles on the roof of the house next door. Next ball brought a stifled appeal for lbw to a bat-pad. To the bowler's amazement, Arthur upheld the appeal. As I departed, the bowler made noises to Arthur which cast doubt upon his interpretation of Law 38 (I *think* it is 38) but there was method in his supposed madness. 'My house was next in line!' he confided.

My naivety as a captain was exposed by a certain man whose name was not unfamiliar in these parts. The fixture was with the Broadhalfpenny Brigands and I was to learn that they were very aptly named. The mantle of captain of this erudite gathering of Winchester dons for the game rested on my shoulders and it weighed heavily. Of course I was anxious, a little nervous even. My opposite number suggested that his troops were not overpowering in batting strength and that perhaps we could ease back if wickets fell quickly. I won the toss and, in my innocence, failing to bear in mind numerous Test match disasters and heedless of the fiendish grin on their captain's face, I inserted the visitors. The pre-match advice came wafting back at 28 for 5 so I took heed and the score duly mounted. At 100 for 5, I thought that we ought to put the brakes on but, as invariably happens in these situations, was powerless in the face of two firmly entrenched veterans, one of whom was the Brigands' skipper. As time slipped by and the score neared 150 for 5, I suggested that we had fulfilled our part of the bargain. I was completely floored when he said, 'Oh, I forgot to tell you that Learie Constantine always said, "If you're silly enough to put us in, you get us out"!'

This delightful world of cricket has no parallel in Australia: the social game that is competitive, but never descends to the level of surrogate war, and that is

Paul Sheahan.

played, apart from this season, in the pastel, filtered light of an English June evening rather than the harsh, uncompromising atmosphere of a burning Australian summer when it is more a feat of endurance than a pleasure to play a game of cricket. Where in the Southern Hemisphere could one play cricket while the spectators partook of strawberries and cream and the strains of a military brass band playing something marvellously melodic carried across the playing field?

Cricket played on pitches that remain relatively docile in the rain — unless 'Deadly' Underwood is playing — rather than the sleeping vipers in the Antipodes that subdue even the stoutest heart in the batting fraternity at the mention of moisture. Cricket played for the 'squire' of Longparish, Johnny Woodcock, followed by a country church service. Cricket played on a south lawn at Blenheim Palace. Is it true that the cricket must cease when the Duke's mallet is seen to wave above the hedge of the croquet lawn? Visits to Arundel Park whose wooded groves surround one of the loveliest grounds imaginable. And so *ad infinitum*.

Perhaps the greatest pleasure that I experienced was the vicarious one of looking after a school team. I had not realised previously that cricket-watching could be such a nerve-racking business. Possibly despite, rather than because of, my coaching, the boys played some very good cricket! How rewarding it would be to see one of them touring Australia in MCC colours or is it now England ones?

One of the really enjoyable games in which I played was the one organised by Vince Broderick, the professional coach at the college and formerly a Northants player of great distinction. Vince rallied many of the past Winchester captains to honour the retirement of the much-loved Podge Broadhurst who *was* Winchester cricket for quite some time. During proceedings I learned that one can rarely get the better of an English pro. At one stage runs were particularly hard to come by in our quest for their total so I caustically remarked to Vince, 'Are you trying to destroy Podge's afternoon by making a draw of it?' Vince's instantaneous retort, 'Looks like it by the way you're playing!' set one smug Australian back firmly on his heels.

They say that you should learn something every time you undertake any activity. If there is one thing that I have learned during the summer it is, to borrow the phrase of a friend, that I could be quite happily laid to rest facing my own bowling!

Bert Oldfield — wicket-keeper to shopkeeper

David Frith

David Frith.

In a house manically cluttered with cricket books and relics, one item has a special sweetness. It is an Australian Test blazer, almost boy's size, from the 1930 tour of England, given to me by Bert Oldfield in 1954. It was given freely and without calculation by an old-world gentleman who was said — so I heard — to be a tight-fisted businessman.

It was a presentation made, perhaps, in recognition of fervid enthusiasm shown by a 17-year-old for a game which unites men of all ages and nationalities. That shop, W. A. Oldfield's, was already a shrine; it now became a magic temple.

It was in Hunter Street, Sydney, a walk from St James station. There was a huge blow-up in the shop window of the classic Hammond cover-drive, with Oldfield himself in perfect position low behind the stumps. Around this giant cardboard cut-out were bats and stumps and brilliant red cricket balls, and inside the shop were stacks of boxes full of boots and sprigs and sweaters in the colours of all the Sydney grade clubs, including the red stripes of my beloved St George.

But these everyday items could also be obtained from Stan McCabe's shop in George Street or Alan Kippax's rather impersonal establishment in Martin Place. Mr Oldfield (he was 'Bertie' or 'Cracker' only to his own generation) went back a lot further. He used to talk of fellow Glebe cricketer 'Tibby' Cotter, a turn-of-the-century boyhood hero of his own. There was a huge enlargement of Cotter by the staircase. He spoke of his fine athletic build and beautiful skin, and when he spoke of his death in the First World War, I couldn't take my eyes away from that cardboard form for several minutes.

I did the rightful thing on one visit to the shop, lashing out on an Oldfield Test Perfection cricket bat. He threw the tin of linseed oil in for nothing and wrote me a letter wishing me luck with the bat. Any wonder I went back as often as I could.

Upstairs was the reclusive Charlie Macartney, who emerged once just long enough to sign my autograph book. It was a place to meet all kinds of cricketing people. An early visit, during the 1950–51 MCC tour, coincided with a call by English cricketers Trevor Bailey (with his Lindwall-broken thumb in plaster) and Reg Simpson, who patiently listened to the meaningless outpourings of a starstruck teenager. At one stage the talented NSW batsman Ray Flockton worked in the shop and it was exciting to talk to him only days after he had taken 85 off the West Indian attack at Sydney.

But the chief draw was always the proprietor, Bert Oldfield, capped 54 times by Australia, holder of 78 catches behind the stumps, with an amazing 52 stumpings to go with them. And he made more than 1400 Test runs. He would, Ray Robinson once wrote, 'have made a fine courtier in Louis XV's day. You could picture him in the ballroom at Versailles, with powdered wig, gleaming shoe-buckles and snowy lace at his wrists'. In complete contrast to the muddy shape retrieved from a shell-hole in Belgium in the First World War, his head broken, the Bertie Oldfield of the 1920s and 1930s was an elegant vision in cream and white. And now, in the 1950s, he moved with brisk dancer's steps around his shop, head high, wide smile, waistcoat perfectly fitting, starched white collar gleaming. This was the man who would have caught you or stumped you almost apologetically and sent you on your way with a sympathetic smile and a word of consolation. The battered fingers were the only clue.

I once saw him keep wicket. He was in his 60th year and he agreed to turn out in a match, at Glebe oddly enough, in honour of the Pakistan High Commissioner. He seemed to crouch not quite as low as in the old photographs, but he moved with supreme grace and ease, and I went home proud and satisfied.

He would talk of Hobbs and Sutcliffe and Hammond, and of England and its castles and theatres, and of the Royalty he had met, and of the many kindnesses extended to him in the Old Country. Once he offered me a lift to the Sydney Cricket Ground in his car. It was like gliding along in a Heavenly carriage. I remember giving in to one brief fantasy as the vehicle cruised down Macquarie Street. I was off to the SCG to open the bowling for Australia, and my driver was my wicket-keeper: Bertie. To hell with the 'Mr'. Hope old Jack Gregory's in good nick today. I don't want to show him up for pace. Expect Bertie will scoop a few up off the edge for me while the ball's new. Amazing how he never seems off-balance, never dives and cavorts around like this Evans chap.

Mr Oldfield must have braked sharply. I was back in the 1950s. Moore Park was up ahead. But elderly gentleman he may have been, he still sounded like a cricketer — and not a bragger either, as he calculated that he had made a century in every country in which he had played. I had to leave the car before it entered the members' gate into the holy of holies. I knew I could see him again in the shop some day. I've forgotten the day's play, but not the transfixing effect of that ride.

It was many years later that, having been resident in England, I walked into the new Oldfield shop in Sydney. He remembered me and took me to lunch at his club. Afterwards, as we crossed Market Street, he did an old-fashioned thing. He linked arms with me, the way sportsmen used to do so uninhibitedly so long ago. And I was so *proud*. Had a speeding Holden descended upon us, I should gladly have put myself between it and this antique little cricketing treasure who had once kept wicket for Australia.

I took my sons to his house in Killara. We had a blissful afternoon tea and hours of talk, not all cricket. He gave them a cricket bat, lovingly signed. Later they could not decide whose it actually was, so I sorted matters out by proclaiming it as part of my collection. That and the 1930 blazer are on daily view, a kind of immortality I suppose.

'. . . one must remember that
Sri Lanka is very much the infant among Test-playing countries.'

The contrasts of Australian and Sri Lankan cricket

D. F. Whatmore

Upon my arrival in Australia with my family in October 1961, I must admit to feeling rather nervous about surviving, let along planning a career in cricket, always my favourite sport.

I soon learnt to survive in inter-school cricket; one had to not only possess ability but also be able to endure to a high degree the competitive content which appeared to be held as a priority. It was in this area that I found the most amount of difficulty in adjusting, particularly when one carried an all-year-round tan and a distinctive accent. In Sri Lankan schoolboy cricket, all aggression was channelled into either punishing a cricket ball while batting, or imparting a terrific amount of spin in order to bowl the unplayable delivery. In fact, the attitude was quite the opposite to Aussie players. Cricketers on the Island Nation did not care too much for playing themselves in as batsmen, rather they believed the ball was there to be hit and they endeavoured to, on the most part, hit it correctly. There are, however, many instances where some of the strokes offered can correctly be described as an open 'old-fashioned slog', albeit effectively executed in some cases.

This calypso-type attitude towards cricket is by no means a reflection of the lack of coaching within the schools. In fact quite the contrary occurs. It can be seen that there is more coaching of technique during the scholastic years of an individual than at any other time of his career. Unlike most Australian schools, sport (rugby and cricket) is given a high priority within the curriculum and many hours are spent by the coach teaching the technique in both batting and bowling. Regretfully this does not occur in our State school system. Indeed it appears that the teaching of cricket is slowly disappearing with either the expulsion of inter-school matches or a very small amount of time allocated to it. Too often coaching is left up to a teacher who has a definite interest in the game and its survival.

The degree to which coaching is held during the schooling years and its effect is evidenced by the performances of the national Sri Lankan schoolboy teams

S. A. R. Silva, the Sri Lanka opener, takes a six off the bowling of Botham, August 1984.

that have played against touring sides on the island. Nearly all visiting teams have struggled to perform to their capability and levels of performance displayed in their domestic competitions. While there are outside factors effecting onfield performances (weather conditions, local food) much of their demise is directly related to the inability to cope with the required technique.

The weather conditions are an obvious difference between these two cricketing countries and one which, when coupled with playing surfaces, directly reflects the type of player that is constantly produced. Because of the very hot and humid conditions in the tropics, we find a lack of pace bowlers willing to bend their backs on unresponsive wickets. Instead they tend to produce some very good spinners who possess the ability to turn the ball sharply with a high degree of accuracy. In contrast, because Australia's climatic conditions are much cooler, we seem to produce more fast bowlers. This type of delivery is more responsive to the harder surface of wickets where great pace can be generated by 'hitting the wicket hard'. Australian spinners seem to have more of a dominant role to play late in the game when the harder wickets begin to crack under the wear and tear of both teams first innings. The spinners in Sri Lanka can expect to share the bulk of the bowling immediately the game begins.

When comparing batsmanship, I always contend that Sri Lankan players possess a tremendous amount of ability in stroke-play. However, their sub-standard mental approach in exercising patience and self-discipline to build a long innings all too often brings about their downfall, thereby denying themselves respectable scores. The Australians, by contrast, adopt a more sober approach towards their batting. Caution constitutes a high degree of the make-up, and stroke-play all around the wicket commences at a time when the batsman feels he is in full control of the situation.

When comparing these two cricketing nations, both of whom are full members of the International Cricket Conference, one must remember that Sri Lanka is very much the infant among Test-playing countries. Having obtained full status only a matter of a few years ago, they have much ground to cover in order to reach a consistent standard of cricket. Their performances to date have been creditable, and with expert help being sought by the authorities it may not be too long before they begin to win their share of the series.

On the Lord's side

Rabbi David J. Goldberg

The England Test team plumbed the depths against West Indies last summer. But painful though those memories are, in my synagogue opposite the Grace Gates of Lord's I benefited in a way that would make any cricket fan green with envy. I have been passionate about the game ever since my favourite uncle finally acknowledged that his only child, a girl, would never become another Frank Woolley, and took me instead to watch Compton and Edrich in that golden summer of 1947 when between them they scored more centuries than most current English batsmen amass in their entire careers.

When, nearly 25 years later, I was ordained a rabbi, job opportunity and location happily combined to provide me with the ideal post at the Liberal Jewish Synagogue in St John's Wood Road. In St John's Wood Road but not on the Lord's side gibe Orthodox Jewish detractors of this 'cathedral' of Progressive Judaism, designed in that style halfway between a Greek temple and the Firestone building that was so popular in religious and cinema architecture of the 1920s.

Whether or not we merit the Lord above's approval, our relationship with the Lord's opposite has always been cordial. The synagogue's first rabbi was a friend of Sir Pelham Warner, and would lunch with him at least once a week. In my mind's eye I have an appealing picture of Israel Mattuck, a small, intent scholar of Lithuanian ancestry, strolling through the pavilion at Lord's with the delicate, languid 'Plum' Warner, the quintessential MCC gentleman, in earnest conversation about the lbw law and its talmudic interpretation.

An enemy bomb partially destroyed the synagogue in 1940 and services were held at Lord's until rebuilding was completed. It was something of a blow to neighbourly relations when the Tavern Stand was erected. Until then, armed with grappling irons, ropes, a pair of binoculars and sense of balance, one could climb onto the Synagogue's roof and get a passable view of the cricket.

Our congregants park their cars at Lord's on Saturdays and festivals, except when a match is in pro-

The pavilion at Lord's.

gress. There was much traffic congestion one September when the Gillette Cup final and the Jewish New Year fell on the same Saturday and I had sneaking sympathy for the member of both synagogue and club whose hopeful suggestion was that we should move the New Year to Sunday.

The reader can imagine, then, my pleasure and surprise when I pulled into the synagogue forecourt on the morning of the one-day international and saw the official West Indies tour coach parked there. Our caretaker explained that it couldn't get through the Grace Gates for the crowds and had asked us to provide temporary asylum. The synagogue secretary, a decent, kindly man but one who doesn't know the difference between a cricket bat and a salt-beef sandwich, had agreed, *but wanted to know how much we should charge for the privilege*!

It was as though all my years of training in biblical criticism, Semitic languages and pastoral psychology had been preparing me for this historic moment. With quiet authority I vetoed the idea of pecuniary gain from

Clive Lloyd and Co. and walked over to the coach. Inside it was somewhat more luxurious than the average living room, the pride of the British Leyland fleet, with every mod. con. from fridge to video.

I demanded to know who was the driver. There was an uneasy silence and a cautious 'Why?' I repeated the question, adding ominously that I was rabbi of the synagogue. Finally someone owned up, but asked why I wanted to know? 'Because I'm not allowing this coach to move from this forecourt,' said I sternly, 'unless and until I receive for my 10-year-old son the autographs of the entire West Indian team and a special one from Viv Richards!'

After much relieved laughter the autographs were duly provided and I invited the coach back for the Lord's Test. Every time I passed during its five days I was hauled aboard for a drink, and congregants grew used to the sight of their rabbi weaving unsteadily from coach to office with a glass in his hand, all in the cause of Jewish-Caribbean relations.

It seemed for a while that bad weather would spoil

*Thomas Lord, creator of the
famous London cricket ground.*

that match, but on the last afternoon Gordon
Greenidge played quite simply the greatest innings I
have ever seen. By the time David Gower — looking,
as the series wore on, ever more like a doomed
subaltern on the Somme — belatedly realised what was
happening, Greenidge was in the mood to destroy
bowling infinitely better than England's threadbare
attack. Even more thrilling than his sumptuous drives
were his back-foot shots through the covers, when he
crouched, then *launched* himself at the ball like a puma
on its prey, and hit it so hard that it was reaching the
boundary fielders 70 yards away too quickly for a run
to be taken.

I dreamed of his innings for three nights afterwards
and preached about it the following Saturday. Since the
biblical portion for the week was the story of the sooth-
sayer Balaam from the Book of Numbers, it was not all
that easy to tie text and innings together sermonically,
but I did so to my own satisfaction, if to patent
mystification of the family of the 13-year-old boy who
was celebrating his *barmitzvah*.

The last time the coach came back was for the game
with Middlesex. I was on holiday by then, but dropped
some papers into the synagogue, to be warmly hailed
and invited aboard to meet Jackie Hendriks, the team
manager. I thanked him for all the pleasure his team
had given even while inflicting such pain on England
and he thanked me for the use of our forecourt, which
had made entertaining so much easier than at Lord's,
with milling throngs trying to peer in. We both agreed
that Greenidge's had been the innings of the summer,
weightier in its context than the devastation wreaked
by Viv Richards in the one-day international at Old
Trafford and fit to rank in years to come with Stan
McCabe's legendary 232 at Trent Bridge when Don
Bradman called his team onto the balcony to witness
such splendour.

In reply to my question about how he would rate the
current West Indies team against, say, the Sobers-
Kanhai side in which he had played, the charming Mr
Hendriks made the point that it was impossible to
assess, because the strengths of the opposition had also
changed; Snow and Underwood, for example, were
more formidable bowlers than Foster and Pringle.

Finally, as thanks for having given the coach parking
facilities, I was presented with Trevor McDonald's
biography of Viv Richards, inscribed by the batsman
himself with best wishes to 'Rabbi David'. It now
occupies pride of place on my bookshelves, along with
lesser treasures such as a Wittenberg Bible and a 14th
Century codex of the Babylonian Talmud.

So, a cricket season of unmitigated gloom for
England provided me with an unexpected bonus. I
assured the West Indians they can park with us again

when they next visit in 1988 and hereby invite the Australians and other touring teams to do the same. All I require by way of thanks is their autographs, purportedly for my son, but really, of course, for me.

This article prompted the following letter: 'May I say how much I enjoyed the article contributed by the Reverend Goldberg (*WCM* [*Wisden Cricket Monthly*] July). It was written with all the whimsicality that is in character with so much Jewish literature. It did leave me with a question, however.

What would Shakespeare have thought about a Rabbi who demanded a set of autographs as his pound of flesh for services rendered?

Cartoons by Jack Broome.

'The Hau Haus were armed with two-barrelled guns and Enfield rifles, and used them to express dissatisfaction with the rate of scoring, or boredom.'

Batting under bullets

Dick Brittenden

Dick Brittenden, doyen of New Zealand cricket writers.

New Zealand cricket has had very few skirmishes with the armed forces; there were a few Army club teams in the Second World War and the first New Zealanders to tour England played the Army at Folkestone in 1927. The opposition in the 1931, 1937 and 1949 tours of England consisted of Combined Services players.

The 1949 match was played at Bad Oennhausen, headquarters of the British Army of the Rhine, and was notable chiefly for the fact that in the Combined Services' second innings, Martin Donnelly was an opening bowler.

Donnelly, a particularly gifted left-handed batsman, was an occasional left-arm slow bowler, but he expressed an interest in having a few overs in the Nobby Clark of Northants mould, so he was given the ball.

The captain, Walter Hadlee and the vice-captain, Mervyn Wallace, stood together in the slips while Donnelly performed. He got four for 68 — and nervous exhaustion. The team's hierarchy, straight-faced, demanded he bowl 17 overs on end, all the while exhorting him to bowl faster and making unkind observations on the level of his bowling arm.

The most bizarre Army match was played at South Taranaki in New Zealand over Easter in 1866, during the Maori wars, between two sections of the British Army Bushrangers — the troopers ('Pigskin Polishers') and the Rangers ('Footsloggers'). The army was at loggerheads with the Hau Haus, a fanatical, religious group of Maoris.

It was played with all the fervour of a Test match, for every ranger and trooper had wagered his tot in support of his side. Only modern cricket could afford a comparison with the protection each player was afforded, for each cricketer was required to wear a holster belt, with his revolver, carbine and 50 rounds of ammunition. At the call of each over, each fieldsman had to pick up his armaments. The umpires — forever beasts of burden — held the batsmen's guns.

The Hau Haus were in the forest, a thousand yards

from the fort, but there were extensive patches of bush within 400 yards of the cricket ground. It was a distinctly unappreciative audience — something like the Roses matches? — which gathered in the bush, but the Hau Haus observed the custom of watching the opening overs in silence.

The Troopers scored 100 runs and the Hau Haus in the bleachers did no more than express disquiet with a haka (war dance), but by the time the Rangers had scored 90 for the loss of nine wickets, all hell broke loose. The Hau Haus were armed with two-barrelled guns and Enfield rifles, and used them to express dissatisfaction with the rate of scoring, or boredom.

On the other field of conflict, attention was focused on a massive Rangers sergeant, a former Varsity Blue. There were only 11 runs to make, but his partner, everybody seemed certain, was about to be bowled by the first ball he received.

The sergeant, perhaps in search of a decoration, hit a huge blow to long-on. The match, it could be safely said, was delicately poised. The sergeant's hit was eagerly pursued by a fieldsman, but he tumbled to the ground while unleashing his revolver. He had time to cry 'lost ball'. It was no time to be a boundary rider, for the Hau Haus had opened a withering fire.

The colonel, who was umpire at the time, ordered a counter-attack. Fieldsmen, batsmen and umpires, assisted by the scorers and spectators, charged the Hau Haus, who made a strategic withdrawal; but they kept firing. The game went on, although the Enfield bullets kept whistling by and the groundsman must have been mortified at seeing the pitch torn up by the fire. All available men, save the players and a tribe of friendly natives, were ordered to keep the Hau Haus at bay, and even when the enemy were 1000 yards distant, they kept up a lively fire.

That, however, was kids' stuff. And the Troopers won by seven runs on 'grog' night. The Rangers' number 11 had received a straight ball. Probably a military policeman.

'When I bowled him out at Lord's in the 1956 Test match he saluted me by saying: "You will do for me." I have never forgotten that tribute.'

Miller the Marvel

Fred Trueman

Fred Trueman — an artist's impression.

Keith Ross Miller will go down in the history of Test cricket as one of the great all-rounders of all time. In my opinion he will also remain the biggest enigma that Australian cricket has ever produced or is likely to. He had the flair, as any cricketer of the highest class must have, to be able to perform great feats that surpass even one's own expectations. He also had a great personality that influenced all who came into contact with him and I do not think that anyone could say they knew how he would react to a situation on a cricket field. That was where his greatness lay.

When he was bowling it could have been an edged shot or something that a player said or a remark from the crowd that would suddenly change his mood. Or it could even have been an important horse race on television that he had an interest in. Suddenly a wicket that had appeared docile and in the batsman's favour would seemingly change into 22 yards of sheer devil-ridden hell. The ball, which had hardly reached the wicket-keeper's ankles the over before, would start coming into the 'keeper's gloves at chest height. The batsman playing and missing as the ball started moving would cause the slips to retreat backwards two or three yards. Miller's influence had to be seen to be believed.

That was the magic of Miller. He had the ability to change the whole course of a match in two or three overs and the crowd would be stunned as the tranquil atmosphere suddenly became one of breath-held tension which you could cut with a knife.

He did not always rely on his pace to get wickets as David Sheppard, now the Bishop of Liverpool, will tell you. In a match at Lord's, just before the close of play, he bowled a googly with the new ball and had Sheppard out lbw. Even the Reverend David looked to the heavens for some guidance!

That was not the only time it happened. I understand from that great Australian captain and my personal friend, Richie Benaud, that Miller did it again in the West Indies to another Test player. In 1955 when Australia were touring the West Indies they were playing in Georgetown, British Guyana. Keith had had his

usual large amount of sleep, which was not easy in the air-conditioned but steamy hotel, before racing up in the first over and bowling a bouncer. Next ball he delivered the 'wrong-'un' and Bruce Pairaudeau played at it three times and was out suffering the same fate as the Rev. David.

Miller could incense a crowd with something he had done and, with one flash of genius that is the hallmark of a great player, would pull something out of the bag and have the crowd purring its pleasure. I remember at the Oval in a Test match watching Miller standing at first slip as the great Ray Lindwall, his partner in fast-bowling 'crime', was running up to bowl. Miller's arms were folded and he appeared to be looking at the crowd and not taking any interest. Lindwall delivered the ball and the next moment Miller was flat on the floor, facing down the wicket, with arms crossed in front of his face holding a magnificent catch in one hand. I'm still trying to work out how he got there!

Miller's explosive batting could also win a match. He believed in hitting a ball and entertaining the crowd even if the conditions were against him. He could hit sixes with ease and grace and I recall that in 1953 at Kingston in Surrey, after England had won the Ashes, I was one of his victims. I was playing for the Combined Services against the Australians when Miller was dropped at leg slip before he had scored and he took full advantage to make 262 not out. He destroyed me. I failed to take a wicket in 14 overs and conceded 95 runs as Miller produced as fine a display of aggressive, controlled batting anyone would want to see.

When characters like Miller are around there are always the inevitable stories to go with them and there is no shortage when you talk about him. Peter Philpott, the leg spinner from New South Wales, tells the lovely story of when he played his first match for the State side in 1954 against South Australia. NSW had batted and made 270 before the umpires upheld a light appeal which incensed Miller. The next day he was supposed to pick up Philpott on his way to the ground and completely forgot about him! Miller suddenly remembered, jumped into his car, and roared back to the arranged spot. Somehow he made it back to the Sydney Cricket Ground just as the umpires were going out. With shirt flapping and boot laces undone he arrived on the field for the first over and proceeded to bowl South Australia out for 27. Harris, the South Australian opening bat, finishes the story by saying: 'Yes, I remember because I bagged a pair before lunch.'

But Miller's exploits don't end there, of course. He was made captain of NSW in place of Arthur Morris, who was a fine skipper but deposed because the selectors did not like a captain wearing suede shoes. On one occasion when Miller was leading the team onto the field, Bill Watson, who made a century for NSW in 1954 against the MCC and Frank Tyson, said: 'Hey, Nugget, we have 12 players on the field.' Miller, without turning his head, said: 'One of you b— off and the rest scatter!' That symbolises his approach to the game.

I have my own memories of him. When I bowled him out at Lord's in the 1956 Test match he saluted me by saying: 'You will do for me.' I have never forgotten that tribute.

His human touch was also reflected in the long-running television program, *This is Your Life*. Before the end of the program Miller was almost reduced to tears when his family and friends from all over the world paid tribute to him. For me it was proof that he is a sincere and honest man with a heart of gold. That is probably why they call him Nugget. He is a man I've been proud to acknowledge as a friend through the golden years.

Keith Miller hits a perfectly executed six over mid-on at the Sydney Cricket Ground against South Australia.

Middle and leg

Brian Johnston

Brian Johnston.

Here are some stories which have been told to fill in time when rain stops play. We all have our special favourites among the great characters which cricket has always produced. I suspect that John Arlott's favourites are George Gunn, 'Bomber' Wells or anyone from Hampshire. My own is certainly the one and only Patsy Hendren. Everyone's favourite seems to be Freddie Trueman himself. I hope that you will find yours among the sample of stories which have been told in the press box.

Dr W. G. Grace had just packed his bag one morning and was ready to go off to play for Gloucestershire when a lady rushed up to his door and said, 'Can you come quickly, Doctor, I think my twins have got the measles?'. 'I'm sorry, Ma'am, but I am just going off to Gloucester to play cricket and can't stop. But contact me at the ground if their temperatures reach 210 for two'.

George Gunn, when playing for Nottinghamshire against Glamorgan, started to walk off the field at half-past one with the impression that it was time for lunch. However, under the conditions for that match, lunch was not due to be taken until 2 p.m. and Gunn was recalled to continue his innings; he lifted his bat away from the next ball, was comprehensibly bowled, making no attempt to play the ball, and as he retired to the pavilion, said 'You can have your lunch gentlemen, when you like, but I always take mine at 1.30 p.m.'

During Len Hutton's tour of Australia, Frank Tyson's tremendous speed caused dismay and destruction among batsmen wherever he bowled. On one occasion when he was at his fastest, he had run through a side until it was the turn of the number 11 batsman to come in. Looking pale and apprehensive, he came down the pavilion steps, but was so nervous that he couldn't close the catch of the pavilion gate. A voice from the crowd shouted: 'Leave it open, you won't be long!'

A batsman had played and missed a number of times. 'Yabba', the famous Sydney Hill barracker, shouted out to the bowler: 'Send him down a grand piano, and see if he can play *that*!'.

In a match against Gloucestershire, Brian Close was fielding at forward short leg with Freddie Trueman bowling. Martin Young received a short ball which he hit right in the middle of the bat. It hit Close on the right side of the head and rebounded to first slip who caught it! Close seemed none the worse but when he returned to the pavilion at the next interval a member asked him, 'That was a terrible blow; aren't you worried standing so near? What would have happened if the ball had hit you slap between the eyes? 'He'd have been caught at cover,' replied the indomitable Yorkshire captain!

When 'Bomber' Wells came in to bat for Nottinghamshire against the Australians at Trent Bridge in 1964, Neil Hawke was in devastating form. The umpire, ready to give him guard, said, 'What do you want, ''Bomber''?' 'Help'.

Arthur Wood, to a batsman who had played and missed at three successive balls, each of which just grazed the stumps without disturbing the bails: 'Have you ever tried walking on water?' And to Hedley Verity at Bramall Lane in 1935, after H. B. Cameron had just hit Verity for 30 in one over, Wood offered this advice: 'Keep 'em there, Hedley. Thou hast him in two minds — he don't know whether t'smack thee for four or six.'

When 'Bomber' Wells was playing for Gloucestershire he was batting one day with Sam Cook. They got into a terrible tangle over a short single, with Sam just making the crease by hurling himself flat on the ground. As he lay there panting he shouted out to 'Bomber': 'Call!' — and 'Bomber' shouted back: 'Tails!'

The Reverend David Sheppard was embroiled one day with 'Bomber' Wells and with edges past slip and short-leg was enjoying a good deal of luck.

'I should think Vicar,' said the 'Bomber', 'that you've been on your praying mat.'

'Indeed,' replied the Reverend. 'But don't *you* pray, Brian?'

'No, I always rely on skill and a bit of luck.'

'Well,' said the Reverend, 'which is showing the greater profit at the moment?'

Alf Gover, Surrey and England, as a 19-year-old, arrived at Lord's for his first Middlesex versus Surrey match. When he got to the old 'Pros' dressingroom, only one other person was there — the great Patsy Hendren.

'Hello, young chap,' he called out, 'what's your name?'

'Alf Gover, sir.'

'What do you do?'

'I bowl.'

'Quick?' said Patsy.

'Very quick,' he answered proudly.

Patsy looked round the room to make sure that he was not overheard, came over to him and said, very confidentially: 'Look, son, I don't mind quick bowling, you can push it down at me as fast as you like, only — another conspiratorial glance round — 'only I don't like 'em if they are pitched short. You know this is my home ground and they like me to get a few. My peepers aren't as good as they were and I can't pick up the ball as fast as I used to, so keep them well up to me, won't you?'

Alf pondered on this self-admitted fear of the great England and Middlesex batsman and decided that there was a great chance for him to make his name.

He happened to be bowling from the pavilion end when Patsy came in and said to himself: 'Ah, here's that old man who can't see and doesn't like short-pitched balls — so here goes.'

His first ball was very short, just outside the leg stump and as fast as he could bowl it. It was promptly hooked for six into the Tavern. 'Fluke,' he said to himself and sent him down a similar short ball, only this time on the middle stump. Patsy took two steps back and cut it for four past third man. 'I've got him scared now — he's running away,' Gover said to himself as he walked back to his mark. Down came his third ball just the same as the other two and it went sailing away for six into the Mound Stand. At the end of the over Jack Hobbs went across to him from cover.

'What are you bowling short at Mr Hendren for, son?'

'He's afraid of them,' Alf replied.

The 'Master' stared in amazement. 'Who told you that?' he asked.

'He did, Mr Hobbs,' said Alf.

'Young man, never do it again,' said Hobbs. 'Patsy is still the best hooker of fast bowling in the world. May I remind you that he's an Irishman and every night he kisses the Blarney Stone!'

On another occasion after suffering from a surfeit of dropped catches in the slips off his bowling, Alf Gover was having a drink with some of the offenders after close of play. After a while one of them said: 'Well, so long Alf, I must be off. I've got a train to catch.' Alf replied: 'So long, hope you have better luck — with the train!'

Patsy Hendren was fond of telling this apocryphal (I hope!) story. Once when travelling in a train on his way to a match he sat opposite an ashen-faced stranger, who had his coat collar turned up around his ears. He looked so ill and thoroughly miserable that Patsy was moved to ask him what the trouble was. In a hoarse whisper — hardly able to speak — the man confided that he was a very keen cricketer, but had recently let his side down badly by making five ducks in a row. Said Patsy: 'Oh dear, oh dear, if I ever made five ducks in a row I would cut my throat.'

The Stranger (in a whisper): 'I have.'

On one occasion Hendren was fielding on the boundary by the famous Hill on the Sydney Cricket Ground. The batsman hit the ball high in the air towards him. As it soared higher and higher, a raucous voice from the Hill shouted, 'Patsy, if you miss the catch you can sleep with my sister.'

Later Patsy was asked what he had done. 'Oh,' he replied, 'as I hadn't seen his sister, I caught the ball.'

Just before retiring Hendren was batting against Derbyshire on a wet pitch that was slippery with mud. Walter Robins was his partner and was batting against the leg breaks of T. B. Mitchell. Robins, who always used his feet to attack slow bowlers, had got into the habit of dancing down the pitch and if he missed the ball, walking straight on to the pavilion without looking round at the wicket-keeper. Mitchell was bowling from the pavilion end and as usual Robins danced down the pitch, missed the ball and continued walking towards the pavilion without so much as a backward glance. Patsy immediately shouted 'He's missed it', so Robins turned quickly round and flung himself on the ground, bat stretched out towards the stumps. There was a roar of laughter from the players and the crowd, as Robins slowly got up, shirt, flannels and pads covered in mud. He looked up to see the bails lying on the ground and Harry Elliott, the wicket-keeper, chatting to the slip, having obviously brought off a neat stumping! When Patsy was asked how Robins had taken it, he said that he hadn't been too pleased! Knowing R.W.V.R. that was putting it mildly!

Leicestershire were playing Nottinghamshire and Harold Larwood was bowling at his fastest and most frightening. The light was very bad and he had taken four quick wickets when it was Alec Skelding's turn to bat. He came down the pavilion steps very slowly, then groped his way along the railings in front of the pavilion, shouting to the members, 'Can anyone tell me where this match is being played . . . ?'

A similar story is told about Jack Newman when he came out to bat with Lord Tennyson, and his Lordship called down the wicket to Newman, 'Why don't you appeal against the light, Jack? They won't listen to me.' To which Newman replied, 'I can hear you, my Lord, but I can't see you . . . where are you?'

On 1 January 1925, Jack Hobbs and Herbert Sutcliffe of England batted all day against Australia in Melbourne, putting on 283 for the opening partnership, in reply to what was then a record Test total of 600 runs by Australia. There were 75,000 people on the ground and as the day wore on they began to barrack their team more and more. (It is worth remembering, perhaps, that the bowlers included Jack Gregory, Charlie Kelleway, Arthur Mailey and Arthur Richardson.) But the barrackers were merciless on them, 'You'll never get 'em out — you'll have to burn 'em out — send for the Fire Brigade, they'll get 'em out — put the roller on — put the clock on', etc. But the culminating point of the whole day's batting came between the tea interval and the close of play. There was a momentary silence which was broken by a terrific, raucous voice (Yabba?) which yelled out, 'Send for Nurse Blank, she'll get the b.....s out!' (Nurse Blank was a well-known midwife

who shortly before the Test match had made the head-lines in an abortion case!)

In 1958 at Bridgetown against the West Indies Hanif Mohammad of Pakistan was playing his marathon innings of 337 which lasted for 16 hours 13 minutes. A West Indian supporter, perched perilously on a branch of a tree, stuck it for most of the day but then fell asleep either from the heat or boredom and fell with a resounding crash to the ground and knocked himself out.

He was taken off to hospital where he was unconscious for some time. When he eventually came round one of the hospital nurses told him he'd been 'out' for two hours. Quick as a flash he exclaimed: 'I only hope Hanif has been too.'

A match to remember

The Lord's Taverners—Les Favell Testimonial Match, Adelaide Oval, 5 April 1987

Dr Donald Beard

There is charm in every piece of ground where a cricket pitch is struck. There is special charm when that piece of ground nestles between St Peter's Cathedral and the River Torrens in Adelaide. There is interest in every game of cricket that is played. There is special interest when that game is a testimonial to a courageous cricketer. Such a game was played on the Adelaide Oval in 1987 in honour of Les Favell, MBE.

The match had originally been intended as part of a sports day organised by The Lord's Taverners of South Australia. It had been the idea of the Chairman, Ian McLachlan, Cambridge Blue, South Australian and Australian cricketer. It was to be a sort of Pro-am for Taverners to participate in tennis, bowls, cricket and the friendship and fellowship for which the Lord's Taverners is renowned. The day fulfilled the ideals.

When Les Favell fell sick in January 1987 and deteriorated in February and it became obvious that his malignancy would advance rapidly, the committee decided to make the day an opportunity to thank him for what he had done for cricket.

Les Favell had been many things. He was perhaps the most dashing opening batsman ever in Australian cricket. It did not matter what was the match, who was the bowler or whether it was first ball. If it was over pitched it was driven and if it was short, it was hooked. In April 1955 he took strike against Trinidad's Gerry Gomez. The first ball went over the mid-wicket fence, the next over the square leg fence, the third was cut for four and the fourth over the long-on fence. Gerry was stunned but Favell grinned.

He played first-class cricket from 1951 to 1970 scoring 12,379 runs with 27 centuries including a memorable 101 for Australia in Madras in 1959. He became captain of South Australia and took them to three Sheffield Shield wins. At times he was criticised that his batting was too risky but as Sir Donald Bradman said, 'What a pity other players don't have the same fault'. In later years, his aggression showed in his captaincy. Victories were gloriously won and losses gallantly and sportingly accepted.

It was as captain of South Australia that Les rose to his greatest heights. His discipline was strict but he was loved and respected by his players, the SACA administration which he later joined and cricket followers. He had everything including wit, charm and dignity. This was the man who would be honoured on 5 April.

It might have been thought strange to have a testimonial for a man with not long to live, but it did not turn out that way. It was not a sad day. Everyone, including Les, lived, breathed and enjoyed cricket and good fellowship.

And so arrangements were started. Who would be the captains? Les would be one, of course, and it was decided to ask another ex-South Australian captain to be his opponent. Sir Donald Bradman had kept out of the cricket limelight since his retirement because of his desire to give younger men greater opportunity. Would he participate? The president and the chairman visited him at his Adelaide home with the request that he come out of retirement for the first time in years. Not only does Sir Donald want to leave the limelight to the younger players and administrators, but if he were to agree to every request to appear at some cricket function, he would have very little time to himself and with Lady Bradman. On this occasion, to our very great joy, he agreed to be the non-playing captain for the day. He said that he would do it because of his respect of Les.

The playing captains would be the Lord's Taverners Chairman, Ian McLachlan, and Dr John Lill, both of whom played for South Australia with Les. Next came the matter of guest players. The three internationals who had played with and for Les were Sir Garfield Sobers, Barry Richards and Lance Gibbs. Sir Garfield was most upset that another engagement would prevent his coming. Barry Richards was contacted in South Africa and said that he would not only be delighted to participate, but might also bring Graeme Pollock with him. Lance Gibbs was eventually tracked down in his appointment as a shipping agent in Miami. There are not many cricket lovers in Miami, but nevertheless, he was given leave.

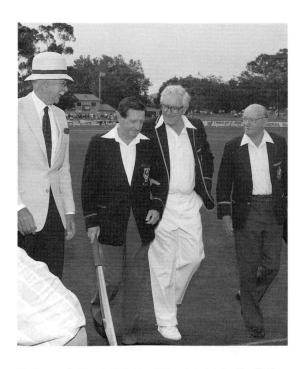

The last match: (From left) Dr Donald Beard, the late Les Favell, Alan Davidson and Sir Donald Bradman at The Lord's Taverners–Les Favell Testimonial Cricket Match. The game was played at the Adelaide Oval on 5 April 1987 between teams with non-playing captains, Sir Donald Bradman and Les Favell. Favell died two months later on 14 June, aged 57. More than 1000 people attended his funeral, including Sir Donald and enough cricketers to establish two Test and four Sheffield Shield teams.

147

Neil Hawke doing his
commentating 'bit'.

Don Bradman, Dr Beard and Les
Favell on the great day.

The peerless Lance Gibbs at the
match.

Ian Chappell executes a classic
forward stroke.

The toss between Les Favell and
Sir Donald Bradman.

Barry Richards copes with a
nasty one.

Neil Harvey gets one away.

The greats relax at the match.
(From left): Dr Beard, Neil
Harvey, Les Favell, Sir Donald
Bradman, Alan Davidson, Lance
Gibbs and Gilbert Langley.

On the Sunday morning of the match, I looked out of my window to uncertain clouds. Surely the sun would shine for Les? An hour before start of play, long queues were forming. This is not uncommon before a cricket match when most lovers of the game like to be there for the teams coming onto the ground and the first ball to be bowled. But in this case there would not be the thrill of seeing a Lillee or Holding or Willis delivering the first ball. The crowd had come to see the toss between Les Favell and Sir Donald Bradman.

One of the executives of a car firm in Adelaide offered to chauffeur Les in a Rolls-Royce for the day. We thought he could also pick up Sir Donald Bradman, who lived nearby, but Sir Donald said, 'No, it is Les's day'. In fact, the Rolls was driving through the Adelaide Oval car park when it came upon Sir Donald walking towards the entrance and it stopped and gave him a lift; so the two great captains arrived together.

In the dressing rooms there was a hush of nervous expectancy. There were some heavy, leather, long-sprigged boots being pulled on. Les sat quietly and said to me, 'Doc, I hope I can make it out to the middle and back'. I promised to be not far from his side. Some of the participants were a bit late getting through the crowd. Ray Lindwall had already played a round of golf and been to church.

Finally the players went out onto the ground and Les gathered his strength. That strength had been boosted by a blood transfusion earlier in the week. In the past there have been players who have felt it necessary to have a couple of pints of beer before a match, but how many cricketers would have four pints of blood in order to participate? Finally Les turned to me, grinned and said, 'Alright, let's go', just as he did to Gerry Gomez 22 years before. Sir Donald Bradman wore his baggy green Australian cap and 1948 Australian blazer. His creams no longer fitted. Les elected to wear his South Australian blazer.

As he went down the steps of the Members' Stand, everyone in the crowd stood and cheered. I could feel Les's arm shudder. On the ground was a guard of honour of the teams, the umpires and his old cricket colleagues including Miller and Lindwall, Langley and Noblet, and beyond that, a battery of television cameras. Les and Sir Donald went on to the middle of the ground, inspected the pitch and made what must have been an historic toss. Les won but could scarcely do otherwise as Ian McLachlan had supplied a double-headed penny. With all his old confidence he invited Bradman to bat. How many captains would have done that? We turned and walked back again to a standing ovation. A couple of times the emotion was almost too much. There was a tear, not only in Les's eye, but in countless others among the players and the crowd. His step faltered towards the top of the long climb at the Members' Stand steps, but he made it, turned and sat down to watch the start of play. Any sadness was over. There was a game of cricket starting and what a joyous, magic, happy game it turned out to be.

A running commentary was made by ex-Australian Test player Neil Hawke whose survival following an operation and multiple complications including gas gangrene of his abdominal wall was a miracle. Neil kept the crowd amused all day. At the same time national radio gave a ball-by-ball description of the whole match including interviews with players who had come from far and wide to pay homage.

Favell opened the batting but it was not Les but his son Alan and he top scored. The opening bowler was another former Australian Test player, Eric Freeman. At first there were some creaking joints but they loosened up and there was some wonderful cricket.

Barry Richards came out to a great reception and there was another cheer when Lance Gibbs took the ball. His black curly hair is turning to silver but as Wayne Phillips said, 'He had the ball on a string and seemed to be able to do anything with it'. Later Ian Chappell wrote to me and said, 'Lance Gibbs was back at the site of his Test hat-trick, 26 years older, a little heavier, with more grey hair and a little wiser. His bowling still contained the two ingredients for which he was famous — flight and accuracy'. Barry Richards played some delightful shots but unfortunately was out too soon to a magnificent catch by Graeme Hole.

Lance Gibbs continued to bowl to Alan Davidson just as he had done in the 1960–61 series. Davo had trouble getting him away but his guard was firm and he then proceeded to take a lot of runs off the bowler at the other end with glimpses of his old driving, pulling and cutting. And then Neil Harvey came to the crease, playing for Bradman as he did 40 years earlier. At the start he was in great difficulties but suddenly some of the old shots came back. No-one who was at the ground that day will ever forget a dancing on-drive for four. David Hookes said, 'I had heard about the Harvey footwork but never believed it until today'. And this from a player who, with Wayne Phillips a month earlier in a Sheffield Shield match, had put on a partnership of 462 in 299 minutes against Tasmania.

Throughout the morning there had been bursts of brilliant sunshine and it was warm with a north-westerly. From the rear windows of the committee room can be seen the western skies and clouds started to bank up in the south-west from whence bad weather comes. They came closer and then there was some rain but the players did not leave the field because they were playing for Les Favell and Don Bradman. The clouds rolled or were pushed away and once again the sun came through and the game went on.

When lunch was taken the Bradman Eleven was 9 for 229. Lunch was a delightful affair. The President of the SACA, Mr Phil Ridings, had handed over the Oval and all the facilities for the day to the Lord's Taverners and to Les Favell. There was much happy talk of memories of matches gone by and the joy of the match in progress. Les's appetite had been failing but it returned with the delicious lunch specially prepared by the caterer, Mr John Selth, and with all his friends and his wife and family around him.

When the players again took to the field, Les sent out his opening batsmen, ex-Test players Gavin Stevens and Rick Darling. The Rolls-Royce then took Les home to rest for the afternoon.

The game went on. Alan Davidson opened the bowling. His first ball moved in the air, cut off the pitch, went between bat and pad and Darling's stumps went over. Luckily for Darling, it was called a no-ball by ex-Test umpire Colin Egar who nonetheless said that a better first ball he could not remember. Wayne Phillips came in and delighted the crowd with some lovely cutting. He was followed by Ian Chappell who had not walked onto the Adelaide Oval for many years. He showed all his old determination and was fighting for his captain, Les Favell.

Somehow the two great footballers Graham Cornes and Neil Kerley lifted their standards from their usual beach cricket to make useful contributions and take a couple of good catches to the joy of the crowd, more used to cheering them for their long kicking and marking.

The score crept up but wickets fell. Finally it came to the last partnership between Lance Gibbs and Les's great old cricketing friend, Neil Dansie. Came the last over, to be bowled by Barry Richards. Two runs were required and four balls had passed before Neil Dansie was able to pull one to the boundary and the Favell Eleven had won. And it was not contrived! It had been a battle all day. Les had just returned to the ground and what a sweet victory it was for him. The tired muscles were rejuvenated by hot showers and cold refreshments and the happy post-match conversation which occurs all over the cricketing world at the close of play.

And finally came the Lord's Taverners dinner to honour Les Favell, MBE. More than 400 guests sat down in a marquee erected behind the members' stand. As is befitting the two captains, Favell and Bradman, sat together and were joined by Neil Harvey and Alan Davidson. Once again Les found his lost appetite and enjoyed his dinner. Afterwards two memorable speeches were made by Barry Richards and Ian Chappell. They spoke of the good things of cricket and how it really should be played to the example set by Favell.

By now, Les's strength was beginning to ebb. He

was neither physically nor emotionally able to rise to reply but his beautiful wife Berry said she would do it for him and she spoke to a hushed audience and said the things that Les would have said himself. In particular she spoke of the many families — of friends and cricketers and the South Australian Cricket Association and the *Advertiser* newspaper for which he had worked. She sat down to tumultuous applause and there were few dry eyes.

The evening concluded with an auction of cricket bats signed by the players from the Bradman and Favell Elevens. Doug Walters had been unable to come over from Sydney but sent his Australian sleeveless sweater and, as auctioneer Michael Brock said, 'it is complete with cigarette stains'.

The successful bid was $650 from a member of the Wudinna Cricket Team which had a 1400km round trip to come to the game and pay their respects. The sweater was pulled on proudly and was probably worn all the way home. Wudinna had been the scene of the country match where England had played on the 1985–86 tour.

There was another charity match in Perth on the same day and there were several players, including Greg Chappell, Graeme Marsh and Ashley Mallett, who would have liked to have been in Adelaide. They all autographed a bat and had it sent over by plane for the auction that night.

Sir Donald Bradman had autographed an enlarged photograph of him playing one of his classic off-drives. When it came up for auction he lent over to me and asked what I thought it would bring. I said, 'about $1500'. He replied, 'But it is only a photograph'. 'No, Sir Donald, it is a photograph of you and it is signed by you.' Barry Richards wanted to take it back to South Africa but was beaten in the bidding by Wolf Blass, the South Australian winemaker, who paid $4500.

And then it was all over. It had been a wonderfully happy day and night. Les and Berry climbed into the Rolls-Royce and as they drove through the gates of the Adelaide Oval, he turned and waved, never to return.

Within six weeks he had deteriorated rapidly. He said to me, 'Doc, I am sad. I don't think I will ever see another cricket match played, but how fortunate I have been to have enjoyed so many and to have had such good friends'. Two weeks later, Les died quietly in his wife's arms with his son and daughter at his side. The great spirit had at last failed but he left behind an example for all of us to follow. At his funeral, more than a thousand came to pay their respects and their thanks for his friendship and for all that he had done for the noble game of cricket.

One of the two bats auctioned at the Les Favell match. All testimonial photos reproduced courtesy of Advertiser Newspapers Ltd., Adelaide.

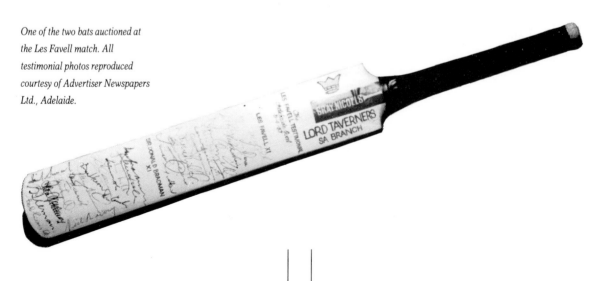

'. . . I am not in accord with the present Law of Cricket which bans the delivery of the ball by the bowler underarm . . .'

Finish of match

Sam Loxton

That's the fella! (Left to right) Arthur Morris, Ron Hamence, Ian Johnson, Sam Loxton, Bill Johnston and Doug Ring identify Loxton in a picture in which he is shown being bowled by the English bowler Pollard in the third Test of the 1948 tour.

The following true story will indicate why I am not in accord with the present Law of Cricket which bans the delivery of the ball by the bowler underarm, although it had its genesis in this country in most unfortunate circumstances.

I was a member of the 1953–54 Commonwealth Team to India managed by the late George Duckworth and captained by the late Ben Barnett, the former Australian wicket-keeper. As the tour was drawing to an end it was decided to play an additional match at Eden Gardens, Calcutta, in aid of Prime Minister Nehru's Flood Relief Program.

The late Jack Iverson was a replacement during the latter stages of the tour for Sonny Ramadhin and C. J. (Charlie) Barnett replaced the late Frank Worrell, both West Indians having to return to the Caribbean.

We had almost reached finality in the match when, the number 11 for the Prime Minister's XI (name long since forgotten) took his place at the crease and confounded all by playing two overs from Iverson without making contact.

While these proceedings were taking place I occupied the silly mid-on position which was not unusual as I was long before appointed to the job by Lindsay Hassett, our Victorian captain. On occasions the position was silly, on others downright stupid, but this was certainly not a time to be asking for danger money.

As the start of his third over was about to take place, Iverson was having a discussion with the umpire and it was observed by all, via Iverson's gesticulations followed by those of the umpire to the batsman, that an underarm delivery was proposed. It was not generally known that Iverson had perfected this delivery.

The scene was set, the delivery made, a gentle arc to perfect length, a nice bounce and lo! contact upon the middle of a prodding bat and this time I did not drop it!

Finish of match.

'Yes,' said The Burden. 'And you get a special prize if you can hit the ball out of the ground on to the island in the middle of the river. Keith Miller was the last to do that'.

Stuff me an innings

Michael Muschamp

Michael Muschamp.

'Young Muschamp has taken five wickets and three prisoners.'

I have, during a long and somewhat mottled career, had little of great pith and moment on the cricket field. But the game has given me great enjoyment in many countries as an enthusiastic but not greatly expert participant and as a spectator at most of the world's great grounds.

I spent some time, aeons ago, as a naval officer. Now, naval officers afloat don't have much chance of cricket practice — or any kind of sporting practice, save the time-honoured one of lifting the elbow with a glass, rather than a bat, in hand.

Back in 1953, the vessel which was unlucky enough to have me as its 'Keen Young Sub', called at Port Moresby. We distinguished ourselves by first ramming the brand new jetty, driving some 1500 tons of frigate two or three feet into 'green' concrete. The locals didn't seem too upset by this somewhat unusual method of stopping one of HM's ships and came aboard with sundry invitations and massive thirsts. One of the invitations was to play cricket against the Army which, in those days, consisted of two Australian battalions.

The Royal New Zealand Navy has seldom distinguished itself on the greensward, if cricket is the game, in contrast to its supremacy (as far as all 'White

155

Ensign' navies are concerned) in the matter of rugby football. Nothing loath, however, we took up the challenge.

I had thought that I was the only officer with claims to cricket ability and was appointed captain. We then discovered a 'sleeper', in the person of the Supply Officer, who had captained one of New Zealand's most famous schools, Auckland Grammar, at both cricket and football. So we put him in the side as opening bowler and batsman, though with a few reservations as far as I was concerned, for his habit of smoking about 80 duty-free cigarettes a day, combined with an almost insatiable appetite for most forms of alcoholic beverages, made me doubt whether he could see out a two-day engagement of any sort, save amatory.

The pitch was, to say the least, unusual. Coir matting had been stretched over some ground whose cross-section resembled the north face of the Matterhorn. The outfield was a strange combination of dense jungle and a kind of New Guinean Simpson Desert.

The Supply Officer's bowling was, frankly, a danger to life and limb. It's the only time I've ever seen six byes signalled as one ball, bowled with even more than usual ferocity, hit about halfway down and soared over second slip's head to carry the boundary on the full.

The Army's opening bats were both, I was assured, Sheffield Shield players and, in desperation, I put myself on. The lunchtime refreshments, which were entirely of a liquid and non-teetotal nature, had wrought their worst on the batsmen, while empowering me with an ability I've not had before or since. I took 5 for 17 and retired to backward square leg to rest a throbbing head. I've absolutely no idea who won the match and I doubt if any of the 22 players or the assembled crowd (numbering upwards of a couple of hundred) either knew or cared.

A few years later, at the end of a five-year stint in London, I selected one match from the fixtures list of the London New Zealand Cricket Club as the most likely to be a 'Good Occasion'. The obvious one was that against the Distillers Company.

Like most expatriate clubs, the LNZCC could sometimes turn out a team which had a number of internationals and not a few Plunket Shield players. On other occasions, the quality of the players was such that Little Binghampton-in-the-Marsh's second eleven could have won by an innings. The match against Distillers produced one NZ cap in the person of a fast bowler (and captain for the day), a couple of Shield players and eight of varying degrees of lack of ability.

The week before the match, I had a liquid lunch at the BBC where two good friends, Neil Durden-Smith (later to be Chairman of the Lord's Taverners) and Corbet Woodall, in his day a very good cricketer indeed (he once hit six sixes in a row in a game playing for Aunty against ITV) told me how lucky I was to be playing at East Molesley, where the Distillers had their ground.

'It's the place where all the touring sides play a friendly match on the first Sunday of their tour,' said Woodall.

'Yes,' said The Burden. 'And you get a special prize if you can hit the ball out of the ground on to the island in the middle of the river. Keith Miller was the last to do that.'

They told me just how to get there, with elaborate details worked out on the back of a beer coaster. So, next Sunday, driven by SWISO (She Who Is Sometimes Obeyed), I headed for the ground. Arriving 10 minutes before the 11 a.m. start I was horrified to see the fielding side going out on to the ground. I rushed into the changing room and, not seeing anyone I recognised, assumed we were fielding and galloped out on to the field to be greeted by the fielding captain.

'Very nice of you to come out and sub,' he said. So I settled down, once again at backward square leg, while SWISO departed homewards.

I didn't recognise the opening bats, but this didn't worry me too much, as the LNZCC by its nature, doesn't have too many players who are regulars from year to year and this was not only the last match of the season, but the first I had played in that year. When the first wicket fell I didn't recognise the number three batsman, I felt it only right to ask the umpire.

'I know this is a silly question, but who's playing who? He looked at me as if I had lost all my marbles.

'East Molesley against Old Tiffinians.'

Not only was I playing on the wrong pitch, but on the wrong ground! I confessed my error to the fielding captain who asked me to see out the over and then arranged for one of the batting side to drive me to the correct ground, about a mile away where I arrived in time to see the LNZCC going out to field. As the time was now 11.30, I knew this was the right place. We never started anywhere near the advertised time.

Not with the ball, this time, but the bat. I went in at number seven and, by virtue of being dropped twice and given not out by our own umpire when I was palpably lbw, amassed 57. The captain apologised for not putting me further up the order, I was plied with sundry liquors from the Distillers' bar and I retired, if not into total oblivion, to the euphoric state which comes to us all, whatever our standard, when we have 'made a few' and been hero for an hour.

I've often wondered if, with the miracles of modern science, it is now possible to 'stuff an innings' in the same way as one gets a taxidermist to deal with a large fish. If such be the case, then my two 'Get Stuffed' requests would be for bowling half the Australian army out in Port Moresby in October, 1953 . . . and for playing in two different matches on two different grounds in England on the same day in August 1964.

Bouncers

Harold 'Dickie' Bird

Harold 'Dickie' Bird.

The mistake I made was to hit Frank Tyson's first three deliveries for four. I might have known the next ball in that match at Scarborough would be a bouncer. As he bowled it, Frank said, 'Hit that bastard for four'.

I was half on the front foot, looking to drive again, when the ball smashed into the side of my jaw and knocked me to the ground. There was blood all over my face and inside my mouth. I was dazed but not completely out. Faintly, I could hear the 'ting, ting, ting' of the ambulance. People seemed to be laughing. I was carried off the field and lifted into the ambulance. At the hospital, the X-ray showed that my jaw wasn't broken but the wound needed a stitch or two. I was patched up and went back to resume my innings.

At the time, Tyson was probably the fastest bowler in England. Not long before, he'd earned the nickname 'Typhoon' in Australia as he demolished the Australian batsmen in the 1954–55 series. He was very fast, but not as fast as Holding or Thomson.

I had encountered bouncers before but this was the first one that had really maimed me. Tyson never apologised. Norman Yardley, the former Yorkshire captain and a member of the committee, said it was my own fault; I should have expected a bouncer. I should have been on the back foot. We were tough in those Yorkshire days.

The other time I was hit on the head was against Hampshire at Ilkley. Butch White bowled a reasonable bouncer in his day and this particular one struck me a glancing blow on the head and went on to bounce off the top of the sightscreen. The umpire signalled four leg byes. I sank to my knees, more in shock than pain and Willie Watson, who was batting with me at the time, said sternly, 'Get up and get on with it. You're all right'.

I might have lost some teeth on another occasion when Lancashire's Colin Hilton bounced one at me in a county match which saw Leicester bowled out for 38 on a dicey wicket. I played it down in front of my face off the knuckle part of the glove, fracturing one of the small bones in my hand.

Perhaps the most serious case of a bouncer injuring a batsman was the Charlie Griffith versus Nari Contractor incident in Barbados when the Indian opener was on the danger list for a week after ducking into a Griffith bouncer. Contractor had a steel plate put in his head and I've been told is still troubled by it today.

Some people are very unlucky. Tom Pugh, once the Gloucester captain, ducked into a bouncer which never got up and was given out lbw. He would have retired hurt anyway because the blow fractured his jawbone. The worst incident I ever saw was in a match at Paignton, when Jeff Tolchard, now with Leicester, was hit in the face by a local bowler. His glasses were smashed and bits of glass went into his eye. He was lucky not to suffer more permanent damage.

The bouncer is a dangerous ball but it is part of the game, and I would never agree with those who say it should be outlawed. It is a legitimate part of the fast bowler's armoury. Without it, the game would be much less exciting. Some of the most dramatic moments in Test cricket come when a bowler drops it short and the batsman hooks it spectacularly for four. West Indians and Australians, brought up on hard, fast wickets, usually rise to the challenge. To stop bowlers bowling bouncers to someone like Clive Lloyd would rob the game of one of its finest sights.

The trouble comes when bowlers start peppering the batsmen with bouncers and the bouncer becomes an intimidating weapon. This happened, apparently, on the final session's play in the England versus West Indies Test at Old Trafford in 1976 when Mike Holding, Andy Roberts, and Wayne Daniel overdid it against Brian Close and John Edrich. Edrich felt so upset about it that he said later he felt like coming off the field. 'Surely cricket hasn't come to this,' he said.

Many deliveries flew over their heads and only 21 runs were scored in 80 minutes. Several times Close was hit about the body and arms as he stood there, often not even trying to avoid the ball. Eventually Bill Alley had a word with the West Indians and later Lloyd admitted his bowlers had bowled badly and had got carried away. There was to be no repetition.

The matter is adequately covered in the Laws of Cricket. The relevant section says, 'The persistent bowling of fast short-pitched balls is unfair if, in the opinion of the umpire at the bowler's end, it constitutes a systematic attempt at intimidation. In such event, he must adopt the following procedure:

a) When he decides that such bowling is becoming persistent he forthwith cautions the bowler.

b) If this caution is ineffective, he informs the captain of the fielding side and the other umpire what has occurred.

c) Should the above prove ineffective, the umpire at the bowler's end must:

(i) At the first repetition call 'Dead ball' when the over is regarded as completed.

(ii) Direct the captain of the fielding side to take the bowler off forthwith. The captain shall take the bowler off as directed.

(iii) Report the occurrence to the captain of the batting side as soon as the interval of play takes place. A bowler who has been taken off as above may not bowl again during the same innings.

Here is the text of a despatch that the British High Commissioner in Canberra sent to the Secretary of State for Foreign and Commonwealth Affairs, Sir Geoffrey Howe, on 17 October 1984.

On delivering a Letter of Introduction from Mrs Thatcher to the Prime Minister of Australia

Sir John Leahy

Sir,

1. In accordance with the instructions contained in the despatch dated 14 September, I delivered my Letter of Introduction to the Prime Minister of Australia on 14 October. This was my second day in Australia and a Sunday. Mr Hawke was dressed in white flannels and an open-neck shirt; I more formally in grey flannels and a blue blazer. I drank beer from a can; he does not do that any more.

2. The occasion was a cricket match between Mr Hawke's selection from his staff and a team drawn from the Parliamentary press gallery. It was also the last occasion when I was likely to be able to see him until after the general election in seven weeks' time, because he was almost immediately setting out on the campaign trail. The assignation was cleverly thought up by the Deputy High Commissioner, Charles Cullimore, and readily agreed to by Mr Hawke himself.

3. When we arrived at the small ground where the match was being played, Mr Hawke was already padded up waiting on his own in front of the pavilion to bat next. We went straight up to him and introduced ourselves. Naturally he had half an eye on what was going on in the middle, but otherwise the conversation flowed freely, if not profoundly, and he was as relaxed as any 54-year-old Prime Minister would be, with a cricketing reputation to live up to and the TV cameramen all waiting to see him get out first ball.

Some of these same vultures turned their attention to the two of us as we talked and I thought it would somehow not be in keeping with the dignity of the Prime Minister's letter if I made a show of handing it over to him then. There was also the practical consideration that Mr Hawke could not easily have read it or given it to anyone before going out to the wicket. With Mr Hawke's agreement I therefore passed it shortly afterwards to Mr Hawke's Private Secretary, who, I regret to report, treated it with even less respect by stuffing it into the back pocket of his somewhat off-white flannels. I feared it might be lost in the wash, but fortunately it survived.

4. I stayed to watch Mr Hawke bat. This he did to great effect — he was 12th man for Oxford when Colin Cowdrey was captain — until, after scoring a brisk 27 runs, he was hit in the eye in attempting an ambitious hook and had to retire hurt. I can only hope that he will not attribute any of the blame for this to my having shaken his hand a few minutes before. Anyway I enjoyed our first meeting and have subsequently heard that he did too.

5. This may seem a somewhat unorthodox way to have delivered my Letter of Introduction from Britain's Prime Minister to the Prime Minister of Australia. But I believe that it provides an apt illustration of the nature of the relationship between Britain and Australia. We should try to keep it that way.

I am, Sir,

Yours faithfully

John Leahy.

Sir John Leahy with Prime Minister Bob Hawke waiting to bat on the 'fateful' afternoon. Mrs Thatcher's letter, referred to in the despatch, is protruding from Sir John's blazer pocket. Prime Minister Hawke's injury in the game is pictured in the section, 'A Premier Game' on page 90. Photograph courtesy Graham Wilkinson, the Canberra Times.

'When I rang my father to tell him I had been selected to umpire Australia versus West Indies at the MCG over Christmas 1984, he very nearly jumped through the phone!'

Thoughts of an Aussie umpire

Steve Randell

Umpire and Lord's Taverner Steve Randell with England Test player Neil Foster during Tasmania versus MCC in Hobart, 1986–87 tour.

Waking at 2 p.m. this Sunday afternoon I knew there was a better than average chance of writing this article. Single, with none of the 'necessities' of life such as television, video, radio, stereo or phone, my life is different to most. Although 80,000 roaring fans at the pressure-cooker Melbourne Cricket Ground is a memorable experience, a quiet Sunday with nothing better to do than sleep is a welcome alternative.

Teaching in a tin mining village called Zeehan on Tasmania's wild west coast is a definite contrast to the summer's umpiring, where you stay in five-star hotels, meet a lot of people and travel continually. Here the local Aussie Rules football team (for which I play seconds) trains on the local airstrip, which hasn't seen a single Cessna in six months. Cricket and football grand finals are played on the famous Queenstown gravel oval — there's not much encouragement for fast bowlers. Pride decrees that gravel rash is not discussed, let alone complained about!

The Sydney Cricket Ground is far removed from Western Tasmania but holds a special place in my heart. I'd never been to Sydney until I umpired my first one-day international in January 1984. Day/night matches start at 2.30 p.m. and finish under lights at about 10 p.m. Immediately I decided one-dayers were okay — I could sleep in! Another advantage is that you are not there next day if you have made any mistakes; you are already travelling to your next match!

The pride I felt umpiring at international level was worth all the sacrifice, suffering and criticism over many years.

Just before Pakistan started chasing Australia's 264, fellow umpire Peter McConnell warned me I wouldn't be able to hear anything but the crowd noise. It's an incredible feeling when 30,315 people roar in unison at the SCG. It's also an incredible feeling when someone 10 metres away shouts at you and can't be heard. I prayed there wouldn't be a close call for caught behind; however the good Lord didn't answer my prayer because Mudassar Nazar almost immediately flashed at a Geoff Lawson delivery and I had to make the decision. I gave him out, which was correct, but this noisy new experience was somewhat scary.

Far from giving me the quiet start in international cricket for which I had hoped, there was further drama just around the corner. The perky Pakistani, Javed Miandad, was trying for a second run on Greg Matthews's throw. Javed had placed his team in a winning position, but on this occasion I adjudged him run out (the replays showed by about six centimetres). Straight away I had 30,315 friends! That was a terrific feeling. And when Javed threw his bat away in disgust, he had 30,315 enemies! Javed apologised during the next match. We had a good laught about it and I didn't even threaten to give him out again!

When we left the SCG at midnight, I took a quick look onto the great ground. Without blazing lights and excited sepctators, it was an eerie feeling experiencing the exact opposite to the commotion of two hours previous. Something fantastic, which very few have the honour of achieving, was over; I only hoped there would be further opportunities.

As the youngest of the panel umpires by 13 years, the other seven members have made me feel completely accepted. Under the chairmanship of former umpiring great Col Egar we have been together now for four seasons. The friendships and understandings we have developed have made the pressures on the field much easier with which to cope. I feel real empathy for any of the others who 'cop a bagging' — there is strength in numbers and we want people to know that we are the united third team on the ground. The only thing which is difficult to explain is why Dick French continues to support the Sydney Swans. As a Carlton supporter my fridge usually becomes fully stocked around VFL finals time!

The ultimate in cricket, as umpire or player, is representation at Test level. When I rang my father to tell him I had been selected to umpire Australia versus West Indies at the MCG over Christmas 1984, he very nearly jumped through the phone! From the earliest days I remember following Dad to every game he played for Kingborough, of which he is a life member. Former Australian Test star Max Walker was playing for rival club North Hobart then — it must have been a fair while ago! I was also lucky enough to play with Dad at South Hobart and I even umpired a game in which he played — I didn't give him a wicket though!

I was 10 and my sisters were 13, seven and four when Mum died. In the ensuing 20 years things haven't always been easy but Dad has never flinched and has supported us to the fullest extent. That's what I call a Dad! Before the Melbourne Test I decided to dedicate the match to my family; I was very proud that my father, Don, and sisters Sandra, Vicki and Julie were there and I wanted to do my best for them. Even now Dad travels to every match; it's nice to know I have his support.

My final two goals were achieved with this game — a Test match and a Test at the MCG (virtually Tasmania's Test home ground). I was too excited and proud to be nervous beforehand and when I walked onto the arena as the youngest Test umpire ever, I didn't know what was going to happen, but I intended enjoying this unique experience. I think I'm the youngest ever. When I debuted I was 28 years, 307 days. Do you think it is worth checking? After a quiet series, Viv Richards bludgeoned 208 in a magnificent performance but Australia brought the Windies long-running winning sequence to an end with a hard-fought draw.

Full concentration at the highest representative level is very difficult. In the last session of this match I was telling myself to keep concentrating when I looked up and saw Australian spinner Murray Bennett staring at me as though I had two heads. After all I am Tasmanian! I felt a real sense of accomplishment and Test representation had been a dream come true.

Increasingly, the topic of video replays is a major point of conjecture among cricket followers. I would love a dollar for every time someone has sympathised with the umpire's lot regarding replays; however, I don't look for sympathy. My belief is that the television

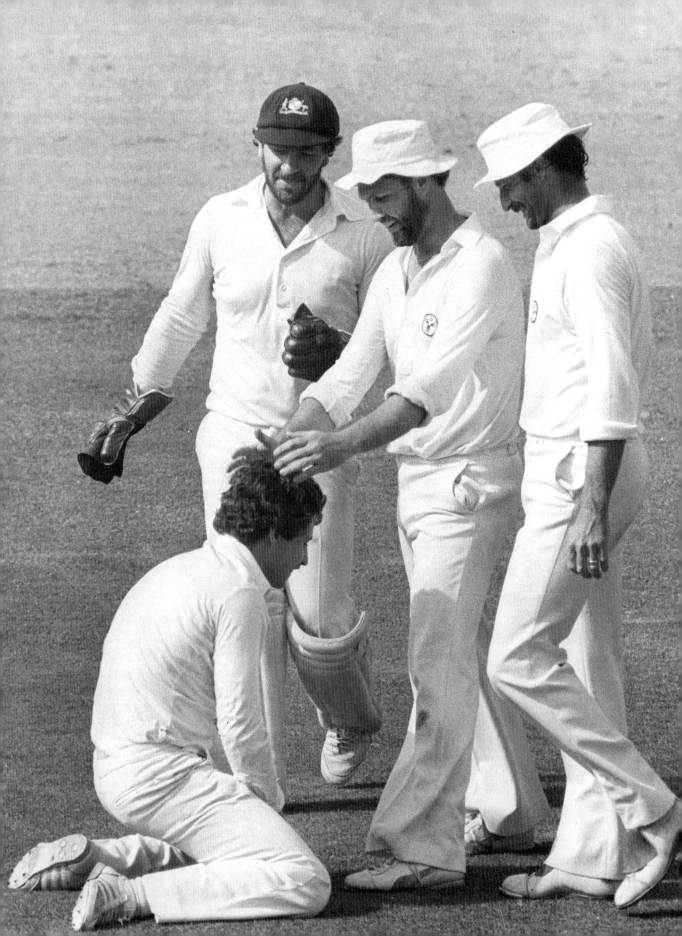

screen shows when you are correct, not incorrect. Positive thought is so important and proper mental attitude is a major contributing factor for success in any top level sport.

There is a school of thought that replays can better determine some decisions than an umpire. Maybe so, but cricket is a human game and the idea of a machine telling me what to do isn't high on my list of priorities; I like the personal challenge that umpiring provides. The panel umpires have often said there wouldn't be many volunteers if all an umpire had to do was count to six, call 'Over' and walk to square leg (especially for five days in 40 degree temperatures).

It is an eerie feeling at the MCG and SCG when 40,000 or 50,000 pairs of eyes stare at the big screens after you have made a decision. There is never any need for an umpire to look as the roar of the crowd soon delivers the message!

There is difficulty in concentrating fully in a Test which sees about 2700 balls bowled. As on-field happenings cannot be kept on-field any longer, no wonder it is highly unlikely that anyone will officiate for a full five-Test series as happened years ago. Australian tele-vision provides a magnificent coverage but with more than 15 cameras at an MCG Test match added pressure is certainly understandable.

Anyway I was led to believe that umpires were blind — they couldn't see replays, could they?

Replays are here to stay, all that can be asked is that a balanced approach incorporating normal speed and the position of the umpire be presented.

There is a growing trend in Australia for younger umpires. Last season Darren Close from Tasmania debuted with four Sheffield Shield matches and the domestic one-day final. At 18 he quickly developed an impressive rapport with the players and displayed coolness under pressure. Darren is setting the basis for a successful career; he couldn't have had a better beginning. Coping with pressure and excellent concentration are necessary characteristics for making correct decisions; whether you are 18 or 58 is of little importance.

What will happen in the future? Who knows. I have been very fortunate — cricket has given me many things. It has enabled me to achieve goals which precious few are able to attain; for that I am extremely grateful.

Blessings on you, boy: Ray Bright gives Graham Wood a pat on the head after catching Botham for a duck. Also in the photo are Rodney Marsh (left) and Dennis Lillee, England versus Australia, Centenary Test, September 1980.

'I usually go where the action is, and although that may sound a little odd, I have a very good reason for choosing short leg or the slips.'

Ease up a bit!

Ernie Wise

Ernie Wise.

As a Yorkshireman, it is natural that I should be interested in cricket. I have played an active part, too: as a child of six I actually lived next to the great Geoff Boycott who lived at a place called Fitswilliam. I lived in Kingsley just down the road from him.

I suppose my love of cricket started in 1959 when I went to see the Test matches in Australia. Mind you, I also appeared in the local theatre in Melbourne and Sydney. I still have a cricket bat signed by the whole team.

I then had many show business teams in the seaside shows at Blackpool, Yarmouth, etc. One of the advantages of being a show business cricketer is that you can get preferential treatment. It seems to be perfectly in order to approach the captain of the opposing side and say, 'Look, old boy, I'm working on stage tonight and it says in my contract that I am not to be injured in any way. I can't put up with bruised legs or missing teeth. My smile is one of my greatest assets.'

It usually works; the bowlers ease up a bit. I remember one particular occasion at a charity cricket match. It was agreed that I be allowed to knock up a few runs to impress the fans. (Yes, there were a few!) I had a marvellous time and hit 35 in as many minutes but my confidence got the better of me. Like a fool, I told the captain he could step up the pace a bit. He did. I was out first ball! I also remember a match at Blackpool with a showbiz team that we shaped into a fighting side. Our first match was with a team from a local school: lads of about 12 years of age. They gave us the thrashing of our lives.

One of the most important aspects of cricket is fielding. I usually go where the action is, although that may sound a little odd. I have a very good reason for choosing short leg, or the slips. The ball is usually flying off the bat at great speed and the chances of ever catching it (at least *my* chances) are slim. Whereas, if I were in the outfield and a batsman skied the ball, I would be victim to that terrible hush that always falls around the ground, as I waited for the ball to come to me — only to drop it to a loud groan. Mind, you get plenty of sym-

166

pathy. People say, 'Well you don't play very often' or 'The sun must have got in your eyes'. That's small consolation if it's a cloudy day.

Yes, I love cricket but I must stop trying to emulate the stylish batting of players like Geoff Boycott or Ian Botham. It looks good but I am always bowled first ball. All I should do is just concentrate on hitting the damned thing!

When I say I played an active part, that was up to two years ago when I went to catch a ball. It hit me on the shin and up came a big lump that lasted a month. I decided from then on I would just watch the game . . .

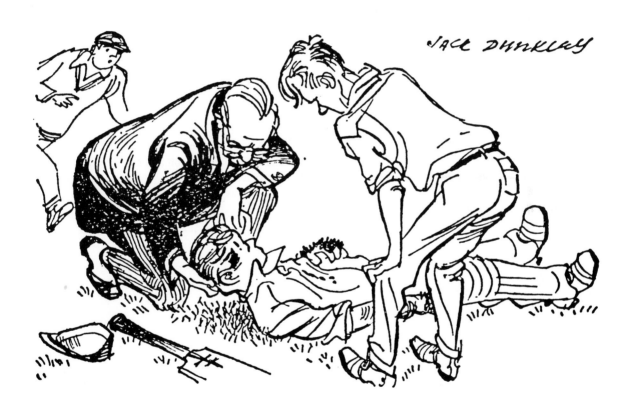

A funny thing happened . . .

Strange and often funny things happen even when serious cricket is being played. Here's some intrusive and lighter moments of cricket happenings.

Cricket at Lord's: Second Test, England versus West Indies, final day, July 1969. A lone spectator hoists West Indies batsman Lance Gibbs after he had hit an impressive four.

An elderly gentleman 'invades' the field to congratulate Bobby Simpson on a century he made during the second Test against India at the Melbourne Cricket Ground, January 1968.

Above: PC Adam Hughes, 23, and a fair damsel of a waitress relax 'in the middle' during the first Test, England versus Australia, June 1985. There had been attempts to vandalise the Lord's ground.

Caught behind: The now-famous Lord's streaker who interrupted the celebrated Test between England and Australia, August 1975, by running onto the pitch as naked as a cricket ball and leaping (very carefully) over the stumps. It was very nearly a case of caught and bowled but when the law took a hand it turned into a matter of 'court and hold'.

Black and white comedy: An intruder on the wicket looks dressed more for the Proms in his tails and training shoes. He raises a protest letter like a baton as umpire 'Dickie' Bird puts out a restraining hand. Umpire Bertie Meyer moves in quickly to assist while batsmen Ian Botham (far left) and Mike Brearley watch unperturbed.

Scarecrow on a wet pitch, Lord's Cricket Ground, August 1970.

'It was our last game before the Centenary Test and defeat by an innings and 76 runs at the hands of a county side amounted to poor credentials for a major confrontation with England's best.'

Ashes to ashes

Allan Border

The 1977 Centenary Test in Melbourne is regarded even by die-hard purists as one of the great Anglo-Australian cricket matches. It was before my international time, but I followed every ball and every stroke from afar. I've seen enough of the replays and the replays of the replays to go right along with the consensus: *that* was a game of cricket.

Both countries had high hopes for the follow-up, the 1980 Centenary at Lord's. If the Poms had stuck strictly to history, the game would have been played at the Oval, scene of the first Test between the two countries in England a hundred years earlier. But to where else but Lord's would you turn on such a game as this?

I was in that 1980 game and, like everybody else involved, envisaged something of a re-enactment of the high drama and excitement the MCG extravaganza had produced. It didn't happen. Rain saw to that. Five days' play was reduced to three and a half, effectively washing out any possibility of a result.

On the flight home, we consoled each other by saying we had been robbed by that unprintable English weather. We were never going to lose, that's for sure, but the record books show the Poms with an honourable draw against their name. Gee, it's hard to win a Test match in England.

The sombreness of our departure was in vivid contrast with the mood of our arrival. Having won the Melbourne Centenary, and with a short, sharp tour ahead of us, we were all systems go. The flight from Australia was routine, but the bus ride from London's Heathrow Airport to the Waldorf Hotel was something else. Rod Marsh and Ashley Mallett sat together and as the bus pulled out, engaged in a physical niggling match. High-spirited guys, those two. I don't know how it started, but it may have been that one had more than 50 per cent of the seat and the other objected. It quickly reached the stage of pulling the hairs on each other's arms, and the hirsute Rodney was at a big disadvantage here.

As a still-young tourist who had tended to idolise both these guys, I was amazed. Was this Rodney

Jubilant Aussie skipper Allan Border after taking a spectacular catch.

Marsh, legendary Australian wicketkeeper, and Ashley Mallett, one of the world's best spin bowlers, behaving like a couple of juvenile delinquents? Could two mature heroes of mine, larger-than-life figures I'd watched so often on TV, be here on a London-bound bus, wrestling, scragging and thumping each other? Yes. Seeing was believing.

The two-man war (for 'man' we should perhaps substitute 'kid') went on all the way to the hotel. Hostilities were adjourned while we checked in, but when 'Bacchus' and 'Rowdy' learned they had drawn each other as room-mates, it was on again — all the way up in the lift and along the passage to their room.

It was there that Rodney called a truce. Ashley accepted, happily, I think, because he was less robust than his foe. 'Okay', he said, 'truce'. And with that he adjourned to run himself a bath.

Rowdy should have known better than to take the word of a devious bloke like Rodney, who hid behind the bathroom door and lay in wait. When Ashley emerged, bath still running, for his towel and soap (and possibly his rubber duck), he was ambushed and the no-holds-barred wrestling match resumed. It was still going strong when the phone rang. 'Management here,' said the caller. 'We'd just like to know if there's something wrong with your toilet or your bath because the guests in the room below are complaining about water dripping all over them through the ceiling.'

'Christ, the bath,' said Rowdy, as he neatly extricated himself from a Marsh headlock which had previously been regarded as a submission hold. Much of the suite was awash. It took about 50 towels and a small army of hotel staff to mop up the overflow. It also took a lot of sweet-talking to get the staff back onside. We never did get to meet the people in the suite downstairs.

It was my first close-up experience of Ashley Mallett and I regret that our careers did not totally coincide because I would like to have spent a lot more time in his company. He was a scream. I've no doubt he would have made a big career for himself as a stand-up comic had cricket not intervened. He was also accident-prone, and his wit and his clumsiness combined to make him an unforgettable character.

You had to be there to really appreciate the value of his presence to the morale of a team. You'd go along to a toffy English function and Rowdy would bung on the best upper-class Pom accent you've ever heard.

He'd mingle with the cream of society and while the rest of us stood back shunning the limelight, he'd do an impeccable impersonation of Lord Ashley Mallett, 'Oh, yes, polo and riding to the hounds and all that. Splendid. Of course, I did a good deal of my schooling at Oxford, you know. And, oh, the boat race . . . yes, thoroughly spiffing! Good-oh! Nice one, that!' He was unbelievable. On the way home, he'd grab the bus driver's microphone and recap the evening for us, sending up everything from the speeches to the cucumber sandwiches. A rare, multiple talent was Ashley Mallett.

Because our mission was the Centenary Test, we took the preliminaries a little light-heartedly. And we paid the price. The first game, against Hampshire, was a nice pipe-opener which we won by 10 wickets. I was happy with my 95 runs. Surrey, at the Oval, was next and the less said about our 59-run defeat the better. We drew with Young England and Lancashire, lost both one-day internationals (at the Oval and Birmingham) and moved on to Nottingham.

Greg Chappell had made a typical Chappell hundred against Lancashire and, understandably happy with his form, took the Nottinghamshire game off. As things turned out, we could really have used him. Notts in those days were a real 'foreign legion'. No import restrictions or South African embargoes for them. South African captain Clive Rice was their skipper and a compatriot, a quick named Watson, was also in the team. So was Richard Hadlee. It was a pretty formidable frontline attack. Their batting line-up was more than just respectable too. It included Derek Randall, who had given us such a hard time in the Melbourne Centenary.

It was a real seamer's wicket at Nottingham and I thought we did well to make 207 in the prevailing conditions. Graeme Wood and I top-scored with 76 and 73 respectively and Watson and Hadlee took eight wickets between them.

We had Dennis Lillee, Jeff Thomson and Len Pascoe in our side and we figured we'd whip right through this county lot. Unfortunately, our guys bowled like up-country amateurs and Nottinghamshire belted them all over the place. Their first wicket fell without a run on the board; their last went down 465 runs later. It was a record score for Nottinghamshire against Australia.

We helped them along by dropping more than a dozen catches, thanks largely to an experiment aimed at improving the side's fielding versatility. Kim Hughes was captain in Greg's absence and he figured every player should have some sort of close-to-the-wicket fielding experience. So, instead of the quick bowlers taking their usual places in the outfield, Kim put them in slips. It was a new experience for Dennis, Jeff and Len and they treated the ball like a live grenade. I reckon they put down eight or nine chances a primary school kid would have coolly accepted. If we hadn't been in such diabolical trouble, it would have been hilarious.

As so often happens when you're facing a huge deficit, we failed miserably in our second innings. We compiled 182 and the fact that I top-scored with 38 was scant personal consolation.

It was our last game before the Centenary Test and defeat by an innings and 76 runs at the hands of a county side amounted to poor credentials for a major confrontation with England's best. Still, this was the game we'd come here for, wasn't it? This would be different. And how different it was!

Obviously influenced by our shocker against Nottinghamshire, the betting people had us 7-1 under-dogs to win the Test. They were ridiculous odds for a two-horse race and right from the outset we made them look silly.

Rain delayed the start and was to cost us almost 10 hours' play in the first three days. Greg won the toss, elected to bat and Wood and Bruce Laird, the Western Australian team-mates, laid the foundations for a big score with a 64-run opening partnership. Graeme went on to 112, but the innings belonged to Kim Hughes. He was magnificent and his 117 was among the best knocks I've seen *anybody* play. There were three sixes and 14 fours in that innings. It was a masterpiece of controlled aggression.

I was on 56 and we were 5-385 when Greg declared. There was no 7-1 on offer about us now, and we were odds-on favourites after we bundled the Poms out for 205. Lillee, bowling superbly, destroyed the top order and finished with 4-43. Pascoe took up where Dennis left off and demolished the middle and lower order. His figures wee 5-59. The last seven England wickets fell for just 68.

It left us enough time before stumps on the fourth day to rattle up 106 for the loss of two wickets, stretching our overall lead to 286. More quick runs (as quick as possible) were the order of the following morning and we added 83 before Greg declared at 4-189.

Again, Kim Hughes was the star. He batted superbly, savaging the attack for 84 runs before sacrificing his wicket. It had been quite a batting performance by Australia; an overall total of 574 for the loss of just nine wickets.

The declaration left England 350 minutes in which to score 370. It wasn't an impossible assignment, but the Poms didn't enter into the spirit of things at all. Lillee trapped Graham Gooch leg before for 16 and Pascoe had Athey caught for just one, and England put up the shutters. They had just the man to do it, too — Geoff Boycott. Without making the slightest attempt to chase the target, Boycott tapped and deflected his way to an unbeaten 128.

At the end, England were 3-244. The game had died hours before. You couldn't really blame them for going defensive to save the game. The Poms do, after all, take quite unkindly to defeat. But I thought that an historic occasion like the Centenary Test deserved better. I thought they may have had a decent sort of whack at the target we'd set them. Ian Botham was their captain and it was contrary to his character to pull the pin. But pull the pin he did. I've no doubt we'd have won had the game run its full course, but there is little real satisfaction in moral victories.

The Test was the last game on that tour. We left England in early September and were back the following May for the 1981 Ashes campaign. All of us involved in that tour will remember it as one of sacrificed opportunities. We did everything but win. We could well have gone home 4–1 winners of the six-Test series; instead we limped back to Australia 3–1 losers. For two reasons, I'm not going to dwell too long on the 1981 tour: millions of words have already been written about it; and it is personally far too painful to relive in detail. You have to be a dead-set masochist to go back over it again and again.

Things were going well for us in the early stages. Rain played havoc with the first four county games, but we won the one-day series 2–1 and took the first Test by four wickets on a seaming wicket at Trent Bridge. It was a real bowler's paradise. The highest score in the four innings was England's 185 in the first, which indicates just how much the ball was moving about.

This was the Test which saw the emergence of Terry Alderman as a champion medium-pacer. Terry relished the conditions and had match figures of 9–130. It was the start of a remarkable series for him, a series in which was to take a record 42 wickets. You look back on that performance and realise just how tragic was that shoulder injury, sustained in a scuffle with an invading spectator at the WACA ground in Perth in 1981, which irreparably set back his career.

Sure, Terry made it back into senior cricket, but he was never to approach those magic heights of 1981; not by a mile. Terry set up that Trent Bridge win for us by taking 5–62 as England's second innings folded for 125. Our target was a mere 132, but on that particular wicket there was no guarantee of anything. We lost six wickets in the process of making the required runs, but

that didn't sour the taste of victory at all. We were rapt. Particularly rapt was Kim Hughes, captaining Australia in Greg Chappell's absence. This is one of the tours Greg chose not to make.

The second Test at Lord's was drawn, a considerable let-down after the Trent Bridge triumph. It had become the pattern for rain to interrupt Lord's Tests, and this one was no exception. It was a highly competitive game but the loss of two hours' play on the second day, plus other weather interruptions, eventually ruled out a result.

England declared at 8–265 in their second innings, setting us 232 to win in 170 minutes. They were in with a real chance, too, when our third wicket fell at 17. The ball was turning appreciably, but Wood played a fine hand for 62 not out and Trevor Chappell dug in for more than an hour for just five runs. We were 4–90 at the finish and rather glad to see the end arrive.

We were still on good terms with ourselves, one up in the series with two Tests gone. The next was at Leeds and to say the wheels fell off is to considerably understate what happened.

I still can't believe it. I can't believe that we could declare at 9–401, bowl England out for 174, have them 7–135 in the follow-on ... and still lose the bloody game. I don't have to remind you what Botham did to us in their second innings: an unbeaten, blistering 149 to lift England to 356.

Botham had resigned the captaincy after the Lord's Test and that Leeds innings was his way of saying how great it was to be relieved of the responsibilities. It was by no means a classical innings and 'Both' had his share of good fortune. More than his share, perhaps. But he survived and he gave our bowlers a father of a hiding. He was awesome. I doubt that I have seen a more savage innings.

Despite it, we were odds-on to win the match and take a 2–0 lead in the series. When the England innings ended early on the fifth day, our target was 130. The ball was seaming, but if Botham could make 149 on his own, we'd collectively bowl over 130. No problems.

And there weren't too many problems early. We lost Wood with the score at 13, but John Dyson and Trevor Chappell took us along to 56 without further damage. There was no indication of the shocking chain of events which was about to follow.

Bob Willis started it by getting Trevor with a rearing delivery. Our demise was under way. Trevor's wicket was Willis's inspiration and he careered through our line-up like a man possessed. Kim Hughes and Graham Yallop both fell for ducks. It was certainly Willis's day. He had been a lion-hearted performer for England for a lot of years and this was his moment of glory; he richly deserved it. I just wished he'd saved the most devastating performance of his career for some other team. Why pick on us?

Willis's figures in that innings speak for themselves: 15.1 overs, three maidens, 43 runs, eight wickets. England had skittled us for 111. They had done the impossible. We had outplayed them for more than three and a half days of a five-day Test, and lost. It was incredible.

It was this Test which produced the infamous Lillee-Marsh bet. The much publicised episode was born at tea on the fourth day. At that stage, England were seven down and still 80-odd short of avoiding an innings defeat. And do you think we weren't slapping each other on the back! We'd wrap this game up long before stumps and the celebrations would start nice and early. And if we had a few too many, it wouldn't matter because we'd have all day tomorrow (a bonus rest day) to recover. It was great to be alive.

We were wallowing in self-adulation when Ladbroke's market on the outcome of the game was flashed on to the scoreboard. England 500–1! It was an absurd price, an absurd situation. Not even the punters among us had heard of such outrageous odds in a two-horse field. But when you looked at England's position it was probably their right price.

The proposition appealed enormously to Dennis Lillee. 'They're unbelievable odds,' he said. 'I reckon the Poms have got a good chance of getting up.' His voice was dripping sarcasm. Out of sheer perversity, Dennis wanted us to put 50 quid out of the team fund on England. You can't do that, we told him. We also told him it would be a stupid bet because we were going to have this game won in half an hour or so. But when Dennis gets his teeth into something, he's like a bull terrier. And he wasn't about to let this one go.

'Well,' he said, 'I'm going to have 10 quid on it.' We told him he was crazy, but Dennis was unmoved. He produced his money and sent it off to Ladbroke's betting tent with Peter Tribe, the team bus driver. Peter is one very nice guy. We called him 'The Geez' because he was forever referring to people as geezers. As we returned to the field for the big kill, Peter was heading for the tent to make this very unlikely bet. Rodney Marsh had obviously been giving that 500–1 a lot of thought because he caught Peter's eye and, in sign language, indicated that he'd have five quid's worth of the action.

When the story broke later, all sorts of amazing allegations were bandied about. The most outrageous suggestion was that Dennis and Rodney had sold Australia out for personal gain, that, having backed England, they played dead. There is only one answer to that: bullshit. I have yet to see two more patriotic Australians. Suggesting that either would give anything less than 100 per cent at all times for his country is both scurrilous and fatuous. Not on, no way.

Dennis and Rod were simply sucked in by the unreal situation. They were as shattered as any of us (and perhaps more so than most) as we sat, shell-shocked, in the dressing room after that horrendous second-innings collapse. They actually had to be reminded that they had won a lot of money; £7500 to be precise. They had, in fact, broken the bank.

By the time The Geez got back to the Ladbroke's tent to collect, the one-pound betters had cleaned out the cash reserves. The loot had to be picked up at Worcester, our next port of call after a fleeting visit to Glasgow for a one-day game against Scotland. The Geez arrived in the Worcester dressing room during a lunch adjournment with the money (all in £5 notes) stuffed into his jumper. I'd never seen so much in one heap. Obviously, the drinks were on Rod and Dennis and they bought plenty. What isn't generally known is that out of their 'ill-gotten gains', they shouted Peter Tribe an Australian holiday. They bought him a return ticket to Australia the following season and he had a ball.

The fourth Test, at Edgbaston, was virtually a carbon copy of the Leeds catastrophe. The similarities were quite eerie. Again we outplayed England for most of the match; again we thought we had them at our mercy; again we were set a piddling target for victory; again we capitulated shamefully — Ian Botham destroyed us.

It was another low-scoring match but our 69-run first-innings lead and a great spell of spin bowling by Ray Bright set us up for what should have been a comfortable win. Ray took 5-68 off 34 overs as England groped their way to 219 in their second innings. We had two days to make 142 and recapture the series lead. We failed abysmally. We started badly, losing wickets at 2, 19 and 29, but Graham Yallop and I managed to call a temporary halt to the rot and at 4-105, we were going to do it comfortably.

Then England skipper Mike Brearley tossed the ball to Botham and our lights went out. We failed by 29 runs. The man who had destroyed us with the bat at Leeds now demolished us with the ball. I don't have to elaborate on his performance, his bowling analysis tells it all: 14 overs, nine maidens, 11 runs, five wickets. He conceded only one run as he snapped up those wickets.

By all things logical, we should have already wrapped up the series 3-0. Instead we trailed 2-1 and were starting to seriously doubt our own ability. The Poms, on the other hand, had been geed up by their extraordinary victories and they applied the *coupe de grace* in the fifth Test at Manchester. We sealed our own, and the series' fate, by collapsing in a style sadly reminiscent of Leeds and Edgbaston, in our first innings after restricting England to a modest score. They made 231; the best we could muster was 130. If

there was a way to get out, we'd find it. And if there wasn't a way, we'd invent one. I was becoming convinced that failure is habit-forming. When England batted the second time, Botham, our nemesis, did it again. He top-scored with 118 and the Poms' total of 404 left us the unlikely target of 505.

It would have been a history-making achievement and after what we'd recently been through, we were psychologically unprepared to rewrite records. We gave it a big of a fly, though, and our 402 was, by one run, our highest score of the series. My contribution, 123 not out, was also the highest by an Australian. I made those runs with a broken finger, sustained in the field in England's first innings. We lost by 103 runs, but I guess we restored a little self-respect.

The series was lost 3-1, with the final Test coming up at the Oval. The pressure was off and we had a little chat and decided we were not going home with a 1-4 scoreline hanging over our heads. We were very determined to do well and, indeed, things were going our way when we ran out of time. It was our most consistent batting performance of the season. We led by 38 on the first innings and our declaration at 9-344 in the second gave England a full day to score 383.

When Lillee had Boycott, a first-innings century-maker, leg before for a duck, we had visions of salvaging something very substantial from the wreckage of that English summer. At 6-144 we had them on toast, but England's salvation came this time in the form of veteran wicket-keeper Alan Knott. Knotty, always a difficult customer to dislodge, held the innings together and was still there, on 70, at the finish. An honourable draw for us but, as I said, moral victories are not worth a crumpet. It was a good Test for me, 106 not out and 84, but it didn't really erase all the unhappy memories.

You try not to think too much about the 1981 series, but it keeps on recurring. You cannot get out of your mind the plain fact that you lost a series you should have won. Personally, I am haunted by the fact that the Australian cause was ravaged by a mate of mine. A bloke named Ian Botham.

Caribbean cricket and then some . . .

Peter McFarline

Peter McFarline.

On the beach at Sandy Lane, in the parish of St Michael's, on the island of Barbados in the coalition of countries known as the West Indies, there is the answer to one of life's great mysteries.

For decades now, the batsmen of the world have ducked and weaved, have cursed and muttered, have shuffled and jabbed and poked ineffectually as an endless line of West Indian fast bowlers tormented their souls and their averages. And around the cricketing stadiums, spectators have 'oohed' and 'aahed', sucked in their breath as they watched the sheer pace and fury of the Caribbean comets reduce once-reliable run-scorers to impotency.

From the safety of the terraces and the members' enclosure, the over-riding emotion has been, 'Thank God it's not me out there'. From the front-line of the popping crease, more often than not, the over-riding emotion has been, 'Why me? What did I do to deserve this?'. And always the unanswered questions. Where do they come from? How do they keep producing them? When will they run out of express pace bowlers?

The line goes back a long time, more than half a century. Back to England in 1933 when Learie Constantine and Manny Martindale revived the spirit of bodyline just as officialdom was beginning to believe it had been laid to rest forever. In hindsight, that was the first clue. Even then the fledgling West Indians could call upon muscular, athletic men with a mean eye and meaner disposition who revelled in the ability to propel the ball at disconcerting pace into batsmen's bodies.

In terms of the evolution of the West Indies fast bowler, there was a lull in proceedings until late in the 1950s when a strapping fellow named Roy Gilchrist began to terrorise batsmen. Unfortunately, big Roy was altogether too nasty even for the sensibilities of his own selectors. His international career was brief. But Gilchrist was the start of a new era, an era that lifted the Caribbean to the forefront of international cricket.

Wes Hall, Charlie Griffiths, Andy Roberts, Michael Holding, Malcolm Marshall, Sylvester Clarke, Colin

Croft, Joel Garner, Courtney Walsh, Tony Gray — all athletes of frightening pace coupled with immense skill and an enthusiastic hatred of the man with the bat at the other end.

Express pace has always been the strongest of cricket's magnets. Every boy who picked up a ball has fancied himself as a very fast bowler. Every coach has spent his days searching for the youngster with the fluid action, the genuine speed, the volatile temperament and physical attributes to bowl straight and hard.

Every so often, men of speed have appeared to leave their particular brand of fire and brimstone on their time. Barnes, Larwood, Tyson, Trueman, Snow, McDonald, Lindwall, Miller, Lillee, Thomson, Procter, Hadlee, Imran Khan, Kapil Dev. . . . In their wake, however, has been not more speed but less. Skill of the medium-fast variety, perhaps, but not speed of the mind-numbing, heart-quaking school. Unless, of course, it was from the West Indies.

I recall vividly a conversation with that marvellous Caribbean cricketer and captain Clive Hubert Lloyd in Georgetown, Guyana, just prior to the first Test of the 1984 Australian tour. Injuries were to keep two of the greatest of their fast bowlers, Michael Holding and Malcolm Marshall, out of that first encounter. Not unnaturally, the Australians were overjoyed at the news, so much so that they reckoned on a winning chance.

But Lloyd was unperturbed. He spent no time at all lamenting the loss of his wonderful pace duo. 'We've plenty more where they came from,' he said with just a ghost of a smile. He was right, of course. Up from the reserves came Wayne Daniel and Milton Small, with no diminution in pace or hostility. Holding and Marshall, once fit, joined forces with Joel Garner to destroy the youthful Australians. Along the way, the West Indies' selectors found time and space to blood another couple of young speedsters, Winston Davis and Courtney Walsh.

That year, and the one that came after it, saw, probably, the zenith of the West Indian cricketing chart.

The giant Garner, having been left out of the previous tour of the Indian sub-continent, ostensibly because he was in the twilight of his career, was venomously determined to put that idea to rest. The broad-shouldered, muscular Marshall was spurred into a fury of blinding pace by some fool's written suggestion that he was no longer the fastest in the world. Holding was contemplating retirement, a contemplation which brought with it the desire to go out on a high note. Four others, Daniel, Gray, Davis and Small, were battling for the greatest sporting prize in the Caribbean: a permanent place in the West Indies cricket team.

Kim Hughes's battling young Australians were cast aside 3-0. Immediately after, the West Indians toured England where they administered a 5-0 thrashing in conditions that were not ideal for their bowlers. Less than a year later, back on their own sunbaked pitches, they repeated the dose, leaving the cream of England's batsmen shell-shocked and unwilling to take more punishment.

Ever since the first genuine paceman appeared on the cricket ground, arguments have raged about the morality, indeed the legality of the art. By the mid-1980s, the debate had reached fever pitch. The West Indies, at first under Lloyd and then his successor, Viv Richards, had employed the fast men to such an extent they had reduced their over rate to a pitiful 12 an hour, a tactic that other countries had copied, basically in self-defence. Worse, far worse, from the purists' point of view, was the intimidatory tactics that had become part and parcel of the Caribbean attack. Three and four bouncers an over had become routine. Sometimes there were more.

Umpires everywhere seemed powerless to react to what was a flagrant abuse of the laws, not to mention the intent, of the game. Cricket authorities, from the International Cricket Conference down, refused to intervene for fear of upsetting the emerging nations of the Caribbean.

Controversies aside, the Caribbean cannonballers had succeeded in lifting their art, trade, call it what you

Sobers in characteristic sweeping style.

will, to the ultimate in fear. And the wonder was, they just kept on coming. It was mass production in sport but a natural process as opposed to the way the Eastern Bloc produces gymnasts and swimmers, and Bulgaria weightlifters. As soon as one retired — as Andy Roberts and Michael Holding had — or one was injured, there were two or three or four, as quick, as mean and as frightening, fighting for the vacant spot.

Sir Gary Sobers, the finest cricketer of my time and perhaps any other, was an integral part of the West Indies' rise to power. He played with Gilchrist as a raw teenager, was at the height of his immense powers while Hall and Griffiths wreaked their mayhem and in his final playing days oversaw the development of Andy Roberts. To Sobers, the only surprise about the development and replenishment of the Caribbean pace stock was that it took so long to happen.

Not long before Australia's 1984 visit to the Caribbean, I had the privilege of assisting Sir Gary in the writing of the foreword to a book on fast bowling. 'Tell us the secret of West Indian pace bowling success,' implored the publishers. Sir Gary well knew the 'secret'. Putting it into words was something else again. 'Man, you'll just have to see it for yourself,' Sir Gary said finally. Which is how, in March 1984, I came to be on the beach at Sandy Lane, in the parish of St Michael's, on the island of Barbados. Not a half a mile from the Sandy Lane Hotel, reputed to be one of the most exclusive, and certainly one of the most expensive resorts in the world; not a mile from a mansion, once owned by British pools and racing magnate Robert Sangster, which can be anyone's for US$1000 a night (including servants), not another mile from the superbly-appointed retirement home of former Australian jockey Scobie Breasley, the West Indies fast bowlers of the future gather every evening.

There is nothing formal about the gathering; there are no coaches, no supervision. Just a group of lithe young Barbadians, from early to late teens. Between them is a battered old community cricket bat, and a piece of timber that acts as the stumps the batsmen

must defend. But each competitor brings with him the ultimate weapon in this game called 'wind ball'. It is a tennis ball which has been carefully shaved so that one complete side is bereft of hair. The idea of the game, played right on the water's edge, is to propel that shaven ball as fast as possible at the batsman, protected only by his bat.

The bowlers, of whom four or five may be operating at one time, match their run-up to coincide with the run-out of the gentle waves of the Caribbean which slide up the beach every 30 seconds or so. By hitting the wet but firm sand — the pitch — in front of the batsman with these shaven projectiles, the bowlers can generate frightening pace, erratic bounce — and a great deal of trepidation from the uninitiated. A young life of practice on such a surface will breed batsmen and fielders of extraordinary reflexes and sound technique; without a combination of both, the bruises and occasionally the broken bones mean certain enthusiasm to find a more comfortable pastime.

It is no relaxation, this game called 'wind ball'. It evolved over the years, and according to Sir Gary Sobers, Clyde Walcott and Everton Weekes, has produced more West Indian Test Cricketers than any coaching clinic, any talent search. The West Indian islands, despite their ascent to nationhood, are still desperately poor. Wind ball gives the sons of the poor, the unemployed and the eager the chance to hone their natural skills without waiting forlornly for the chance to practise on turf wickets, in white clothing, with pads, and gloves and helmets.

Walcott, for years a national selector, regularly calls by the beach to check the form. Throwing is allowed, which merely makes the lot of the batsmen more difficult. Usually there is a cordon of four or five slips, standing alongside the bare-handed wicket-keeper. And three or four in close-catching positions on the leg-side. A snick from a fast-moving windball travels at tremendous velocity, yet on Sandy Lane beach, a dropped catch is more than a sin. It can cost a turn with the ball or worse, a chance to bat. Tourists, I suppose, have

Keith Boyce of the West Indies and
Essex lets go a fast one as umpire
Harold ('Dickie') Bird looks on.

been watching this strange game for decades but strangers are rarely invited to join.

For three fascinating evenings, I watched· these superb young athletes emulating their heroes and preparing themselves for future glory. Occasionally, uninvited, I did a bit of outfielding and once, obviously to the amazement of all, held a difficult running catch at long-on. This unusual feat had its results. There was a brief 'team' meeting, then a strapping fellow, with Rastafarian hair, asked me gruffly, 'Want a hit, man?'. Of course I did! At least I thought I did until I heard one of the bowlers mutter to his mates as I faced up, 'Let's draw blood, man'.

Years before, as a teenager in Brisbane, I had faced the great Wesley Hall and made a handful of runs. But that was on a wet wicket and the great man, fearful of the approaches, had bowled gentle off-cutters. On Sandy Lane beach, the wicket was wet alright but the approaches were not. And so in the interests of a story, I had my baptism of fire.

By some strange fortune, I hung in for some time, not scoring many runs — if you weren't adept at the hook or the cut, runs were almost impossible — but hanging on, to the intense annoyance of one bowler. By the time I surrendered, thankfully, I was a mass of bruises and, yes, blood had been drawn. Time and again, the back defensive stroke brought nerve-deadening thumps to the left side and the left arm. Once, going forward, the ball caught me on the fore-head, between the eyes. Later, after my ordeal, I brought some beer back to the beach and the young Bajuns shared it, and not a few cricket stories about the great men they had seen play at Bridgetown and the wondrous dreams they had for themselves.

None were regular club players but they knew that local officials often dropped in on their unofficial games. They were hoping, each and every one, for the call that would one day put them into a club side, a chance to open the bowling, a chance to become yet another in the line of West Indian fast bowlers.

They gave me, as a souvenir, a shaven tennis ball. I took it back to the Australian camp and soon the cricketers and the journalists were playing their own inept version of windball. A few weeks later, in Antigua, we were battling away on the beach when Michael Holding strolled by. He asked for one delivery. Naturally, we were delighted — proud — to oblige. I'll swear I saw it out of the hand. But once it hit that sodden, firm sand I never saw it again, only heard the impact of shaven tennis ball on timber which rep-resented middle stump. Holding kept walking, and grinning. As he passed me, he said, 'That's the way I learned my cricket, man'.

All around the cricketing nations of the Caribbean, they play a version of windball although none is as deadly as the one played on a beach where the waves lap gently to give the bowler a hard, damp surface at which to aim. And while they play windball, the West Indies will keep on discovering demon fast bowlers. And keep on winning.

During our discussion Bill offered to pass on some advice about captaincy.

The toss

Greg Chappell

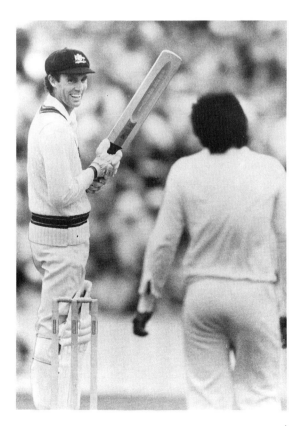

When I moved from Adelaide to Brisbane in 1973, I joined the South Brisbane District Cricket Club and was made club captain. Apart from residential qualification, which allows you to play for the club in whose district you live, or for the club either side, I chose 'Souths' because of their sound administration as well as their good facilities. Some of the club's former players included Bill Brown, Ken and Ron Archer and Wally Grout as well as a large number of Sheffield Shield players. Pride and tradition are vital ingredients for a happy and successful club.

First match of the season was a 'friendly' between past and present members of the club at which many former players were present. After the game, which the current players just won, a cocktail party was held in the club rooms. During the function I spoke to Bill Tallon, brother of the famous Queensland and Australian wicket-keeper Don Tallon. Bill was a former club captain who had represented Queensland on a few occasions. He was more renowned for his sense of humour than his outstanding cricket ability, and his stories were made funnier by the fact that Bill had quite a pronounced stutter. Having heard so many of the tales attributed to Bill, and having heard him tell a few of them on the one previous occasion we had met, I was delighted to meet up with him again.

During our discussion Bill offered to pass on some advice about captaincy. I was eager to learn as much as I could, but when Bill said 'w-w-when I-I-I w-w-was c-c-captain I-I-I n-n-never l-l-lost t-t-the t-t-toss w-w-when I-I-I c-c-called'. I was expecting to hear tales (or should it be tails?) of two-headed coins. When I enquired how he could possibly have achieved such an incredible record, he said 'w-w-when t-t-the c-c-coin w-w-went up I-I-I j-j-just c-c-called t-t-t-t-t-that's it!'

Greg Chappell in characteristic good humour at the crease.

The frail cricketing genius

Jack Pollard

The late, lamented Ray Robinson.

At best, Ray Robinson was among the finest writers on cricket from any country and was only challenged by Jack Fingleton for supremacy among Australian cricket writers. He never attempted the dramatic prose of Neville Cardus, nor the racy, self-confident, scalpel-like commentaries of Fingleton. He built his portraits of players painstakingly and it was the final mosaic that lingered in memory rather than the brilliance of his phrase-making. John Arlott called him the most under-estimated of all cricket writers; Cardus called him 'X-ray Robinson'.

He was probably the most meticulous notetaker in sportswriting. He left a house full of notebooks and stray pages reminding himself of the habits and style and eccentricities of hundreds of cricketers. He left, too, hundreds of letters from Test players in which they answered his queries about how they held the bat, why they licked only one finger before bowling, how they developed a characteristic routine in taking block. I remember driving him home not long before he died when he apologised for keeping me waiting. 'I've just confirmed with Imran Khan that Richard Hadlee was barred from bowling under the intimidatory law half-way through the Pakistan-New Zealand Test at Karachi in 1976,' said Robbie. 'It was the only time in any country umpires have invoked that law.' He was like a small child who had just discovered Santa Claus.

To the end of his life he kept querying delegates to meetings that decided some of cricket's most conten-tious issues on how they had voted. It took him 25 years to discover how the selectors decided to omit Don Tallon from Australia's 1938 tour of England. It seldom took him long to discover that an apparently trustworthy administrator had lied to him about what had happened behind closed doors. All of his discover-ies went into his notebooks, which became a vast store-house of cricket's past for use in one of the thousands of articles he wrote for magazines and newspapers around the world.

The miraculous thing was that for all his factual accuracy, he remained on friendly terms with everybody in cricket, for he had a way of taking the barbs out of his criticisms. The late Jack Fingleton was often cruel in his criticisms of Ray Robinson, claiming he could not possibly write well about cricket because he lacked experience as a Test player. Robbie refused to retaliate. 'Fingo always has something interesting to say on the game,' he would say. 'And Fingo has written some of the game's finest books.' Always fair, never overawed, Robbie kept trying to find good qualities in cricket's villains.

Raymond John Robinson was born on 8 July 1905, the eldest of three sons of a butcher who conducted his business from a shop in New Street, Brighton, Victoria. One of his brothers, Frank, also became a butcher, but Ray and his younger brother Andrew ('Drew') went to work for the Melbourne *Herald*, Ray as a copyboy, Drew as a compositor. Ray attended Brighton State School and was regarded as a model student. He played a lot of junior cricket and dabbled in golf, squash and Australian football. He originally planned to become a teacher but fell ill while he was sitting for the entrance exam and failed.

The founder of this Robinson clan migrated from Surrey in England, arriving in Fremantle on the *Palestine* in 1852 to take up a position as overseer for Sir George Shenton. Over the next two generations the family spread from Perth to Kalgoorlie to Melbourne. Ray and many of his uncles played for the Brighton Cricket Club. All the Robinsons were right-handed batsmen who liked to thump the ball hard, and were dedicated supporters of the Essendon Australian Rules football club. Another uncle, Alec Robinson, captained the Goldfields XI against MCC at Kalgoorlie in 1924-25, and a cousin, Dr George Robinson, captained Western Australia against the 1946-47 MCC team captained by Wally Hammond. Ray Robinson, the Test batsman from Newcastle in the 1936-37 series against England, was not related to Ray Robinson the writer — whose best was the First XI of the Brighton Club in 1925-26.

The Melbourne Robinsons were extremely friendly with their second cousins, the Bailey brothers, who worked for the *Sporting Globe* newspapers, and when Ray left school one of the Bailey's, E. N. ('Ernie'), got Ray a job as a copyboy on the *Herald*. Ray was given a cadetship and worked through the early 1920s as an Australian football and cricket writer. In 1925 he wrote to Pelham Warner, editor of the authoritative English magazine *The Cricketer*, saying he was horrified by the poor coverage of Australian cricket in the magazine. Warner invited him to submit his own reports on events in Australia and from 1926 until he died Robinson seldom missed an issue.

Initially, Ray had planned to be a cartoonist. Once, travelling home from work on the bus, he sketched the conductress, Ellen Jessie Gilbert, whom he learned was from Tasmania. He gave Ellen the sketches as he got off. From this a romance developed and they married in 1927. Ellen Robinson, who preferred to be known by her middle name, Jess, later worked on the *Bulletin*, writing for children under the pseudonym 'Sister Sadie'.

The Robinson's first child, Brian John, was born in 1930 on the day that Phar Lap won the Melbourne Cup. Ray was not present for the birth, he was away chasing Don Bradman for an interview, and his absence started a problem which worsened throughout the marriage. Jess believed that when children were born his place was by her side. But when their second child, Audrey Clarice, was born, Ray was in Naples en route to England with the 1934 Australian team.

Ray had worked on the Melbourne *Herald* during the bodyline series in 1932-33 and he always believed he was the sub-editor who picked up the word 'bodyline' and made it a headline when Hugh Buggy used 'cablese' to condense 'in line with the body' in a telegram to the *Herald* from Brisbane.

When a group of journalists helped start the *Star* newspaper they immediately recognised Robinson's talents by offering him the cricket writer's job. He went to England with the 1934 Australian team but had to contribute his articles through the London Press

Agency and at first was not allowed to travel with the team. His reports of the team's London matches so impressed the press agency, however, that he was commissioned to accompany the team for the later matches on the tour. He made further tours to England with Australian teams in 1948, 1953, 1956 and 1961; toured South Africa in 1957–58, the West Indies in 1954–55, and made a number of tours of India and Pakistan for the *Times of India* and *Sportsweek* in Bombay.

He moved to Sydney in 1939 at the invitation of Frank Packer and spent the war years sub-editing for the *Daily Telegraph*, Sydney. When I first met him in 1943 he was part of a brilliant sub-editors' table that included superb journalists like Richard Hughes, King Watson, Peter Gladwin, Forbes Miller, and George Illingworth. When Packer began to produce a supplement for the *Sunday Telegraph* called *Time* he chose Robinson and Jack Paton to edit it. In his spare time Robbie worked on his first book. At the end of the war he showed the manuscript to Neville Cardus, who had worked as a music critic for the *Sydney Morning Herald* through the war years. Cardus sent the manuscript of *Between Wickets* to William Collins in London, urging them to publish it.

Robinson and Paton left the Packer organisation together to edit a supplement called *Fact* for the rival *Sunday Sun*, and in 1948 Robinson went to England with Bradman's famous team despite the attitude of newspaper proprietors who regarded good sub-editors as more valuable than reporters. He had never been a full-time cricket writer until that tour, although he had ghosted people like Alan Kippax, Bill Ponsford and Bill Woodfull. A major reason for his departure from Packer's newspapers was Packer's preference for ghosted cricket reports by Test cricketers, which Robinson abhorred. He prepared for the 1948 tour by producing an amazing notebook containing minute details on all of Bradman's players, a procedure he followed on all his subsequent tours.

This tour threw him together for the first time on an overseas tour with Tom Goodman, of the *Sydney Morning Herald*. They formed a formidable duo, far superior I always thought to their English counterparts, great all-rounders, neat, polished and reliable in all they did, accurate reporters with a descriptive flair. Sadly, Goodman, who had been with the old *Evening News* in Sydney after the First World War, never persevered with book writing.

The publication in 1946 of Robinson's *Between Wickets*, followed in 1951 by *From the Boundary*, established Robinson's international reputation and alerted cricket-lovers everywhere to his exceptional gifts. But Robinson's talents made no impression on the *Sun* organisation's chief executive, Eric Kennedy, who, like Packer, rated him more valuable on the sub-editor's table and persuaded a former Adelaide lawyer, R. S. ('Dick') Whitington to give up law and become the outfit's cricket writer. There were many who believed Kennedy's judgement was at fault, for Whitington was not a trained fact-gatherer and his material was full of errors.

The competition for the cricket writing job and the desire to live up to the big reputation he had won with his books did cause Robinson to stumble, however, and for a time he became slow almost to the point of tedium in producing his copy. He spent far too long working out telling phrases for sub-editors thirsting for copy back at head office. I remember one day when he scratched around for a special effect and finally at the end of the day confided that he had got it: 'Yardley's perfume of batsmanship.' In this period he missed deadlines and was not wanted by afternoon tabloids, a fate he shared with the great English writer R. C. Robertson-Glasgow, whose copy was mercilessly cut by over-zealous Australian sub-editors.

Robinson was saved by the overseas newspapers who were eager to receive his copy. His syndication department always knew they could recoup most of the cost of sending him on tour with the fees he attracted from journals throughout the cricket world. His children did not see much of him because of his touring and Jessie Robinson's ire over his absences increased even after he bought a block of land at Northbridge in Sydney in 1948 and built a house there. His daughter Audrey became a cadet journalist on the *Sydney Sun* after attending the exclusive Wenona School on Sydney's North Shore. His son Brian went to North Sydney Boys' High School, where he was an outstanding student before graduating in science from Sydney University and taking a Ph.D. at Cambridge.

In 1966, Robinson's Sydney doctors sent him to the Retina Clinic at Boston, Massachusetts, for operations for detached retinas on both his eyes. The New South Wales Cricket Association passed an emergency loan of several thousand dollars to allow him to make the trip which it was believed would fully restore his sight. The operation on the left eye was successfully concluded but before doctors could operate on the right eye Robinson developed a severe gastric complaint. He was moved to the nearby Massachusetts General Hospital and there it was found that he had an hereditary stomach complaint. He was required to pay at least $3000 for blood transfusions needed during the stomach operation. He could not afford that amount, but Australian journalists stationed in New York were organised by *Sydney Morning Herald* chief Allan Dobbyn to go to Boston and donate the 15 pints of blood required.

The vomiting associated with his gastric complaint detached the retina of the right eye completely, and no further attempt was made to repair it. Back in Australia his son, Dr Brian Robinson, had to read the final proofs of his father's book, *The Wit of R. G. Menzies*; this book was commissioned and published in 1966 by the editor of the *NatWest Boundary Book*. It topped the Australian best-seller lists, staying there for 28 weeks. He had just finished the task when he learned that his father was returning home, doomed to a future of failing sight and a worsening stomach disorder. Robinson retired as a full-time journalist in 1970. He began another book, *The Wildest Tests*, delving into his notebooks for accounts of the dramatic events of cricket in the upheaval of the postwar world.

He was then awarded a Commonwealth Literary Fund fellowship and a grant from the Literature Board of the Council for the Arts. Ray threw himself into the task of creating a new book on Australia's cricket captains. He knew his time was short and that there was not time now for studied phrase-turning and he developed a facility that made his writing flow in a manner which some of his previous work had lacked. His wife Jess died in 1973, aged 73, feeling to the end that cricket had cheated her. Two years later Robinson's finest book, *On Top Down Under*, appeared — a marvellous piece of fact-gathering with the pace of a first-rate novel. It won the English Cricket Society's Literary Award for 1976. He flew to London to accept the award and was photographed chatting with his friends E. W. Swanton, John Arlott and the other leading English cricket writers.

Then he returned to live alone in his house at Northbridge overlooking Cammeray Bay, occasionally enjoying visits from his grandson Anthony. Every day Ray worked on articles for cricket magazines and on revisions to his books. Bill Frindall, the English cricket statistician, stayed with him for a summer, and old friends like Bill O'Reilly, Bill Hunt and Keith Miller called to see him, but mostly he was alone, refusing his son's suggestion that he move to a nursing home or somewhere where people could take care of him; he wanted to be near his notebooks and files in a place where he could find them despite near blindness caused by a cataract on his one good eye. In the cricket season he travelled to grounds on public transport with his customary large file of notes, as enthusiastic as a junior reporter at his first big match as he hauled his frail, wizened, grey-haired frame up the pavilion steps. With little sight left, he peered out at the players on the field through binoculars, pecking out his pieces with fingers that had lost all strength.

Most Fridays I took him shopping, stocking up on tins of baby food, eggs and blackcurrant juice, which was all his stomach would hold. I was working on a 1200-page cricket book at the time and he told me to come armed with queries. He was a man who never had any rivals and shared his remarkable knowledge of cricket eagerly and honestly. You asked him about Bill O'Reilly and he would tell you of how O'Reilly fooled great players so badly with his remarkable flight and spin that they often looked about the field trying to find out where they had been caught. Talk to him about Jeff Thomson and he would say, 'The most alarming bowler we have had'.

Bodyline remained a vivid memory. 'It was very disturbing to me because fellows who were friends of mine were subjected to great peril,' he said. 'Nobody was killed but there were some nasty injuries. One time Bill Ponsford had 10 bruises behind the shoulder. Ponsford and Woodfull took some terrible blows.' He loved to talk about Jack Ellis, the Victorian wicket-keeper in the 1920s. 'The Victorian batting was so strong, with Woodfull and Ponsford opening, that if they won the toss and batted, Ellis used to go and inspect various contracting jobs he and his men were working on around Melbourne.'

Then there was the time Robbie was in the West Indies when a pace bowler named Hilton was sentenced to death for the murder of his wife. A West Indian fieldsman, John Holt, dropped three catches off Australian opener Colin McDonald. Within minutes a macabre banner was erected: 'Hang Holt, save Hilton.'

He wrote five cricket books: *Between Wickets*, *From the Boundary*, *Green Sprigs* (published in England as *The Glad Season*), *The Wildest Tests* and *On Top Down Under*. There are wonderful lines for every cricket lover in all of them. Jimmy Burke enjoyed his reference to Jeff Thomson's bouncers: 'In a couple of overs Thomson can turn a thigh pad into Vienna Schnitzel'. Bill Hunt liked: 'Watching Bill Lawry, as you have ample time to do, you sense that he loves batting. If he is not actually wedded to his art everyone can see he is going steady.' John Arlott liked: 'Kippax modelled his stance at the wicket on Trumper's. Cover the heads on photographs of each awaiting the bowler and there are

few clues to tell one from the other. The similarity extends even to the shirtsleeves folded halfway up the forearm.' My favourite was his account of how, after the Second World War had shortened his career, Sid Barnes eliminated all risky shots from his exciting repertoire. 'Often,' wrote Robbie, 'Barnes seems to get bricked up inside his own run factory.'

Ray Robinson was inordinately proud of his son's success as a senior scientist for the CSIRO, involved in the excitement of space age astronomy at the radio telescope at Parkes. He was proud, too, of his granddaughter Anne, an outstanding schoolgirl athlete. Taking a look at the honours on her blazer, he said, 'It looks like the credits for a TV epic'.

Towards the end of June 1982 his son and daughter-in-law, Jill, convinced Ray to spend a while in a private hospital. On the night before he was due to be admitted Ray fell, broke two ribs and punctured a lung. He was rushed to hospital, where doctors found that he was also suffering from an intestinal blockage.

For two weeks he seemed to rally under treatment, read the one Dickens novel he had never read, and chatted animatedly with many cricketing friends, drawing on his unlimited store of cricket stories. But the stomach problems could not be solved and doctors put him on morphia to dull the pain of his final day. There was a great sense of sadness that Ray Robbie, who had endured so much, had finally, 'laid aside his pencil'.

When his son went back to Ray's house, he found a half-finished obituary about his mate 'Slasher' Mackay in Ray's typewriter. It was full of the old Robinson magic. 'Not once in an innings of 203 did Mackay justify his nickname; the drone of the bagpipes was still in the background of strokes that rang out with trumpet-like clarity,' he wrote.

Robbie may have endured marital problems, chronic stomach problems, virtual blindness, and a little loneliness, but he never relented in his devotion to his art — cricket writing. I believe his life was a triumph.

Over the rainbow

Sir Brian Rix

Sir Brian Rix.

I've actually seen the Lord's Taverners in action in Australia — and very impressive they were too! It was Old Australia versus a load of other old cricketers and they all looked good enough to walk straight back into Allan Border's team. Good enough, that is, until you saw them in the dressing room afterwards. Pink faces and moans of pain made it clear that old cricketers are like old actors — great at keeping going in front of the audience, but badly in need of a large gin when the curtain comes down. But bless 'em, they'd all helped to raise a sizeable sum for a charity and that's what the Taverners are all about.

I used to play once with the old, great and the good; when I was an actor. And they are all lovely — particularly to someone like me, who fancied himself as a bit of a goer and was fed a succession of long-hops by such heroes as Jim Laker or Alec Bedser. No, come to think of it, Alec never could bowl a long-hop — but he'd give you one off the mark, anyway. On the other hand, Eric was kinder — just as kind as Jim, in fact. And I've got 75 at the Oval and 54 at Lord's to prove it!

Furthermore, I reckon those two scores made up two of the happiest days of my life. Daft, isn't it? But that is the secret of the Lord's Taverners. They give the crowd just about the right mixture of reasonable cricket, famous faces and fast and furious fun. And the actors love mixing with the cricketers and vice versa.

After that Lord's match, I was asked into the holy of holies — the Committee Room — to have a drink to celebrate. I explained I had my 16-year-old-daughter with me and, to my surprise and delight, she too was asked in. 'You know, my dear,' said one red-faced old committeeman as my daughter entered, 'you ought to feel very proud. The only women who usually get in here are the Queen and the cleaners'.

And that says it all. The highest of cricketers and the lowest of actors can mix successfully in the Lord's Taverners. Long may the old flourish in the land of Oz. They need that crock of gold over the rainbow. There are so many children in need of support. You're giving yours by buying this book.

Lightfoot, cricket and pen

Garry Lightfoot, the highly talented illustrator of the *Sydney Morning Herald* and other Fairfax publications is 36 years old, married with nine-year-old twins, Mark and Joanna. He played grade cricket in both Perth and Sydney where, he claims, 'I couldn't bat to save my life!'.

Garry has drawn just about every major sportsman one can think of and has collaborated with soccer players, a world-champion surfer and Dennis Lillee on illustrated sport publications. He recently completed a fine illustration of Australia's best-ever cricket team.

He owns about 300 cricket books. His favourite authors? Ray Robinson, John Arlott, Frank Keating and David Frith — all of whom are represented in this book.

Garry Lightfoot.

190

BORDER

GRAEME WOOD

191

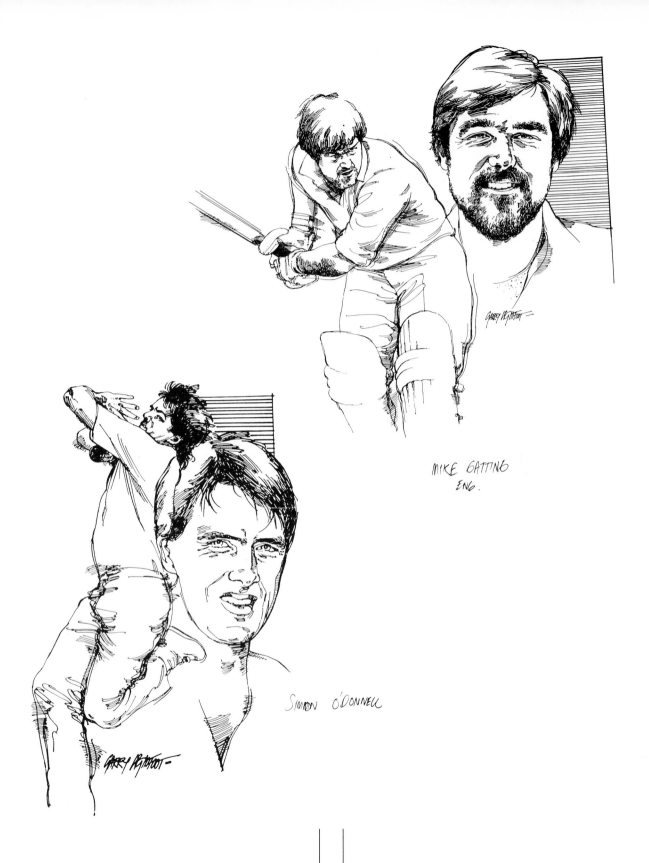

MIKE GATTING
ENG.

SIMON O'DONNELL

R. HADLEE
NZ.

IAN BOTHAM
ENG

A message to the Lord's Taverners Australia from Honorary Taverner, His Serene Highness, Prince Rainier of Monaco, especially for the *NatWest Boundary Book*

His Serene Highness Prince Rainier of Monaco.

Palais de Monaco

       Cricket is essentially a British game, but it has amazingly spread over the last two hundred years to many countries and now finally reaches our shores.

       Naturally, quite an effort is required in order to become familiar with Cricket, and even as one «learns» it, it remains somewhat difficult for us to fully understand the spirit behind this typically British game!

       Cricket is slowly but surely, I hope, making a home for itself in the Principality of Monaco, and I look forward for it to be played here in the true British style during the summer season if, however, we can still find space for the lawn! -- that will be the main problem!

With all best wishes,

RAINIER, Prince de Monaco

The toast is the Taverners

John Darling, Chairman, The Lord's Taverners, Australia

John Darling.

It is almost six years since the Lord's Taverners Australia was incorporated in August 1982. We had received the permission of our sister organisation in the United Kingdom to use the name and begin as an independent body but with similar objectives.

Our only tangible common link is His Royal Highness, Prince Philip, Twelfth Man to both organisations. He carries the drinks here in Australia, too!

Most people interested in cricket know that we are now firmly established in six States and the ACT, with more than 1500 members throughout the country. Each branch is now getting about its business of supporting and developing young people in disadvantaged economic circumstances through cricket.

The funds we raise all go back into the game. Raised in various ways, they are invested in many projects and in the process a lot of Taverners have shared enjoyment and seen value for their efforts. It is, however, of the future of which I write.

Organisationally, we have yet to develop the Northern Territory as a branch. Thereafter the task will be to develop, as simply as possible, a number of regional sub-branches in each State. As it was necessary to have a national body with branches in the States and Territories to encompass the problems of the geography of our large continent, so too, is it necessary to decentralise still further to cope with these same geographic problems of vast distances within the States.

The main benefits of such a Taverner's organisation are twofold. Firstly: the ability to keep both the cost of administration and travel to an absolute minimum, thus ensuring the greatest possible percentage of all funds raised being ploughed back into the objectives and projects.

Secondly: it will create greater opportunity for personal contact between Taverners in the smaller towns and between Taverners and the schools and youth that are remote from opportunity. From now on a lot of the work of the national body and the State branches will be to this end.

Our major thrust, however, in all State branches is

The popular Lord's Taverners' corner in Sydney's celebrated Regent Hotel. The cases contain interesting memorabilia of The Lord's Taverners' beginnings — including a copy of the first Boundary Book.

to help develop youth cricket: bringing boys from remote areas for coaching in the cities, the provision of junior equipment to schools in country areas; in certain suburbs in bigger cities, the introduction of cricket to young men in a prison farm with results that have surprised the authorities; the sponsoring of State junior carnivals, and so on.

Perhaps one of the most significant decisions that the national council made in 1986 was to select in each State annually a 'Junior Taverner of the Year'. This is to be a lad between the ages of 14 and 18 who will be recognised by the award of a Lord's Taverners cap and plaque. The choice will not be made just on cricket ability but on character, the embryonic qualities of leadership, sportsmanship, and behaviour both on and off the field.

Apart from the fact that we all wish to see young boys growing up and emerging into State sides and the Australian Eleven, it will be one of the ultimate tests of our efforts, indeed success, if a junior Taverner achieves the same distinctions. We would hope, by his example, that he will influence others of his age to conduct themselves well, both in Australia and in overseas countries, and to set a standard of behaviour that succeeding sportsmen can build on and so gain public respect.

The number one honorary member of the Lord's Taverners Australia is Sir Donald Bradman. He exemplifies all these qualities and has inspired many, many young people of his day by his outstanding conduct.

I do not see these aspirations as some idealistic reason for our existence; we are a body of people who care about the way things are done, not just what is done. The fact is that we can all have an influence in helping youth find some of the real values of life: values that have largely been discarded in the rush for monetary gain and materialism.

John Varley, chief executive and secretary of The Lord's Taverners Australia.

In cricket terms some examples would be: the value of putting the team first and oneself last; the grace of taking what might appear to be an unfair decision and not showing it; the value of that important quality, honesty. How much do we admire the man who owns up, saying it was *not* out? Or the batsman who walks? We occasionally see rare instances of this sportsmanship and when we do it restores our faith in human nature. These examples set the standard for all to follow and allows the umpire to develop a trust. The opposite of course is equally true. Constant appealing, very much in evidence today, can only have one motive: to get decisions that are often not correct. I and many others deprecate the use of 'sledging', a word that should be eliminated from the game. Moreover, the target should be the stumps and not the man.

Lest anyone think that we have shallow objectives, I hope that I have shown that our ideals and desires are correct and loftier in the long term. Given the enthusiasm of members, so evident in this early period, I know we can go on and be a really effective organisation to help many young people, who otherwise would be throwing stones rather than cricket balls, were we not to provide an alternative.

We do, however, need help to finance our whole organisation. We need the sponsorship of committed corporations and individuals to support the State branches and the national organisation. To date we have existed with the backing of a founding sponsorship and above all, the 1500 members throughout Australia who have put the backbone into the organisation.

The Lord's Taverners Australia are set fair to do a fine and lasting job for the youth of this country. And that, precisely, is what they are going to do.

My mate Marsh

Dennis Lillee

GARRY LIGHTFOOT—

He stands only 5ft. 8½ ins., but his stockiness gives his body an indestructible look. He may only come up to your shoulders, but you'd think twice about insulting him because there's something about the thickness of his physique which suggests you might be a lot better off being his friend.

He plays tennis and golf right-handed, but bats left-handed. He learned the piano as a kid and still sings because he refuses to be musically ignorant. As his country's 'keeper, I've lost count of the time he has hovered mid-air, body outstretched, fingertips clutching the ball.

There has only ever been one Rodney William Marsh.

You have heard a lot of stories about Rod Marsh and what he has meant to me, as a mate and my associate in what has been described as one of the most successful fast bowler wicket-keeper partnerships in cricket history. Let me tell you another . . .

The scene was certainly depressing enough. I was sitting in a corner of the dressing room at Launceston, Tasmania, when I should have been out there playing for W.A. Like Dame Nellie, I had attempted another comeback, or should I say attempted again to overcome a withered right leg and a knee joint which kept filling with bone fragments and fluid.

I had bowled well during the first spell, taking a couple of wickets, then tried to come back for a second and couldn't. I managed to finish the over and when I limped dejectedly from the ground, I must have looked like a broken-down gunfighter no longer game to walk the streets.

Rod was the first to come up to me after the day's play.

'How is it?', he asked.

'Not too bloody good', I said.

I suppose I could have used a bit of sympathy, particularly from my old mate Bacchus. But no, he took the other tack.

'Well, I suppose that's it. You can't make it back now. I reckon you ought to give it away', he said.

I couldn't believe my ears. We'd had our verbal gymnastics before, but they only really ever masked our mutual affection. Now here he was laying down the 'retirement' law as though he knew all about it. There wasn't a hint of kindness or understanding on his face. He just shook his head and said: 'No way. Forget it, pal.'

It worked, of course. I have always thought of Rod as a very shrewd man. I'll show the bastard, I thought to myself. In the cool of the evening later, I knew exactly what Rod was trying to do. In a way, realising just that made me even more determined not to let him down. Not to let Australia down. And not to give up and let myself down. There was no way I was going to sky the towel and limp into retirement. Not after Rod's subtle psychology. He'd have never forgiven me.

In many ways, Rod Marsh is a much-maligned character. Just about any cricket journalist in the land will tell you he is not the most polite man on earth. He is, if anything, inclined to call a spade a f------ shovel rather than merely a spade. There are no half-measures about him, but make a friend of Bacchus and you have a great, lifelong mate. I'm biased because our mateship goes back a long, long way.

I first laid eyes on him when I was about 17, which would have made him about 19. He was playing for University and I for Perth Cricket Club in a grade match at the University ground.

Now Rod, until late in his career, was never what you could call dapper. Certainly he looks the part these days in a suit and tie, but even on the cricket field, while his whites are white and his keeping something to behold, he can still manage to look a touch untidy at times.

Well, when he was a youngster he looked bloody dreadful. He had one shirt sleeve rolled up, the other down. In fact, the shirt was his big problem. He could never really find a way of keeping it tucked into his trousers. On reflection, the stomach overhang was the root of the shirt dilemma. He also looked as if he had been dieting on cream pudding and dumplings for most of his younger life. A more corpulent human dome I'd never seen on a cricket field. I was, however, about to learn that extra weight didn't count for one ounce with Rod Marsh.

He opened the batting in those days, and when I ran in to bowl the first ball, I couldn't help but wonder how a bloke so slovenly could get a game of cricket in a top grade side. Then again, it was University, so he must have some talent. They let beatniks in, so why not this fella?

I made a classic mistake that day. Keep in mind I was young and raw, concentrating only on bowling fast. The words 'line and length' had been mentioned to me but, hell, speed was my go. Well, that slob Marsh started to carve me up. He despatched my shorter, faster balls to all points of the boundary. I kept thinking to myself that surely a bloke who looked as bad as he did couldn't keep playing shots like that. But he did. I wished I'd never laid eyes on Rodney Marsh, whoever he was.

I didn't see much more of him either until we both found ourselves in the W.A. team. He made it first and when I followed, you could hardly have called us close mates. In fact, my very first close-up impression of Rod was that he was a little above it all. I was certainly in awe as I ventured into the first-class scene. There I was all of a sudden unpacking my bags with guys I had idolised. But Rod was a particular sort of animal.

In those days if you didn't do what he did, then you didn't fit into his group. You see, Rod drank a bit. I didn't. Rod played golf. I still don't. Rod was one of the boys. I was a novice trying to take it all in. In short, I didn't seem to fit in.

I suppose it should also be pointed out that our backgrounds were quite different. Rod was a university graduate. I left at high school stage and became a bank johnnie. It could hardly be expected that we were going to be bosom buddies right away.

Rod was also a schoolteacher and schoolteachers were not my favourite people. I never had a great respect for most teachers. I always thought they were

Here they are: Rodney Marsh (left) receives exuberant congratulations from his mate Dennis Lillee.

fine in theory, but not so good in practice. I had that theory for a long time and, over the years, I really haven't seen any concrete evidence to change my mind — though I'm sure John Inverarity, an assistant headmaster in Adelaide these days (and a close buddy) would like to argue that point with me, as would another pal, Tony Mann.

I think Rod and I always respected each other's ability. Certainly, I respected his. The bloke just didn't let anything by him and he took 99 catches out of a hundred, which hardly gives you room for complaint.

I suppose the first bonds of friendship were forged when we began touring overseas together with Australian teams. We obviously got to know what made each other tick. The friendship blossomed. We roomed together, we joked together, we fought together and we were always more than just partners on the cricket field. Well, almost always.

While Rod has been a permanent fixture in the Australian and W.A. teams, he has been a real nomad in terms of his commitments to grade cricket. He had played with no fewer than seven grade clubs in Perth, which must be some sort of a record. One of them was the Perth Cricket Club, where he played under my captaincy.

I wasn't bowling at all at the time. I was directing traffic from mid-on or mid-off and trying to improve my batting while nursing myself to recovery from a serious back injury. The fact that I wasn't able to bowl really didn't curb my natural instinct to win. It was always a serious business as far as I was concerned.

On this particular day, a batsman played a ball out into the covers and I had to run around the field. There was absolutely no chance of a run-out but to set the right example to the lads I sprinted around, gathered in the ball and fired into Bacchus a return that would have winded the sphinx.

While it all looked very nice, as the ball thudded into Rod's gloves, it didn't impress him one bit. He threw off his gloves and slung the ball back at maximum velocity. The only problem was that rather than cut me in half, as he had obviously intended, the ball flew about 10 feet over my head to the boundary. The words exchanged could never be printed. To this day, I haven't asked Rod why he threw that ball.

While Bacchus, like all of us, had his moment of controversy, I cannot think of anyone who better typified the fighting spirit on a cricket field, whether it be a grade match, a Sheffield Shield game, or wearing his favourite green-and-gold. And I'm certain few people are aware of the pain he suffered and the sacrifices the man made just to play cricket.

In later years, he would limp into the rooms after each session in a day behind the stumps and pack his arthritic knee in ice. It had really troubled him for years, but he never complained. He would even pride himself on being able to sprint over 40 or 50 metres against the young blades and hold his own.

His hands took a terrible pounding, too, never more so than in the 1974–75 season against Mike Denness and his Poms when Jeff Thomson was at his glove-thudding best. Again, no complaints. Nothing — certainly nothing so mundane as injury or pain was going to interfere with his involvement with Test cricket.

Much — and all of it detrimental — was written and said about Rod's debut for Australia, in the first Test of the 1970–71 series against England. No-one (least of all Bacchus himself) was impressed. One respected English scribe, John Woodcock, wrote with all the authority in the world that Rod must be replaced after just that one Test. I wonder what Mr Woodcock thinks of his own judgement now.

It was from that inauspicious debut that Bacchus earned the famous nickname 'Irongloves'. And for it we are indebted to, of all people, Ian Chappell, his team-mate who was to become his skipper. It was all in fun, of course, but it stuck. And in those early days of Rod's international career, it hurt.

The wit of Doug Walters was to make mileage of it years later, when Rod broke Alan Knott's world record for wickets taken by a Test keeper. Walters was heard to remark that 'Rod would have broken it a long time ago if he'd accepted all those chances in his first Test'.

What a tragedy it would have been for Australian cricket had the selectors heeded the howls for Rod's sacking after that rather unfortunate debut, although I'm sure he'd have quickly fought his way back into the Test team and made the critics eat their misguided words. I'm sure, too, that the 'Irongloves' tag made him all the more determined to prove the rubbishers wrong. And did he do that!

Rod's decision to join World Series Cricket allowed Steve Rixon, John Maclean and Kevin Wright the opportunity to play for the A.C.B.'s Australia. But let's face it, the real action was with W.S.C. I can tell you it was a bloody sight tougher than what they were facing.

When the wounds and egos healed and Kerry Packer and the A.C.B. got together, there were many critics who thought that Rod should have to prove himself all over again to dislodge Wright. What a load of rubbish! Behind the stumps, Marsh was on a planet all of his own. He was the incomparable.

I think it's fair to say that Rod's batting fell away a little towards the end of his career and I'm sure that the constant bombardment by the West Indies pace brigade had something to do with that.

When you think back, the Australians who joined World Series Cricket and then stayed on the scene after the Packer-A.C.B. compromise have had little respite from the Windies speed blitz. We had two years of W.S.C. and when Clive Lloyd and his speed squad weren't out here, we were facing them on their home turf. Since the compromise, they've been back here three times. A few of their quicks have come and gone, but their standards haven't dropped at all. Neither has the pace. Better batsmen than Rod Marsh have wilted under such relentless pressure.

Despite Rod's relatively poor form with the bat by the earlier standards he set, he was — until Wayne Phillips joined him in 1984 — the only Australian wicketkeeper to hit a Test century. He made the first of three Test hundreds against Pakistan, another

against New Zealand and who will ever forget his 110 not out in the Centenary Test in Melbourne in 1977?

Poor old Bacchus has also been criticised for the lack of stumpings to his credit during his long career. I have always thought this criticism most unfair. Some people try to tell you that he lacked the skills to stand up to the slow bowlers. The truth is that he lacked the opportunity.

It used to be unheard of to go into a Test match with four fast bowlers. Today, if it's not four, it's three and this emphasis on pace certainly limited his opportunities to show how well he could keep to spin. Alan Knott was probably a better keeper to spin bowling. And why not — he had so much more of it to handle. 'Deadly' Derek Underwood's 290-odd Test wickets provided more than enough opportunities.

But give me pace — and that's what my story is all about — and I'll have Bacchus any day of the week, thank you.

Certainly, he will take some replacing, not only on the field, but in the dressing-room and away from the cricket arena altogether. It is really quite difficult to put into words exactly how I feel about the man and his effect on the Australian team. I know the dressing-room will be a poorer place without his wit and comradeship. I won't be there either. Neither will Greg Chappell. But while I can see things surviving without Greg and me in the rooms it's hard to imagine them without Rod.

He was one who always had a word when it was needed, as well as an ear. A sort of modern-day Father Confessor, if you like, and it is this aspect of the man that many people in the game are going to miss.

Bacchus was an aggressive competitor and he always tried to instil this into team-mates. He was always straightforward, which didn't leave anybody who was listening to him in any doubt about what he was saying. But while Rod Marsh always had a way with words, I prefer to think of him as a man whose actions always spoke a great deal louder.

I repeat, there will never be another Rod Marsh. Mate, thanks for the memories.

'A truth that will remain is that Perth has given to cricket a fast bowler of hawk-like countenance and perfect physique for his purpose . . .'

Dennis Lillee

David Frith

'It's true, then, Fred—they <u>have</u> got a demon bowler . . .'

There have been faster bowlers than Dennis Lillee, but not many. There have been more hostile fast bowlers, but not many. Spofforth, Ernie Jones, Constantine, Heine, Charlie Griffith, Andy Roberts, Jeff Thomson — all have brought menace, even terror to the bowling crease. Lillee concedes nothing to any of them.

He is one of the great fast bowlers of the 20th century, possessing a full set of gear changes, a knowledge of aerodynamics equal to Lindwall's, an abundance of stamina and determination, and more courage than is given to most.

He needed that courage in 1973 and '74 when he set about achieving one of sport's most impressive comebacks. The four stress fractures in the lower vertebrae would have finished many a career. Lillee, having dramatically bowled his way to fame, was faced with six weeks in plaster and a long and gruelling fight to full fitness. He withstood the punishment and handsomely repaid those who had worked with him and believed in him. He played cricket again, though only as a batsman. Then he put himself on to bowl. No twinges. At the end of the 1973–74 season his hopes were at least as high as the highest of his notorious bouncers.

England arrived next season to defend the Ashes in six Test matches. Lillee pronounced himself fit and dismissed Ian Chappell two or three times in early-season interstate fixtures. Australia selected him again. And in the first Test a new extermination firm was formed: Lillee and Thomson. England's batsmen at Brisbane would just as happily have taken their chances in the company of Leopold and Loeb, or Browne and Kennedy, or, at the end of the day, Burke and Hare. It was devastating, still fresh in memory.

Australia's opening pair took 58 wickets in the series out of 108 that fell to bowlers — this despite Thomson's withdrawal through injury halfway through the fifth Test and Lillee's after six overs in the final match with a damaged foot.

The full force of this controlled cyclone was felt in the 1975 series, though England's sleeping pitches absorbed some of the energy. This was when Lillee's other bowling skills asserted themselves. As in the 1972 series, when he took a record 31 Test wickets, Lillee beat batsmen by change of pace and with his wicked away-swinger. Rod Marsh and the ever-expectant slips cordon did the rest. He had more support now: from the tireless Walker, from Gilmour (who would have strolled into any other Test team in the world) and from Thomson whenever he had his rhythm.

Interrupted only by pleurisy, he went on to torment and punish the West Indians, taking his hundredth Test wicket in the process. Still that remade and wonderfully broad back held up against the pounding constantly dealt it by its owner.

Dennis Lillee's inspiration, when only a boy, came from a West Indian: Wes Hall, the genial fast-bowling giant. The young fellow from Perth, born on

W. G. Grace's 101st birthday (18 July, 1949), clambered with all the fervour of a Beatles fan into the members' enclosure at the WACA ground just to be near his idol. There was also Graham McKenzie, the pride of Perth, to fan the flames of his ambition. And Fred Trueman. And Alan Davidson.

Not that this was enough. There had to be an inherent talent. The tearaway with long sideburns, who stormed in over a long distance and hurled his wiry body into delivery with every ounce of his might, eventually played for Western Australia. By 1970–71 he was considered good enough to play for Australia — one of the hopes in a reshaping of the national eleven. He took 5 for 84 against England at Adelaide in his maiden Test, opening the attack with another young aspirant, Thomson — Alan ('Froggy'), not Jeff.

A season in Lancashire League cricket with Haslingden followed. Next he bowled against a con-

A sequence showing Dennis Lillee's delivery stride and the moment after the ball has been sent on its way.

glomerate team billed as the Rest of the World. In Perth he decimated them with 8 for 29, including 6 for 0 in one red-hot spell (when he wasn't feeling too well). Gavaskar, Engineer, Clive Lloyd, Greig and Sobers were among the victims. The wider world at last took notice and wanted to know all about him.

He was learning all the time, especially when trying to bowl to Sobers during his indescribably brilliant 254 at Melbourne, when straight-drives came bouncing back from the boundary before the bowler had raised himself upright in the followthrough. Yet he continued to harass the tourists, not by any means now trying to bowl every ball at top speed, and if England in the spring of 1972 thought Australian claims of Lillee's bounce and penetration were exaggerated, the threat was soon a vivid reality.

He has sometimes attacked batsmen with his tongue — and been denounced for it. Brian Statham used to let the ball do all his talking. Fred Trueman's ripe language was somehow not the antithesis of geniality. Dennis Lillee's 'verbal aggression' has been something else in its spirit of near-hatred. One could name others in cricket history who have gone about their business in this way, only to be left with the feeling that in each case the bowler has failed in one respect to do himself justice. Lillee was a central figure in Australia's re-emergence as a formidable side, and a great deal has continued to be expected of him. The chanting of the crowds, the persistent publicity, the inescapable type-casting, the need to transpose celebrity into a real-world security — all this must take a man away from himself, at least in part.

A truth that will remain is that Perth has given to cricket a fast bowler of hawk-like countenance and perfect physique for his purpose, whose flowing approach and superb athletic action have been a thrilling spectacle for young and old, male and female, pacifist and warrior.

'Harold Larwood lives in Sydney. I must have his name in the book. How do I contact him?'

One for the book!

Leslie Crowther

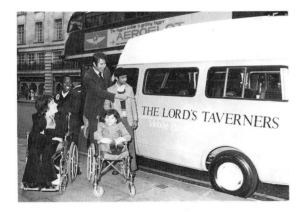

Leslie Crowther, with some youthful beneficiaries, presents another Lord's Taverners' coach to physically handicapped and under-privileged children in London.

Autograph hunters have to exercise a great deal of tact, tenacity, patience and diplomacy. I know — I'm one myself. Christopher Martin-Jenkins's *Complete Who's Who of Test Cricketers* has provided me, and hundreds like me, with the perfect reason for collecting the autographs of former and current Test players, written across their potted biographies in the book.

But you do need to use *tact* — never ask the Test player for his autograph in the company of his county team mates who have never made the Test arena.

Tenacity — always carry the book with you, as you never know when you're going to bump into one of the players you haven't 'got'. I caught up with Jackie McGlew at a boxing night! *Patience* — you may have to wait for what seems like hours outside the players' entrance. And *diplomacy* — never charge up to your victim as he stalks off the field having made a 'blob'; you'll either be told to go away (or words to that effect) or what you get will be sweaty, smeared and illegible.

Shall I tell you about my greatest coup? Yes. My Jean and I were in Australia on business at the start of 1987 and, following the triumphal progress of England from ground to ground, I naturally carried the book with me all the time. In Sydney, I said to Jean, 'Harold Larwood lives in Sydney. I must have his name in the book. How do I contact him?'

'Ring him up,' she said.

'I don't know his number,' I muttered. At which Jean, with that clarity of thought for which she is renowned, said 'Look in the telephone directory'.

I did, and sure enough Larwood, H. was featured, along with his number and address. With a fast beating heart, I rang him. Eventually a voice at the other end of the line said 'Yes?'

'May I speak to Harold Larwood please?' I said.

'Harold Larwood speaking,' said the voice of the great man. I nearly passed out with excitement. Well, I managed to persuade him that I wasn't a newspaper reporter or a nutter, that I *was* a genuine autograph hunter *and* a fellow Nottinghamian, and that I would like to meet him.

'I'm in all day,' he said. 'From now on it's up to you.'

When I arrived at his house, he was waiting for me on the doorstep. He ushered me in, signed the book with great care — he is nearly blind; I had to point his hand to the appropriate page in the book. He then took me round all his trophies and memorabilia. By far the best was a sterling silver ashtray — Harold Larwood smokes like a chimney — on which were engraved the words: 'To Harold, for the Ashes, with Thanks from your grateful skipper D. R. Jardine.'

When he was *totally* convinced that I wasn't dangerous, he introduced his wife Lois. She had been hiding in the kitchen and emerged shyly to the enquiry of 'Shall you come out here a moment, Lois luv?'.

Eventually I left them, but before leaving I recited the following poem. The original, handwritten by Thomas Moult, hangs in the pavilion at Trent Bridge, marking the centenary of cricket on that lovely ground.

Top: The incomparable (and controversial) Harold Larwood at his Kingsford, Sydney, home. Bottom: Harold Larwood with some of the Aussie team during a Trent Bridge match, July 1968.

Trent Bridge — a hundred years old

Trent Bridge Centenary, 28 May 1938. Specially composed and published for this historic occasion by Mr Thomas Moult.

So small a space, so lost this slip of earth
When we spread out the map that spans the shire;
Only an oasis in a city's dearth,
A spark still left in long extinguished fire;
But men have gathered here and given their praise
To many a battle, many a Notts-shire team,
Stored up great sunlit deeds; then, going their ways,
Have seen Trent Bridge for evermore in dream.

They helped to build a Game, those cricketers,
The Gunns and Shrewsbury, Daft and Flowers,
Batting and bowling down the golden hours
On this old hallowed turf. Surely today
Their ghosts come back where once they loved to play! . . .
No cricket ground hath nobler visitors.

As I left, I fancied that Harold Larwood's near sightless eyes were misted up. I know mine were.

That bodyline bloke

Douglas Robert Jardine (1900–1958), a Winchester and Oxford man, was born in Bombay, the son of M. R. Jardine, who made 140 in the University match of 1892. Tall and angular, Douglas was invariably the wearer of a Harlequin cap and a back player of the highest class. Captain of England, he devised and directed the controversial bodyline tactics during the England tour of Australia in 1932–33, tactics which nearly alienated a continent. Steadfast in crisis and a remarkable player of fast bowling, he was always upright and correct in his demeanour. He first played for Surrey during the Oxford season in 1921 and continued to do so until 1933, captaining Surrey in the last two years. He is seen here during his Surrey innings of 74 not out against Yorkshire, pulling a ball to leg on 23 August 1923 at the Kennington Oval.

_p: The 'leg-trap' as used by Harold Larwood in the 1933 fifth Test
Sydney. The five fieldsmen are Allan, Ames, Sutcliffe, Jardine and
yland as Oldfield plays Larwood to leg._

_Bottom: England's 'leg-trap' field of the controversial bodyline Tests in
Australia. Larwood is bowling to Stan McCabe. The other batsman is
Don (now Sir Donald) Bradman._

'. . . Ironmonger pulled a dirty piece of rag from his side pocket and waved it vigorously for all to see . . .'

A sidelight on the bodyline bit

Bill O'Reilly

It is hard to recall even one pleasant feature of that horrifying Adelaide Test in January 1933 which went down in cricket history as *the* bodyline blow-up, but I have done so.

Bertie Ironmonger, then in his 51st year, lined up in the Australian Test attack to deal out his highly-accurate, orthodox, left-handed spinners on a pitch which then, as now, was notoriously unsympathetic to his type of bowling.

'Dainty', as he was known by every first-class Australian cricketer (and a few privileged English ones, too!) was a 'nuggety' six-footer weighing 15 stone — and a man of few words. Two of his spinning fingers had pieces missing from them, the consequence of a fracas he had with a circular saw in his younger days in Queensland, the place of his birth, before he became employed as a professional gardener by the St Kilda City Council in Melbourne.

To see him dress in a quiet corner of the players' room before a big match was a memorable event for a young player eager to be 'out in the middle'. Slowly and methodically, he would pull on two pairs of heavy woollen socks, then came the elastic knee-guards followed by two rolls of rubber, one for each leg, which he wound securely around his thigh muscles. Having watched the dressing process, one marvelled at the horse-power generated by those highly-protected legs. He bowled 77 overs in that Adelaide Test of 1933.

England batted first, Douglas Jardine having won the toss, on a water-logged pitch that contained more liquid than one had any right to expect in Adelaide. The groundsman, Alby Wright, had probably over-reacted to the weather forecast which had prepared us all for a typical century plus north wind blowing in from the direction of Oodnadatta in Central Australia.

In no time, Australia had four wickets in the bag. Herbert Sutcliffe, Jardine, Walter Hammond and Les Ames were out by lunch and Maurice Leyland and Rob Wyatt had begun their 156-run partnership.

Then Leyland, facing Ironmonger, spoke to umpire George Hele asking him to enquire of Dainty whether

Sharing a joke: Bill ('Tiger') O'Reilly with The Taverners' Twelfth Man, the Duke of Edinburgh, in 1953.

he was using resin to help him grip the ball. The Australian fieldsmen quietly sniggered — for many years it was well-known that Dainty was partial to a bit of help in that direction.

Highly indignant, Ironmonger pulled a dirty piece of rag from his side pocket and waved it vigorously for all to see — it would have been difficult not to see the white powder flying from the soiled linen — and in his deep, guttural voice, old Bert said, 'No, I'm not using resin. I have kerosene sprinkled on this rag to keep away the flies'.

Not many believed him but the popular Leyland had had his joke which most of us enjoyed.

Dainty's was the last wicket to fall in that memorable match. I am sure that Gubby Allen will not have recorded the fact in his diaries that it was he who bowled the 'old man' for yet another of his accustomed blobs but he will have certainly remembered Dainty's final gesture.

As the stumps scattered, Dainty grabbed them, clasping them to his chest as he tried to snaffle the two bails to complete the job. As the players left the ground, crowding through the boundary gate, Leyland, of all people, tried to wrest one of the stumps from Ironmonger's grasp. Quick as a flash, up came Dainty's bat, at a completely unaccustomed speed, and Maurice hurriedly moved out of reach!

I affectionately remember Dainty as a brave and cooperative bowler who, had he been born in England where left-armers have always ruled the roost, would have gone down in history along with Wilfred Rhodes.

213

Philosopher, historian, dramatist, teacher, journalist and writer of what is arguably the best book on cricket, Beyond A Boundary, *C. L. R. James has given much to the game. He is here interviewed by the editor of* The Journal of the English Cricket Society.

C. L. R. James on cricket and cricketers

Clive W. Porter

C. L. R. James.

*W*hat *particular gifts did Sir Frank Worrell and Clive Lloyd bring to the captaincy of the West Indies?*

Historically speaking, Worrell created West Indies cricket as a concept. Lloyd inherited it. From the bottom Worrell built a team, a team that would do anything for him. He was a superior person, a man who saw in cricket far more than a man bowling a ball. He made a team that mattered; it was a conscious act. The West Indian history of the territories shows a subordination to leaders. In the past the white man had led. Now a black man was born for the post and after a struggle, he took it, with the support of his community. He was a product of Harrison College, a most distinguished classical college. As a black man he was one of us — but he was as well educated as any of them. He was the people's captain. The ordinary West Indian had not much to live by. The white ruling classes were remote. The church and cricket meant much — they both taught morality.

Sir Garfield Sobers followed Worrell. How would you assess him?

The greatest cricketer I have ever seen, heard of or written about. I know him very well. In everything but cricket he is a simple, straightforward man. On the cricket field he was very gifted. Worrell did his best to ensure that Sobers succeeded him as captain. He gave him experience and guidance. His accession to the office was not unopposed in the West Indies. He came from an ordinary background. A very decent person who was not ashamed of his origins, he earned great respect. He could have played for any Test team in any period as batsman or bowler. He remained through it all a totally genuine man. As regards the captaincy he may have been given it too early. He did not have the cricket authority of time and custom. Too much was expected of him; it was a heavy load. Perhaps he didn't live up to that.

Do you think Vivian Richards will join the ranks of the great captains?

I can make no judgement on the matter. There is not enough material to go by. To see how good a captain is, you must see him in conditions of adversity. He is unquestionably a very great batsman.

What is your opinion of consistently short-pitched fast bowling?

I don't believe the laws should be changed. The laws cannot be constructed to accommodate every circumstance. The umpire is empowered to intervene and should do so. The short-pitched ball *is* a legitimate ball but persistent short-pitched bowling upsets the game. The captain ought to act. Crowds don't like such bowling. It all depends on the moral outlook of the players. If it is not stopped it will do great harm to cricket.

Is there any change in the laws you would like to see?

I don't feel really qualified to comment as it is so very long since last I played and one has to experience the conditions but there are two points: When they changed the lbw law in 1934 they should have included balls on the leg side as well. I don't care where it dropped but if a ball hits a batsman on the foot in front of the wicket then he should go. That I would like changed. The other point concerns a return to a natural, uncovered wicket. Obviously the materials for making wickets have changed over the years so they have become better. Batsmen, after the first few overs, can bat for ever. Constantine and Headley used to tell me strongly how they deplored the perfect wicket. They always felt three days was plenty for a match and thought little of five-day Tests.

Do you think spin bowling is finished as a force in world cricket?

I am always cautious about announcing such a death. It has been said before and we have seen recently how well a good spinner can bowl in Tests. I would always want a slow spinner in my side. He will beat the batsman who can play the fast bowlers well. There is a tendency for slow bowling to be on the wane in the Caribbean where the fast bowlers hold sway.

Captains such as May, with Lock, and Worrell, with Griffiths, must have known they sometimes threw the ball. Why did they not act?

No doubt both those bowlers occasionally threw but it was not a regular habit. The captain has much to do. It is not reasonable to expect him to take on this responsibility in addition to all others.

Your writing about Barnes led to employment with the Manchester Guardian. *What do you remember of him?*

A formidable man, reserved but militant. He could make the ball curve in from the off and then snap back on a leg-break that was unplayable. Bradman said it was a ball impossible to play. Barnes himself told me he did not know he was going to bowl this ball in advance but once he had done it he knew it. He had sense; he didn't exhaust himself playing first-class cricket. He was a very serious man, self-contained.

Other great bowlers?

McDonald the Australian had complete control. There was something sinister about the way in which he walked back to his mark. McDonald gave you nothing. Talk with old players leads me to believe that for a few overs there was nothing quite like the pace of Larwood, but he could be tamed. McDonald could not be.

You mentioned Bradman.

In the first over he was vulnerable every innings. Each time I saw him this was so. It was purely psychological. He would play forward nervously and the ball would be in the air on the leg side but there was no one up to catch it. He was uncomfortable against Verity. Bradman was a murderous batsman, especially in the area between short-leg and mid-on. Drawing back he would slash the ball through there. Always on the alert he was not at his best on a difficult wicket, unlike George Headley.

What about Headley?

Headley preferred to bat on a damaged wicket. He said

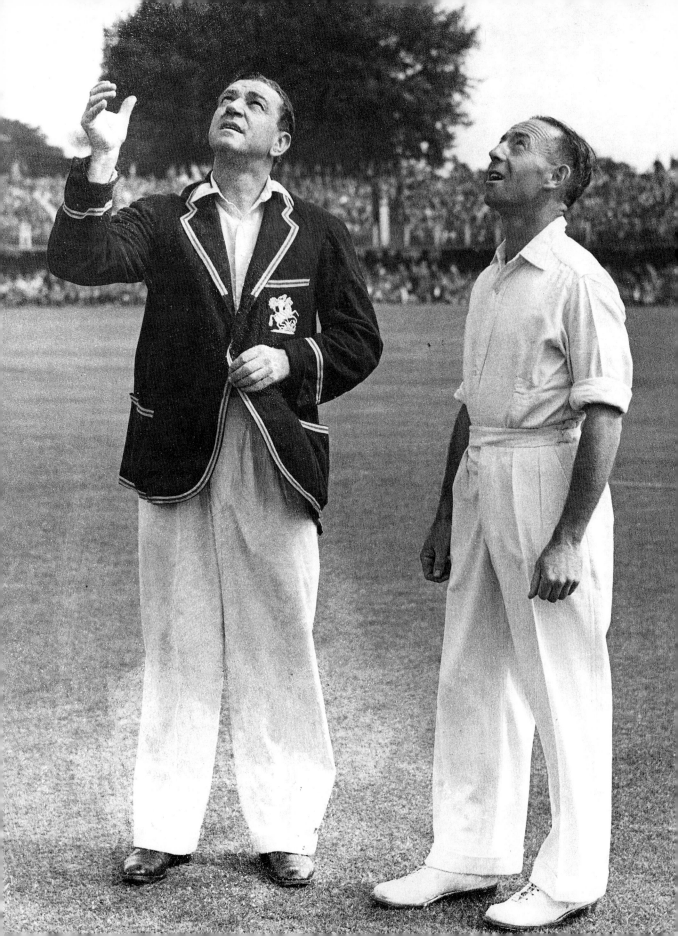

to me: 'You go right forward and drive or right back and hook. There is no other possibility if you are to make runs.' He played with absolute certainty. Nothing ever worried him. Test cricket to him was like playing with his son using a tennis ball. Never, at any time, did he show anything other than a mastery. He was all ease and grace. Constantly on the back foot he had two special strokes: a fierce cut past second slip and, to the ball that others might be content to push away, a glance to leg, very fine, for four runs. A modest and moderate man in all that he did, he had supreme confidence in his cricket ability. Once we watched together O'Reilly bowling to Hammond in a Test. Tremendous bowling. 'That fellow really can bowl,' said George. I asked him if he would be in trouble against him. 'Oh no,' he replied simply, 'I'm *never* in trouble with a bat in my hand.' His powers of intense concentration made everything else subordinate to his batting.

How did Hammond compare?

I like a batsman you can rely on. Often in England in Tests, Hammond did not show the form he produced abroad. But in 1938 at Lord's he removed all my uncertainties. I have never known a finer innings. He walked in with complete authority.

Another story I have to tell about Hammond involves Bradman as captain. Later that season, at Scarborough I think, Hammond came out to bat. Bradman moved midwicket in close. The fielder was not keen — even though O'Reilly was bowling. Bradman motioned once more; the fielder turned his back. O'Reilly bowled and compelled the great Hammond, who had of course seen all this going on, to play the ball in the air on the leg side. The fielder stretched, one-handed, to take the catch. Had he gone where Bradman wanted him it would have been an easy two-handed matter.

What is your opinion of modern English cricketers such as Gower and Botham?

Gower is the most gifted cricketer in England at the present time. There is no bowler who can dominate him; a fine stroke player. And yet I am disappointed that he has not extracted the highest value from his undoubted qualities. There is a little something lacking — not in terms of technique; perhaps it is a matter of inner confidence.

Botham I don't criticise. Such players are laws unto themselves. You must not try to alter fundamental qualities. Botham is what he is. Nobody can bowl him a ball he cannot hit. On and off the field he may be a man without complete control of himself but he is the finest all-round cricketer England ever had. To interfere with that character and personality is a complete stupidity.

You wrote once of the 'clash of race, caste and class' stimulating West Indian cricket. Is that still true?

It is not so sharp and vicious as it used to be with the coming of self-government for more blacks. You must understand the blacks feel intensely: 'You can't let the race down.' It is a pro-black feeling, not an anti-white one. It dates from the days of slavery. It is an intense pride in racial identity. White cricketers have suffered a loss of status in society and in the game itself.

What has given you most pleasure in cricket?

I was overwhelmed by the certainty with which I saw and *read* the cricket of George Headley. I would go anywhere to see a century by Sobers. He made me understand there is no limit to the achievements of a gifted individual.

At the time of this interview in late 1986, it was not known that the authorities would decree that the County Championship should be played on uncovered wickets. This must surely be seen as one of the most imaginative and positive measures of recent years taken by those in control of the first-class game in England.

It is also to be hoped that, if it is a wet summer, everyone keeps his nerve. Uncovered wickets must be the order of the day for at least five years, if a new generation of spinners is to be given the opportunity to develop under the tender, loving gaze of those rational pragmatists, the county captains.

Captains Walter Hammond and Lindsay Hassett toss before play in the fourth 'Victory' Test, at Lord's, August 1945.

Poetry of cricket: six of the best

Some years ago my definitive anthology, *The Poetry of Cricket* (Macdonald, London), was published, a tome of some 531 pages. It was received with much praise from press and public which was reward enough. But any book which is 'definitive' is only thus until the next of similar ambition comes alone. Since that time, 1964, none has. One day, perhaps, I'll produce an updated volume which will surely be enlarged with at least a further 200 poems, so quietly prolific are those imaginative sentinels of the game — the Poets of Cricket.

Meanwhile, I have been persuaded to ponder on the inclusion here of a mere handful of that romantic breed. But which poets and poetry should I choose faced with such a formidable list of *litterateurs* ranging from William Blake to Edmund Blunden, Alfred Cochrane to Sir Arthur Quiller Couch, Cecil Day Lewis to Lord Dunsany, E. V. Lucas to Thomas Moult, A. E. Housman to Alan Ross, Keats to Byron, *et al*?

An impossible task. *Quite* impossible! I therefore chose six poems — yes, excluding Francis Thompson's *At Lord's!* — that I particularly like. You are here invited to share my choice, slipping in as I do (at extra cover?) E. V. Lucas's trenchant and charming writer's song, *Alleviation*, with which I completely identify!

— *Leslie Frewin*

More mighty than the bat, the pen,
And mightier still as we grow old.
And hence I needs must scribble when
I'd fain be bowling — or be bowled.
Yet thoughts, whate'er the task, will stray;
To work they never wholly yield,
And mine, on every sunny day,
Are in the field, are in the field!

The season opens

A Tower we must have, and a clock in the tower,
Looking over the tombs, the tithebarn, the bower;
The inn and the mill, the forge and the hall,
And that loamy sweet level that loves bat and ball.

So a gray tower we have, and the centured trees
Have arisen to share what its belfry-light sees,
The apple-plats riches in spring-song of all,
Kitchen-gardens and the field where they take bat and ball

The stream with its moments of dance in the sun
Where the willows allow, runs and ever will run
At the cleft of the orchard, along the soft fall
Of the pasture where tourneys became bat and ball.

And now where the confident cuckoo takes flight
Over buttercups kindled in millions last night,
A labourer leans on the stackyard's low wall
With the hens bothering round him, and dreams bat and ball;

Till the meadow is quick with the masters who were,
And he hears his own shouts when he first trotted there;
Long ago; all gone home now; but here they come all!
Surely these are the same, who now bring bat and ball?

— *Edmund Blunden*

The game that's never done

Soft, soft the sunset falls upon the pitch,
The game is over and the stumps are drawn,
The willow sleeps in its appointed niche,
The heavy roller waits another dawn —
　　Bowled is the final ball again,
　　Hushed is the umpire's call again,
The fielders and the batsmen cease to run —
　　But memory will play again
　　Many and many a day again
The game that's done, the game that's never done.

In happy dreams we'll see each ball re-bowled,
And mend the fault that robbed us of some prize,
In dreams we'll hold the catch we failed to hold,
And see our duck's-eggs swell to centuries —
　　In dreams we'll take the field again,
　　In dreams the willow wield again,
And set the red ball spinning in the sun —
　　Ah, memory will play again
　　Many and many a day again
The game that's done, the game that's never done

— Eleanor and Herbert Farjeon

In the spring

Grass begins to grow,
　　Winds to be more civil,
Rollers press the pitch
　　For to make it level:
Thrushes pipe a stave
　　In the budding thicket;
Snowdrops point to pads,
　　Crocuses to Cricket!

Soon will stand the Slip
　　Crouching for a capture;
Soon the slogger slog
　　Four and fives in rapture!
Soon the curly lob
　　Find its love, the wicket;
Snowdrops point to pads,
　　Crocuses to Cricket!

Urchins in the road
　　Bowl with oblong pebbles,
Sending to each mate
　　Bursts of happy trebles:
In the words of slang,
　　Summer is the ticket!
Snowdrops point to pads,
　　Crocuses to Cricket!

— Norman Gale

The First Game

There comes a Day (I can hear it coming),
    One of those glorious deep blue days,
When larks are singing and bees are humming,
    And Earth gives voice in a thousand ways —
    Then I, my friends, I too shall sing,
    And hum a foolish little thing,
And whistle like (but not too like) a blackbird in
        the Spring.

There looms a Day (I can feel it looming;
    Yes, it will be in a month or less),
When all the flowers in the world are blooming,
    And Nature flutters her fairest dress —
    Then I, my friends, I too shall wear
    A blazer that will make them stare,
And brush — this is official; I shall also brush my
        hair.

It is the day that I watch for yearly,
    Never before has it come so late;
But now I've only a month — no, merely
    A couple of fortnights left to wait;
    And then (to make the matter plain)
    I hold — at last! — a bat again;
Dear Hobbs! the weeks this summer — think! the
    weeks I've lived in vain!

I see already the first ball twisting
    Over the green as I take my stand,
I hear already long-on insisting
    It wasn't a chance that came to hand —
    Or no; I see it miss the bat
    And strike me on the knee, whereat
Some fool, some silly fool at point, says blandly,

        'How was that?'
Then, scouting later, I hold a hot 'un
    At deep square-leg from the local Fry,
And at short mid-on to the village Scotton
    I snap a skimmer some six foot high —

Or else, perhaps, I get the ball,
    Upon the thumb, or not at all,
Or right into the hands, and then, lorblessme,
    let it fall.

But what care I? It's the game that calls me —
    Simply to be on the field of play;
How can it matter what fate befalls me,
    With ten good fellows and one good day? . . . But still,
    I rather hope spectators will,
    Observing any lack of skill,
Remark 'This is his first appearance'. Yes, I
    hope they will.

                                    — A. A. Milne

O Willow

O Willow, in our hours of ease
    (That is to say, throughout the Winter),
I take you sometimes on my knees,
    And careless of the frequent splinter,
Caress you tenderly, and sigh, and say,
    'Ye Gods, how long till May?'

And so as soon as April's here
    I do not sob for Spring to show its
Pale daffodils and all the dear
    Old flowers that keep the minor poets;
I sing it just because a month (about)
    Will find *you* fairly out.

Revered, beloved, O you whose job
    Is but to serve throughout the season
To make, if so it be, the Blob,
    And not (thank Heaven!) to ask the reason —
To stand, like Mrs. Hemans' little friend,
    Undoubting to the end.

Old Willow, what a tale to tell —
    Our steady rise, from small beginnings,
Ab ovo usque — usque — well,

To eighty-four, our highest innings
(Ah, me, that crowded hour of glorious lives —
   Ten of them, all from drives!)

Once only have you let me in,
   Through all the knocks we've had together;
That time when, wanting four to win,
   I fairly tried to tonk the leather —
And lo! a full-faced welt, without the least
   Warning, went S.S.E.

A painful scene. In point of fact
   I'm doubtful if I ought to hymn it;
Enough to say you went and cracked,
   And left me thinking things like 'dimmit'
(And not like 'Dimmit'), as I heard Slip call
   'Mine!' and he pouched the ball.

Do you remember, too, the game
   One August somewhere down in Dorset,
When, being told to force the same,
   We straightaway started in to force it . . .
For half an hour or so we saw it through,
   And scratched a priceless two:

Or how the prayer to play for keeps
   And hang the runs, we didn't need 'em,
So stirred us, we collected heaps
   With rather more than usual freedom;
Fifty in fourteen minutes — till a catch
   Abruptly closed the match?

Well, well — the coming years (if fine)
   Shall see us going even stronger;
So pouring out the oil and wine,
   Let's sit and drink a little longer;
Here's to a decent average of ten!
   (Yours is the oil. Say when . . .)

— *A. A. Milne*

Close of play

How shall we live, now that the summer's ended,
And bat and ball (too soon!) are put aside,
And all our cricket deeds and dreams have blended —
The hit for six, the champion bowled for none,
The match we planned to win and never won? . . .
Only in green-winged memory they abide.

How shall we live, who love our loveliest game
With such bright ardour that when stumps are drawn
We talk into the twilight, always the same
Old talk with laughter rounding off each tale —
Laughter of friends across a pint of ale
In the blue shade of the pavilion.

For the last time a batsman's out, the day
Like the drained glass and the dear sundown field
Is empty; what instead of summer's play
Can occupy these darkling months ere spring
Hails Willow once again the crowned king?
How shall we live so life may not be chilled?

Well, what's a crimson hearth for, and the lamp
Of winter nights, and these plump yellow books
That cherish Wisden's soul and bear his stamp —
Time's ever-changing, unalterable score-board,
Thick-clustered with a thousand names adored:
Half the game's magic in their very looks!

And when we've learnt those almanacks by heart,
And shared with Nyren . . . Cardus . . . the distant thrill
That cannot fade since they have had their part,
We'll trudge wet streets through fog and mire
And praise our heroes by the club-room fire:
O do not doubt, the game will hold us still!

— *Thomas Moult*

Keeping cricket alive

Grace Garlick

'In Cromwell's time cricket was more advanced in Ireland than England and Cromwell ordered the destruction of all the cricket bats in Dublin because the game was encouraging his troops to fraternise with the Irish.'

The speaker is an Irishman named Pat Mullins who lives in suburban Brisbane and carries in his head an encyclopaedic knowledge of cricket that inspires awe in all the pilgrims who come to consult him.

'Did you know,' says Pat, 'that Joh Bjelke-Petersen made rubber cricket bats? That was 62 years ago and they weren't a success.' Pat wrote to Sir Joh to check the legend and includes it in the book Pat has written with Philip Derriman, *Bat and Pad, writings of Australian Cricket 1804–1984*. Published in 1984, the book marks the first time Oxford University Press has turned out a book devoted to cricket. The Australian edition has quickly sold out.

A second book is on the way, *The Cradle of Australian Cricket*. Pat, working with fellow cricket enthusiast Brian Crowley, has put together all the writings of Thomas Patrick Horan, who wrote under the pseudonym of Felix, to be published by Macmillan next year.

Pat Mullins is a quiet and courteous authority on cricket whom most other authorities call when they are stumped for an answer. The dates and the details of cricket's long history come alive when Pat Mullins talks about it.

'That's a picture of the Australian cricketing team for the first Test match in history. The game was in 1877, between England and Australia, in Melbourne,' says Pat, pointing to one of the framed pictures on his wall. 'The team includes Thomas Horan, the first Irishman to play cricket for Australia.'

The picture is framed by a door to the sacred place in his home, Pat's library. He has one of the world's eight best collections of cricket memorabilia — books, pictures, cartoons, music, neckties, balls, plates and posters. The collection is priceless. And Pat is going blind. His condition, *retinitis pigmentosa*, diagnosed in

1957, has reduced his peripheral vision to just a few degrees.

'The collection should be properly housed somewhere,' he says. 'It should be catalogued and continued — hopefully at the Queensland State Library. Something I've learned over 40 or 50 years is that it needs the attention that only such a library can give it. It's a bit hard for me to get up and down the bookshelves these days.'

The collection fills the walls and overflows the quiet room. The bookshelves are built to the ceiling. There's a 1949 Brisbane *Telegraph* poster on his wall, 'Bradman writes for the Telegraph'.

Pat was born in Townsville in 1923, the son of an Irish publican. He lived in Tully to the age of 17. He still has the pocket of his Mount Carmel, Charters Towers, school blazer. He played in the first eleven in 1937, '38 and '39.

'There was no wireless then. We heard people talking about cricket and we read about it in the papers. That's how we heard of players like Bradman.'

He started his collection with cuttings from newspapers used to wrap bottles sold at the pub.

Pat went to war in 1942 from the New Guinea Force training school. He came to Brisbane to finish law studies and returned to Tully to help his parents. In 1948 he bought a radiola so he could listen to cricket. 'I was addicted,' he says. 'In 1940 I listened to Neville Cardus. He was music critic for the *Guardian* in Manchester and his editor told him, "You shall go out and report cricket". That's how Cardus began his life-long love affair with the game.'

Pat collected all the writings of Cardus. Cricket writers have developed a special literature of their own. 'Prime Minister Robert Gordon Menzies wrote about cricket, too. He wrote, "Cricket is a summer game for the player and observer; but a winter game for the reader and thinker, who sits by his fireside and evokes imperishable memories".'

Pat married Betty Gardiner in 1955. By now he was reading about cricket at the rate of one book a night.

For a while he concentrated on Bradman, becoming an authority on Bradman's career. He saved every edition of *The Cricketer* from England and searched out any other book or magazine that had a reference to cricket.

The strength of Pat's collection, according to library authorities, is that there are all sorts of bits and pieces — from a teatowel of 1848–1915 Test teams ('No one ever washes up with that one,' he says) to a Bradman Toby jug. He even has a photograph of horror-movie star Boris Karloff playing cricket in Hollywood.

By 1977 Pat was contributing to E. W. Padwick's *A Bibliography of Cricket*. 'Some collectors are selfish with their knowledge,' he says. 'I've always been pleased to share mine.'

As his interest in cricket expanded, it became insatiable. Pat's hobby was now his whole life. He progressed from cricket books to books that explain cricket books. 'No other sport has literature like cricket,' he says. He pulled out a printed program featuring the Australian team on a Canadian-American tour in 1926. Nearby was a prize copy (number 70 of a limited edition of 120) of Neville Cardus's *The Summer Game*.

There's a book on Arthur Coningham, the first player from Queensland to play for Australia against England in 1894–95. Coningham took a wicket with the first ball — it was the only one he took in the whole game. 'He once lit a fire at Lord's to keep himself warm — at *Lord's*.' Coningham became a bookmaker later in his life and wore an apron identifying himself to punters as 'Coningham the Test cricketer'.

Pat Mullins is in no doubt about the greatest cricketer of all time: 'It has to be Bradman, number one. With Bill O'Reilly as bowler and Don Tallon as the 'keeper.' Pat recalls the bodyline era: 'In 1933, my dad was interested in the bodyline series for two reasons — one that it was us versus the Poms, and the other because there were four Irish names involved: McCabe, O'Reilly, Fingleton and O'Brien. Dad had told me that Fingleton's rosary beads were crushed when the ball hit him. He always had them in his pocket when he went to bat.

'In 1933 the fourth Test was in Brisbane and the fifth in Sydney. Jack Fingleton and O'Brien were batting together on the Sydney Cricket Ground and Fingo held up his hand and stopped play because Mo (O'Brien) had lost his holy medal. The Englishmen joined in the search, although they weren't sure what they were looking for. Archbishop Duhig of Brisbane had given all the players St Christopher medals. Imagine stopping a cricket match to look for a medal today!'

Pat turned to his sheet music. 'Here's a precious piece: *Every Day Is a Rainbow for Me*, music by Don Bradman, published in the 1930s.'

Pat Mullins doesn't want to discuss night cricket or some recent cricket developments. 'Real cricket,' he says, 'is played in the backyard. That's the true spirit of cricket.'

He produced some words in *Wisden Cricket Monthly* by editor David Frith: 'A visit to Australia's premier cricket collector Pat Mullins was tinged with sadness since his library is destined for sale. This generous man for whom cricket is a genuine freemasonry showed me rarities that added substantially to the revised bibliography, a timely reminder that cricket is not all run-rates and coloured costumes and floodlights.'

'What, by whom, off whom, for how many?'

'Tibby Cotter, a trooper in the 12th Light Horse Regiment, bowled with the wind behind him, and the Tommy officers never saw which way he went.'

Cotter's last match

Extract from *The Evening Sun*, Melbourne, Saturday 15 November 1924

The following sidelight on cricket history is contributed by Miss Lloma Lewis who was handed an ancient newspaper by her neighbour, a Mr Frank Dunn. Painstakingly put together the result records a game in the desert which was often referred to in the years 1919–25. I have no knowledge of seeing it recorded elsewhere and the article is published again here as a rare item of cricketana. (Editor).

DOES DOUGLAS RECALL?
TEST MATCH ON SINAI
COTTER'S LAST GAME
UNKNOWN CRICKET HISTORY
(By 'SERGEANT')

When Johnny-Won't-Hit-Today Douglas comes to write his memoirs, 'My 97 Years of Cricket at Home and Abroad', I bet he won't remember a certain cricket match played on the sands of the Mediterranean coast of Southern Palestine between the British Yeomanry and the Australian Light Horse. Both divisions were having a short rest and a clean up on the coast. The Yeomanry, led by Gentlemen from the Very Best Families of England, sent the Light Horse Commander a challenge to a game of cricket. Our scouting parties had seen the Tommy officers sporting themselves in flannels in the cool of the evening. Anyhow, we took them on.

Douglas was a Colonel of the Yeomanry, although I never rightly knew whether he was in the Warwicks, the Worcesters, or the Gloucesters. He was always there when it came to a cricket match or a fight according to the Marquis of Queensberry.

The Dress

We had a few sets of cricketing tools bought out of certain regimental funds — never mind whose funds. The desert sand, watered and stamped with tibbin by the Kamleelah wallahs, made a pretty fair concrete pitch.

The Yeomanry team, all officers, was a treat to see in spotless flannels. The officers were always punctilious about appearance and cleanliness even on the desert. How they carried their boudoirs about the desert was a marvel.

Our team looked like a mob of Murrumbidgee whalers who had lost their swags. A few of the officers were in khaki slacks and shirts, and the other ranks wore their old blue-grey flannel shirts, riding strides with the knees out for the most part, no leggings, and their knitted socks hanging down over their ankle boots.

Our fellows won the toss, and had a bat. They put up only 57, Douglas getting most of the wickets.

Then the Yeomanry took block. That's about all they did take. Tibby Cotter, a trooper in the 12th Light Horse Regiment, bowled with the wind behind him, and the Tommy officers never saw which way he went. They just walked in and out in a dazed manner. We had four men behind the stumps to stop any risks of byes getting into double figures.

A Sinister Silence

Clive Single, Colonel of our ambulance, bowled from the other end. He had been high in Grade cricket in Sydney and had a good University career — as far as cricket went, anyhow. He bowled a mixed over of slow and medium balls breaking in from both sides.

Cotter and Single bowled the Yeomanry all for 4, including one bye.

'Who is this Cotter man?' they kept asking.

Douglas had spotted Cotter the first time he made his characteristic long run before bowling, but thought it wise not to break the news to the batsmen beforehand.

They took it like sportsmen when they knew. It hardly seemed fair. They squared it off with us later — but that is another story.

Poor old Tibby Cotter was given out at Beersheeba later. He was in the front of the mounted charge.

Young Australian all-rounder Stephen Waugh during his second-innings 73, versus England at the SCG in January 1987.

West Indies 'keeper Jeffrey Dujon gets one off his legs during the second Test versus Australia at the SCG in January 1982. 'Keeper Marsh, slip G. Chappell, bowler Geoff Lawson and non-striker Larry Gomes are also in view.

*England's left-arm spinner Phil Edmonds wheels in to bowl during the
first Test versus Australia at the 'Gabba, November 1986.*

Australian orthodox left-arm spinner Ray Bright bowling against New Zealand in season 1985–86.

Former New Zealand captain Jeffrey Crowe batting during the 1985–86 season when the Kiwis at last won a series against the Aussies on Australian soil.

Fourth Test Australia versus England at the MCG, December 1986, and Botham, Richards and Athey appeal for the wicket of Geoff Marsh.

England wicket-keeper Jack Richards batting during his century in the
second Test versus Australia at Perth, November / December 1986.

Off-break spinner John Bracewell of New Zealand cuts during the Test versus Australia in November 1985.

Botham and Border in deep conversation in early 1987. Their
professional and personal friendship was to be severely tested during
Botham's unsettling summer spent playing with Queensland under
Border's captaincy in 1987–88.

Opener Bill Athey of England on his way to a half century in the drawn
third Test versus Australia at Adelaide in December 1986.

Australia's number three batsman Dean Jones clubs a ball through mid-
wicket during a one-day game versus India in season 1984–85. Jones
averaged 68.10 that season and has continued his good form.

Sir Donald Bradman in Rolls-Royce leads the 'Living Legends' around the Sydney Cricket Ground prior to the drawn Bicentennial Test in January/February 1988. In the 'computer Test' run concurrently with the 'real' one, Sir Donald's second-innings century and Bill O'Reilly's six wickets helped Australia to a 37-run victory.

In the Bicentennial Test, Chris Broad's mammoth innings of 139 ended on a controversial note when he clubbed his stumps in disgust after deflecting a Steve Waugh ball off his body onto the wicket. Broad's public apology satisfied the purists but his 365-minute innings put precious little fire into a dull game.

*Australian all-rounder Tony
Dodemaide fires one in during the
Bicentennial Test as non-striker
and England captain Gatting and
Australian match-saver David
Boon prepare for action.*

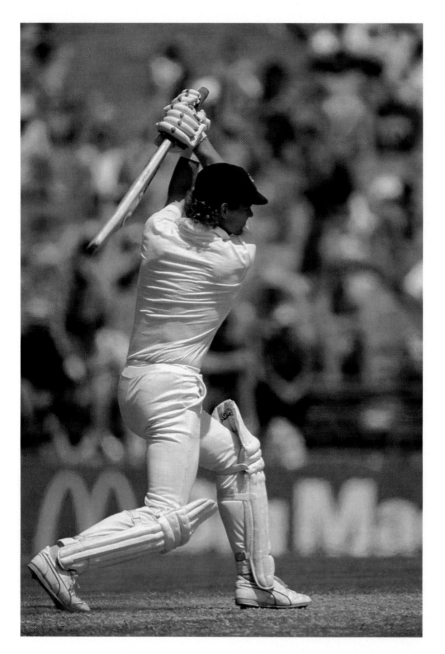

Dean Jones top-scored with a cautious 56 in Australia's miserly first innings total of 214 in the Bicentennial Test. Here he hits one of only four fours. Jones, Marsh and Border helped David Boon hold out for a draw on the final

*Gritty opener Boon plays forward to an Emburey ball during his match-
and face-saving 184 not out in the Bicentennial Test. Boon's one-man
rescue mission saw him occupy the crease for 492 minutes with his
personal-best top-score coming off 431 balls with 14 boundaries.*

Two of the young men upon whom
Australia's future Test hopes lie:
all-rounder Steve Waugh and fast
bowler Craig McDermott. In the
Bicentennial Test, Waugh made
third top score in the first innings
as well as claiming three England
wickets (Broad, Gatting and
Dilley). McDermott bowled well
but without luck.

Cotter's last 'bowl'

'Blue'

I was 'Tibby' Cotter's cobber in the 12th Light Horse and on the night of 30 October 1917, we were at Khallassa, in southern Palestine, the most remote portion of the southern position. We watered our horses there, and prepared to move off in the attack on Beersheba.

Tibby was one of the best foragers in the A.I.F. He would come to light with a bottle of champagne in the middle of the desert, and the lads in the section all looked at him to turn up with something unusual.

'Tibby' Cotter in action.

About 1.30 on the morning of the attack, Tibby, who had received instructions to report to Echelon on a guard, turned up at the unit. He said to me: 'Bluey, I've skittled a Turk in one hit; and what do you think he had on him? Here it is — a yard of ling.' He wasn't going to Echelon, he insisted, but said he would treat the boys to a Stammell fish supper in Beersheba, and be damned to the consequences.

We moved off at 4.30 a.m. from Khallassa and attacked Beersheba that afternoon. Tibby was next to me on one side in the charge, Trooper Jack Beasley on the other. Rex Cowley was there also. The other three were skittled by a machine gun, and after we had cleared the Turks out, the troops went back half an hour later to bury the dead.

Tibby was still alive when I got to him and he recognised me. 'Blue,' he said, 'You can have the fish supper on your own.' He died shortly afterwards. He should never have been in the charge. Had he obeyed orders, he would probably have lived.

Just before we left Khallassa, Tibby — who, in a bowling competition at Tel-el-Fara, bowled over 18 single stumps at full pace out of 24 — took up a ball of mud and, throwing it into the air said: 'That's my last bowl, Blue; something is going to happen.'

— *NSW Cricket Association Archives*

Albert (Tibby) Cotter, 1883–1917, was born in Sydney. Before the First World War, Tibby was an idol of spectators because of his habit of breaking batsman's stumps. He was a furious pace-bowler, Jack Pollard claims, as dangerous at the end of a hard day as at the start. Born of affluent parents, he went to Forest Lodge Primary school and Sydney Grammar School. He played District cricket for Glebe. A menacing batsman, he hit 152 runs in an afternoon against Waverley which included 16 sixes and six fours in only 70 minutes. He toured England with the 1905 team after making his debut for NSW four years earlier. He returned to England for a second tour in 1909 when he took 64 wickets at 29.09 in all matches.

Evading a bouncer: This prize-winning photograph of Western Australian Mike Veletta shows him ducking under a bouncer from Victorian fast bowler Merv Hughes at the WACA Ground, Perth, in December 1986. The picture won the 1987 Rothmans National Press Photo Award in the Sporting Section. Photographer: John Campbell. Courtesy of the West Australian, *Perth, WA.*

'O'Neill was in to face the might of England — a pace attack of Trueman, Statham and Tyson, plus spinners Laker and Lock.'

The enigma of Norm O'Neill

Sydney *Daily Mirror*, 1987

When the Australian cricket selectors left Norm O'Neill out of the 1957–58 tour of South Africa, the youngster exacted savage revenge and turned in some Sheffield Shield performances that had the fans talking of a second Bradman.

The 20-year-old from the Sydney suburb of Carlton proceeded to thrash some of Australia's best bowlers in a series of displays that overshadowed the Test team in South Africa. The pinnacle of that devastating season came at the SCG in January 1958 when O'Neill hit 233 sparkling runs in 244 minutes for NSW against Victoria.

The fans had seen nothing like this since the heyday of The Don. They cheered all the way as O'Neill took to the bowling. He blasted 38 fours on the way to his first century, with four successive boundaries when experienced Victorian skipper Sam Loxton brought on the bouncers. Loxton was forced into a rapid change of tactics, but he could do nothing to stop the flow of drives through the covers.

If the crowd liked O'Neill, the press just loved him. One writer was moved to say: 'He's another Bradman. Even a blind man can see it.' But, unfortunately for NSW and Australia, he was wrong.

O'Neill had many of Bradman's skills, but he turned into an enigma — one of the greatest riddles cricket has known. He suffered terribly from nerves and that stopped him from scaling the heights that Bradman reached. The defect meant O'Neill often got out for low scores when he should have been blazing centuries, but his golden moments came often enough to write his name into the record books.

Norman Clifford O'Neill was born in the Sydney suburb of Carlton on 19 February 1937. By the age of eight his uncle, Ron Campion, was coaching him, realising the potential of his young nephew. Campion was a fast bowler with Glebe and by the time O'Neill was 16, he was facing his uncle in first grade. That first grade confrontation with his uncle, Ron, did not have the fairytale ending O'Neill would have liked. He snicked an outswinger into the slips and was caught for

3. 'Sorry, son,' said Campion, as the disappointed youngster strode back to the pavilion. 'I would have liked to see you get 50.'

When he was nine, he joined a St George District under-13s team called The Dragons. He had to add a year to his age to make the side, but was a good match for the older boys. His batting strokes shone through even then and, by the age of 13, he was scoring prolifically at Kogarah High, finishing the season with a batting average of 130.

A year later, he made the St George fourth grade side, where he scored 300 runs in his first season. He was also starting to show the athletic ability that would make him a superb fielder and a useful leg break bowler. Cricket could have missed out on some rare talent, because O'Neill also showed huge potential at baseball, golf, tennis and swimming.

At school, his teachers thought he could be a topline golfer, as he twice helped his team win the NSW Schoolboys' Championship. But he soon established his place in first grade cricket, although it took him some time to master the State and international players he came up against. That first season was nothing to shout

about, but the second time around he scored a total of 350 runs and his first century came in 1955.

There was plenty more where that came from and O'Neill also made the Shield side that season. Again, the elation was tempered by disappointment as he was relegated to 12th man for the first five matches. When he did get his chance against South Australia, he missed out. Those nerves beat him and he lasted only seven balls before Don Gregg bowled him for a duck.

O'Neill divided his teenage attentions between cricket and baseball. During the winter, his baseball form for NSW earned him international recognition. He was picked for the side to go to the Olympics, but then fate stepped in once more when the Olympic committee ruled him out because he was a professional.

They based that decision on the $6-a-day expenses he earned when he toured with the NSW Sheffield Shield team. O'Neill turned that disappointment into a

'You chaps mind terribly if I have a look at him, too?' (Cartoonist Rigby, of the Perth Daily News, *gives his impression of O'Neill's first appearance against MCC in Perth.)*

concerted charge towards cricket fame and he made South Australia pay for the debut duck with a sparkling 127, his first Shield century. It was the start of the golden era as the ton came only days after a hurricane 108 in 32 minutes in a Sunday game at Waverley Oval.

O'Neill had everything going for him — aggression, physique, a superb range of strokes — and, on his day, he was the most entertaining batsman in the world. When he controlled his emotions, he was unstoppable. He finished the 1956-57 season with 501 runs at an average of 41.75 and earned a place in the side to tour New Zealand. He scored an unbeaten century in the third Test and headed the tour averages with 72.66.

O'Neill seemed a certainty for the trip to South Africa and it was a body blow when the selectors left him out. They could only sit and ponder as O'Neill took to the Sheffield Shield opposition with a vengeance. The 233 against Victoria was the highlight as he rattled up 1005 runs for the season, the first time a NSW player had passed the 1000 mark, at an average of 83.75.

He opened up with a blazing 175 in 208 minutes at the MCG and followed that with two centuries against South Australia. Back in grade, he smashed 201 not out against Waitara and, just for good measure, he took 26 wickets to head the Shield bowling averages, too. Not since the Bradman days had there been such excitement in cricket and this time there was no hiccup when the team to take on the MCC was announced.

O'Neill was to face the might of England — a pace attack of Trueman, Statham and Tyson, plus spinners Laker and Lock. It was a baptism of fire and O'Neill came out blazing with a battling 104 for a Combined XI in Perth. He opened with successive fours off Laker and continued to take the fight to England in the Test series. In the first Test in Brisbane, he scored 71 not out and tipped a finely balanced match Australia's way.

It was all so easy for the youngster as he went off on the 1959-60 tour of India and Pakistan, where he teamed up with Neil Harvey to carry the batting. His first Test century came against Pakistan, when he

smashed 134 and he averaged 68 in the Tests, and 85 for the tour. O'Neill really let rip against the President's XI at Ahmedabed with a career best of 284.

Back home, he took on the West Indies and starred in the 1960-61 tied Test in Brisbane with a dashing 181 in the first innings. He was the highest scorer on either side, but the nerves were starting to show more and more. He seemed to suffer attacks of the jitters at the start of every innings. The brilliance was still there, but O'Neill peppered his play with rash shots that often led to his downfall.

He seemed to rely on a series of superstitions to rev him up and would never eat lunch if he had to bat afterwards. His concentration faltered and he was constantly tugging at his cap, walking around the crease and brushing imaginary specks from the wicket.

O'Neill was going through the horrors and it showed on the 1961 tour of England, where his average slumped to 40.50. Worse was to follow when Ted Dexter's team came to Australia the following year. O'Neill's average this time was only 34.44 and it seemed that the golden flow of runs was drying up. He did score one century against England in Adelaide, but this was his last Test ton. He played 15 more matches for Australia, but never recaptured the form of the early days.

It was the beginning of the end of his international career when he went to the West Indies in 1964. He scored 266 in four Tests, but launched a vitriolic attack on pace bowler Charlie Griffiths when he returned home. He labelled him a 'cheat and a chucker' and vowed he would never again play against the West Indies. The selectors seemed to take notice of this outburst and left O'Neill out of the side to play in South Africa in 1966.

Once more, he set out to prove himself and his form returned. He smashed 180 and then 80 against South Australia in the Shield, but then everything went wrong again. This time it was injury and doctors warned him he would need surgery on his knees if he continued to play. O'Neill had been plagued by knee

Norm O'Neill in fiery form.

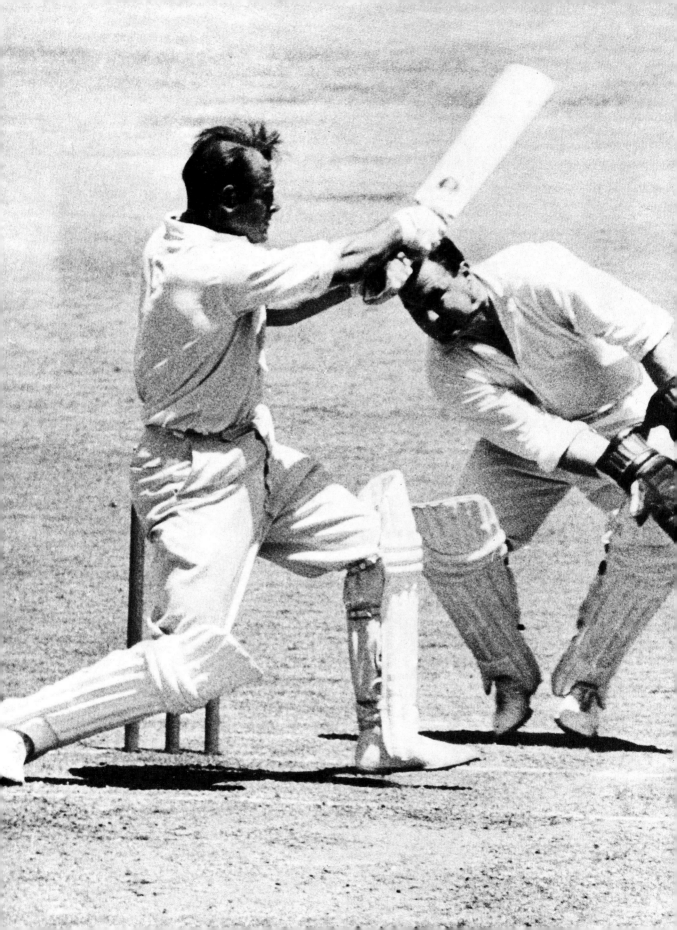

injuries for years, but this time there was no answer and he finally drew down the curtain on a bitter-sweet cricketing career in April 1967.

O'Neill may have been finished as a great player but he stayed in the game as a commentator and his authoritative comments have added a great deal to ABC radio. He has ripped into today's players verbally just as he did physically with the bat years ago.

When Pakistan turned on their go-slow tactics in the SCG Test in 1984, O'Neill voiced the thoughts of the masses. 'It was shameful,' he said. 'Sarfraz in particular gave no thought to the people who had paid big money to see a good game of cricket. Mudassar also bowled well wide of the off-stump to try to slow down the onslaught of Greg Chappell and Allan Border.'

In 1982 O'Neill sprang to the defence of Chappell who ran into so much criticism over the under-arm bowling incident. Chappell's captaincy was under fire but O'Neill said: 'He is a fine man and I see a lot of strain on his face. Take into consideration what he has done in the past. He would be a great loss to the Australian cricket scene.'

Now O'Neill's son, Mark, has taken over the family cricketing tradition and has been on the fringe of the Australian team for several seasons. When he emerged as one of the brightest young Shield batsmen in 1980, Norm spent one of his most harrowing days as Mark crept to his maiden first-class century for Western Australia against the touring Indians.

'There is just one thing that would make me completely happy,' said Norm. 'One day I would like to be remembered as Mark O'Neill's dad.'

Stories of rural Australian cricket

Robin Letts

Terry Green.

The Green Ghost that haunts Granite Flat

Take out a map of Victoria and look for the towns of Donald and Charlton in the north-central area. Having found them, imagine you're driving east from Donald to Charlton. Turn off to the left at the Jeffcott Public Hall, 20 kilometres from Donald, and travel about five kilometres into the wheat country known as Chirrup Swamp.

You'll come to a paddock which, until 1974, was the home ground of the Granite Flat Cricket Club. From the turn of the century, with breaks only for world wars, Granite Flat had always been 'competitive' in the Donald District Cricket Association, even if it had not won an A grade premiership.

Doubts as to that competitiveness, however, must surely have begun to surface in the 1969–70 season when a 16-year-old player from the Litchfield club, Terry Green, took block for the first time against Granite. In that innings Terry scored 97 not out, including 12 fours.

He did not play in the 1970–71 season, but in the next three summers his scores against Granite Flat were: 1971–72: 103 not out (including 10 fours) in 75 minutes; 1972–73: 230 not out (26 fours, 8 sixes) in 120 minutes; 1973–74: 110 not out (9 fours, 5 sixes).

In all, in four successive innings against Granite Flat, Terry Green scored 540 runs *without being dismissed*! At the end of that 1973–74 season Granite Flat decided to disband and throw its lot in with the Charlton club.

Whether or not Terry Green unwittingly hastened that decision, the story is not without its happy ending. Several of those former Granite Flat players have since taken a major role in the considerable success enjoyed by Charlton, including a number of A grade premierships.

As for Terry Green, now 35 years old, his batting statistics for Litchfield (and later Litchfield-Watchem)

237

stand at 7773 runs at an average of 46.2 He has also taken 278 wickets and 116 catches. It is his intention to play until he turns forty.

Granite Flat may never again suffer the fury of Terry Green's blazing bat. But other sides most assuredly will!

Shock for Dr Grace

Even now, a mere mention of the late Dr W. G. Grace, famous English Test batsman, seems to engender in Australian enthusiasts a special interest.

One of Australia's best-known all-rounders and Test representatives against England at about the turn of the century, the late George Giffen of South Australia, produced a very readable book on his experiences in the great game.

The book is long out of print, but for any enthusiast able to have access to it the time spent in reading it would prove enjoyable.

Much discussion on the voyage to England centred on the great Dr Grace and the possibilities of dismissing him for adequately moderate totals. As a fast medium-pacer Giffen had a special interest in this, and a fair share of confidence and hope that he would be able to help in finding a solution.

He relates how in his first encounter with the 'W.G.' he was able to write, with evident gratification and satisfaction, 'I bowled his middle stump'.

Value of practice

George recalls an amusing incident regarding the team's 'Demon bowler', Frederick Spofforth, who was also a wizard slips fieldsman. Many young admirers sought his signature.

Spoff had no difficulty in coping with his methods of training for slips. 'Well,' he said, 'in Australia we have lots of boxthorn hedges. I give the boys sixpence to throw stones into them — and as the sparrows fly out, I catch 'em.'

Swift retribution

It is natural that in rural Australia, country cricket provides the 'pepper and salt' ingredients for the discussion that distinguishes the intervals between weekly matches. Fortunate it is, also, that so many reminiscences survive for retelling. The charm of such stories lies often in the fact that many are true, and this is so in the following instances.

Shortly after the Second World War an important match was listed in a Victorian well-performed country competition and the town team's party included, by invitation, several government visitors inspecting shire roads. On the trip out the town captain reminded his bowlers that they could encounter some queer umpiring decisions. One could come from an elderly member of the opposing club.

His technique included marking on the bat under his arm the balls in each over. Any appeal for lbw by bowlers opposing the bush team's batsmen would most likely hear, 'Sorry, I didn't see it, I was marking the bowls on the bat'.

No names, no pack drill in this narrative. The towns opening bowler, a 6 ft 3 in clergyman and a real 'gentle giant', commented incredulously, 'But surely no man would do that?' 'You wait and see,' said the captain.

Now, many of the district's summer baked pitches were still smoothed by a heavy iron wagon wheel. A single matting concealed deficiencies which demanded respectful concentration. The players had never believed that the 'sky pilot' had bowled at his top.

They did not have to wait long to find out. The opening batsman had scant success and in due course 'the Reverend' quietly lodged one of his infrequent appeals. The umpire did not lose his nerves. 'Sorry Sir, I didn't see it. I was marking down the bowl.'

Resuming the toil, he dismissed the team for 11 runs, with the inevitable match result. As one of the visitors remarked, 'It was worth the trip out' to be even a passive part of the proceedings.

'On my three tours to Australia as a player the journey by luxury liner was down to 20 days. Now it is a matter of hours . . .'

Love affair

Alec Bedser

In the 35 years over which my memory sweeps, cricket has undergone many changes. The game we play today is scarcely like the game of my boyhood. There have been silent revolutions transforming cricket in many directions, improving it in some ways, and in others robbing it of some elements of its charm.

So wrote Dr W. G. Grace, the great English cricketer of Queen Victoria's days, in 1899. The words might have come from the players of my post-war generation though I would opt for 'strident' rather than 'silent' revolutions.

Who would have guessed when I started my international career in 1946 that one-day matches would be an integral part of every touring program, that cup competitions would be highlights of domestic seasons, or that a newly-born state, Pakistan, would compete on equal terms with Australia and England? Pitches have altered. Bowling, alas, is all too often intimidatory, attacking the batsman's person instead of the stumps, and batsmen walk to the crease almost anonymous figures behind their helmets, visors, arm guards and heaven's knows what. Even fielders are padded and protected.

But probably nothing has changed the ways of cricket and cricketers more than the invention of the jet engine. In 1873 it took Grace's side 52 days to sail to Melbourne from Southhampton, and involved a change of steamer at Ceylon, now Sri Lanka (and surely Grace would never have visualised Ceylon as a Test-playing country!). The actual tour began on 23 October when the *Mirzapore* left England, and ended on 18 May after another seven weeks at sea.

On my three tours to Australia as a player the journey by luxury liner was down to 20 days. Now it is a matter of hours, which was some comfort to me as chairman of England's Test selectors if a player had to be replaced. We had four on 24-hour standby in case of an injury, and I still boggle at the thought that it is possible to be in London one day and in Sydney 24 hours later.

Inevitably, instant travel to all parts of the cricket world has led to a glut of Test matches. In the course of two years a regular international can play in more matches than the pre-jet player managed in the course of his entire career. I sometimes think Test cricket has become like a dog chasing its own tail. To pay the players and meet the cost of travel and staging a series it is necessary, even in these days of sponsorship, to have a non-stop program without a breathing space.

Modern tours are, of course, much shorter but in some ways the players miss a lot. A journey to Australia, involving stops at Port Said, Aden, Bombay and Colombo, was an experience to be savoured and never forgotten. The advantages were also apparent — one could rest after a domestic season and get to know the other members of the party. Such a difference from today's dash between continents and the equally hectic to-ing and from-ing across Australia once the match program begins.

When I was England's manager in 1979–80 the tour was so overcrowded that a great deal of the time was swallowed up flying in aircraft and being driven in coaches with overnight stops in hotels that it was scarcely worthwhile unpacking one's luggage. At one point England flew from Perth to Brisbane, from Brisbane to Sydney and back to Brisbane on the following day — all for limited-over matches. I reckoned if all the time we spent in the actual travelling, waiting at airports and checking in and out of hotels were added together we could have played another five-day Test match. Clearly cricketers cannot give of their best under such strain.

On my first trip in 1946–47 England travelled on the *Stirling Castle* which was still under the control of the Ministry of War Transport. The passenger list contained many wives and brides-to-be of Australian servicemen but the old sea dogs complained the voyage was not up to the usual standard. For me it was utter luxury and to be going to Australia was sheer bliss. I grew up in a Surrey dressing room in which those lucky enough to have toured Australia told tales to stir my ambition and imagination. To be chosen to go to Australia was the Everest of every career and I look back on my initiation to Australia at the port of Fremantle as one of the most magical moments of my life. It began a love affair with Australia and Australians that has never dimmed with the passing of time. I thought the people were the friendliest I had ever met and I still do.

I was able to see more of the country when I and my twin brother Eric did some coaching up-country. With no disrespect to the magnificent modern cities of Sydney, Melbourne, Perth, Adelaide, Brisbane and Newcastle, the visiting cricketer in these days sees only one part of Australia. With Wally Hammond's side we travelled by train taking 36 hours to cross from Perth to Adelaide. Air-conditioning had yet to arrive either in train compartments or hotels. But who cared? It was the experience of a lifetime, and no one was in the hurry of today.

Now there is no time in the helter-skelter itinerary to play up-country matches, a fact which I much deplore. Playing against country districts teams gave tourists an opportunity to see another side of life, served as a fillip to local cricket (and were not Sir Don Bradman and Bill O'Reilly among greats who originally came from the country?) and extended the bonds of friendship. I always thought the festive atmosphere and the marvellous meals and hospitality said a lot about the Australian people.

In 1962–63 I was assistant to the late Duke of Norfolk, whose appointment to manage the England team provoked unusual interest, as was to be expected. It is not every tour that the Premier Duke and Earl Marshal of England acts as a cricket manager! He loved the up-country occasions from the moment he went to Kalgoorlie and had to queue for his morning shower at the hotel's communal wash house.

He was less impressed, however, at the end of another match when he was persuaded to attend a 'special' reception at which he was to be offered a present. He wasn't prepared to be taken 20 or so miles

Alec Bedser (left) watches Alan 'Davo' Davidson welcome Mike Denness (right) to Australia.

away and, after some speeches, the now-tired Duke was handed his present — an empty jar said to contain 'our fresh air'!

One local umpire persistently no-balled John Snow, England's fast bowler, for over-stepping. At last John turned and said, 'Give me a break, this isn't a Test match you know'. The umpire replied without hesitation, 'It is for me, mate!' Ah, happy days, those matches.

Australia's grounds and pitches have also changed much in my time. When I first bowled there the pitches were bone hard without any grass — like a bald man's pate. After a few overs the shine on the ball had gone and eventually, perhaps after 50 overs, it resembled a piece of rag. Every side, too, had a leg spinner and an off spinner or a slow left arm bowler was a rarity. The leg spinner banked on getting turn as the match progressed and, importantly, he could get a degree of bounce which, over the years, defeated many of England's finest batsmen. It was unheard of for an off spinner to turn the ball as they are able to do now. For many years England never thought of choosing an off break bowler for Australian conditions.

The essential difference between the batsmen of the two countries in playing leg spin was that the Australians were prepared to leave the crease. The English played from within the crease and now it is a valid criticism to say that hardly any batsmen use their feet to attack slow bowlers.

I have to say I preferred the Sydney ground before the advent of floodlights and I have a special affection for Adelaide, a truly lovely ground, and if somebody whispers 'isn't that where you bowled the Don for a duck', I would nod with pride. I had my triumphs and failures against Australia and I count my old adversaries on the field as some of my most cherished friends.

And isn't that what Test cricket should be all about?

'. . . I was one of the crowd that was to witness the second day's cricket in the ninth Test match . . .'

The greatest test match

Sir Neville Cardus

A remarkable late 19th century photograph showing spectators outside Lord's Pavilion in the heyday of W. G. Grace. The celebrated doctor is seen in the foreground in striped blazer, and beard.

On a bright day in the spring of 1921 I went to Lord's, hoping to see the first practice of the Australians. But the place was deserted, save for the man at the gates. He told me Armstrong's men were being entertained that afternoon somewhere in the City and that they wouldn't be in the nets till after tea. Still, he added, with a touch of human nature not too common at Lord's, if I liked I could enter the ground and sit and enjoy myself in the sun till they came.

I sat on a bench with my feet spread out so that they touched the soft grass. A great calm was over the field. The trees beyond the Nursery were delicate with fresh green and the fine old pavilion seemed to nod in the sunshine. It was an occasion for a reverie and I fell to affectionate thoughts upon the great days of cricket, of the history that had been made on the field which stretched before me. I thought of Grace, of Spofforth, of Hornby, of A. G. Steel . . . maybe I dozed for a while. Then I was conscious of a voice. 'Would you mind moving up a little? This seat is rather congested.' I

looked around and saw sitting by my side a man in a tight black coat which buttoned high on his chest. He had sidewhiskers and wore a low turned-down collar and a high bowler hat. A handkerchief was showing from a breast pocket in his jacket. Not quite awake yet, I moved up. 'Thank you,' he said. "I'm sorry I disturbed you. A nap carries one comfortably through a long wait at these matches. What a crowd there is!' I looked round. I was in the middle of a big crowd indeed. In front of me sat a parson. He was reading *The Times*. I glanced over his shoulder and saw the headline: 'Egyptian Campaign: Sir G. Wolseley's Dispatch.' The man at my side said, 'Were you here yesterday, sir?' and before I could reply he added, 'It was a considerable day's cricket, and the *Post* has an excellent account. Perhaps you've seen it?' He handed me a copy of the *Morning Post* and, thanking him, I took it. The paper was dated 29 August 1882. In a column headed 'England v. Australia' I read that, on the day before, Australia had been dismissed for 63 by Barlow and Peate, and that England, captained by A. N. Hornby, had made 101 in reply. Then I understood my situation. And what is more I now understood it without the slightest astonishment. Even the aspect of the ground, which told me it was Kennington Oval and not Lord's, did not embarrass me. It was enough that I was one of the crowd that was to witness the second day's cricket in the ninth Test match — the most famous Test match of all.

I gave the *Post* back to my companion in silence. 'A considerable day's cricket indeed, sir,' said the parson. 'But England ought to have made more runs. Our batting was distinctly mediocre — almost as bad as the Australians'.' A loud cheer disturbed his argument. Down the pavilion steps walked the England Eleven in single file, led by Hornby. With him was 'W. G.', and he passed along the field with an ambling motion and the wind got into his great black beard. He spoke to Hornby in a high-pitched voice and laughed. Then he threw the ball to a tall graceful player just behind him and cried, 'Catch her, Bunny'. Following Grace and Hornby were Lucas, C. T. Studd, J. M. Read, the Hon. A. Lyttelton, Ulyett, Barlow, W. Barnes, A. G. Steel and Peate. The crowd quietened, awaiting the advent of Australia's first two batsmen, and I again heard the parson's voice '. . . The English total was distressingly poor. Rarely have I seen poorer batting from an All-England Eleven. The fact is, sir, that for some little time now English cricket has been deteriorating. Our batsmen don't hit the ball as hard as they used to do, and even our bowling . . .' Another cheer drowned his discourse. 'Bannerman and Massie,' said my companion. 'I should imagine Bannerman's the youngest man in the match.' The parson was prompt with his correction. 'I believe S. P. Jones, who was 21 on the first of the month, is the junior member of the two teams. Studd is, I fancy, 11 months older than Jones. Bannerman is 23 at least, and Giffen is six days younger than Bannerman.' My companion was silenced, but I ventured a question. 'How old is Spofforth?' Pat came the answer, 'Twenty-seven on the ninth of next month'.

'No, you be Denis Compton — I'll be Neville Cardus.' Cartoon by Bernard Hollowood

243

The crowd, including even the parson, went as quiet as a mouse as Barlow began the English bowling to Bannerman. Lyttelton, behind the wicket, crouched low. It was exactly a quarter past 12. The next half-hour was a tumultuous prelude to the day. Bannerman was all vigilance, while Massie played one of the great innings of Test cricket. He hurled his bat at every ball the slightest loose and his hits crashed ponderously to the boundary. He was the living image of defiance as he faced the Englishmen, glaring round the field his challenge. At one huge drive from Barlow's bowling my companion murmured, 'I've never seen a bigger hit than that at the Oval'. But the parson overheard him. 'When the Australians were here in '78,' he said, 'W. H. Game, playing for Surrey, hit a ball from Spofforth to square-leg right out of the ground.' Still, he admitted, this Massie fellow hit them quite hard enough. In half an hour England's advantage of 38 was gone. Hornby called up bowler after bowler, Studd for Barlow, Barnes for Studd. Steel tried his hand at 56 — the sixth bowler in less than three-quarters of an hour. When Australia's score was 47 Massie lifted a ball to long-on. 'Lucas is there,' said the parson, 'he'll get it all r---. Good Lord!' For Lucas dropped the ball and blushed red as the crowd groaned out of its soul.

'Sixty-six for none,' murmured the man at my side, 'they're 28 on with all their wickets intact. If Massie prevails — ah, bravo, sir; well bowled, well bowled!' A ball from Steel had tempted Massie and just as he jumped out it broke back and wrecked the wicket. Massie walked to the pavilion, roared home by an admiring but much relieved crowd. His innings was worth 55 to Australia, made out of 66 in less than an hour.

Bonnor came next and the English outfields dropped deep and had apprehensive thoughts. Would not Massie's example make this bearded giant a very Jehu? But Hornby has an inspiration. He asks Ulyett to bowl instead of Steel. And Ulyett moves to the wicket like a man ploughing against a breaker, puts the last ounce of his Yorkshire strength into a thunderbolt of a ball that sends Bonnor's middle stump flying. The crowd is only just getting back the breath lost in approval of this feat when Bannerman is caught by Studd at extra mid-off. Bannerman has batted 70 minutes for 13. 'Quick work for him!' says the parson. And with the broad bat of Bannerman out of the way the English bowlers begin to see daylight. Peate's slow left-hand deliveries spin beautifully, as though controlled by a string. The Australians now, save Murdoch, are just guessing. The fourth wicket falls at 75, the fifth at 79. Australia are all out 122. 'Only 85 to win,' says the parson. 'It's our game after all, though Lucas did his best to lose it.'

It was a true autumn afternoon going to its fall in grey light when 'W. G.' and Hornby went to the wicket to face Spofforth and Garratt. The crowd filled the ground, but so silent was it as Grace took his guard that one could hear the tink-tink of a hansom cab coming closer and closer along the Vauxhall Road. Spofforth's first over was fast — he let the ball go with a quick leap, dropping his arm at the moment of release. Blackham 'stood back' when Grace was batting, but crept up for Hornby. 'Beautiful wicket-keeping,' murmured my companion. 'Pinder was not less gifted,' said the parson. And he added, 'I have not seen Spofforth bowl as fast as this for some time. He has latterly cultivated medium-pace variations'. Both Hornby and Grace began confidently, and at once the tension lifted. Hornby made a lovely cut from Spofforth and a dainty leg stroke for a couple.

Spofforth uprooted Hornby's off stump with England's score 15 and with his next ball clean bowled Barlow. The crowd gave out a suspicion of a shiver, but the advent of bluff George Ulyett was reassuring, especially as Grace welcomed him with a fine leg hit from Garratt for three and a beautiful on-drive to the boundary from Spofforth. 'Thirty up,' said my companion, 'only 55 to get.' England was still 30 for two men; Spofforth crossed over to the pavilion end. Now I was behind his arm; I could see his superb break-back. And he bowled mainly medium pace this time. With each off-break I could see his right hand, at the end of the swing over, finish near the left side, 'cutting' under the ball. Sometimes his arm went straight over and continued straight down in the follow-through — and then the batsman had to tackle fierce top-spin. There was the sense of the inimical in his aspect now. He seemed taller than he was a half-hour ago, the right arm of him more sinuous. There was no excitement in him; he was, the parson said, cold-blooded. Still Ulyett faced him bravely with Grace, at the other end, time after time moved from his crease with a solid left leg and pushed the ball away usefully. 'Fifty up,' said my companion, 'for two wickets. It's all over — we want only 34 now.' And at 51 Spofforth bowled a very fast one to Ulyett, who barely snicked it. It served though; Blackman snapped the catch, and his 'H'zat!' was hoarse and aggressive. Lucas came in, and with two runs more 'W. G.' was caught at mid-off. 'What a stroke,' said the parson. 'I'm afraid he's not the Grace he was.' Four for 53 and Lyttelton and Lucas in. Lyttelton hits out big-heartedly, but the field is like a net tightly drawn. It is suddenly understood by every man of us that the game is in the balance. 'The wicket must be bad,' says somebody.

Lucas stonewalls, with a bat as straight as a die. Spofforth bowls a maiden; Boyle bowls a maiden; Spofforth bowls another maiden. The air is growing thick. 'Get runs or get out, for the Lord's sake,' says somebody. The field creeps closer and closer to the wicket. Spofforth and Boyle are like uncanny automatons, bowling, bowling . . . Six successive maidens. 'This,' said the parson, 'This is intolerable.' One's heart is aching for a honest boundary hit . . . And the human bowling machines send down six more successive maidens. Think of it; 12 successive maidens, and the game in that state, the crowd in that purgatory. 'When Grace was a boy of 18 I saw him make 50 on this very ground and he played every ball he got.' It was the parson again, but he sounded a little strained, a little unhappy. At the end of the twelfth successive maiden, a hit was purposely misfielded that Spofforth might have a 'go' at Lyttelton. The batsman fell into the snare.

Four more maidens, and spinning is Lyttelton's wicket. 'Anyhow, that's over and done with!' thankfully breathes the crowd. Better all be dead than dying! England five for 66 — 19 needed. Steel comes next and Lucas hits a boundary. Roars the crowd 'Bravo!' then catches its breath. Steel caught and bowled Spofforth none — Maurice Read clean bowled second ball. England seven for 70. 'Incredible!' say 20 000 people in dismal unison. Barnes, the next man, hits a two. Thirteen to win. Heaven bless us, Blackman has blundered! He allows three byes. Run Barnes, run Lucas! Spofforth is inscrutable as the crowd makes its noises. His next ball is too fast for eyes at the boundary's edge to see. Lucas comes down on it, though — hard and determined. And the ball rolls ever so gently on to the wicket and disturbs the bails. Poor Lucas bows his head and departs, and blasphemy is riot throughout the crowd and is communicated by stages to the outer darkness of Kennington Road. The stars are set against England — our cricketers are for the first time on English soil face to face with a victorious Australian XI. With 10 to struggle for, Blackman catches Barnes off his glove, and the last man is here — poor Peate, who is the best slow bowler in England and not a bit more of a cricketer than that, and what good are his mysteries of spin now? Studd is there yet, though; only 10 runs and it is our game. Perhaps *he* — Peate has hit a two. It was audacious, but maybe the ball was a safe one to tackle. A bad ball's a bad ball at any time. Peate has nerve (so we are telling ourselves, desperately): he's the right man: he'll play the steady game to good stuff and leave the job to Studd . . . The stark truth is that Peate hit out wildly yet again at a slow from Boyle, missed it, and was bowled. There was a hollow laugh somewhere as the wicket went back, but whether it came from this world or the next I couldn't say. Studd did not get a ball. 'Why, man, did you try to hit: why couldn't you just stop them?' they asked Peate. 'Well,' he replied, 'I couldn't trust Maister Studd!'

As Peate's wicket was broken, ten thousand people rushed the rails and hid the green field. Spofforth was carried shoulder-high to the pavilion and there the mob praised a famous man. I, too, wanted to get up and shout, but somehow I was rooted to my seat. I was probably the only man in that multitude on the pavilion not standing up, and as I sat there I had a strange sense of making a lonely hole in a solid black mass. The parson was standing on the seat beside me. His boots were not more than two feet from my eyes and I could see the fine ribbed work on the upper edge of the soles. The cheering came downwards to me, sounding remote. I lost grip on events. It seemed that I sat there till the ground was almost deserted, till over the field came a faint mist, and with it the vague melancholy of twilight in a great city. Time to go home, I thought . . . a great match . . . great days . . . great men . . . all gone . . . far away . . . departed glory . . . A hand of someone touched my shoulder and I heard him say: 'The Orsetralians are on the way and they'll be in the nets at four o'clock. Nice in the sun, isn't it?'

The legendary Hornby.

'But the passengers were counting on playing their own trump card. For their skipper had scoured the passenger lists and found the magic name: F. H. Tyson. When the "Typhoon" raged, the officers' stumps and all their hopes would be shattered.'

Cricket at sea

(or How they stopped the Typhoon Raging)

Ewan Letts

Ewan Letts and his sassy Taverners' tie.

In the original *Boundary Book*, John Clarke's story of a sea voyage to Australia with the MCC touched fleetingly on the bookmaking and pool-combing successes of England fast bowler Frank Tyson. It also referred to the ship's captain's order that first class passengers should keep out of the tourist section, where especially cricketers 'had been known to find congenial company and less formality than forrard'.

Taking advantage of the rule allowing the Archives to be opened after 30 years, I can now reveal that the 'no mixing' order worked very rigidly in the other direction during the *Orsova*'s journey to Europe in early 1958. That is, it worked rigidly when it suited the cricketing ambitions of the British vessel's officers.

It began with Lord Nuffield's cocktail party. The motor magnate was a regular sailor between England and the Antipodes. He was the most approachable of men, especially when resting from one of his daily marathons around the upper decks. He was also an enthusiast for England's cricket achievers and thus looked forward to the pleasure of the company of his country's fastest bowler at the reception which Nuffield gave jointly with a group of Australian naval officers on their way to training at Portsmouth.

The invitations were duly issued. Obscure officials and other Government-paid freeloaders in first class received one. So, naturally, did Frank Tyson, who was taking his Australian bride to his native land and had a cabin in the tourist class. It never entered the hosts' heads that a man who had made the doughtiest Australian batsmen tremble in their Stamina creams — Ian Chappell is even said to have forgotten to adjust his box when facing the 'Typhoon' — would be stumped by the boycott of a pretentious, pink-faced Orient Line purser.

But so it happened. The pink purser said no to the cocktail appearance of the touring Tysons. Appeals over his head to the captain brought no change of heart. This boycott, like its Yorkshire namesake, was immovable.

The disappointment shook Nuffield to his foundations. He began to circumperambulate 'A' deck in the reverse, anti-clockwise direction, pausing only to toss the occasional tarred quoit through the purser's (unopened) porthole. No one knew then that worse, much worse was to come.

The real highlight of the sporting and social calendar on the good ship *Orsova* was the cricket match: Passengers XI versus Ship's Officers. The game was played under a strong rope net pitched high above the players' heads and fastened between the funnel and poles projecting from the ship's railing. The rubber ball used was thus able to be saved from a watery resting place in the Indian Ocean and the players were spared the indignity of donning life-belts before attempting a diving catch, or launching the life-boats after one.

The officers, all British, were togged out in splendid uniforms, carefully pressed by the domestic staff. They were very jealous of their appearance and their playing reputations. The passengers, mostly Australians, were a mixed bag of young and old, attired in a motley collection of jerkins, jeans, and gym shoes. They lacked the cachet of their opposition; an unkind steward said they would have trouble catching anything except a tropical disease.

But the passengers were counting on playing their own trump card. For their skipper had scoured the passenger lists and found the magic name: F. H. Tyson. When the 'Typhoon' raged, the officers' stumps and all their hopes would be shattered.

With the artlessness of the true amateur, the passenger skipper gave the officers the courtesy of his team list before the match. With the ruthlessness of professionals, the officers struck out one name, *the* name, and sent the list back. Without a ball being bowled, Tyson was dismissed.

Quickly the land-lubbers formed a delegation. The nets had almost been erected on deck before the ship's captain received them: 'Delighted that you have mounted a challenge for the *Orsova* Ashes, but I can't change the company rules. You will have to replace that tourist class ring-in with someone from first class.'

The calm of disappointment descended on the passengers, the calm before the storm which never broke. The time bomb was defused, the secret weapon disarmed without the firing of a shot.

The officers prevailed, of course: 6 for 90 declared v. 75 all out. One passenger player, an Irishman, had tried to sneak beneath the stone-walling purser's guard by bowling under-arm, but was ruled out of order by the sole umpire, an Anglo-Catholic priest. The cleric, who saw himself as one of the ship's company, turned out to be more Anglo than Catholic in his sympathies.

So Britannia continued briefly to rule the waves, and the wickets above them. But the skulduggery of her methods was not lost on the defeated passengers. Nor was it lost on Prometheus chained, the feared and shunned Frank Tyson. Between clenched teeth, he made a vow to return Down Under and train Aussie quicks to beat England.

He kept the vow. Some say he composed the dirge of the '70s, intoned behind the backs of departing England batsmen:

> 'Ashes to ashes, dust to dust.
> If Lillee don't get you, Thomson must.'

I think the credit for that really belonged to a leading Australian cartoonist. But the inspiration, the breath that fanned the Australian bushfires, was Frank's.

And now you know what caused the nemesis. It was the high-handed hubris of British officers who thought they could tame a typhoon. In the end, they reaped the whirlwind.

Ewan Letts, is Secretary of the Lord's Taverners, Australian Capital Territory. Frank Tyson was until 1987 President of the Lord's Taverners, Victoria.

'Note, again, that Melbourne was several steps ahead of Lord's. Marylebone were not responsible for an English touring team to Australia until they sent Plum Warner's in 1903.'

The Melbourne age of cricket

E. W. Swanton

Considering that cricket was so well-established a pastime in England in the 18th century (its origins, of course, go back as far as 1300), it is significant how much of the impetus behind the early Anglo-Australian contests came from Australia, and in particular from Melbourne. It was the colonials who seem to have made most of the running; who attracted the leading professionals to bring teams, playing first against odds; who employed them as coaches; and who eventually enticed across the world W. G. Grace himself — at a price. In 1872 East Melbourne and South Melbourne combined with the Melbourne Cricket Club to guarantee £1500 plus expenses for the doctor, £170 apiece for the pros. But, lo, is it not all written — this rather shaming detail included — in Keith Dunstan's classic history, *The Paddock that Grew?*

However 'W.G.' did his stuff. A tour not without its disputes multiplied Australian enthusiasm, which in turn led to the accommodation of larger crowds. And so it was that in 1877, a mere 40 years or so after John Batman had proclaimed the first village settlement on the banks of the Yarra, it was the Cricket Club of Melbourne, not Marylebone, that staged the first instalment of the most famous serial in the history of sport.

Note that it was men rather than representative institutions who were the early organisers of international cricket, Melbourne Cricket Club apart. It was James Lillywhite's initiative that brought the 1876–77 side to Australia and which organised the Australian visit to England in the following year. Lord Harris followed Lillywhite, and then came the Hon. Ivo Bligh and the story (by now surely a little tedious) of the urn and the ashes.

'The Australians loved Ivo Bligh,' so Dunstan tells us, 'and this was the happiest of all tours' — his book was with the printers, by the way, when Frank Worrell and Richie Benaud were contesting the great series that set the modern standards in sportsmanship and high endeavour. Moreover Bligh, like many a sensible Englishman since, married an Australian girl, and it was largely he who persuaded the Melbourne Cricket

Club to undertake the responsibility for overseas tours. Thus there enters the formidable figure of Ian Johnson's predecessor at only the second remove, Major Ben Wardill, secretary of MCC 1878–1911, manager of the Australians in England in 1886 and often thereafter.

Note, again, that Melbourne was several steps ahead of Lord's. Marylebone were not responsible for an English touring team to Australia until they sent Plum Warner's in 1903. Since then, of course, cricket has been democratised to the extent that the English ruling body is now the Cricket Council while at the turn of the century Australia — and with what difficulty and heart-burnings — set up its Board of Control.

One might speculate, by the way, why recently the 'Control' has been dropped, but I am due to move on and to salute the game and the players of today and yesterday as I have known them in the 30 years bar one of my visits to Australia.

It is usually the first impressions that stick longest and my abiding memory of the Melbourne Cricket Ground is of the start of the Victoria-MCC match in '46: a workday Thursday it was, 31 October, and near 30,000 somehow got there to see Walter Hammond's team and in particular the two men they had been waiting to appraise ever since they had made history against Don Bradman's side of '38. Len Hutton had been only 22, Denis Compton just 20, when each made hundreds in their first Tests, at Trent Bridge. Denis next had saved his side at Lord's, and then Len at the Oval had even put the Don's 334 in the shade.

England were outplayed in 1946–47 (out-led chiefly), but these two great batsmen, applauded on that Melbourne morning all the way to the middle, took 151 not out and 143 respectively against Victoria, Denis in the first innings, Len in the second. The warmth of their greeting was surely, as it seemed at the time, a reflection, with a special Melbourne emphasis, of the appreciation felt by all Australians of burdens lately shared and perils overcome.

Raucous though they can be, I have never since that

Colin Cowdrey has spread himself a little since Jim Swanton's observation. Here is Cowdrey as seen by comedian and caricaturist Willy Rushton, a faithful Lord's Taverner in England.

first occasion had cause to doubt the generosity of the Melbourne crowd, whether in victory or defeat. I think of the second Test of 1950-51, an agonising game won by Australia by 28 runs though the crowd surely (my memory can't be all that senile?) were *willing* England home because they had been cruelly robbed by the storms at Brisbane.

Colin Cowdrey's reception (aged 22, 102 out of 191 all out) in the first of the Melbourne Tests of 1954-55: Frank Tyson's devastation a few mornings later: Cowdrey again, with Ted Dexter, the future Lord Bishop of Liverpool, and Fred Trueman sharing the honours of a great win in 1962-63: and not least England's extraordinary innings win wherein Mike Denness settled a few accounts in the last match of my reporting life a few years ago: *of course*, human nature being what it is, it's the victories one remembers.

Another reason is that they've been fairly infrequent. In the eight tours since the war I've seen Australia win 18 times to England's nine, with 15 draws. That cannot be accounted for in a few words, but at least I have the chance to salute a few of those whose marvellous skill and personality and aggressive sense have upheld the high standard of Australian cricket in my time.

One can only begin with Sir Donald, whose successive feats in 1930 in England I saw and marvelled at. He says that that 254 at Lord's was his best innings, and no one ever doubted it, least of all the England XI. Quickness of eye and foot, unerring judgement, uncanny reaction to danger, and apparently inexhaustible stamina were the ingredients of his batsmanship: all this and a mighty strong will to succeed.

The Don and the finest of all spinning combinations as between Clarrie Grimmett and Bill O'Reilly dominated Australian cricket in the 1930s. Afterwards, to England's discomfiture, the little man girded himself for the fray once more, and built around his experience and unique prestige a talented and invincible side. Since the war Australia's chief advantage has been the presence until lately of two and often three all-rounders of the highest class. You can scarcely pick an indifferent side if you start with Ray Lindwall, Keith Miller and Richie Benaud. And in Richie, right out of the blue, a captain emerged in the Bradman class.

Twice Alan Davidson, young and coming-up, played for Australia with all three of these in Test Matches — as fine an all-round quartet as ever played simultaneously for any country. To the Englishman brought up on the steadier fare of county cricket there is generally an enviable flair about the top-ranking Australians. Partly, of course, it is the warmth and the climate and the true pitches which encourage both batsmen and bowlers to attack. Certainly the crowds, impatient for action, are less easily satisfied than those at home.

How I got Compton out twice in an innings

John Cleese

John Cleese.

'So why should we listen to your opinion on the subject of cricket?' you ask. Well, I'll tell you why. Because I once got Denis Compton out twice in an innings, *that's* why. '*Twice* in an innings?!' you cry.

Now, I should make it clear that I believe that getting Denis out once in an innings would not be that much to write home about. A cause for momentary joy certainly, particularly in 1947, but not something that one would necessarily want on one's gravestone. After all, a lot of people have done it. Lindwall, Miller, Bedser, Laker and Bertie Buse, to name a few. But to dismiss the brilliantined genius twice in one knock is something else. Here is how it happened.

Denis came down to play against Clifton College, a West Country sports academy, in 1958. His son was a pupil there. So was I, I was in the team as a slow off-spinner, because during June I was more or less unplayable. This was because for these four weeks the pitches were in line with a huge red-brick building called School Hall. Being six foot five, my arm cleared the sight-screen easily and so if I bowled the ball from the right end with the right trajectory the batsman was lucky to get so much as a late glimpse of it. During June, this was. Compton came in July.

He'd been in about 10 minutes when I was called upon to bowl. He'd not had much of the strike and needed about four for his 50. He was coming down the wicket in a way I'd never seen before. In first-class cricket I'd seen him leave his crease as the bowler bowled. On this day he was setting off at about the same moment that the bowler started his run-up. There was a danger with the quickies that he was going to strike the ball before it left the bowler's hand. I'm very sorry, I'm exaggerating. Let's just say he was non-creasebound as it is possible to be.

As an off-spinner I had one advantage over and about School Hall. That was our coach, Reg Sinfield, ex-Gloucs and England. He was quite my favourite person at Clifton, funny and wise and kind. I'm afraid he showed most of the masters up dreadfully. Anyway, Reg had told me to bowl very wide at any batsman running down the wicket, so just before my first over I said to the wicket-keeper, One Pickwoad, 'Third ball, I'll bowl him a very wide one. Be ready for it, we might get a stumping.' 'You can bowl him a wide one if you like,' said Pickwoad, 'but I'm not stumping him. I want to watch him bat.' This was a blow.

I don't remember what happened to my first two deliveries, but they were eventually retrieved. I ran up to bowl the third ball. Denis Compton left his crease and I bowled him a wide one; so wide that it surprised him, passing him yards down the wicket. It pitched, leaving him stranded, and proceeded at a gentle pace and comfortable height towards the waiting Pickwoad. Pickwoad calmly rotated his wrists through 180 degrees and thrust the back of his gloves at the ball. The ball shot up in the air. 'Damn!' cried Pickwoad towards the master-in-charge, umpiring at square leg. But to my amazement the ball landed, spun sideways and bumped against the stumps, dislodging a bail, with the King of the Sweep still yards out of his ground. I'd got him.

Time passed. I became aware of a strange stillness. It occurred to me that no one had appealed. Denis had wandered back to his crease and now stood there, slightly puzzled. Pickwoad was replacing the bail. The other fielders seemed absorbed in their personal problems. Pickwoad picked the ball up and tossed it back to me. 'Bad luck,' he called. Then I realised I'd blown my chance. If I'd appealed straight away it could have been put down to youthful excitement. But to do so now was cold-bloodedly to spoil everyone's afternoon. I'd got Compton out and no one would ever know. It was a sad moment. I turned, walked back to my mark, ran up and bowled the next ball, a slow, high full toss on the leg stump. Spectactors started taking cover.

Whether Denis was distracted by the sight of a bowler openly weeping in his delivery stride, or

Vicky in the News Chronicle

whether he took it upon himself to right this particular wrong, I shall never know, but painstakingly he hit a catch to mid-on. Mid-on was Ken Whitty, playing in his first match for the XI and consequently the only other man in the ground with an interest in the catch being taken. Had the ball been edged to Pickwoad, it would no doubt have been thrown over the sightscreen for six. Whitty grabbed glazedly at the ball and suddenly stood there triumphant, the ball securely wedged between his chin and his forearm.

Compton, D.C.S. c White b Cheese, the *Bristol Evening Post* later announced . . .

P.S. Pickwoad now lives in Canada. Serves him right.

253

'Father Done also received some favourable treatment when he was reinstated to the wicket after being bowled. Umpire Kingston later explained it was a no ball, but even divine intervention could not help Father when he was caught minutes later by a country fieldsman.'

A wish for my sons is a love of the game
That my dad passed on to me.
May I do for my sons . . .
What he did for his sons, all three.

— *William M. Ellwood*

Bush cricket — the home of enthusiasm and humour

Ian Ferguson

Ian Ferguson.

Bill Ellwood is a farmer from Bethanga on the Victoria and New South Wales border in southern Australia. He was a fine player in the Albury and Border Cricket Association during the 1920s and 1930s, and he has always had a deep affection for the game.

This verse is from his poem 'Cricket Memories'. It echoes the great enthusiasm millions have felt for cricket all over Australia since the earliest days.

Lachlan Macquarie, Governor of NSW from 1810 to 1821, was one of the early enthusiasts. He was keen to have fine, substantial buildings erected in early Sydney town. Cricket was also a priority and he encouraged his son to play from an early age. The Governor even commissioned a local carpenter to fashion a cricket bat from native Australian timber for the exclusive use of his son.

The young colony had a passion for cricket. By 1862, the first English team to visit our shores arrived in the famous Victorian gold mining town of Ballarat for one of their early games of the tour. The England XI had travelled by horse and cart from Geelong. When they arrived at Buninyong, on the outskirts of Ballarat, they were met by the strongest team that the locals could select — all 22 of them.

Together the two teams 'partook of ginger beer and apples to the joy of a large excited crowd', said the *Ballarat Star*. The English players were agreeably surprised by such a spontaneously warm welcome, which almost reached the status of a royal visit when the accompanying bands from Ballarat played 'Rule Britannia' and 'See the Conquering Hero Comes' as the team travelled on to their destination, 'cheered all along the way by an excited population'.

A public holiday was declared in honour of the match at Ballarat's Eastern Oval, and Sam Costick, representing the local 22, distinguished himself by 'flogging a sixer over the grandstand'.

This first English tour of Australia was a great success, even though our convivial hospitality was apparently more impressive than our cricket standards. 'Oi doan't think mooch of their play, but they're a wonderful lot of drinking men,' was England player Roger Iddison's comment on his return home at the end of the tour.

Big Victorian rural crowds also enjoyed matches at Sandhurst (Bendigo) and Ararat on the next England tour in 1864. It was reported that one country cricket enthusiast walked nearly 300 miles to see the return Ballarat match against England. If this devotee of the great game had read the *Ballarat Star*'s report about that 1864 match, he would have noted that Englishman Bob Carpenter was given not out caught during the game because the umpire decreed that it was a 'bum ball'!

The third England cricket tour to Australia in 1873–74 was captained by the legendary W. G. Grace, who vividly recalled the match he played at Ballarat that season. 'It was about the hottest day in which I ever played cricket,' said 'W. G.' 'The heat was almost unbearable, dry sultry and exhausting. The seats for spectators became so hot that people wouldn't sit on them.' The local writer agreed: 'The sun shone infernally, the XI [England] scored tremendously [470], we fielded abominably, and we all drank excessively.'

During that same tour, Grace's team also played in the Victorian town of Stawell, and 'W. G.' was unimpressed by the playing conditions. He enquired where the wicket was when he walked on to the ground and the locals told him, 'You're standing on it'.

England suffered a memorable defeat in that match, as Stawell won by 10 wickets. *Scores and Biographies* said, 'The wickets were simply disgusting, newly made

and no grass on' and cricket historian Jack Pollard still cannot believe the result. 'It was unbelievable,' he wrote. 'The might of England beaten by a country town!'

In far more recent times, other international teams have also struck rare playing conditions at country town venues. In February 1964, a southern New South Wales team played South Africa at Cooma in conditions that were almost as unbelievable. The afternoon before the game, a violent rain and hailstorm saturated the Cooma showgrounds, which had been in perfect condition for the town's first international cricket match. Parts of the oval were under water, after 100 points of rain. The local organising committee, under the leadership of John Whitehead, refused to allow the elements to defeat them. That night at the floodlit Cooma showgrounds, Whitehead and his volunteer helpers toiled until midnight, painstakingly sponge-drying the wet outfield with hessian bags. So desperate were they for Cooma's inaugural international match to proceed, that they even soaked the pitch with petrol and set it on fire in an effort to absorb the moisture! The gamble succeeded — the surface of the wicket was dry in an hour.

Early next morning the volunteer workforce was on hand again, spreading sawdust on the bowling approaches and rolling their 'barbecued' wicket. Miraculously, the game was able to start shortly after 1 p.m. The Springboks must have considered the wicket would still contain plenty of fire. They insisted that southern NSW bat first — even though the country captain had won the toss! Batting first was far from an easy task and the Country XI was bowled out for 117.

There were many memorable performances in this game. Bob Le Fevre, a 20-year-old leg spinner from the Snowy Mountains town of Tumut, captured two wickets in two balls, before finishing with the splendid figures of 4 for 22. Denis Lindsay, the South African wicket-keeper batsman, also delighted the crowd of about 3000 with some powerhouse hitting which brought him four huge sixes in his innings of 35. All of these highlights, however, fade away compared to the

A sign of the times.

image of those flames leaping from the Cooma pitch on the eve of that eventful match.

There has not been an international cricket game at Cooma since 1964. Perhaps the locals' unique method of salvaging rain-affected wickets produces a surface that is too fiery for any touring team to handle. However those rural Australians must be given credit for their ingenuity.

Cricket had become a part of our nationalism, our Australian way of life, as early as the 1860s. 'Not to be interested in cricket,' wrote R. E. N Twopenny in *The Coming Australia*, amounts to a social crime.'

The earliest recorded bush cricket games in Tasmania were in the Macquarie Valley, just west of Campbell Town in the early 1830s. By the 1860s the game was popular in South Australian bush towns such as Jamestown, Gawler, Orroroo and Kadina and as the 19th century progressed, rural cricket became increasingly popular right across this huge continent.

By the early 1900s, West Australian Jack Rogers was exhibiting this keenness for cricket that many fellow Australians in country areas came to share. His daughter, Mrs Betty Loukes, now lives in Bunbury and she remembers her father rising at 4.30 a.m. to milk the cows by hand before he set off in a horse and cart to captain the Scotsdale cricket team. When Jack arrived

home after the game at about 7 p.m., he knew the cows would be there, waiting to be milked once more.

A decade later, and on the other side of the continent in central NSW, Ray Buckley would think nothing of saddling up his horse after a hard day's work on the farm to ride eight miles and practise cricket with the Webb brothers, Merrick and Gwynn of Tarana. They laid mats over a gravel pitch fashioned on the family farm near Bathurst and would play together long into the summer evenings. Ray Buckley's keenness was well rewarded — his fast bowling prowess earned him the local nickname of 'Terror'. Today, bush cricketers all over Australia exude similar enthusiasm for the game.

George Smith and his son Kim from Western Australia are modern-day examples of dedicated bush cricketers. They have to travel at least 100 km over some rugged, rough, unsealed roads, in the searing heat to represent the Sandstone Cricket Club in the north-eastern Goldfields region. They are celebrity players in the area. When they are available, Sandstone usually win. But when they are not, the town's XI expects the worse.

Grafton cricket administrator Eric Brumby was so dedicated that when the North Coast played NSW at Grafton's Fisher Park in October 1951, he slept the night on the eve of the game near the pitch, to ensure the sacred turf would not be touched. Fisher Park in Grafton also had special significance for Ted Haggar, a former president and umpire in the Upper Clarence Cricket Association. After his death, his ashes were scattered over his beloved cricket ground, fulfilling his last request.

This same enthusiasm for the game has been consistently shown by women throughout country Australia. When the first women's cricket match in Australia was played at Bendigo in 1874, the players — all miner's daughters — wore long calico dresses and red and blue tops. By the 1890s, strong teams were established such as the Warrnambool 'Forget-Me-Nots' from Allansford, the 'Snowflakes' from Garvoc and the 'Seafoams' from Nirranda. Women were warned to tie their hats securely. Catches were often dropped when women tried to hold their hats in one hand and take a catch with the other! Some tried to stop the ball with their petticoats — a practice considered unsporting.

In one of the earlier games recorded in Australian women's cricket history, the 'Forget-Me-Nots' played the Avoca Fire Brigade men's cricket team. The gents had to bat, field and catch with their left hands and bowl nothing more than right-arm under-arms. The girls, resplendent in costumes of cream flannel with pale blue ties and sashes, won 18 boundary hits to eight, but the scores could have been closer as several of the fire brigade XI, including their captain, had to leave early to catch the steamer to Melbourne.

There was so much regular competition that the Victorian Women's Cricket Association was formed in 1905 and a State match against Tasmania organised. And in 1927 the New South Wales Women's Cricket Association was founded. By the 1930s, Jean Williams and other young women in the western part of that State participated in Mumford Cup games.

During those years Jean Williams had many happy and successful times in country cricket. She remembers sitting with her teammates, on a long stool in the back of a truck, travelling with the Gilgandra women's side to various cricket venues. Some of the ovals were very rough. One ground was called 'the scalded plain' because of the complete absence of grass on the oval's parched surface. Jean overcame the difficult playing conditions to become the best woman all-rounder in western New South Wales. She scored 215 not out against Dubbo in one Mumford Cup game, and later captured 6 for 28 against Bathurst. Local newspapers began referring to her as 'Gilgandra's Lady Bradman'.

In those early times in her hometown, local cricketers were very ecumenical. After Sunday matches, they often attended each other's church services. On one occasion when Norm Bennesconi led his cricketing comrades into his local catholic church for the evening service, one of the cricket brethen — from another religious denomination — was walking behind Bennesconi and was caught unprepared when Norm suddenly knelt in the aisle before the altar. He toppled over the kneeling figure and crashed onto the church floor. 'I notice the cricketers have arrived,' was the father's dry observation, as the congregation broke out into laughter.

Many annual social cricket matches are still enjoyed all over rural Australia. Between Albury and Corowa, on the New South Wales and Victoria border, a match that reminds one of the peaceful charm of past days is played each New South Wales Labor Day in October. It is the Bungowannah parish cricket match. Often one can hear the cockatoos shrieking among the river gums while the stall specialising in damper and 'underground mutton stew' (rabbit) does a roaring trade each year, as the Rector's XI and the Country XI battle for the Bungowannah 'Ashes'.

During the early years of this century, this Labor Day picnic match was a major social occasion for the good folk of the Corowa Anglican parish. However, the match was discontinued for many years after the Second World War intruded, and many of the cricketers were taken away from their local playing fields to overseas battle fields. For some years then the old cricket mats lay mouldering and forgotten underneath the nearby St Marks Church, until the parishioners decided to revive the event in 1984.

As before, in the first 'renaissance' match teams were chosen on the spot and included grandfathers, young men, little boys in short pants, women and girls. When the match started even the hint of a bumper would have been declared a very poor show indeed by the crowd, who sat watching while they sipped tea and munched chocolate cake in this peaceful Murray River setting. Good sportsmanship was an attitude which seemed entirely natural to such gentle people.

Mind you, it must be admitted that there were some questionable tactics employed in the 1985 match, when the Country XI defeated the Rector's XI. The Rector played 18 batsmen that day and umpire Fred Kingston took a brilliant catch to dismiss a key country player. Father Done also received some favourable treatment when he was reinstated to the wicket after being bowled. Umpire Kingston later explained it was a no ball, but even divine intervention could not help the father when he was caught minutes later by a country fieldsman.

Now the 'Ashes' (the stumps, bails and bats burnt after a game 50 years ago) have been returned to the crypt at the Bungowannah church until the next annual parish cricket match.

A more 'robust' attitude is adopted by those who participate in matches for the Wave Hill Cricket Club. Wave Hill is a small settlement on the Northern Territory and Western Australia border, not far from the town of Halls Creek. Ringers, camp cooks, mechanics and others travel for miles to play in a Wave Hill cricket match, which can last for as long as a week when the 'social activities' associated with each match are included. Transport to the venue is usually by four-wheel drive, bed and breakfast facilities are your own swag and tucker box, and visitors sleep out in the open — 'the starlight motel'.

The centre of culture and entertainment at Wave Hill is Frank's Bar and Grill, which is the local name for the licensed premises that adjoin the cricket ground. Frank Dalton, the licensee, is a keen supporter of the cricket club. The number one ticket holder is ex-Test player Rod Marsh.

Peter Young became involved with the Wave Hill cricket club when he was stationed nearby, with the Northern Territory police force. His poem about Wave Hill captures the companionship, humour and enthusiasm which are characteristic features of so many cricket venues in outback Australia:

You may tread the hallowed precincts
Of the Oval or at Lord's,
You may see a Test in Sydney
Or join Melbourne's teeming hordes;

But you've never seen a cricket match,
I fear you never will,
'Til you've seen the boys in action
On a clay pan at Wave Hill.

Now Brisbane has the 'Gabba,
While Sydney has its Hill,
But the place that they all envy,
Is Frank's famous Bar and Grill.

You may speak about Don Bradman,
O'Reilly and Clem Hill,
But their exploits tend to pallor
With the mention of Wave Hill.

Our Number One is Rodney,
A keeper of great fame,
But we'd like to see him out here,
Just to polish up his game.

With their spirit never daunting,
Their fervour not denied,
I'm sure they'd play each other,
If it came to one a side.

The Wave Hill Cricket Club (Peter Young is centre rear with the straw hat in hand).

You must take an extra cooler
If you've n'er been there at all,
'Cause you'll find that when you're leaving
One is hanging on the wall.

There's a reason for this practice,
As I'm sure you'll quickly learn,
See, you've always got a cooler,
Whenever you return.

They'll collect for causes worthy,
Or a mate who's down and 'flat',
And they'll gather up the proceeds
In Buck's old battered hat.

But when they've bowled the final over,
Or bad light has stopped play,
To Frank's Bar and Grill inviting,
They wend their weary way.

Where the atmosphere is friendly,
Abounding with good cheer,
And we quaff the gallons lustily,
Of cold and welcome beer.

But the memories I will cherish,
I know I always will,
Are the hours playing cricket,
On a clay pan at Wave Hill.

Another outback cricket match is held every Easter at the remote Central Mt Wedge Station, 250 km north-west of Alice Springs. Each year since 1968 the Alice Springs 'townies' and the Northern Territory 'bushies' have enthusiastically competed for the Mt Wedge Cup — a battered old aluminium chamber pot.

More than 100 people travel by light aeroplane and in four-wheel drive vehicles each year to attend this match. Bill Waudby, the station manager, is always keen to provide some unusual attractions in the day's program. (He has had sky divers from Alice Springs drop in to deliver the new ball prior to the start of play!)

However, the most unusual highlight in Central Mt Wedge history occurred on Easter Sunday in 1980. At 3.30 p.m. play was unexpectedly halted and the crick-eters called from the ground. A shiny Mercedes-Benz, decked with white ribbon, was driven slowly onto the dusty, grassless oval, and a bride stepped out of the car. Cheers broke out in the crowd as she was escorted slowly down the pitch to join the marriage celebrant and her husband-to-be. Then, after the umpires had reverently removed the bails, an outback wedding took place — on the pitch, close to the normal silly mid-off position.

George Formby, the marriage celebrant, had been flown in from Alice Springs for the occasion and about 150 people witnessed the 10-minute marriage cer-emony. After the nuptial vows had been exchanged, the crowd joined the happy couple in celebrating the occasion with both traditional and bush champagne.

Why did Malcolm Wolf and Anne Thompson choose an outback cricket match for their wedding venue? 'We wanted to give our friends a wedding they would never forget,' said Malcolm. 'Anyone can have their wedding in a church or a home but we wanted something a bit different and we were going to the cricket match any-way . . .'

Not that they are great cricket fans. 'We only go to the station matches to escape the noise of town life and to have a good time,' said Malcolm. Despite this 'sac-rilegious' attitude to cricket Malcolm and Anne have been involved in an unbroken partnership now for seven years. They live in Alice Springs.

Like the 19th hole in golf, drawing stumps at the end of the day in country cricket areas often sparks the start of more action — the post-match socialising.

As many a cricket widow can testify, the hours of play for this second game can often outdo the first!

John Forbes recalls one amusing result from a typical match 'post-mortem' when he was playing in the South Australian town of Port Lincoln. 'After the weekly attempt at the world beer drinking record had been given yet another scare, 'TB', a local identity, needed a push start to guide his utility over the two-kilometre obstacle course to his home,' Forbes said.

'Max, the team's fast bowler, happily obliged and put his considerable weight to the task. He made the mistake, however, of taking too firm a grip on the tailgate of the ute. 'TB's' vehicle sprang to life and roared off with Max still on the supporting frame. He had to hang on for dear life.'

The steel caps on Max's boots provided many illuminating sparks from the road in the 2 a.m. gloom. It also served as a useful protection for his toes and he somehow survived the entire journey. Later when he was plodding back through the darkened streets, he wasn't surprised to find his boots just a little airier than usual.

Arrangements for beer to be available for thirsty outback players is always addressed with meticulous attention to detail by those involved. Nowhere is this more true than at Ambathala station, 700 km west of Brisbane in outback Queensland.

Every Boxing Day, intrepid cricketers travel over a bone-shaking, corrugated track to participate in the annual picnic match and in 40-degree heat, it is not surprising that they look forward with eager anticipation to a large, cold keg of beer arriving from the nearest town by the end of the day's play.

However, on one never-to-be-forgotten occasion an unforeseen disaster nearly ruined their day. Unfortunately the keg had been stored at too low a temperature in the hotel at Charleville and it would not flow — the beer was frozen solid! However, the cricketers refused to accept defeat. Showing typical outback initiative and determination, they lit a fire underneath the keg to free the precious contents and all the beer was consumed before the crowd finally dispersed. What's more, no one admitted that the beer was warm and flat that night. Beer, whatever its condition, is nectar from the gods on such occasions in the outback.

Thus humour and enthusiasm are constant ingredients in all Australian bush cricket and it seems that nothing, not even a serious illness, can stifle the enthusiasm of some of country cricket's most avid supporters. In Maryborough, Victoria, the recently deceased Ron Sinclair compiled a history of the Maryborough and District Cricket association during the latter years of his life.

It was a monumental task, not only because it took him two and a half years to research and complete the 900-page manuscript, or that it included the names of everyone who had played cricket in Maryborough between 1857 and 1970. What made it a more remarkable feat was that much of it was typed with one finger, after Ron became crippled with acute arthritis.

No one exuded more enthusiasm for country cricket than Sinclair. He was the 'Mr Cricket of Maryborough'. He played with distinction for 25 years in Maryborough, scoring 207 and 151 in two successive final series. Thirteen years later in the 1954–55 season, he won his club's bowling average, with his best performance, a stunning 8 for 9. He was a respected coach and administrator and he had a local oval named after him. He was also a life member of both the Maryborough Knitting Mills Cricket Club and the Maryborough and District Cricket Association.

In the Leeton District Hospital in New South Wales there is another fine example of bravery and enthusiasm. Allen McCormack has been unable to walk or speak since he suffered a stroke three years ago. However, his mind is full of cricket memories, such as the time he represented a Riverina team against a side which included the mighty Don Bradman. McCormack has the use of one finger and a special typewriter to record such memoirs and he is now contemplating compiling a history of cricket in the Leeton district.

Cricket is indeed a great game when it can inspire such fine examples of courageous enthusiasm.

'I cannot accept that the great fast bowlers such as Lindwall, Miller, Hall, Lillee and Larwood, to name a few, needed to resort to intimidation to succeed.'

Conduct of the game and players

Lou Rowan

Top: Lou Rowan (right) with Alan McGilvray (centre) and Colin Egar at Adelaide in 1967.

Bottom: 'This photo shows Illingworth, Snow and Greg Chappell taken at Sydney as I warned John Snow after Jenner was "decked" and a few minutes before Ray took the team from the field and says it all on the point of arguments with umpires.'

— Lou Rowan

When the game of cricket came into being, participants and supporters alike recognised the need for laws to govern the conduct of the game. From the outset, it was to be regarded as a sport in which the highest degrees of sportsmanship would be evident, with ample opportunities for players to demonstrate the best of character and, as circumstances dictated, to suffer defeat in fair competition without complaining.

Laws were framed to determine the number of players on each side; the number of ways in which a batsman may be dismissed; the method of bowling; scoring; and so on. The game has always been governed by a series of codes or laws.

The legislators and students of the game, recognising the frailties of human nature, introduced laws to control players to ensure they complied with what was envisaged as the epitome of sportsmanship. The Marylebone Cricket Club, since its formation in 1787, has had the sole authority for the drawing up of the code. The present code was adopted on 7 May 1947.

Since 1947, there have been numerous changes and variations to the laws. There are rules and conditions for all manner of games, mostly as the result of the introduction of limited-overs matches. Conditions that apply in one match may well have no application in another. If it was the intention of administrators to confuse all and sundry, they have succeeded.

The reasons behind many of the changes are obscure to both players and umpires alike. When one considers the calibre of some who, from time to time, emerge as 'law-makers', it is a wonder the game has survived. The confusion surrounding many laws is solely the fault of administrators, many of whom have never made a study of existing laws (and the reason for such laws) and who have not had involvement with cricket at top level. Fortunately, in Australia, the game has had as one of its administrators the greatest batsman the world has known, Sir Donald Bradman. No man has a greater knowledge of all aspects of the game and the finer points of all laws than Sir Donald. Yet, I know he had extreme difficulty at times in convincing others to

accept his considered views. Indeed, there were times when his views and advice were ignored.

Some may wonder why such was the case. To find an answer to that, it should be borne in mind that so many of the administrators lack a proper appreciation of the points of law. Some become administrators through manoeuvring for status, a boost to their own ego, and have a limited knowledge of what the game is all about.

In theory, the role of the umpire is quite simple: he must have a sound knowledge of all aspects of the game; the laws; the capacity to interpret what has been laid down, and the ability to assess the facts and apply the laws.

Some may wonder why I mention the interpretation of the laws by umpires. To almost everyone this would appear to be normal procedure. But, in my home State of Queensland, umpires have been told all too frequently that the administrators interpret the laws and that umpires have nothing more to do than apply them. How anyone could be expected to apply some law, the interpretation of which escapes him, is quite beyond me. To my mind, administrators should be available to explain, if necessary, what was intended by certain legislation, but commonsense dictates it is the umpire who must interpret the laws he is to apply. How could it be any other way? With few exceptions, I would like the laws left alone.

The leg before wicket law has seen many changes over the years and, if only to avoid further confusion, it should be left alone. Bowlers and batsmen are now accustomed to the law as it stands. It is this particular law that causes so much trouble to the junior players; to the picnic players and to some administrators who have not figured out what the game is about.

The application of this law causes little trouble to top umpires these days. Some commentators are prone to make bold statements on each decision they happen to see (or are told of). As a rule, former players are circumspect in their comments.

Of all the Laws of Cricket, those relating to the no ball law; the leg before wicket law, and the law dealing with duties of umpires ensuring that the conduct of the game (and the implements used are in accordance with the laws) invite most interest.

The no ball law with the front-foot rule has reached the stage where it is plain stupid. In the early years of its application, changes were the order of the day. Umpires were to ensure that the front foot did not touch the popping crease and, later, they were directed to permit the front foot to touch the popping crease provided some part of the foot was grounded behind the line or was here, or there, or somewhere else at the point of delivery, and so on. No one knew exactly what the administrators had in mind because I am sure they did not know themselves. Sir Donald Bradman, Colin Egar, Bill Priem and I were convinced the front-foot rule was a bad law. We remained in the minority on that point. It seemed so stupid that some administrators who could not bowl a hoop downhill with the assistance of a following gale could rave on about the advantages of a rule they would not know how to apply. Sam Loxton always argued that 'Froggy' Thomson was harshly treated by umpires because he was, in fact, a 'wrong foot' bowler. Perhaps Sam had a point. I feel sure that had 'Froggy' been a Queensland player, the local administrators of that time would have had a field day. However, despite my dislike for that particular law, it remains.

When legislators framed the law dealing with the conduct of the game and empowered umpires to take steps to ensure the implements used were in accordance with the law and that play would be fair, it is more unlikely they foresaw the abuse the laws would be subjected to, or just how far some players and administrators would stretch the law.

The incident at Perth where Lillee was prevented from using a cricket bat made from some metal alloy demonstrated the need for umpires to take a stand. The game was held up while Lillee argued with the umpires and resumed only after he had thrown the bat away and selected a conventional bat. What was his captain doing while this was going on? Surely that whole unsavoury incident could have been avoided? Yet another example of the sheer inability of some officials to enforce some discipline.

There can be no doubt that the most important duty imposed on umpires — apart from adjudicating on appeals — is the matter of ensuring fair play. The same duty is imposed on captains but that has long been a lost cause. In recent years, most captains have not the slightest interest in just how the game is played or how their team members conduct themselves, concentrating rather on the ready flow of money for their services. The spirit of the game seems secondary if it rates a place at all. If this is not the case, then how do they explain their tolerance of obscene and abusive language directed at their opponents; the disgraceful spectacle of bowlers making indecent gestures to opposing batsmen; bowlers exhibiting resentment at the umpires' decision; the persistent bowling of short-pitched deliveries aimed at the batsmen; and a whole list of incidents that have done nothing but harm to the spirit of the game?

Would anyone suggest that the terrible battering taken by Ken Barrington at the hands of West Indies bowlers was within the guidelines for the conduct of play within the spirit of the game? Would the flooring of the umpire by a West Indies fast bowler in New Zealand, or the knocking down of Sunil Gavaskar in England meet the standards sought by the legislators? Could those incidents stand alongside the action of Wally Grout in refusing to run out an England batsman flattened by an Australian bowler? Would the underarm delivery at Melbourne rank with the attitude of Brian Booth and his players who declined an appeal when Geoffrey Boycott handled the ball batting in a Test at Brisbane? I suggest it is time players and officials reflected more on spirit and less on money and winning.

It is not to the credit of our present-day captains and officials that we no longer see exhibitions of sportsmanship. They have permitted the display of open hostilities, all in the name of the game that was once regarded as the epitome of sportsmanship. It would seem that the keen rivalry and sense of fair play belongs in the past.

If captains were all to accept their responsibilities we would never have known that diabolical scheme which resulted in bodyline. A plan was devised to combat the sheer batting skills of one man, Bradman, who, although far from a fit player at the time, still managed a batting average that remains the envy of some of the healthiest players the game has known. The bodyline plan could not have been executed without the total co-operation of the then England captain, Douglas Jardine, who, I suggest, abandoned all pretence of sportsmanship in his quest for victory at all costs.

I know that many England supporters of the game do not like being reminded of what happened during that infamous tour, but they, and all connected with cricket throughout the world, should bear in mind that history will judge us all, and now is the time to take a stand against practices that bring the game into disrepute. Who would ever have thought that in reading a copy of *Wisden*, long accepted as something of a 'Cricketer's Bible', the reader would find an article dealing with a meeting held to discuss a player's conviction for a drug offence? It makes one wonder just what type of conviction would be necessary to result in the banning of a player from representing his country and wearing that country's colours.

The bodyline series left in its wake resentment that has been lessened only by the passage of time. The players and those who witnessed the events of that series cannot forget the sight and the sickening sounds when Bill Woodfull and Bert Oldfield were struck terrible blows. Could anyone suggest play was conducted within the spirit of the game?

Then, in the 1970–71 series, we saw an England captain who gave every indication of adopting the win at all costs policy, even when it meant intimidatory bowling to tail-end batsmen resulting, finally, in Terry Jenner being felled after being struck on the head. I would suggest his main bowler was good enough to succeed without resorting to such tactics. Here, again, administrators must look for more in a captain than playing skills and luck with tossing the coin.

Administrators have made numerous changes to the law regarding intimidatory bowling but no amount of legislation, no formation of words, will have any impact if administrators are to continue in their hypocrisy in ignoring the failure of captains to ensure that play is conducted with the spirit of the game as well as within the laws. One wonders just when administrators last raised such a point with captains.

Fortunately, the game has always had the capacity to produce captains who have had a deep sense of sportsmanship. In my time, the game was served by captains such as Brian Booth, Mike Smith, (England) Peter Burge, Les Favell, Trevor Goddard, (South Africa) and Richie Benaud, all of whom played the game hard but always as sportsmen and always within the laws.

There have been others with, perhaps, greater leadership qualities but who lacked what I believe was a true sense of sportsmanship and composure. The sledging and language used by some and permitted by others would debar them from my list of good captains.

I reserve my strongest criticism for umpires. They have a clear responsibility and, indeed, a duty to ensure the proper conduct of the game. It is unfortunate that we seem these days to have umpires who are not prepared to take a stand to ensure the proper conduct of the game. Again, no matter how careful legislators are in framing laws and regulations their efforts are in vain if an umpire shirks his responsibilities; if he seeks refuge in some ambiguity in the law and uses this as a convenient peg on which to hang his conscience.

For a number of years, the game has been brutalised by those who substitute fast bowling and intimidation for sheer skills. I remain totally opposed to such tactics! Where is the real skill and sportsmanship in intimidatory bowling? Skill and sportsmanship must not be separated by brutality such as intimidatory bowling.

It remains my belief that Lillee and Thomson were permitted far too much latitude in the 1973–74 season in Australia where they subjected the England batsmen to what seemed an unending flow of bouncers. In the face of such bowling, the England batsmen seemed to spend more time avoiding injury than playing shots. Why wouldn't they?

Away from the game, batsmen will almost always insist they don't mind bouncers. Perhaps they live in hopes of retaliation. Having watched so many of them at close quarters, I am not convinced, regardless of how few bouncers were bowled at them. The only time they relish such bowling is when they are in complete control and the bouncers are ineffective. Peter Burge relished every short delivery in his immortal innings of 160 at Hedingley in 1964. He will now tell anyone that the only way to handle intimidatory bowling is to remain at the bowler's wicket. How true!

I cannot accept that the great fast bowlers such as Lindwall, Miller, Hall, Lillee and Larwood needed to resort to intimidation to succeed. Although Lindwall and Miller bowled a lot of bouncers, they never used such tactics against tail-end batsmen. One could not say the same of West Indies bowlers of recent times.

I believe that fast, accurate bowling is a joy to watch. There is nothing attractive in a batsman being struck. It is all very well for people to claim that it is the fault of the batsman if he is struck. There are occasions in all manner of contests where judgement fails and dire consequences result. It is gross stupidity to suggest that the batsman was at fault if he is injured, maimed or killed as the result of being struck by a ball aimed at him. Such conduct by bowlers shows a failure to use skills correctly and a failure to preserve the best sporting traditions. Where is there any evidence that intimidatory bowling ever did anything but damage the image of the game?

The tennis world embraced misconduct by certain players and the image of that game has suffered. Imagine anyone taking children along to watch the antics, the disgusting conduct and indecent gestures of some of the loud-mouthed players of today.

It seems that officials and promoters alike want such conduct to continue otherwise direct action would have been taken years ago. Are cricket officials going to permit in cricket the conduct we see even at basketball games where coaches run up and down the sidelines ranting and raving like people demented? Will the game reach the stage where runners enter the players' arena with messages for them as is done at Australian Rules football games? I will concede that some of our modern captains seem detached and disinterested in the game and, perhaps, could do with some advice.

The conduct of some players in accepting decisions is disgraceful. By what right do they presume to stand their ground in open disagreement with the umpire's decision? Fortunately, I did not experience that type of reaction, mainly because such conduct would not be accepted by me.

It would be difficult to see anything more offensive to standards of decency and propriety than a bowler making indecent gestures to batsmen. And what do the administrators do about it? When Lillee kicked Miandad, during a Test at Perth, he should have been called from the field of play and summarily dismissed from that and future games. When Greg Chappell resorted to the use of an under-arm delivery in a game against New Zealand at Melbourne, he insulted the true spirit of cricket. Ian Chappell was suspended from the game because of misconduct. All forms of misconduct are so unnecessary and do nothing more than demonstrate the contempt the guilty parties have for standards and tradition.

Great bowlers like Bill O'Reilly never resorted to abuse and obscenity. He had spirit and determination seldom equalled. He never quit and his greatest battles were against the might of England. I challenge the right of any player to bring this game into disrepute. By what right do they do these things?

I challenge administrators to stand up and be counted; to take a stand against those reprehensible practices and thus demonstrate to players and public alike that there is still some decency; that standards and traditions must not be scorned and spat upon.

What is the real purpose of intimidatory bowling? The answer is simple — it is designed to put the batsmen in such fear for safety of life and limb as to be unable to display normal batting skill and technique. Some teams have a proliferation of fast bowlers, all of whom demonstrate undisguised hatred for batsmen and total disregard for the consequences of aiming the ball at them at high speed.

Sport is as good only as the characters it produces and participants will be best remembered for ability and sportsmanship, not for unfair practices and hatreds.

'Hollywood was the first cricket club to permit ladies in the pavilion, which decorated their Sunday afternoons with Olivia de Havilland, Greer Garson, Gladys Cooper, Merle Oberon and Evelyn Laye. I wonder if they made the tea?'

Cricket and the American Revolution

Dr Richard Gordon

I love Hollywood. It so reminds me of Bromley. Its rectangles of neat suburban houses in pretty gardens erupt vast hotels and glittering restaurants, as though the Dorchester and Le Gavroche had replaced our British Home Stores and the local. Rodeo Drive tempts with the world's most expensive shops — diamonds, fashions, art, uniforms for your servants — all as modest as Bromley's suppliers of camping gear or pet foods. The criss-crossing streets have homely names like Brighton Way, Hillcrest Road and Elm Drive. Like Bromley, Hollywood has buses, polite policemen and a delightful cemetery.

Hollywood is famous as the home of American cricket. In 1931 C. Aubrey Smith of Cambridge and Sussex arrived to act for MGM. He had appeared on the field with Abel and Ulyett and on the stage with Ellen Terry and Mrs Patrick Campbell. He was from Hove, a doctor's son like W. G. Grace, against whom he played. He performed for England in the first Test ever against South Africa, at Port Elizabeth, scoring three and taking seven wickets. He was the captain. He was never picked again. That was in 1889. Now he was pushing 70.

Like any cricketing Englishman in outlandish surroundings, he speedily established his essential sport. C. Aubrey Smith was tall, heavy-browed, sweeping-moustached, pipe-smoking and left-arm medium-paced — 'Round the Corner Smith' from his run-up. Four years captaining Sussex had perfected a blunt, good-humoured, forceful, generous way of getting people to do exactly what he wanted. He soon scrambled into a team of fellow-exiles the good eggs like Ronald Colman, Errol Flynn, P. G. Wodehouse and Nigel Bruce, who batted in a brown trilby.

The first fixture of the Hollywood Cricket Club was the following season of 1932, versus San Fernando Valley in North Hollywood Park. Shortly Hollywood CC moved to the Fenner's of Los Angeles, the UCLA campus lying between Beverly Hills and the ocean. In 1936 the club, like Lord's, arrived at its third and eternal resting place. Griffith Park is near Universal Studios,

'The Monster was such a gentle creature,' Boris reflected over his pint at the Oval. 'If he shuffled about killing people, he simply knew no better.'

where today conducted tours of their startling special effects allow you to enjoy in comfort the adventures of train smashes, armed hold-ups, typhoons and being eaten by sharks.

They rechristened it the C. Aubrey Smith Ground. They built a pav, housing a shield emblazoned with the founder's cricketing career from Charterhouse, the credits including Gentlemen versus Players, and with justifiable generosity the captaincy of England versus Australia in 1888, when he was only playing the lead in one of Shaw and Shrewsbury's two XIs on tour in Australia that summer. When they ceremonially opened the pavilion, Smith blubbed.

Hollywood CC produced world-famous cricketers. Sir Cedric Hardwicke, David Niven, Alan Mowbray the eternal butler, Basil Rathbone the eternal Sherlock Holmes, Herbert Marshall, Roland Culver, Frank Lawton, Laurence Olivier, H. B. Warner, who was Jesus Christ in the Cecil B. DeMille version, and George Colouris whose dream was a theatrical touring company capable of a quick-change act into a visiting cricket team, and who came home to enliven the *Doctor* movies as a peculiar patient.

Hollywood was the first cricket club to permit ladies in the pavilion, which decorated their Sunday afternoons with Olivia de Havilland, Greer Garson, Gladys Cooper, Merle Oberon and Evelyn Laye. I wonder if they made the tea?

Once in Hollywood on some business, I implored first to see the cricket ground. They stopped the studio limo, the film people withdrew — traffickers in emotions know when to leave a man to his own. I gazed at the turf. I felt like a toiling English cleric viewing the missionary chapel radiating his faith in the heathen jungle.

With the Second World War C. Aubrey Smith did his duty. He directed the chaps to join the colours. And David Niven did. His ground now degraded to equestrian sport would have made him shudder, like show-jumping at Lord's. He was knighted in 1944 for services to Anglo-American relations, complicated when they

Raffles rides again! The celebrated fictional character created by E. W. Hornung, as portrayed in an early Hollywood movie by Ronald Colman, 'Raffles' was, of course, the legendary amateur cracksman of literature who, when not rifling elegant country houses, usually turned to a game of cricket for relaxation.

were winning our war and taking our money. He died four years later, aged 85.

He appeared in 100 films like *Lives of a Bengal Lancer, Little Lord Fauntleroy* and *The Prisoner of Zenda*. Also as Sir Ambrose Abercrombie, with his Eton Ramblers' blazer and I Zingari boater, the 'false and fruity' self-centred scheming stage-Englishman President of the Hollywood Cricket Club in *The Loved One* — the book.

Actors watch cricket matches with the childlike enthusiasm they apply to all public spectacles — which appears charming or touching depending on the quality of the show. They are easily spotted. They applaud like

270

Max Beerbohm's Zuleika, who 'In the way peculiar to persons who are in the habit of appearing before the public, held her hands well above the level of her brow, and clapped them with a vigour demonstrative not less of her presence than of her delight'. All actors leave during the tea interval. Those performing are obliged to work waiters' hours, the others are terrified people might imagine they are not.

In the years when Surrey CC and the rest of the country never had it so good, I enjoyed the honour of sitting below the immemorial gas-holders and sharing my packet of sandwiches with a star player of C. Aubrey Smith's Hollywood XI. The glittering Hollywood magnet has many facets. It draws genius, ability, looks, sexiness, craftiness, and ambition and hope, if equally empty. Boris Karloff appeared in Hollywood because it was at the end of the railroad track he was being paid to lay. Then requiring alternative employment, he turned to driving trucks of cement, and acting.

Boris Karloff was William Henry Pratt. He was the brother of Sir John Pratt of the British Foreign Office. He readily won selection for the side from C. Aubrey Smith, having been to Uppingham. Tall, square-jawed, romantic-looking, he first made hearts throb rather than flesh creep. He became the Monster of the Universal make-up man — the face which frightened several growing generations is studio copyright. He changed his name. Whoever heard of a Monster called Bill?

'The Monster was such a gentle creature,' Boris reflected over his pint at the Oval. 'If he shuffled about killing people, he simply knew no better.' He was gentle himself, unloquacious, amusing, thoughtful, knowledgeable about the game, the ideal man to discover sitting in the next seat. The single-minded application of the players to cricket is widened by important personages with a boyish delight in talking to cricketers. Some of these personages are dreadful bores. Luckily, the game provides a higher education in tolerating boredom.

Stewart Surridge's conquering side of the 'fifties saw refreshing Boris as another former player. Boris was as constrainedly proud of sitting on the team dressing room balcony as of winning an Oscar. He had a thoughtful wife who met him at the Hobbs Gate on the close of play with a dry martini in a thermos in the glove compartment. He was my fellow-clubman like Ben Travers and Ken More — who used to come on the bus until the conductress kept refusing his fare. Ken asked why. 'Because I love you,' she said.

At the 1964 Oval Test against Australia when Fred Trueman took his 300th Test wicket (Hawke c Cowdrey 14), Boris complained mildly to me that he was falling to bits. The surgeons patched his body together, but sadly not as magically as Frankenstein. He died five years later, aged 81. He achieved one of the 48 foot-square black and gold plaques in St Paul's, Covent Garden, the actors' church. It is inscribed rightly with Marvell's 'He nothing common did nor mean Upon that memorable scene', and is positioned at second slip from Ivor Novello.

His memory is as immortal as the ghouls he played. The man from the *Sunday Times*, his mind straying during Sir Michael Redgrave's memorial service, startled himself with the image of Boris with billowing cloak and bared fangs brightening the ritual by rising screaming from under a slab.

C. Aubrey Smith was anticipated by settlers among the Redskins. New York saw cricket before Broad-Halfpenny Down. Cricket and the English language in 1776 were proof against revolution, and the New England XI of 1850 make a handsome bunch on the pavilion walls at Lord's.

The first English touring side, which sailed in 1859, had John Wisden complaining that 'The sea needs ten minutes of the heavy roller'. In August 1872 W. G. Grace — 'the Babe Ruth of cricket' — brought an XI including Lord Harris and A. N. 'Monkey' Hornby aboard the 400-ton *Samaritan* in storms so violently vomitory that W. G. busied himself with his will — necessarily to dispatch in a bottle — while Monkey piled luggage against cabin door to stem the Atlantic, and left-arm Lancashire bowler A. Appleby enthusiastically cheered the white-faced groaning side by singing repeatedly *A Life on the Ocean Wave* and *Home Sweet Home*.

The England XI played the New York, Philadelphia and Boston XXIIs. They generally won by an innings. Cricket and communism never caught on in America, neither suiting the national character.

Cricket spread like the Australian gumtree under the bright skies of the British Empire. Who knew not the Bodyline Controversy for real in the 1930s cannot know how an Englishman wore the idea of Empire as unthinkingly as his clothes. We were everywhere.

Listening to the Test 50 years ago you knew the BBC was bringing it all the way from Australia. 'Whoooosh whoooom Larwood's running to the wicket eeeepppp wowowowowow Bradman's turned him to leg, good krkrkrkrk, sir!' crackled from the receiver on dim icy mornings to families silent over their porridge. Play stopped when you went to work, a radio being a motoring luxury as *outré* as a cocktail cabinet, and a portable wireless was the size of a mobile commode.

Those times when flannels were made of flannel, appeals were *sotto voce*, and the Oliver Cromwell was as taboo as the clap, Australians were known only as wearers of green gorblimey caps who said stumps instead of close of play. In 1950 I achieved my childhood dreams: I watched the Test at the Gabba at Brisbane (sticky wicket, England declared 68 for 7 in their first innings, Australia at 32 for 7 in their second and won by 70).

I had arrived embellished with brass buttons, doctor aboard a cargo ship. In Australia then, afternoon tea meant steak and eggs, there was nothing to drink but beer and the police threw everyone out of the pubs at six. Entertainment was 'swy', the gambling game of two-up, which only Australians can appreciate, like their hot meat pies which on biting squirt a gravy like sump oil. Women had their place in Australian society, codified by defining a wife as 'a gadget you screw on the bed and it does the housework'.

I returned much later as a Literary Gent, to discover Sydney all skyscrapers, opera house, oysters Rockefeller and Great Western champagne. It has dinner parties so polite you forget there is nothing between your tulled hostess, who is slicing the pavlova, and Darwin but abos and kangaroos.

Women are now admitted to be part of the natural order less curious than the native duckbill platypus, the only mammal that lays eggs. Sydney has discovered vice. While the panting pre-breakfast joggers picked their way through the crumpled tinnies and huddled drunks of Kings Cross, I found ladies of the night facing the morning like bleary vampires. I confessed to an inviting blonde in a black leather bikini it was a trifle early in the day for a Pom. 'But it comes cheaper, sport,' she explained helpfully. How typically practical of Australia, providing sex at matinée prices. I wondered if she gave half fare to OAPs.

Near Hobart hangs a road sign, DEVONSHIRE TEAS. The southernmost tea and crumpets in the world. Which is the charm of Australia. It assures you there'll always be an England, even if it is in Tasmania.

Before the First World War half of Britain's savings were invested abroad, much in the Empire. Before the Second World War British overseas investments paid for a quarter of our imports. Rightly or wrongly, we lived off the world nicely — until we had to sell the lot to America to pay for the war against Hitler. As we were both on the same side, this seems hardly cricket. Without the Empire we should never have enjoyed the vaguer values of the Commonwealth, nor this poem in the *Pink 'Un* after the 1896 Old Trafford Test:

> For 'twould have been a sorry game
> Without those runs of Ranji's;
> And Father Thames was glad to claim
> His tributary Ganges.

(Prince Ranjitsinhji made 154 not out.)

A Prince among players

The Twelfth Man of The Lord's Taverners doesn't play much cricket these days — he's settled for a coach-and-four for a bit of exercise. But he is still the redoubtable champion of the Taverners and never misses an opportunity to bolster their efforts, at the same time poking a bit of gentle fun at the actor-cricketer band of brothers. Just for nostalgia's sake, here's a two-page pictorial replay of some of his Royal Twelfthmanship's games in days of yore. Even by today's standards he measures up quite nicely, doesn't he?

'If the game tilted sharply towards Australia after tea Knott made it clear that they were not going to have it all their own way.'

A dish to set before the Queen

Colin Cowdrey

Colin Cowdrey (courtesy Sydney Morning Herald).

Melbourne, 18 March 1977: As the light began to fade after five gloriously sunny days of enthralling cricket, Knott was dismissed by Lillee, his fifth wicket and 11th in the match, and Australia had won the Centenary Test match by 45 runs.

By some coincidence, on 18 March 1877, a hundred years to the day, England were set a target of 154 and also lost by 45 runs. Today it was a stiffer task. In scoring 417, England achieved the highest total in the fourth innings of an Anglo-Australian Test match and in doing so have won all hearts.

The last day began with England needing to score just 272 to win — 90 in each session, a task by no means beyond them on the slow, easy-paced pitch. Provided that the early overs were negotiated safely only the clock might have presented a problem. As the ball becomes softer on this slow outfield, a batting side can so easily get bogged down. So it was important that they did not lag behind and at lunchtime were well in contention.

The first hour was fascinating, for Chappell had a problem. With Gilmour injured, Lillee was the trump card. He had to be thrown in to the fray to make the early break, if possible, but the new ball would be due in 12 overs. O'Keeffe bowled tidily and took two vital wickets later on. Walker, faced with the prospect of some marathon spells later in the day, was discarded temporarily.

Needing just 13 for his first Test hundred, Randall was confronted with a burst from Lillee. If he was nervous he showed no trace of it. Brearley had provided the helpful word early in his innings and now he was fortunate to have the steadying influence of Amiss at the other end. In the event he played quite superbly, a deft sweep, a glorious late cut and he was soon on 99, facing Lillee. He tucked Lillee away to fine leg for his first Test hundred and became the 14th batsman to score a hundred in his first Test match against Australia. The Yorkshireman Willie Watson was the last to do so, in 1953.

I was delighted for him after his rigours in India

where his previous best in a Test match had been 37, but he had made a huge contribution to the team's success by his enthusiasm. It would have been understandable if Randall had shown the odd lapse of concentration in the excitement of his achievement but he just played better and better as he went along. He is something of an irrepressible jack-in-the-box, both in batting and fielding, but today he assumed a responsibility to fit the occasion. His timing never left him; only fatigue slowed him down and, in part, contributed to his downfall.

All the while Amiss looked a class player with plenty of time. He seems to have the broadest bat in English

Past memories: The young Queen Elizabeth at Lord's in 1953 where she watched a match between Australia and Middlesex. She is shaking hands with Lindsay Hassett, the Australian captain.

Another Royal event: The Australian cricketers, led by Don Bradman, were guests of the King and Queen at Balmoral Castle in September 1948. Bradman is seen introducing members of his team to the then Queen Elizabeth, and young Princess Margaret.

cricket today and Lillee did not ruffle him as much as I expected. His sudden dismissal by a ball that kept rather low was the turning point of the day. True, while Greig and Randall were together we could still have won but somehow I had the feeling that we were beginning to live too dangerously.

When Randall made 161 he edged Greg Chappell low and wide where Marsh appeared to have scooped his glove under the catch. As he rolled over and over the umpire upheld the appeal and Randall departed a disconsolate figure. Without delay Marsh leapt to his feet and rushed down the wicket to tell his captain that the ball had bounced. The umpires conferred and Randall was recalled. It was indeed a chivalrous gesture at such a critical moment of the match.

Just before tea England were slowed down by some good bowling from Chappell himself and he elected to gamble with O'Keeffe. In his first over, Cosier dived full length to take a magnificent catch off bat and pad and Randall's historic innings had closed on 174. The whole ground rose to him.

Through the tears of joy he went out through the wrong gate, finding himself at the end of the path leading to the special box where the Queen and the Duke of Edinburgh were sitting. Within a few yards of them he discovered his mistake and stopped in his tracks and, much to the amusement of all, bowed before beating a hasty retreat across the public seats. It was a happy touch, for the day had belonged to him.

It might be argued that Lillee's great bowling could have earned him the prize of Man of the Match, but without doubt Randall was the man who had made the match complete. There were not four gladder hearts in Melbourne today than Larwood, Voce, Hardstaff and Simpson, giant names from Trent Bridge. If the game tilted fairly sharply towards Australia after tea Knott made it clear that they were not going to have it all

their own way. He played a series of astonishing shots, treating Lillee with utter contempt. He is a genius of improvisation.

But the day finished with Lillee summoning up energy and fire from I do not know where. He was bowling faster at the end than he was at the beginning and deservedly he was carried aloft, first by players and then by some of his ecstatic countrymen, while a dozen or more policemen surrounded him to keep him intact.

But alas, his medical advisers have determined that he is not quite intact, although you could never have guessed it today. Sadly for the English public but to the relief of the English batsmen, he has withdrawn from the forthcoming tour of England.

We have had a remarkable week and life will be rather flat until we have had time to absorb it all. I do not know when I have enjoyed the last day of a Test match more than this one. It had everything, both captains playing their part in the challenge, both wicket-keepers making their mark, some wonderful fast bowling, good sustained spells of leg spin bowling, some fine fielding, a generous gesture and a large crowd. The result was open until near the end. When Randall and Greig were raking the embers just before tea, there was still the prospect of an English victory. What a dish it was to set before the Queen.

Australia 138 (G. S. Chappell 40) and 419 for 9 dec (R. W. Marsh 110 not out, I. C. Davis 68; C. M. Old 4 for 104).

England 95 (D. K. Lillee 6 for 26, M. H. N. Walker 4 for 54) and 417 (D. W. Randall 174, D. L. Amiss 64, A. P. E. Knott 42, A. W. Greig 41; D. K. Lillee 5 for 139).

Australia won by 45 runs.

'The SCG will always hold a fascination to me . . . Sydney and its ground will always be my home.'

Sydney Cricket Ground

Alan Davidson

Alan Davidson in action.

It was always my ambition even as a small boy to play at the SCG. The ground, as a young boy in the 1930s, was regarded as the finest cricket ground in the world and all my readings exhilarated me in the feeling of one day walking where the greats of cricket had performed such feats.

My first visit to the SCG was at the age of 10 to see NSW versus Victoria, under the guidance and care of an aunty. I watched with awe as NSW batted against a keen Victorian attack led by fast bowler Barry Scott and Australian representative Maurie Sievers. The highlight of the day was an innings of 49 by Stan McCabe, a man I had read about so much. Two shots live in my memory, one a hook high over fine leg for six and a thumping four forward of point off the back foot — both off the pace of Scott.

My second visit was some years later, at the end of the Second World War, when NSW met a Queensland team with Bill Brown and Rex Rogers the openers. The magic of Bill O'Reilly saw him take six wickets cheaply and the control he placed over the game impressed me.

My next visit was a 'wagged' day from school where with my uncle I went with the hope of seeing Don Bradman bat. The occasion saw the great Don walk to the wicket and the expectation and hum from the crowd was stimulating and gave me the feeling that I would one day play a Test match against England at the SCG. Bradman scored just 12 runs before being bowled by Douglas Wright but in that short innings I marvelled at his incredible footwork.

I was but 17 years of age but already my mind was made up. Some two and a half years later, having travelled from the country to the city, I was to play my first representative match for a NSW Second XI versus the Victorian Second XI but regretfully not on the SCG but the number two ground at the rear. My first-class career had to wait another few weeks where in Adelaide I played my first Shield match against South Australia. Another match versus Victoria in Melbourne and then my third match for NSW was versus Queensland — at last on the SCG.

It was my first long look at Ken 'Slasher' Mackay who was later to become one of my teammates, roommate and great characters of international cricket. He top scored with 76 and his ability to let balls go so close to the line of the stumps was fantastic. The match gave me great pleasure as I bowled Bill Brown with a ball that swung back and clipped the leg bail. Brown had just returned from the 1948 Bradman team and to meet a player of that class meant a great deal to me. Following the game an Australian Second XI team was chosen for a tour of New Zealand with Bill Brown the captain and myself in the side with greats such as Don Tallon, Jack Iverson and Doug Ring.

The following season was a memorable one as the MCC toured Australia. I looked forward to having my first game against England at the SCG. It was a high-scoring match with NSW closing at 3 for 509, Keith Miller scoring 214. It was also my first opportunity to see the big-hearted Alec Bedser in action. One of the great memories was of Miller straight driving Bedser's first delivery with the new ball clean over the sight board.

When MCC batted I received a rude awakening of my inadequacy and skills. My figures of 0 for 63 were unimpressive but I had the opportunity of looking at the technique of players such as Hutton, Washbrook and Compton. It was a telling lesson.

Fortunes through the years were good to me for in 1952 versus Western Australia I picked up 6 for 13 and was lucky enough to receive great words of advice from Ray Lindwall, the greatest bowler I have seen. Another bowling performance that gave me enormous pleasure in Sydney was my 4 for 54 and 5 for 25 against England in 1962–63 but perhaps the greatest joy was a century versus Victoria in 1961–62. On the fall of the ninth wicket NSW 'keeper Doug Ford arrived, with my score at 46 not out. In the next 23 minutes we added 61 in which Doug faced three balls, got one leg bye and my score went up to 106 before holing out to cover. In the dressing room Doug complained that I had thrown my wicket away just as he was getting set!

I have mentioned Keith Miller's 214 versus the MCC but it was his performance in a match against South Australia in 1955 that will forever mark Keith as one of the most incredible players the world has seen. NSW had declared at 8 for 215 on the first day because of bad light but Keith had bowled just four balls before stumps. The next morning after the first over I joined him at slip where he said, 'There's nothing in this wicket. I'll just have one more over and then you can take over'. His next over claimed three wickets and he finished the innings with 7 for 12, South Australia all out for 27.

The SCG in my time from 1949 to 1963 was a special hunting ground for NSW cricket. In those 14 years we won the Sheffield Shield 11 times, nine in succession. Out of that time and place came marvellous leaders. Keith Miller was certainly the greatest all-round player I have seen. Arthur Morris, one of the greatest of '48, was not only one of the most gifted opening batsmen of any era in Australia but certainly throughout the cricketing world. Another such player and captain was Richie Benaud; his record was spectacularly successful. He and I first met in school cricket in the mid-1940s and our careers dovetailed till my retirement in 1963.

Richie as a captain knew his players so well and developed a team which automatically moved as one. Some of his bowling performances for NSW and against touring teams on a turning wicket in Sydney, just as he did at Manchester in 1961, meant victory against the tide of the game. Richie as an all-rounder developed his skills by hard work and often under the stress of injuries but always as the example for his team to follow. I well remember his natural flamboyancy and exuberance on the field when taking a wicket, which several officials disapproved of keenly. No doubt today this would be mild compared with some but certainly the Benaud psychology never failed to lift his team to greater heights.

The SCG will always hold a special fascination to me as Lord's may do for all England players, Sydney and its ground will always be my home.

Jeffrey Robert Thomson had a large and noisy following all over the world. 'Facing Thomson on a fast pitch that gives him bounce can be a shattering experience, not only through his extreme pace but because of his unique delivery', so claims cricket historian Jack Pollard. Born at Greenacre in Sydney's western suburbs, Thomson was one of five sons who claims he learnt his bowling action from his father. A bit of a renegade against the establishment he is, nonetheless, one of Australia's favourite cricketing sons.

Aboriginal influence

Ken Piesse and Ian Ferguson

Aboriginal cricketers of 1868 — the 'All Blacks'

To Britain they came from the land of the South
  As strangers for honour and glory,
And now as true heroes intrepid and bold
  Will their names be recorded in story.

For not with the sword did they covert renown,
  The battle they fought was at cricket,
In lieu of grim weapons of warfare they strove
  With the bat and the ball at the wicket.

— Anon
(from Leslie Frewin's *The Poetry of Cricket*)

On 13 October 1951, Victor Richardson, a former Test captain, unveiled an important memorial in Australian cricket history. The two-metre granite slab he revealed that day to those assembled at the Edenhope Consolidated School was inscribed with the names of the first Australian cricket team to tour England in 1868 — the Aboriginal tour.

The monument to these cricket pioneers can be found on a small oval at the Edenhope school, near the shores of Lake Wallace in Victoria. Only about 1000 people live in Edenhope, 31 kilometres from the South Australian border. Most of this first Australian team came from the Lake Wallace area. The remainder, apart from the English-born captain, Charles Lawrence, came from nearby Hamilton.

Few professionals were as active in promoting the game as Lawrence. His early career was distinguished. At 17 he gained his first professional engagement, at Perth, in Scotland. Three years later, in 1849, Lawrence, playing for XXII of Scotland versus the celebrated All-England XI at Edinburgh, captured all 10 wickets in an innings, dismissing the renowned left-handed 'Felix' with a shooter which knocked all three stumps out of the ground. He was then associated with the founding of the United All-Ireland XI. From 1854 he played either for Surrey under a residential qualification at Mitcham or for Middlesex, the county of his birth. He bowled with success for the All-Ireland XI versus the MCC at Lord's in 1858 and at the close of the 1861 season, during which he had been appearing for Middlesex, he became a member of H. H. Stephenson's team, the first band of cricketers to visit the Antipodes. The following spring, when the remainder of Stephenson's tourists returned home, he decided to settle in Australia and accepted an engagement in Sydney. Lawrence was the first English professional to coach Australian cricketers. He appeared for New South Wales on several occasions, representing that State against the second English visiting team, captained by George Parr in 1863–64. His next achievement was as coach of the Aboriginal team, whose skill at various sports, boomerang throwing in particular, was noteworthy.

Lawrence found there were more Aborigines playing cricket in the Harrow-Edenhope area of Western Victoria in the 1860s than in any other part of Australia. They had been introduced to the game by the first European pastoralists. By the early 1860s the skills of some Aboriginal players were well advanced. Many of these early games were played in country areas. In early 1866, the Aborigines defeated a European team at Bringalbert, 45 kilometres north-west of Edenhope. By Boxing Day the team was popular enough to attract 10,000 to the MCG.

Early in 1867, a Sydney entrepreneur advanced the idea of sponsoring an English tour for this Aboriginal team. The tour did not eventuate, due to poor organisation and lack of funds; the team was stranded in Sydney without the finances to return home. Charles Lawrence then took the leadership reins. He helped organise a series of matches to fund the Aboriginal team's return to Victoria. One game was staged in April 1867, at Wollongong, on the NSW south coast.

Many details of this match and another later game were recorded in *The International Aboriginal Cricketers v Illawarra*, a book researched by A. P. Fleming of the Illawarra Historical Society. The book relies heavily on the files of the Illawarra *Mercury*. The newspaper's reporter was surprised, and impressed, by the obvious talents of some of the Aboriginal players. 'Mullagh played in a style seldom ever witnessed on the ground and certainly never surpassed,' he wrote. He was also enthusiastic about 'the masterly dexterity with which Cuzens handled the willow, defying the white bowlers' best aimed balls'.

In a rain-affected match, the Aborigines gained a resounding victory by 96 runs. Mullagh top-scored with 45 out of 116. Illawarra was dismissed for a dismal 20. During the same year, the Aboriginal team returned to Wollongong for another two-day match on 6 and 7 November.

By then, definite arrangements had been completed for the English tour in 1868. The organisation and promotion of the team was much more professional. One innovation was the various coloured caps worn by the Aboriginal players, so that they would be more easily distinguished by spectators. Mosquito wore a dark blue cap, Jim Crow pink, and Bullocky had chocolate brown headwear.

The Aboriginal team had another easy victory. They dismissed Illawarra for 27 in the first innings and 102 in the second. In return they scored 86 and 2 for 45 — victory by an innings and eight wickets. Crowds at Wollongong and other centres did not gather just to watch the Aborigines' prowess at cricket, they were also entertained by their ability at athletics and at spear and boomerang throwing.

The most unusual event at Wollongong was 'event four: throwing cricket balls at Dick-a-Dick'. When this event began, spectators watched in amazement as Dick-a-Dick dodged some of the cricket balls thrown at him and parried away others with a shield grasped in his left hand. His skills enabled him to evade or fend off balls thrown by three men at a time. There is no record of him ever being hit by a ball during any of these demonstrations, either in Australia or later in England.

The Aborigines trained by Lawrence belonged to the tribe of Werrumbrook, between the Wimmera and Glenelg Rivers. There were only 650 Victorian Aborigines by the year 1901, so the cricket team which visited England in 1868 came from the smallest community from which a touring side has ever been selected. From being famed boomerang throwers, the Aborigines became powerful cricketers and one of them, King Billy, threw a cricket ball 140 yards at Clermont in Queensland in 1872 — one of the longest throws on record.

The historic team of 1868 consisted of 13 Aborigines, with Lawrence as captain. The tour had been arranged as a speculative venture by Messrs. Hayman, Graham and Smith. W. R. Hayman (Devonshire) and T. W. Wills (Kent and Victoria) assisted Lawrence in the training of the Aborigines, whose cricket experience was limited. Some had played for two or three years; others for not many months. the team was as follows: C. Lawrence (captain), of Middlesex, Surrey, Scotland, Ireland and New South Wales XIs; J. Mullagh, J. Cuzens and Bullocky, of Victorian XIs; Twopenny, of NSW; Red Cap, Tiger, King Cole, Peter, Dick-a-Dick, C. Dumas, Mosquito, Jim Crow and Sundown, of the Western District. Their real names were considered 'too polysyllabic and not very euphonious' for convenient use in cricket scores and reports.

The preliminary practice of the 1868 touring Aborigines, who landed at Gravesend on 13 May — took place at Town Malling. Fixtures were hard to come by until the MCC granted them a match at Lord's in June. After this there seems to have been no difficulty in organising a most comprehensive tour. No fewer than 47 games were fixed at 40 different centres in 15 counties, the towns visited ranging from Hastings in the south to Newcastle in the north; and from Lincoln and Norwich in the east to Swansea in the west. The tour began and ended at the Oval with games against the Surrey club. Several strong Gentlemen XIs were included in the list of opposing sides.

A curious feature of the tour was the number of matches arranged after the end of August — 11 in September and six in October. The summer of 1868 was an exceptional one; the heat was tremendous, and the climatic conditions and arduous program proved rather trying to the Aborigines, two of whom, Jim Crow and Sundown, left for their homes in August, while another, King Cole, was taken ill and died of lung disease at Guy's Hospital, London, on 24 June. This left only 10 players to take part in the tour from the middle of August onwards.

On King Cole's death, an ode appeared in his memory:

To Britain he came from the land of the West,
　As a stranger to honour and glory,
And now as a hero intrepid and bold
　Will his name be recorded in story.

For not with the sword did he covet renown,
　The battle he fought was at cricket,
In lieu of grim weapons of warfare he strove,
　With the bat and the ball at the wicket.

Now run out for nought in the innings of life,
　By the grave of the good is he sleeping;
Yet sad are his comrades, though reckon they will
　How safe is their mate in our keeping?

If ever you travel old ocean again,
　Take care of the bloody uprooter,
For death may be chartered to bowl in a match,
　And trundle you down with a shooter.

Twenty-two matches were played in a row without a spare member of the team to act as 12th man. It became necessary to call on the services of W. Shepherd, an old Surrey professional who had been accompanying the team as umpire, to fill the gap. Shepherd actually played in seven games, leading the team in the absence of Lawrence. Two other English players also completed the XI in two fixtures — W. S. Norton (Kent) and G. H. Shum-Storey (Northumberland).

The opening match of the tour took place at the Oval on 25–26 May against the Surrey club, which fielded a strong eleven. This was the first match ever played against a team from the Colonies. A local paper said the Aborigines 'cut a highly respectable figure'. On their arrival at Kennington, they were presented with a new bat and a copy of the *Cricketer's Pocket Book*.

Public enthusiasm was high and more than 7000 people attended: 'These included a large number of handsome equipages filled with gaily dressed ladies, and numerous pedestrians, who testified their satisfaction by frequent and enthusiastic plaudits at the prowess of the interesting strangers,' said the local papers.

'Many and confused were the ideas generally entertained respecting these Aboriginals [sic], both as regards their cricketing requirements and their physical conformation. Their beards are long and wiry, their skins vary in shades of blackness, and most of them have broadly expanding nostrils, but they are of the true Australian type. Having been brought up in the bush to agricultural pursuits under European settlers, they are perfectly civilised and are quite familiar with the English language.'

The picturesque appearance of the Aborigines in the field was accentuated by the addition of coloured sashes tied to each man's shirt. This was done to assist spectators in distinguishing the players. Bullocky wore maroon, Tiger pink, Mullagh dark blue, Red Cap black, Dick-a-Dick yellow, Peter green, King Cole magenta, Jim Crow brown, 'Charley' Dumas light blue and Cuzens white.

An extract from a contemporary account:

The match started at 12.15 p.m. As the two leading Surrey batsmen approached the wickets the Aborigines received them with vociferous cheering. Mullagh and Lawrence commenced the bowling, and kept a steady length. Later on Lawrence tried some lobs, off which Jupp was cleverly stumped by Bullocky. The fielding was good, at times brilliant, and Bullocky at length stumped Mr. Baggallay in a style worthy of Lockyer. Only one extra, a bye, was con-

ceded in a total of 222. Long before Tuesday's business began, The Oval presented an unusual gathering of spectators. Mullagh batted two hours and 10 minutes for his 73, a highly meritorious innings, entitling him to the ovation which followed, for he was intercepted on his way to the dressing-room and carried by the crowd to the pavilion, where the usual talent money was awarded him amidst the cheers of the multitude. Mullagh made brilliant cuts and drives, but he lost some runs through the ball being stopped by the spectators.

In those days, all hits had to be run out. There were no boundaries. The Aborigines made 83 and 132 in reply to Surrey's 222. Cuzens, the tourists' best bat, was ill and didn't play. On the Aborigines' return to their native country, they played several matches before finally going home.

Cuzens was engaged for some time as professional bowler at the Melbourne club but he died of dysentery in 1871. His correct name was Zellamach and Mosquito was his brother. Mullagh died in 1891 at Harrow, Victoria, aged 50. He was regarded as one of the best cricketers in Victoria in the 1870s. He top-scored for Victoria with 36 against Lord Harris's All-England XI in 1879. He was generously rewarded by the crowd that day; they presented him with a gold watch and 50 pounds. He was appointed as a professional cricketer with the Melbourne Cricket Club, but soon returned to the country, preferring the life in his tribal territory, where he was a highly respected figure. A cricketer to the core, he was buried in his Harrow Cricket Club colours. His real name was Muaarrimin.

Charles Lawrence returned to Australia after the tour and for many seasons, to the end of 1898, was coach to the Melbourne club. He died in 1917 aged 88. 'An excellent judge of the game, he retained his keenness to the last. What is more, he imparted his enthusiasm to others,' said *The Cricketer* magazine.

Of the others, only Twopenny again played firstclass cricket. He represented New South Wales once against Victoria at Melbourne in 1870. He later worked as a station hand near the present site of Canberra, before excessive use of alcohol caused his death in 1883.

Since then, only four Aborigines from country areas have played first-class cricket in Australia: Jack Marsh, Alex Henry, Eddie Gilbert and Ian King. Marsh, a dapper dresser, and Gilbert were the fastest and best known.

Marsh came from Yugillar in the Clarence River district of northern New South Wales and had a brief, successful and controversial career at the turn of the century. He gained exceptional speed from an easy approach to the wicket. Cricket officials of the time were conducting a 'witch-hunt' against suspicious bowling actions and Marsh became an unlucky victim. He played as a three pound a week professional with the old Sydney club.

Prominent administrator Syd Smith said Marsh was 'very fast and could turn the ball, but his action did not always please the umpires and he was no-balled for throwing on several occasions. Once he stalked off and had his arm put in splints. We onlookers were amazed at his speed and accuracy even with the splints on. He was a remarkable character. He could neither read nor write and club secretary, Alf Dent, found him a constant source of anxiety. Every Saturday morning during the season Alf would take him to Gilham's Restaurant (where the Lyceum now stands) for two three-course meals; total cost, one shilling.

'When he met Alf again he would invariably be rubbing his stomach and saying, "Oh, I feel wonderful Mr Dent. I'll bowl like plurry hell this afternoon". And he would too! Marsh was always immaculately dressed, even if his clothes were on the flashy side. After a match he presented a splendid sight as he left the SCG in his everyday clothes, lovely white teeth glinting.'

He did particularly well in the 1900-01 and 1901-02 seasons. In interstate cricket he took 24 wickets at 22.37 in 1900-01 and at club level the following season his performances were also excellent, and included 2 for 27 and 7 for 19 for Sydney against Leichhardt-

Balmain, 7 for 27 and 3 for 32 against Central Cumberland and 8 for 34 against Burwood. At one stage against Burwood he had 5 for 0.

Picked for the Western District XXVIII against England at Bathurst that season, Marsh had to withdraw at the 11th hour after England captain Archie Maclaren objected to his selection for the local side on the grounds of his doubtful delivery action, and that he did not wish to risk injury to his men before the (fourth) Test match. The local authorities gave way. Marsh disappeared from the first-class scene after being no-balled 19 times in the second innings of a Sheffield Shield match in Sydney in 1901.

After leaving Sydney, he gained permission to play against the 1903-04 England tourists for a Bathurst XI, in February 1904. During this match he captured 5 for 55 and the England cricketers pronounced his action 'perfectly legal'. Several said he was the best bowler they faced on that Australian tour. Marsh demonstrated his bowling skills in a travelling circus for some time afterwards, before he was killed in a drunken brawl at Orange in New South Wales.

The most famous Aboriginal cricketer so far has been Eddie Gilbert, who Sir Donald Bradman once described as being the fastest bowler he faced. Gilbert hailed from the Barambah Aboriginal settlement. His rise was meteoric. His performances were sensational and included 7 for 16 at his first appearance at Brisbane country week. He was named for the Country Colts against City and for the Queensland Colts against South Australia. After taking 6 for 82 in this game he made the Sheffield Shield side.

In 1930-31 he shaped better than any other Australian fast bowler, according to *The Australian Cricketer*. 'Gilbert has a very short run to the wicket, only six yards, adopted on the advice of Andy Ducat, the English coach,' said the magazine. 'Gilbert relies a lot on body swing, and swings the ball on occasions. For a fast bowler, he bowls a very good length ball, and is very difficult to score from in front of the wicket. In lower grade cricket he has taken as many as 80 wickets in a season at an average of 6. He has also made a lot of runs with the bat. As is still a learner, his future should be bright.'

Next year, in the opening match of the 1931–32 season, Gilbert and Bradman had their sensational confrontation at Brisbane. On a fast, green wicket, Gilbert dismissed Wendell Bill with his very first ball. Next man in, Bradman, had his cap flicked off with the first ball he faced, his bat knocked out of his hands by the extreme pace of another and on the sixth delivery he was caught behind for 0.

'Luckiest duck I ever made!' said Bradman. Later he declared: 'I unhesitatingly class his short burst as faster than anything seen from Larwood or anyone else.' (Bradman was out for 0 only 15 times in his first-class career.) Gilbert's thunderbolt deliveries also were on show against Queensland country players. Gilbert could not find suitable employment in Brisbane. Consequently, when he was not on State duty, he still opened the bowling for Barambah in the Kilkivan-Murgon association.

Gilbert was treated like a god by the people at Cherbourg after he 'cleaned up' Bradman. But his presence in the local league greatly disturbed local cricket administrators. The executive moved to have him banned from playing on the concrete pitches. They considered his bowling too dangerous on any surface except turf. The Barambah club responded by threatening to withdraw from the competition, so a compromise was suggested — Gilbert would be allowed to continue in the competition if Barambah promised he would bowl at half pace!

This suggestion was also refused on the grounds that Gilbert would be prevented from obtaining the proper practice necessary for his first-class cricket engagements. Nothing could be resolved and Gilbert continued his dual interstate and Queensland country cricket career.

Gordon Bourne from Goomeri in Queensland was one who sympathised with both Gilbert and the administrators. This stylish country batsman was selected to represent Queensland in the 1930s, aged 18. He also played in the same rural area as Gilbert and saw him perform at both levels. There were some frightening stories about Gilbert's pace on local concrete wickets but Bourne stressed that Gilbert usually operated below top pace against bush batsmen. He only 'let them really go' on country wickets if something had annoyed him.

In one game in rural Queensland, Gilbert was stirred to bowl at his fiercest. A local batting star was depicted in white cricket clothing on a poster advertising the game. Beside him was an Aborigine wearing a loin cloth and holding a boomerang. 'Come and see Jones against Gilbert', read the caption. Poor Jones did not see much of the action at all next day. Gilbert, infuriated by the blatant racism of the poster, demolished the local side taking 9 for 1 in a fearsome display of pace bowling.

Bourne remembers Gilbert as a shy, but friendly person who possessed freakish gifts as a fast bowler. 'He only ran in eight paces, but had unusually long arms and delivered the ball with a very quick, whippy action,' he said. This 'whippy' action caused much controversy. There were many, including Bradman, who considered Gilbert's bowling action suspect. He was no-balled for throwing by umpire Andy Barlow of Victoria in a State game six weeks after Bradman's sensational dismissal. Despite continuing suspicions, this was the only time Gilbert was 'called' in his first-class career. He continued to represent Queensland until 1936. During his Sheffield Shield matches he took 87 wickets for his State at an average of 29.98. He never represented Australia.

Gilbert could be very sporting. When West Indian Learie Constantine hit Gilbert for six at Brisbane, they met in the centre of the wicket and shook hands. Gilbert was unheard of for many years after he left the top cricket arena, until cricket journalist David Frith discovered he was a patient at the Goodna psychiatric hospital. He had been there for more than 20 years and by then his illness had left him a withdrawn, lonely figure without memories. Gilbert was 69 when he died on 9 January 1978. He was buried at the Cherbourg Aboriginal Centre cemetery.

Tragedy has luckily not dogged the life of Phil Minnekin, though some of his admirers claim he was harshly treated by his State's cricket selectors. Minnekin is a Torres Strait Islander. Like Gilbert, he is a product of Queensland country cricket. Minnekin was raised in Cairns, far north Queensland, where he was plucked from obscurity and became a local star all in one match.

Jim Bratchford, the former Queensland all-rounder, was captain of a Cairns side when he was a bank manager in the town. Before one game in 1963 his team was a player short. He had noticed a barefoot boy helping at the team's practice and the lad was offered a game. Sandshoes and cricket gear were found and Minnekin walked onto a cricket field for the first time. His first match is now part of local cricket folklore — he captured seven wickets in a dream debut.

By 1965, Minnekin was playing for the Queensland Country Colts. Shortly afterwards he joined the Wynum Manly club in Brisbane, where he was a great success. He topped the bowling average on four occasions and was regarded as the fastest bowler the competition had seen since the days of the great West Indian, Wesley Hall. He was a regular selection in the State practice squad, but was never chosen to represent his State, despite his consistent performances. Many people in Queensland cricket circles — where he is much admired and respected — are at a loss to explain his rejection. Others are more forthright. 'There was no problem about Minnekin's claim for State selection that couldn't have been solved by a bucket of whitewash,' was one blunt opinion. Others believe the Queensland selectors were reluctant to choose Minnekin because of problems created by another Aboriginal player. Minnekin is now the father of seven children and works as a building tradesman in a Queensland country town.

Many gifted Aboriginal athletes have a nonchalant approach to their sporting achievements. Few epitomise this laid back attitude to country cricket more than Arnold Von Senden, a part-Aboriginal lad who once played in the Northern Territory town of Katherine. His short but dynamic cricket career is well remembered by many — especially by Gary McCauliff, who employed Von Senden at Baruwei Enterprises while Arnold was living in Katherine.

For years cricket in Katherine had been completely dominated by Bob Pemble, a fast bowler of outstanding ability. McCauliff was very pleased to recruit Von Senden to his local side, as Von Senden proved to be a handy fast bowler in the games leading up to the big clash involving Pemble's team. Pemble's long, smooth, gliding approach was very impressive. He was soon cutting a swathe through Baruwei's batting until Von Senden, the 23-year-old Aboriginal 'ring-in', ambled to the wicket.

His batting until then had been indifferent, but his past failures were soon forgotten when he smashed 22 runs from the local champion's first over. Von Senden completely demoralised Pemble — and all the lesser lights in the opposition that day. He carved out 139 runs in only 70 minutes and this match-winning rampage included a last-wicket partnership of 85 with Paul Gunn, who was 0 not out when Von Senden's lightning innings ended!

An elated McCauliff greeted Arnold with much enthusiasm as Katherine's new cricket hero strolled from the ground. 'Congratulations Arnold! What an innings! I've never seen him treated with such little respect. What did you really think of Pemble's bowling?'

'Which one was Pemble?' replied Arnold casually to his stunned audience — a comment which is now as famous in Katherine cricket circles as the fine innings Von Senden played that day.

Allen 'Dusty' Armstrong was another happy-go-lucky part-Aboriginal player who became a cricket legend around the Roebourne area in the far north-west of Western Australia. This class player, who had a bat-

Former Australian Test player Bruce Yardley watches as one of his Aboriginal charges, Barry Demi, bounds into his delivery stride at a Lord's Taverners' training camp in Perth, WA.

ting average of 260 during one of his many fine seasons, died tragically in a 1983 house fire. He was only in his early 40s. Many cricketers of the Pilbara region were among the large crowd which attended his funeral at Roebourne. The sportsmen's bar at the local cricket club was named after him. Visitors to the Roebourne facilities, which constitute part of one of the oldest cricket clubs in Western Australia, will notice that 'Dusty's' cricket cap hangs above the bar named in his honour.

Sam Anderson and Alec James were two other fine Aboriginal players who were honoured by fellow cricketers, both during their playing days and after their deaths. Anderson exhibited freakish all-round ability in the upper Clarence area of northern New South Wales. He crashed many centuries and in one game in the Casino area, he once stumped several players as a wicket-keeper, before capturing four wickets when he was later given a bowl.

Anderson and James were very close friends. They were inseparable on or off the field. They had many undefeated partnerships when they batted together for the duration of their side's innings. The two friends were buried side-by-side in a cemetery on the north coast. Local admirers had two crossed cricket bats sculptured on their gravestone.

Part-Aboriginal Neil Bulger is another highly regarded country cricketer. He was once described by the *Canberra Times* as 'the most brilliant all-rounder to ever play in the ACT'. Bulger was born in the NSW town of Tumut in the Snowy Mountains and became the dominant player in local cricket. In one semi-final match for Wyangle against Tumut Plains, he hammered a record 218 not out with 28 fours and two sixes. The opposing captain described his knock as 'the finest innings I have seen in the Riverina'. Bulger finished that 1977–78 season in the Tumut Association with a mammoth 1013 runs: average 202.6.

In 1979, Bulger, a left-arm medium pacer and aggressive middle order bat, returned to the ACT. Here he rejoined the Queanbeyan club, with whom he had previously played in the 1972–73 season. He has been a stalwart of the club ever since and has won nearly every award possible in Canberra cricket.

The 1980–81 season was the pinnacle of all his years in cricket. His preparation for that summer was very thorough. He began pre-season training at the Canberra Indoor Cricket Centre in the previous July and developed an outswinger to complement his inswingers. The rewards for his hard work were numerous. He won the Player of the Year, as well as both the bowling and batting averages for the association. Queanbeyan won their first flag for 23 seasons. In the final against East Canberra, Bulger took his first-ever hat-trick.

Another highlight for Bulger in that year was winning the Man of the Match award against the touring Indians. With powerful drives and pulls against an attack which included Kapil Dev, Roger Binny and Shivlal Yadav, the powerful left-hander raced to 50 in an hour and finished with 58 not out. Bulger believed he had then achieved most of his cricket ambitions and eased out of representative cricket.

Canberra cricket officials did not forget his fine con-tribution to the game and in 1984 he was honoured by being made 12th man for the Prime Minister's XI against Clive Lloyd's mighty West Indian team. He regards that selection as one of the highlights of his career. Bulger commutes by bicycle to Canberra each day to work with the ACT Parks and Gardens. He has now settled with his young family in Queanbeyan. He and his wife LeeAnn are highly respected for their active involvement in Queanbeyan club activities.

Mullagh, Marsh, Gilbert, Minnekin, Anderson and Bulger are just some of the many fine Aboriginal players of the bush who have emerged in Australian cricket. It is significant that not one Aboriginal player has so far represented Australia. Perhaps we haven't fully tapped a reservoir of talent that has been, and still is, available.

In his foreword to a book about the 1868 tour of England, the first edition of *Cricket Walkabout*, by D. J. Mulvaney, former Australian captain Ian Johnson says: 'When we read Mr Mulvaney's account of the prowess of Mullagh and Cuzens, there is a temptation to feel that we have surely bypassed a budding Gary Sobers.'

'. . . I can tell you a few things. He took six wickets in his last game for Queensland. Terrific bowler — only ran half-a-dozen steps.'

The oblivion of Eddie Gilbert

David Frith

The Queensland Aboriginal cricketer Eddie Gilbert, famed for his bursts of express bowling during the 1930s, had not been heard of for so long that I took it upon myself when in Brisbane to track him down.

An old-timer in the suburb of Red Hill, where Eddie was last seen, thought he had died about five years before. We checked in the general store run by a cricket fan of some 60 summers: 'I'd just about swear to it. Old Eddie went right out of circulation and we never heard nothin' of him for ages. I reckon he must've died 10 years back at least. They had him in Goodna for a while.'

I drove out to the psychiatric hospital along the Ipswich Road in the hope of establishing the truth of the matter. The superintendent, barely concealing his surprise at my questions, led me through to the records office, where he produced Eddie Gilbert's hospital history card. 'Eddie was admitted on 8 December 1949. His age was shown as 37.'

I thought he would have been slightly older than that; perhaps the paperwork was completed hastily that sad day. 'If you're writing about him,' the superintendent volunteered, 'I can tell you a few things. He took six wickets in his last game for Queensland. Terrific bowler — only ran half a dozen steps. He got the knack from boomerang throwing. Some reckoned he chucked, but I never thought so. It was just his funny wrist action. Wish we had somebody like him right now.'

Some weeks earlier Bill Hunt, the prewar New South Wales player, had been in no doubt about it: 'Eddie threw *me* out! By cripes, yeah! And later on I deliberately did the same to him. And d'you know what he said? I'll tell you, he put his arm round my shoulder and said, "Well bowled, Bill. That was a beauty!" So you see, the little fellah couldn't tell a bowl from a chuck anyway! Nice chap, but . . .'

It was Hunt's contention that Stan McCabe, whose name will live for his three classic Test innings, considered his best hand to have been a 229 not out against Queensland at Brisbane in 1931 after Eddie Gilbert had

Eddie Gilbert in action.

served Don Bradman with the 'luckiest duck I ever made'. Bowling with horrifying hostility on an under-prepared pitch, Gilbert had New South Wales in ribbons at 3 for 31, with Alan Kippax in hospital after a dreadful blow on the temple from a mistimed hook off Thurlow. At that point McCabe took command.

So long ago. Now here was I seeking to trace the conclusion of a life story. The superintendent glanced up from the history card. 'He was married at the time he came here. Nobody's visited him for ages. He used to be violent occasionally, but he's all right now — no trouble. But he's bottled right up within himself. You won't get him to talk. We've tried everything. He'll

never change. Just as well perhaps. If he went out again he'd be back among the plonkies down at the Adelaide in no time.'

'You're telling me he's here — alive?' He nodded. 'As I say, he's completely withdrawn. It's impossible to get through to him. He walks the grounds all day — he's content in his own private world. We've tried to interest him in some kind of recreation. His reflexes are still sharp. But when we put a cricket ball in his hand he just stared at it.'

It came as a shock. Eddie — still ticking after all. Even the locals had seemed so certain. I had fallen into line with them and quietly and briefly mourned their

291

popular hero of long ago, the fast bowler to whom they had bellowed encouragement to 'give Jardine a taste of his own bodyline medicine'.

In *That Barambah Mob*, David Forrest's amusing blend of fact and fantasy, Eddie has already been immortalised: on the top of Henry Stulpnagel's head was imprinted in reverse 'nufactured in Austra', a living souvenir of a Gilbert bumper. 'When that ball hit the concrete,' he exclaimed, 'she'd smoke!' Mr Stulpnagel also knew why Eddie never became a Test cricketer: 'He made an ape of Bradman, and he was black, and he was born in Queensland, and they didn't like the look o' that whippy wrist of his.'

I made my reverent plea to the superintendent: 'I'd like to see Eddie.'

'It's no use. He won't talk.'

I pressed him. I had to see the historic cricketer. He picked up the phone and asked the attendant at the appropriate wing to 'find Eddie'. We walked across the sunlit lawns, past slumbering patients, small-talk lost in the insistent buzz of insects. The coolness in the outer block was a relief.

Eddie was some time in coming. Sitting in the office, I scanned the grounds through the open window. Suddenly a male nurse was standing at the door and behind him, reluctant to advance, was a thin man in a maroon T-shirt and black shorts. His hair was white and close-cropped, his skin glistening ebony. It was unmistakably Gilbert.

He shuffled into the room, head to one side, eyes averted, impossible to meet. His physique would have been insignificant beside Tom Richardson, Miller or Trueman, yet he was not the midget legend has depicted. Five feet eight, with long arms: the devastating catapult machine he must once have been was apparent.

'Shake hands, Eddie,' his attendant urged kindly. The hand that had propelled the ball that had smashed so many stumps was raised slowly; it was as limp as a dislodged bail. He was muttering huskily and incoherently, gently rocking his head side to side.

'Want a fag, Eddie?' the nurse asked softly. Eddie grunted, watched the cigarette begin to smoulder and puffed at it. His legs, typical of his race, were thin. He turned on them restlessly. He was an outdoor man; a room was a cage. When I asked the nurse if Eddie could write his name for me he coaxed him to pick up a pen. At the end of an agonising minute Eddie backed away, leaving only a tortured 'E' on the paper. His squinting eyes, deep-set and bloodshot, flashed briefly across all of us.

I thought then of what Archie Jackson, Australia's batting genius, had written about Eddie Gilbert in 1933: 'The adulation he has received has not affected his mental equilibrium. Such a player is an ornament to the game; may he continue to prosper!'

Eddie walked off, still breathing his wheezy monotone; he wandered through the meal hall and the last I saw of him was as he drifted, a desolate individual, across the parched grass.

'We moderns, for a number of years now, have been passing through an era of excessive short-pitched speed bowling which I find during my frequent travelling still remains an emotional talking point wherever cricket is taken seriously.'

Short-pitched bowling — a blight or a blessing?

Frederick W. Bennett

Fred Bennett, immediate past-president of the Australian Cricket Board.

Ever since the late Douglas Jardine applied what has been referred to as 'his tactical genius' on the playing arenas of Australia in 1932–33 much has been said and written about persistent short-pitched fast bowling.

This potentially lethal form of attack has also, somewhat emotively, been referred to over the years by terms ranging from the less offensive 'bouncers' to the more derogatory 'bodyline', coined by a journalist during that controversial Anglo-Australian Test series.

History has vividly recorded all the gory details associated with bodyline which aroused so much ill-feeling that the Prime Ministers of both countries become involved and threatened the strong ties that linked the two oldest and strongest Test nations. Fortunately, in due course, an honourable truce eventuated but only after a firm resolve by both authorities to have certain sections of the laws amended (particularly those laws relating to field placements) to prevent any repetition of the fiasco. Even the usually laconic Arthur Mailey said that bodyline 'would have been distinctly dangerous in any era of cricket'.

But one wonders how much have administrators, umpires, coaches, captains and players generally throughout the expanding cricketing world really learned from all this? We moderns, for a number of years now, have been passing through an era of excessive short-pitched speed bowling which I find during my frequent travelling still remains an emotional talking point wherever cricket is taken seriously.

Discussion frequently hovers between the belief on the one hand that it is an infectious *blight* on the game particularly if effective retaliation is not a viable option and on the other hand that it is a captain's *blessing* in the form of a tactical weapon if he has the armoury to maintain a high degree of fire power.

Obviously, I am inclined very strongly towards the former of these alternatives while freely admitting in comparatively recent times that Australia must share the blame for developing this form of attack. For some time I have held the view that persistent intimidatory bowling is placing our grand game in jeopardy because of the likelihood of Test cricket becoming so tarnished that it will become secondary to the limited-over frolics.

If, as a result of many overseas visits and discussions with many players and administrators, I felt that I was becoming the sole crusader against the excessive use of head-high bouncers, I would not be waxing so determinedly but I have found that a surprising majority of devotees very close to the game share my sentiments.

For instance, in supporting Sir Donald Bradman's contention that 'all great bowlers have one common characteristic: they are predominately attacking bowlers who make the stumps their prime objective', no less an authority than John Woodcock in the 1985 *Wisden* made this assertion: 'It should be a cause of real concern to cricket administrators that the batsman himself has become as much a target for the pace bowlers of the world as the wicket he defends. The viciousness of much of today's fast bowling is changing the very nature of the game.'

Woodcock is an extremely well qualified observer and seldom loses an opportunity to express his opposition to the excessive use of this form of attack because it is undermining the charm and, indeed, the spirit of the game and therefore if allowed to persist unchallenged could do untold damage to the continuance of its acceptance among devotees throughout the world. Furthermore, I have not the slightest doubt, judging by the mass of statistical evidence available to fans everywhere these days, that it is the major contributing factor to the decline in over and run rates, particularly at the Test match level.

Innate fear and self-preservation are constantly in conflict with the batsman's realisation that he is out there in the middle essentially to score runs and in many instances gets himself out through frustration as a result of his need to get his bat somewhere near the ball which he has only a split second to calculate is somewhere near or above his head.

In addition, the growing tendency to give the less talented tailenders the same kind of unchivalrous treat- ment — considered in many quarters as bordering on bad sportsmanship — must surely qualify for the 'blight' category in anybody's fair-minded language.

To change tack a little, it should be made clear that the decision taken at the 1986 ICC to force teams to bowl a minimum of 90 overs per day (although I personally believe at least 105 per day would not be unreasonable) should help markedly to minimise deliberate go-slow tactics of which, without any doubt, monotonous speedy short-pitched bowling was, and still is, one of the chief culprits. But I'm firmly convinced there is still much to be done.

Without intending to be hypocritical of any particular group, I contend that administrators, captains and umpires have indirectly allowed persistent short-pitched bouncers to get out of hand by not enforcing the laws precisely to the letter as they presently stand, rather than standing by awaiting additional specific amendments. This, in my view, is tantamount in an obscure kind of way to aiding and abetting the tarnishing of the true spirit and the inherent charm of the game.

At the risk of being regarded as staid and old-fashioned, I have no hesitation in declaring that a meaningful, universally-accepted phrase such as 'It isn't cricket' cannot be allowed to fade into oblivion as a corny, anachronistic joke . . . there is far too much at stake.

For this very reason, over recent years I have directed my efforts both in Australia and overseas wherever there is a forum prepared to listen, particularly at the international level, to encourage courageous in-depth investigations into the ultimate damage that some so-called modern tendencies are inflicting on the game. I do so because I remain convinced that with the right type of committed co-operation freed from parochialism, we can eliminate the 'harm' from arenas that are in danger of virtually becoming battlefields, and re-establish the 'charm', the many attractions and the genuine sportsmanship that has been synonymous with cricket for more than 300 years.

Apart from the acute damage that is being done to the intangibles of our game, we are being forced to tolerate the unsightly use of a vast variety of helmets and bulky, unseemly protective gear such as sophisticated boxes, chest guards, rib guards, thigh pads, arm guards and even teeth guards, depriving the players of their individuality and creating an appearance typical of the hooded gladiators fighting for their lives in ancient Rome — and all with the same common objective of making sure that 'it will be the other fellow's blood and guts and not mine that will provide the gory spectacle for the fanatics in the bleachers'.

The most frightening thought of all is that it appears certain that these survival kits will be deemed essential equipment while selectors favour teams which have the fastest and the most potentially lethal battery of thunderbolts.

It has been said that this policy has paid rich dividends if the winning of Test matches is the only yardstick. Unfortunately, it has also proved detrimental to the game as a spectacle because it has markedly reduced the value, effectiveness and entertainment value of the spinner, with a few exceptions. 'A well-balanced attack' was a complimentary oft-quoted expression down through the years. Nowadays it has become somewhat underused.

Coaches have a most important role to play in helping to restore sanity to many phases of cricket. One of them is to discourage youngsters not possessing the physique or the natural aptitudes to become speed merchants from aspiring to become prototypes of the truly gifted champions who wreak their particular brand of havoc. Nevertheless I must hasten to add that in my concept of 'well balanced attacks' there will always be a place for a few spearhead bowlers hopefully capable of calling on their reserves of strength and energy to occasionally make a delivery or two *lift off a good length*. The history of the game is studded with the names of many champions with the ability to do this at will. It is part and parcel of the game and should be retained and even encouraged if the talent is there.

It was interesting to assess the tactics of all teams that participated in first-class cricket last season in Australia. There was a noticeable tendency to discard out-of-form fast bowlers in favour of well-balanced attacks and as a result some very attractive encounters were witnessed.

To return to my references to the policy of enforcement through democratic legislation, let me make it very clear that I am not suggesting that nothing has been done in the immediate past or planned for the near future. All that seems to be lacking is solid universal agreement on a few vital issues. The ICC has already had several fruitful discussions without the emergence of any clearcut resolutions in areas causing the most concern. At the 1986 conference there were promising signs of general acceptance by several senior cricket countries who considered that far too many short-pitched, head-high deliveries were being bowled in international matches of all types.

Australia was of the view that such a persistent deliberate form of attack should be outlawed. England, on the other hand, inclined to favour a limited number of bouncers in each over. Following lengthy discussions it was generally agreed that 'every effort should be made' to have the umpires enforce the law consistently, as it now stands, so that some measure of uniformity will be assured irrespective of where the matches are being played. But, as we have previously noted, no specific resolutions arose; just promises for further discussions in later conferences.

In unofficial discussions I have had with other administrators, there seems to be complete agreement (covering the difficulty of umpiring consistency) that if the relevant laws are too ambiguous, or are overly stressing the intimidatory factors at the expense of associated aspects such as deliberate time wasting and ball-out-of-reach theories, then amendments and clarifications should be made as soon as is practicable. These clarifications should be stated in ultra-specific terms so that offending players will not have to wait for an umpire's interpretation to find that they are trans-

gressing, just as surely and as quickly as they know they are out when they have had their stumps knocked out of the ground by a fair delivery.

I'm very confident that these adjustments will eventually be made because the senior nations appear to be on the same rehabilitation course. The pressing need for them is to convince the other ICC members who have a say and a vote at the conferences that a solution to an unsavoury problem through legislation is desirable and enforcement through appropriate areas of officialdom is imperative.

Those who need some convincing will gain some comfort from the knowledge that both Sir Donald Bradman and Sir George (Gubby) Allen, who were very much involved in the bodyline series, firmly believe that if cricket is to retain its oft-quoted ranking as 'The Greatest Game of All', any tendency to condone persistent short-pitched, head-high bowling as an integral part of the game should be squashed as soon as possible. Alec Bedser in his book *Twin Ambitions* supports their contention.

Naturally there are many past and present players and a few administrators who do not feel as strongly about this issue but after seeking authoritative opinions

from all over the world I am confident they are in the minority. So, in order to validate my assertions that we are dealing in the main with a blight rather than a blessing, irrespective of the number of Test matches that have been won as a result of its implementation (not excluding Australia and England), I can do no better than recall John Woodcock to the rostrum. Remember this? 'I am less in sympathy with umpires for the way they have allowed fast bowlers to resort ever more frequently to the thuggery of the bouncer. This has got so badly out of hand that for all but a few highly talented batsmen it is now madness not to have a helmet handy. The viciousness of much of today's fast bowling is changing the nature of the game. A day's play in the West Indies when the West Indians are in the field may be expected to consist of the minimum requirement of overs, if there is one, and as many as three bouncers an over (perhaps 250 per day) so long as the pitch has anything in it. To add to this menace many of them are bowled from around the wicket. I am not saying the West Indians are the only offenders, but they are the worst. The TCCB's decision taken at their December meeting to *dispense with* the agreement allowing only one bouncer an over in domestic English first-class cricket was a setback to those who see intimidatory bowling as a curse of the modern game. Already, each season ends with more broken fingers and cracked ribs than the one before. One day a white line may have to be drawn across the pitch as a warning mark to bowlers.' (1984 *Wisden*.)

This carefully considered indictment published in the most prestigious and most widely-circulated cricket periodical in the world must be accepted as factual, so it follows that if we cricket administrators and other relevant groups fail to rectify matters then let it be clearly stated that it's time we all handed in our credentials and sought better ways of spending our summers, and in many cases our winters, in serving a once very proud institution called 'International Cricket'.

'The answer to the "call of nature", of course, is for the umpire to grab an apparently damaged stump and head very quickly for the pavilion to change same.'

The other side of the TV screen

Robin Bailache

Robin Bailache during an international one-day match, West Indies versus Australia, Adelaide Oval, January 1987.

During my cricket umpiring career two questions have constantly been put to me — firstly, what do you need to be an umpire? That is, what are the ingredients of the umpiring 'pie'? Secondly, do I enjoy umpiring Test matches and the like? (This second question is usually prefaced by comments like, 'I wouldn't be in your shoes for quids, how do you manage not to get bored, how do you stand out there all those hours with the heat and the flies, what do you do when nature calls, etc.?).

The simple answer is that two of the ingredients needed for the 'pie' are surely for the intending umpire to be both a masochist and stupid. The answer to the 'call of nature', of course, is for the umpire to grab an apparently damaged stump and head very quickly for the pavilion to change same! One of my fellow umpires undertook this course of action on one occasion only to be very promptly met at the players gate by a very efficient curator with another stump in hand. I have no doubt that the poor curator was most upset when it was suggested where he should put said stump.

On a more serious note, what makes an umpire? I consider there are three basic essentials; I call them the three 'Cs'. The first is *courage*, the courage of your convictions. The courage to stand up and pay them as you see them and not be influenced by players, crowds or the hometown situation. It takes courage to stand there and shake your head and say 'not out' in response to yelling, bounding appeals from most members of the fielding side, not to mention the crowd, knowing you may have, just possibly, missed something. After all, umpires are only human and like the players, they *do* make mistakes. I guess it could be said that the best umpire is the one who makes the least mistakes.

In any event, one has to make the decision and live with it. In the meantime the TV media is replaying the incident from every angle possible, straight on, from behind, from square leg and even overhead. From the umpire's viewpoint, forget it, get on with the game and wait for the next one; it could be the very next ball or not at all.

The second 'C' is *commonsense*. This is quite difficult to put into words because it deals basically with those grey areas of player attitude, player conduct and those areas where an umpire is obliged, under the laws of cricket, to take remedial action. This great game is played by all colours and creeds and sometimes it can be quite difficult to get the message across without appearing to be a policeman or 'trying to get into the game' as the media like to describe it. Areas such as bowlers running on the wicket, intimidatory bowling, time wasting and substitution are laws that need to be enforced from time to time. Obviously, captains and players vary considerably in their understanding of these matters and a small amount of talk coupled with a lot of commonsense can, in most cases, eradicate the problem. Of course, there are no guarantees that they will agree with your actions or your methods, but I guess that's life.

Finally, we have *concentration* — self-explanatory, of course, and an absolute necessity. An umpire could recite the laws of cricket word for word from front page to back page, but without adequate powers of concentration, and the ability to maintain concentration over many hours, he will always find the going tough.

Please excuse me if the above comments give the impression that cricket umpiring is all hard slog and a demanding and thankless pastime. Far from it. Sure it has its bad spots, when one is bound to feel like one of the soldiers at Custer's last stand and mutter 'what am I doing here?' These spots are far outweighed by the many fine hours of entertainment, excitement and memorable incidents involving many great players. There are many humorous incidents also — strangely, most of the humorous incidents seem to feature fast bowlers. To be a fast bowler in Australia surely needs a certain amount of humour — one runs 30 metres to bowl and is then no-balled because he is a centimetre or two over the line, it's about 40°C in the shade, somebody has dropped a catch off his bowling and the umpire (blind) has just knocked back a plumb lbw!

I have a very deep affection for fast bowlers and I certainly do not subscribe to the definition of gross stupidity as being 144 fast bowlers. One Australian fast bowler was heard to mutter (expletives deleted) to a batsman who had consistently played and missed, 'There are three things wrong with you Poms, you're overpaid, over-rated, and over here'. Another similar type was prone upon being hit for four to walk down towards the offending batsman and indicate the sign of the cross on the batsman's forehead. I think it can be safely assumed that there was no religious or spiritual intent, most likely a veiled threat that a decent bouncer was on the way.

I mentioned memorable incidents — how can I ever forget umpiring in front of 88,000 people at the MCG on Boxing Day during the 1975–76 West Indies tour of Australia or Doug Walter's century in a session in the Perth Test of the 1974–75 England tour of Australia? More recently, the exploits of Viv Richards and the vast array of West Indies talent, Dennis Lillee, the Chappells, Allan Border and many too numerous to mention from all parts of the cricket world have all provided great moments.

Strange things can happen to umpires — I once received a quite worn, much-travelled batting pad through the mail. It was wrapped in brown paper, tied with string and had no forwarding address. Attached to the pad was a scribbled message, 'From me to you, guess who?' I found out, quite accidentally, that it had been sent to me by a now-retired English opening batsman who I had given out lbw on more than one occasion. I guess he thought that as I was so interested in his pads I may as well have one! I wonder if he knows that I know?

Greg Chappell, effortlessly upright

Kate Fitzpatrick

Kate Fitzpatrick and Ian Chappell in the commentary box at the 'Gabba in Brisbane.

From 11 a.m. Friday morning until sixish on Monday evening I watched the Sheffield Shield match between Queensland and New South Wales. I was supposed to be interviewing Greg Chappell when he wasn't fielding or batting.

But as Mum says, 'The road to hell is paved with good intentions'. All we did was reminisce. I went into a four-day trance; watching cricket is as near as I'll ever get to meditating; and was swamped by waves of nostalgia.

I guess it had something to do with being the same age as Greg and coming from South Australia. Greg Chappell's old school, Prince Alfred College, had the same maroon colours as Queensland. It was strange last weekend, a time warp back to school matches between PAC and the blue and white boys from St Peter's.

When I was at school, PAC boys were considered a bit fast — glamorous Protestants who were not forced to confess experimenting with the one, two and three minor league mating steps out of a possible (but unthinkable) 10. SAC (my old school) girls were considered a bit fast themselves, but anything more than three (or fourish) was beyond the pale and *we* had to confess.

I was safe. Apart from never getting any offers, I was far too busy chaperoning my friend Viv to muck around. She had a crush on a tall, blond, handsome PAC football star with a red MGA. Simon was *very* glamorous. At Victor Harbor over Christmas he took us for 100 mph car rides with the roof off. This was before breath tests, seat belts and kilometres. Wherever he went, Viv went and so did I.

The 'Gidget goes sporty' romance lasted for two years. We watched all the PAC cricket and football matches and attended every dance. I don't remember seeing Greg Chappell. I know he was there. We probably even danced together . . . but made absolutely no impression on each other.

I can't imagine why, he's pretty impressive these days. Tall, lean, erect, proud, dark, strong and silent.

He looks broody and mysterious. He has an absolutely wonderful back, completely straight without being rigid, and no wings. Ray Robinson described him as a poplar, upright in growth with little spread. Effortlessly upright, he gets taller as you watch him.

It's hard to imagine him ever joining the rest of us as we curl, curve and collapse back to the all fours of our beginnings. He bends in all directions, even falls backwards, and instantly returns, springs back to an absolute centre. Even leaning on his bat he is perfectly balanced. The hand on his hip corresponds with the leg crossed in front. The straight leg echoes his stiff arm, with its bat extension. Exactly half of him is either side of a plumb line. And he's resting!

He was probably carried, and then walked, never crawled. He has thick, dark, very curly hair and big, deep-blue eyes that miss nothing. 'I have an American friend who is amazed when I can tell him what time he arrived at the ground and where he was sitting. You can see a lot out there. You get used to it.' He can tell you if (and when) you nodded off or wrote something or cracked a joke. 'I don't miss much — just the odd ball . . .' He thinks he's pretty good at reading people and situations.

He has long legs, arms, small wrists and very beautiful long-fingered hands, which he uses economically, deftly, like a good mime artist. They are very strong and quite tough looking. One has a permanent scab that he keeps worrying and knocking. And the other has a bone broken taking an amazing catch to dismiss David Gower. Occasionally they become side flippers which he raises to acknowledge a 'Hey Greg' or 'Good on you Chappell'. Nothing else moves, just his hands — from pointing down to parallel to the ground, wrists still attached to his thighs.

It's great fun trying to work out his field placement signals; to watch him and Allan Border practising what seems to be fly casting or elegant tennis forehands, and wonder if it's a trap. On the opposing team his brother Trevor seems to turn away as if he doesn't want to see them and feel obliged to tip off Dirk Wellham at the other end. His mood on the field changed from day to day . . . lean, boyish jumping around, head-butting the ball one day . . . still, severe, tougher, older, meaner looking the next.

Going to a Shield match is a bit like attending a school play or sports day. Most of the audience are players' friends or family on comps. Waiting for guest tickets to be brought down to the Members' gate, you can pass the time by trying to guess which cricketer has what relation. 'I bet that's Dirk Wellham's brother.'

On the third day, huge white clouds behind the empty Hill looked like snow-covered mountains and the idle, suspended cable cars like a ski-lift . . . cricket in Switzerland . . . Edelweiss, Leiderhorn, the Matterhorn, cow bells and red balls. As my mind wandered off, my companions joked about feeling like cricket groupies and discussed the other regulars there permanently positioned under the players' window, and the 16-year-old down the front today featuring a plunging white bathing suit top and modest skirt ensemble.

Suddenly he's with us again, jumper on, towel around his neck like a thick scarf, and would not be drawn into a conversation about cricket bats. We start on childhood again. 'I didn't grow much until I was 16. I was very short, then all of a sudden I shot up over the Christmas holidays. It probably has to do with the fact that I never ate much. Not much at breakfast, still don't. And I never ate lunch. I used to throw my Vegemite sandwiches away behind the shed. Mum'll kill me when she reads this. It was a waste of time; I was too excited to eat. I wanted to play cricket. You had to stay in the shelter, *sitting down* for 15 minutes! I couldn't stand it. But I was always exhausted at the end of the day. I'd ride my bike home and on the way stop off at a friend's place to do a bit of boxing. I was fine until he hit me in the stomach, then I was history.' Half joking, he says: 'I sometimes think I started to grow when I started eating lunch.' His son, Stephen, is the same. 'Only not sneaky like me, he brings his home untouched.'

He says he doesn't hold grudges, but remembers

Greg Chappell looks as if he's praying for deliverance after missing a chance at slip to catch his brother, Trevor, for 22 off Dymock during a New South Wales versus Queensland match at the Sydney Cricket Ground.

every mean thing ever done to him, from the age of three, in the most astonishing detail. Mrs Boxer, a grade three teacher, hated smelly little boys and accused him of passing a rude note. 'I was at cricket practice, not even there.' He was supposed to tell his mother, didn't and sweated for 10 days waiting for a parental showdown after the PTA meeting. Nothing happened. Either Mrs B forgot or his Mum ignored it. 'Anyway, none of us were very smelly.'

Another teacher, Mrs Thompson, kept him in after school and forgot him. His worried parents arrived at the school and found him still sitting, alone, in the dark classroom. He was 'pushed' off a fence at seven, by someone he remembers but won't name, and hurt his arm. His mother said it looked all right and to stop whingeing . . . just the way my Mum did to my sister after a game of 'Rockets to the Moon'. After three days of little weeps under the tankstand, and less sleep, a doctor announced he had a greenstick fracture. Momentary triumph that something really was wrong with him changed to frustrated boredom when he wasn't allowed to bat. 'It drove me crazy. I kept arguing that it'd make things better, like wearing an arm pad, but my coach wouldn't wear it.'

Queensland declared at 405. I glanced back at him behind the glass and never found out what he meant. The pitch is being flattened by a dear little motorised roller, squeaking slowly up and down, missing the stumps. Two other groundsmen with buckets, spades and brooms come out to fix the potholes. They look like the grave diggers in *Hamlet* . . . rough, very casually dressed, leaning on their spades, cracking jokes.

He didn't like school. Never read a play or finished a book but still passed. 'It wasn't hard. The teachers relied on a few of us getting through to keep their jobs. They usually gave you the questions, went over and over the main points until something sank in. I'm not proud of it but I didn't want to be a doctor or a lawyer. I just wanted to play cricket. Anyway, after cricket practice I was too bloody tired to read.'

He reads a lot these days, novels, autobiographies, golf magazines. Currently *A Retreat From Radiance* by Ian Moffitt. 'I thought he was showing off to start, but as I get more towards the climax I'm loving it.' Before that, *An Indecent Obsession* by Colleen McCullough. 'Didn't bother with *The Thorn Birds* . . . everyone else had. Didn't go for the Beatles much either. I never wanted to do or like anything just because everyone else did. It put me off. I'm still the same. I like the Dave Clark Five and the Hollies.'

The men in green coats seem at a loss — powerless to stop guests sitting in front of the Members' Stand. They give up finally and decide to join their families, cushions and Thermoses, and watch. Very shiny, clean men with red faces, and brilliantly-oiled short back and sides, with a perfectly-combined breaker wave in the front, they are much nicer on slow Shield days. It's a bit like Hitler's Dad's Army during Tests or the Benson & Hedges games.

Allan Border comes to the door, baulks when he sees someone, backs off inside, has a *good* look, and then comes out with a cup of tea. Greg's back. He says he's not demonstrative, overtly affectionate or emotional. Wasn't encouraged to be. 'We were told to win and lose gracefully — that's it really. Ian's the most volatile. Says what he thinks. Trevor's had the advantage of learning from both of us.'

Warm hands, cold heart. 'I try not to hurt people. I'm amazed how people can hurt others. I'm sure I've done it. Mine'd be acts of omission more than anything else. I think of sending my wife or my mother flowers when they're ill, for example, and remember late at night or on a plane. I've got a great memory, but forgot my shoes on my wedding day, had to borrow my brother-in-law's. They hurt.

He loves his family, his brothers, his wife, *all* children, especially *his*; cricket and Dennis Lillee. He was very upset by a newspaper report about a two-year-old girl drowning in a backyard pool. He lives with the natural parental fear of something happening to his kids. The only time he remembers crying (described as 'near to tears') was the day his first child, Stephen, was born. He was at Lord's in England, batting. His wife was in Australia. When drinks were brought on the twelfth man handed him a wire service photograph of his wife, Judy, and his new son. It made me teary hearing the story.

He is adamant that money or a 'win at all costs' attitude had nothing to do with the Melbourne underarm incident. He was frustrated and annoyed. It was a protest about bad conditions. The administration was taking no notice; 'Nothing's wrong'. 'Would actors go on with holes in the stage and a leaking roof? There was no consideration for players. We had no right to an opinion. Look, six off the last ball was a one in a million chance ... a three or a four wouldn't have helped them. Winning for us meant a couple of days off, a luxury, that's all. It *was* wrong. I regret it. I wouldn't do it again. I was shattered at the outrage and screaming chaos that followed. I'm stuck with it ... but it wasn't illegal.' So he went to New Zealand the following year and was voted Man of the Series.

He is very pleased that his children are musical and artistic like his wife. 'The only thing I regret is not learning to play the piano.' When he has finished playing cricket he intends taking it up full-time and playing golf. He says his son is the best seven-year-old cricketer in the world. 'He's had a bat in his hand since he was born. If that's what he wants I'll help him, but I won't force him. I'm happy he's learning the piano.'

On the afternoon of the fourth day while NSW batted, an old man had a heart attack — the Members filled up with police, doctors, paramedics and ambulance men with respirators, injections and little flat-iron, heart-starter jumper leads. Elderly spectators moved away and looked steadfastly ahead, cricket wiping out fears of mortality. The players turned every now and then to check progress.

When I announced that I was interviewing Greg Chappell I dimly remember various people saying, 'He's difficult, taciturn, secretive, humourless or hard'. He must have hated those people or been bored witless.

'I feel I'm quite misunderstood — that's OK.' Somehow I didn't believe him. He admits to being deter-mined, ambitious, going after and getting most things he wants. He says he's not much of a businessman, just good at picking partners. He likes writing but thinks too fast and gets frustrated. On the other hand he can't stand being ghosted. He does have a phenomenal memory — long and short-term — quotes conversation verbatim and remembers in detail what happened and what everyone wore. He'd be a great witness.

He is very grateful for the encouragement, help and sacrifice of his parents and refutes the story of his grandfather's (Victor Richardson) apparent lack of interest. 'That's rubbish — he was very keen on us playing and doing well. I remember playing with him once on a turf wicket behind his house. It must have been when Trevor was born.'

The only time Sir Don Bradman ever spoke to him was to tell him to change his grip. 'I was strong on the leg side — not the off. Sir Don was a South Australian selector — he didn't speak to anyone really except Ashley Mallett, the best spinner I've seen. Anyway he walked through as usual and I said, "Good morning, Sir Donald".

'He stopped, turned and said, "You'll never be a good player with a grip like that". I asked if he had any suggestions. He did and showed me and said it'd feel uncomfortable at first but it would be easier with practice. He then walked off, stopped at the door, turned and said, "I've only given this bit of advice to one other player. He didn't take it. He's no longer in the team". I rushed to the nets. It *was* uncomfortable but it got easier. It's the grip I use now. I've used it ever since.'

He has ears that join without lobes — like mine. It's supposed to indicate criminal tendencies. 'I think I would have been a criminal if I hadn't been a cricketer.' Yeah I bet — a hit and run merchant no doubt. He is warm, friendly, charming, well-mannered, humorous, sensitive, devoted to his wife and family, earthy, honest and a lot older and younger than 34.

He's a very Aussie hero, a bargain whatever way you look at it. Mrs Chappell is a lucky woman. I didn't ask about the ducks. May he never have another.

'Sobers hates the use of batsmen's helmets. He, like Viv Richards today, would never have worn one.'

The point is to protect yourself with the bat, man

Frank Keating

Sobers uncharacteristically misses a slip catch.

24 September 1982: There can have been no more satisfactory or romantic finale to any cricket season than the clamorous curtain call staged by the Oval last weekend.

On Saturday the last shafts of a summer sun beamed down as a congregation of 13,000 West Indians and Ian Botham celebrated a Caribbean carnival: on Sunday in the misty, still opaque damp of an English autumn, middle-aged men became for a brief hour or two once more the champions of childhood. Time for olde tyme! Those, indeed, were the days.

As Sir Garfield Sobers walked back after a superlative innings — admittedly against avuncular bowling — there was, somehow, an echo of lamentation and desolation rising up from the fond and heartfelt tribute. Everyone sensed that we would never see him bat again; never see that lissome tread, that jungle cat's mix of jaunty, relaxed serenity and purposeful, businesslike intent; never see again the cavalier's smile fringed by the upturned collar, the pure arc of his golfer's follow-through after the cover drive, or on-drive, or that genuflecting, exhilarating front-foot square cut played late and cleanly murderous.

And in the evening drizzle, Ray Lindwall bowled. I had never seen him before. The nearest I got was the firm promise of a schoolmaster-monk to be taken to Worcestershire for the Australians' opening match of 1948. Then, on the eve of the trip, something came up and the black-cowled swine reneged. I wondered on Sunday whether, even at the age of 61, Lindwall could muster just a glimmer, a sense of the outline and structure of what old men still say was the most perfect bowling action of all. He did, too, though the arm was low and the run was short and sciatic. But I'd seen Lindwall bowl at last.

At the evening celebrations, four Aussies seemed very pleased to be back. They sat contentedly with their wives and their well-wishers. There was Bobby Simpson, patient bat and supreme snaffler of the slips; Neil Harvey, boy wonder who confirmed his promise a hundred-fold, and now in dark glasses, still smiling, and looking forward to a touring holiday in Devon and Cornwall. Also Ray Lindwall, strong blue eyes and strong square shoulders and off next day for a Continental holiday; and Gary Sobers, now with a whispy grey mandarin's goatee under his gap-toothed smile. He now has Australian citizenship, but not an Australian accent.

Lindwall and Sobers just overlapped. At the end of January 1955, Lindwall and Miller having laid waste the West Indian batting in the previous three, came the fourth Test at Barbados. A slim 19-year-old, who had been picked as a left-arm spinner, was sent in as a stop-gap to open the batting with J. K. Holt. Lindwall and Miller paced out their runs. Said a West Indian supporter: 'Ooh, dear, dey feedin' de poor boy to de two tiger cats to slacken off dey appetite!'

Lindwall admits he and his black-maned mate didn't know what, literally, hit them. Sobers hit six sumptuous boundaries in his first 25. In half an hour the boy had scored a breathtaking 43 and seen off the dreaded duo before Johnson had him caught. 'We were punch-drunk,' admits Lindwall, still shaking his head at the memory. Across the table, Sobers grins: still the sheepish grin of a found-out schoolboy.

Seven years before, at the Oval, Lindwall had, quite simply demolished England. They were swept away; 52 all out; Hutton 30; Lindwall 6 for 20. It was the catching that was responsible, he says, recalling blinders by Tallon and Hassett and Morris. With gentle modesty, he explains that earlier in the week it had been rainy and the pitch was under-prepared and damp. 'England's batsmen were distrustful of the pitch and expected the ball to fly from a length. Actually it went through at a uniform height. At least four of them were bowled by yorkers.' Hutton had played wonderfully well — 'First in, last out, caught by Don Tallon off a genuine leg glance.'

Hutton was the great and admired foe. Once Lindwall gave Hutton a lift from the Sydney Cricket Ground to the England team's hotel: 'We didn't speak a word to each other, apart from saying "goodnight"! By actions in the middle we had told each other a good deal about each other's play. What was there to say after all that?'

At the Oval in 1948, Lindwall clean bowled England's last three tailenders, Evans, Bedser and Young. He does not condone present habits of bumping non-batsmen. 'If a fast bowler cannot bowl out numbers nine, 10 and 11 without resorting to intimidation then he ought not to be wearing Australia's colours.'

Sobers hates the use of batsmen's helmets. He, like Viv Richards today, would never have worn one. 'The point of cricket is to protect yourself with the bat, man.' He says that if they had been worn in his day, 'there would have been no point in bowling at the likes of Kenny Barrington or Slasher Mackay: we'd have taken months to get them out, man; years, probably'.

Sir Garfield, you fancy, had a massive regard for Barrington's dogged, stoic fidelity to his cause. Of the great quartet of postwar English batsmen, May and Cowdrey, Dexter and Graveney, you feel he admired, and warmed to, the latter brace far more. Of the bowlers, Fred Trueman — 'What hostility! What a trier!' — was his sort of fellow, and also India's mesmerising leg-spinner of the '50s, Subhash Gupte, who seemed to be as inventive and experimental and as accurate — even more so — as the Pakistani who both enchanted and bamboozled the English this summer, Abdul 'the Bulbul' Qadir.

Sobers leaves. Lindwall nods goodbye. There is a sudden, awed hush in the room as Sir Garfield eases his way out, down the stairs, and across the Oval concourse for, perhaps, the very last time. The lights go out. It is, in fact, the end of many, many summers.

'Girls just drool over him. It's a purely animal attraction . . .'

Imran Khan — the Muslim idol

A. Read

Victory over England in the Test series is a big deal in Pakistan. Imran Khan is already a national hero there, but this triumph has ensured him a permanent place in his homeland's folklore, the first man to lead his country to a series win in England, on the territory of the colonial masters who invented the game.

This weekend, after Pakistan's massive first-innings score in the fifth and final Test in 1987, the best England could hope for was another draw — the fourth. Pakistan won one Test and that victory ensured Imran's immortality. Hundreds of thousands of people, probably millions, cheered him when he returned home to Pakistan, repeating their recent pleas that he change his mind about retirement.

Imran, 34 pushing 35, insists that after nearly two decades of first-class cricket he has had enough. He had already won a Test cap by the time he went to Oxford in 1971 and always reckoned on leaving the game at 34 while still at the top. The pressure on him to change his mind — both from team-mates and back home — will have little effect on the man. His strength as a captain stems largely from his confidence in his own judgement, an attribute often mistaken from his early years as a sign of arrogance. He rejects the criticism but now accepts that the stigma will never entirely go away.

In truth, the aloofness he is charged with has done little to damage his image, either at home in Pakistan or away on tour. The team has a long history of internal feuding which was never controlled by the succession of captains in charge before Imran. The Pakistani batting hero Javed Miandad provoked much mutineering in the team when he was skipper, a stark contrast to the settled side of today under Imran's aggressive and authoritative control.

The respect he inspires from the team is due in part to a prodigious talent, both with bat and ball. At Oxford, he captained a side with the likes of England's Chris Tavare and brought panache to the Parks with graceful strokeplay and a bowling action both smooth and deadly, swinging the ball both ways. It is testimony to Imran's determination to use all his potential that he later converted that easy, medium-paced action to a fast style of bowling which overnight put him alongside the Lillees and Holdings — with many commentators judging him the quickest of the lot.

The long run-up and the leap in the air at the crease has caused injuries and has often resulted in him just batting. But as he proved at the Oval with a century, described by BBC commentator Richie Benaud as a 'real delight', he is more than worth his place for that alone.

It's not just men who flock to watch him play. Since his Oxford days — he managed a respectable degree in politics and economics — he has had numerous girlfriends and remains today a constant source of stories for the steamier gossip columns. He is six foot tall, just under 13 stone, has broad shoulders and a dark, brooding face; features which dominate advertising hoardings on Pakistan's street corners.

In Britain, Imran enjoys the advantages those good looks give him. He is a non-smoking Muslim, yet he is at ease in London's trendy clubland, within easy access of his flat in South Kensington. He insists, however, that he will marry only a fellow Muslim, as tradition dictates, by his parents. In the meantime, he is, say women friends, thoroughly enjoying his bachelorhood.

Women just drool over him. 'It's a purely animal attraction,' says one. He is particularly popular among that circle of pampered young women who divide their time between shopping, nightclubbing and holidaying. Women friends, all of whom insist on anonymity, say he is good-natured but vain (his kitchen at home is plastered with 'action' shots of him bowling). Others report fondly that he is a one-dimensional conversationalist who talks only of cricket. His club, Sussex, reports that he receives an extraordinary number of telephone calls from women, the majority of whom he has never met. He has, by far, the largest mailbag of any player in England.

Imran is the latest in the distinguished line of great cricketers to come to England from the sub-continent and conquer both the game and society. There are cru-cial differences, though. Imran is not an aristocrat, unlike most of the great Indian and Pakistani players of the past. By birth he is a Pathan, the warrior race that inhabits the Northwest Frontier and Afghanistan.

The game which has made Imran so famous bears little resemblance to the more dignified sport played 20 years ago by men such as the Nawab of Pataudi, who also graced the Sussex turf. It has been hyped and glamorised by the marketing and publicity experts. There have always been superstars but now their fame extends far beyond cricket. Imran seemed destined for fame. His father, a successful civil engineer, had the money and the social connections to send Imran to Lahore's best school, Aitchison College. There the cricket coaches immediately spotted that he had inherited the gifts of his cousins, Javed Burki and Majid Khan, two of Pakistan's greatest players.

Unlike many brilliant sportsmen, Imran never had to struggle. He was driven not by the need to make a living from the sport — he thought of a career in cricket when he was in his late teens — but by the desire to be the best. He first appeared in his national team when he was 18 but he did not become an international star until he played as a member of Kerry Packer's WSC 'circus' in Australia in 1977 and 1978. The Packer experiment revolutionised cricket, forcing the world's conservative cricket authorities to acknowledge that they would have to adopt Packer's slick, high-profile methods. 'Packer deliberately set out to attract women television viewers and Imran was ideal for that,' says Mihir Bose, the cricket writer. 'That is what made him.'

At the same time he had switched counties. He left Worcester because he found living in the county intolerably dull and moved to Hove to play for Sussex, within a bus ride of Brighton's smart restaurants and just 50 miles from London. He had a lengthy relationship with Emma Sergeant, a young, well-connected London artist. Friends say that she introduced him to a new set. 'He became a member of that circle who play backgammon and holiday in Bali,' says one friend.

Imran Khan sends down a sizzler.

His cricket career flourished as much as his social life. He became captain of the national team, appointed as a compromise candidate after friction between Lahore and Karachi camps in the squad. A niggling leg injury prevented him bowling for many months and although he has recovered he has lost that extra half-yard of speed which could make him unplayable. Yet he has lost none of his ambition.

He led Pakistan to its first-ever victory in Britain and has already led it on a successful tour of India. It is hard to see what he can do now to satisfy his competitive urges. He has talked vaguely of politics but it does not appear to interest him. And the scope for non-military leaders is still limited in Pakistan, even for a nationalist such as Imran. He could never, he has said, endure the tedium of diplomacy or the civil service. Since he does not need the money he is not likely to waste his time as the tame frontman of a corporation.

It is, of course, the eternal problem which eventually faces all great athletes: how can life be anything but an anti-climax after all that glory and adrenalin? He might well postpone the day when he retires.

'Australian spectators have a reputation for the quick-witted piece of barracking which happily the mindless yelling of thousands of okkers in recent seasons has not altogether snuffed out.'

The humours of cricket

Christopher Martin-Jenkins

The most famous example of the humour of cricket crowds was the admonition by one Aussie barracker to the unpopular England captain Douglas Jardine on the bodyline tour of 1932–33.

It was a hot day and the flies were constantly buzzing around the captain's immortal Harlequin cap. As he swatted energetically at one particularly persistent fly a voice, which had been administering advice to the players all day, rose again above the hubbub: 'And keep yer bloody hands off our flies, Jardine.'

Amateur cricket is for players first, spectators second, but there is a good case for that order of precedence to be reversed if the game is to continue as a professional sport. All too often players (and umpires) who ultimately rely upon spectators to pay their wages break faith with them by looking too concerned about getting back to the dressingroom in uninviting weather conditions. Sometimes, of course, it is an illusion: playing conditions may be genuinely impossible when the sun has come out after rain — even though there is no reason apparent to inadequately informed spectators why cricket is not taking place. Bad public relations and a failure by players and umpires to be seen to be doing their best to get the game going are often to blame for the crowd fury which leads to riots among volatile onlookers, like those in the Caribbean and to the kind of fracas which demeaned the Saturday of the Centenary Test at Lord's in 1980.

It is usually the occasional cricket watchers, not the regulars, who make most noise. At such disappointing moments the hardened spectators, at least in England, tend to react with a philosophical smile. The real devotees — those faithful zealots who spend much of their summer watching county cricket and many of their winter evenings talking about the game as members of their local cricket society — are well prepared for rain. An umbrella goes up, a plastic macintosh is unrolled and put on, a cheese roll comes out of the basket and a book on cricket is read or the crossword patiently attended to until the fatal announcement that there will be no further play today.

Spectators reflect the region or country they come from more clearly than players. One southern enthusiast up to watch a Test in Leeds was unwise enough to go off to get a sandwich and a beer at lunchtime, leaving his hat on his seat to show that it was taken. When he got back a thickset miner was firmly established and no other space was visible. The hat was on the ground near the miner's large black boots. 'Excuse me,' said the southerner politely, 'but I think you are sitting in my seat by mistake. That's my hat.' The miner fixed him with an icy stare and replied: 'Up 'ere lad, it's bums what bags seats, not 'ats.'

The cricket supporters of Yorkshire are second to none in their enthusiasm for and knowledge of the game. They can take a bit of time to get to know you, though. I have kindly been asked to make several visits to address the famous Wombwell Cricket Lovers' Society, which is run from Barnsley with breathless energy by their secretary Jack Sokell. On my first visit I was presented with a handsome glass mug on which a local artist had cleverly engraved a very good likeness of my face. Attempting to break the ice, I began my talk by saying: 'First I must thank you all for presenting me with this ugly mug.' I meant, of course, my own, but as I looked along the serried ranks of sturdy miners, not a flicker of amusement showed on any face.

Nothing so inhibits a speaker as one of his jokes going down like a lead balloon, but the first impression was wrong. I soon found out that the men (and a few women) of the Wombwell society are warm people with a lively sense of humour. So too are the members of the Northern Cricket Society, the Sheffield Cricket Lovers, the Lancashire, the Stourbridge, the Hampshire, the Essex ... The movement has grown rapidly in recent years, all over Britain and in one or two other countries too. The Cricket Society itself, father of them all, now has some 2200 members. Their members are the faithful souls who would rather go without bread than give up membership of their county club and who make sure, when England are touring Australia, that the alarm is set to go off five minutes before the early morning broadcast begins. No doubt that same philosophical smile greets every England batting collapse.

Some of the more wealthy or adventurous of this ilk have in recent years taken to spending their holidays watching MCC — or England, as they now are — battling it out overseas. The players do not wholly approve. Whereas their leisure activities off the field used to be watched in the old days by a few journalists, they are now also under scrutiny from critical holiday-makers, some of whom think it wrong if the players are not in the nets all day and living quiet, abstemious lives by night. Even journalists sometimes feel that their private reserve has been intruded upon. These people should be back at home reading and listening, not coming out to see for themselves! This may sound a mean and illogical feeling, but I can only say that I have shared it; in a way it is because a cosy party has been invaded, and also because people joining a tour for only a fortnight or so tend to make instant judgements about what is going on without knowing the whole picture.

In the 1981 Barbados Test a whole stand at the Kensington Oval was filled with British supporters and it was said that half the rest of the crowd were relatives of Roland Butcher! It was different when only a few could afford to follow the tour. The 1970–71 series in Australia was watched from first match to last by two well-to-do English gentlemen, John Gardiner and Geoffrey Saulez. The former became the driving force behind the 'ICC Trophy' which brought the little cricket nations of the world to England to play in the World Cup, and the latter has since become England's regular scorer on overseas tours, paying most of his own expenses. So fanatical is Geoffrey Saulez that he scores for Pakistan or the West Indies or any country that will have him when his own is inactive.

He is a large, intelligent man with a nose like that of Mr Punch and he sometimes terrorises fellow-scorers during matches overseas if they do not come up to his high standards. He also reads every hotel bill with the same fastidiousness, and usually finds an error! He is probably the ultimate cricket spectator because I believe he must see more cricket matches each year than any living man.

Australian spectators have a reputation for the quick-witted piece of barracking which happily the

'Yabba', the legendary barracker of The Hill, Sydney, was christened Stephen Harold Gascoigne. He died in 1942, at the age of 64, a grandfather. A first-generation Australian, he was born in the inner suburb of Redfern and was the son of an Englishman and a Sydney woman.

mindless yelling of thousands of okkers in recent seasons has not altogether snuffed out. The first time Derek Randall batted in Australia after his triumph in the Centenary Test in Melbourne was in a country match early in the 1978–79 tour. He studiously played a maiden over, whereupon a bearded man near to where I was walking round the boundary put down his can of beer, cupped his hands and shouted: 'Aw, come on, Randall, you couldn't get a kick out of an electric chair!'

It was on the previous tour that Colin Cowdrey had come bravely out to face the fury of Lillee and Thomson exactly 20 years after taking on Lindwall and Miller on his first tour. As the first of many bouncers whistled past Cowdrey's left shoulder an encouraging voice said: 'That's the spirit, Thommo, rattle out a tune on his false teeth!'

All Pommy players are fair game. Trevor Bailey,

who used to win grudging admiration from Australian crowds for his bloody-minded batting, had a habit of bowling one imaginary ball when he came on to bowl in order to get his run-up correct. He did this when England took the new ball 10 minutes from the end of the day at Brisbane in 1954, Australia having lost only two wickets in humid heat. As he completed his practice run a man shouted: 'And that's the best bloody ball you've bowled all day, Bailey.'

Freddie Brown got the treatment on the previous tour. He had been front-page news one morning after hitting a lamp standard in a car the previous night. When a wild swipe at a Lindwall outswinger failed to make contact by some distance, the reaction was swift, if predictable: 'Pity you didn't miss the lamp too, Brownie.'

Another England captain, J. W. H. T. Douglas, whose initials the Melbourne crowd believed stood for 'Johnny Won't Hit Today', drew the agonised plea during a long, defensive innings: 'Fetch a cop someone and pinch that bugger for loitering.' And Trevor Bailey, batting at Sydney, was once asked two pertinent questions: 'Why don't you drop dead Bailey? Or are you?' When it comes to slow play, in fact, Australians themselves do not escape. 'Slasher' Mackay, Queensland's stubborn left-hander, was told by a bored spectator: 'Blimey Mackay, you'll never die of a stroke', and Jimmy Burke was informed during a patient rearguard action: 'Burke, you're like a bloody statue. I wish I was a pigeon.'

'Yabba', the humorist of the Sydney Hill before the Second World War, used to be an entertainment in himself. He it was, I believe, who first suggested to a bowler who was continually beating the bat: 'Send 'im down a grand piano, mate, and see if he can play that!' To less successful bowlers he would yell: 'Yer length is lousy but yer *width's* pretty good.' When Charles Kelleway took a long time to get off the mark and finally did so with a quick single he shouted: 'Whoa there, he's bolted.' And when Maurice Tate, always having trouble with his boots, bent once again to do up his laces, Yabba called: 'Thank goodness he's not a flaming centipede.'

But the last word shall be with an English spectator. In the Lord's Pavilion they tend to be either very knowledgeable or very ignorant about the game. The Lord's Taverners once had a match at headquarters during which Norman Wisdom got himself into a succession of hilarious running tangles in partnership with Roy Castle. An elderly gentleman with a moustache and panama hat, obviously not quite sure what match he was watching, turned to his neighbour with a half-smile and said: 'That chap ought to be a comedian, y'know.'

The game's the thing!

Alan McGilvray

Alan McGilvray.

It is fair to say, I suppose, that through 60-odd years of active involvement in cricket, I have seen a few things change.

For 50 of those years I worked as a broadcaster and in that area I saw perhaps more change than in any other. I am often amused to look on the changes in the game itself, about which we hear so much these days, and for which there seems to be so much genuine regret, and marvel at how miniscule they really are compared to the changes that have overtaken cricket broadcasting.

Certainly the game is not the same. One-day cricket, commercial cricket, and changing attitudes have made the game a somewhat colder and less convivial pursuit than the one we played at a more seemly pace between the wars. But it is still cricket. It still rewards skill and dedication and those fine qualities of touch and subtlety that were first forged on the village greens of England.

Undoubtedly, one of the more severe influences to have modified current approaches to cricket, by players and public alike, has been the huge impact of television. Television has thrust the game into living rooms everywhere. It dissects every umpire's mistake and strips it bare with a single replay, more than we ever could on radio with a thousand words. It occasionally portrays the players less as sportsmen than as gladiators, highlighting the confrontation and the aggro and planting in the minds of young players everywhere, to the game's cost, that this is the accepted way of things.

Yet television has found for the game new status and new supporters. It was the genesis of night cricket and the genesis of one-day cricket. It has brought more money into the game than we ever imagined in our day and it has given players an unprecedented star status. Some of them do not earn it, for certain, but it remains a fact that cricket these days is projected as a popular, public entertainment that draws mushrooming attention wherever it is played.

To those of us who were involved in the infancy of radio broadcasting of cricket, the current emphasis on television is a wonder to behold. I just hope, though, we do not forget the power of radio. There is a special quality to word pictures that even real pictures cannot usurp.

In the early days of cricket broadcasting, word pictures were everything. I think, even now, as I look back on so many wonderful cricket experiences, the early times I had in radio were the most striking. Cricket has given me many great experiences. Captaining New South Wales in a time when cricket was in the midst of a golden age was certainly one. Batting with the immortal Bradman, once in a partnership somewhere near 170 was a special joy. Knowing and playing with people like Alan Kippax, Stan McCabe, Bill O'Reilly and an army of others at that time, was a rich experience. But of all the experiences of those years, the one that gives me most pleasure was the pioneering work we did in broadcasting in the winter of 1938, when Don Bradman's Australian team was in England.

This was the series of the 'synthetic' Test broadcasts, which represented to the Australian Broadcasting Commission at that time, to the Australian public at large and to the game of cricket, an exercise in adventure and imagination that modern TV crews, with all their technical wizardry, could never hope to achieve.

In those days before the Second World War, radio was well short of the technical excellence of today. Space satellites were science fiction and the shortwave broadcasts from one side of the world to the other were lucky dips, in which the signal went up and down like a yo-yo. Listening to a broadcast from England, at times, was like listening to a radio that had been dropped in the bath.

Bradman's 1938 team came along at a time when cricket was at an absolute zenith in Australia. Bradman had carved up England in England in 1930 and 1934, and such a legend had built up around him that the nation followed his every move. The ABC at the time was pouring more and more emphasis into sport and the broadcasting of so important a series became a matter of high priority.

But how? How could they cope with the vagaries of shortwave transmission, yet feed the interest of a nation they knew would hang on every word? Charles Moses was in charge of ABC sporting broadcasts in the early 'thirties, and was later a long-term general manager of the commission. He was a man with a passion for sport. He played first grade rugby in Sydney and had a wide interest in all sports. Cricket was certainly one of them and when the 1938 Australian tour of England was so much in the mind, it was Moses who determined that the games simply had to be broadcast.

He hit upon the idea of synthesising the broadcasts. If shortwave was not good enough to get the commentary to Australia live, we would simply have the information transferred by cable and manufacture the commentary in the studio. Moses would not listen to those who said it could not be done. His concept was brilliantly simple, yet breathtaking in its scope and it is fair to say it so captured the nation that in the end people had convinced themselves it was real. In some cases, they did not want to hear otherwise.

The modus operandi was simple but polished. A reporter was despatched to England to cable information to Sydney at the end of each over of the Test matches. In the studio, a commentary team was assembled comprising the former Australian captains M. A. Noble and Vic Richardson, Hal Hooker and myself.

A picture of the ground at which the match was being played was mounted in front of us, just for atmosphere. A scoreboard operator maintained a board. A sound effects man was on hand to supply crowd noises and the lusty crack of leather on willow we supplied ourselves by tapping a pencil on a wooden block. And Moses hovered over all of us, like a mother hen protecting her chickens.

An ingenious code was invented to get the information to us as fully and as precisely as possible. A decoder then wrote it out more fully and we put the finishing touches to it at the microphone. A typical cable might read: 'BRIGHTENING FLEETWOOD

HAMMOND FULL FIRSTLY TWO HASSETT SEC-
ONDLY FULL FOUR STRAIGHT UNCHANCE BOWLER
THIRDLY NO BALL FULL TWO OFFDRIVEN RUN
APPEAL HUTTON FOURTHLY FOUR SWEPT BOWLER
KEEPER OFFPUSHED.'

This established that the day was brightening and
Fleetwood-Smith was the bowler. The first ball to
Hammond was pitched up and driven, Hassett fielded
and the batsmen ran two. The second ball was pitched
up and driven straight and was almost a chance for the
bowler but went for four.

And so it went on. The longer we were at it, the
more we started to believe in it ourselves and even now
as I look back on the 1938 tour I can see as much of
that in my mind's eye as any of those I watched at
much closer quarters in subsequent years.

Moses made sure we all lived it. We had to eat at the
same time as the players, take tea at the same time as
the players and treat the nights largely as if they were
balmy English summer days. It played awful tricks
with our body clocks and I doubt that I have ever been
so desperately tired as I was at the end of some of those
long winter nights in the ABC Sydney studios.

But it was pure adventure. Wherever we went we
discovered people simply shut the fact that they were
synthetic broadcasts out of their minds. They wanted
to hear the cricket and this was done well enough, with
enough expertise and authority to do the job. Such was
the public acceptance that Moses actually went to great
lengths to have a newsreel film made to explain to
people how we were doing the broadcasts, lest there
was any suggestion that we were trying to deceive. It
was a brilliant concept and a piece of broadcasting history which to me has always reflected the innovative
genius within man that is often swamped in the highly
technological world of today.

A lot of water has flowed under the bridge since
those pioneering days of 1938. Repeatedly I am asked
what was the best innings I saw, or who was the best
player, or what was the best match. I shy away from
most of those questions, particularly those that relate to
the quality of players, because every era has its
different conditions and its different pressures, and you
can't really judge one batsman against another unless
he plays against the same bowling in the same condition at the same time.

I do, however, have fairly fixed in my mind the
innings I regard as the most memorable I have seen
played and these I am often happy to discuss, for to me
they capture the very heart and soul of cricket, and
paint the game in its best Sunday finery.

Four innings stand out in my memory (though there
were myriad others whose memory I treasure nevertheless) as ultimate reflections of the batting art. First
there was the day at Headingley, Leeds, in 1948 when
England set Australia 404 to score in less than a full day
to win the fourth Test. Left 345 minutes to do the job,
the Australians achieved a target considered impossible
with 15 minutes to spare and seven wickets still
standing.

Arthur Morris hit 182 and Don Bradman remained
not out 173, and their second-wicket partnership of 301
was perhaps the finest batting performance on any
given day I have had the pleasure to witness. Morris
was superb, but there was something special about the
inimitable Bradman. In measuring such deeds I look at
technique, brilliance and ability, but more especially
the purpose embodied in these feats and the value they
represent to a side.

By this measure, the last of Bradman's 29 Test
centuries stands as the ultimate reflection of batting
excellence. The pitch had worn badly, the task was
widely considered unthinkable and Bradman perceived
a real danger in the off-spinner Jim Laker, particularly
when he was bowling to the left-handed Morris.
Bradman manoeuvred and manipulated to keep Morris
away from Laker in an innings which represented total
control over a great many factors working against him.
Yet he still scored runs at a match-winning pace.

Perhaps the next best I saw for sheer triumph over
adversity was the innings which Bill Edrich played
against Australia in Brisbane in 1946. Bill found him-

self caught on a diabolical 'sticky' and facing an Australian total of 645. He made only 16 and people tend to look at me rather peculiarly when I nominate this as one of the finest innings I saw played. But Edrich was courage and character itself in this innings, holding out against Keith Miller and Ray Lindwall on a pitch that made the ball rear and kick like a rodeo steer. His position was impossible, yet he held out for a long time in an innings of incredible concentration.

Then there was Ian Botham's 149 not out for England in 1981 which turned a Test match and provided an innings of belligerent power unlike any I had seen previously. England were on their knees when Botham went to the crease and the sheer audacious brilliance of the hand he played that day had to be seen to be believed.

The fourth innings I will nominate was that played by Gary Sobers in the tied Test at Brisbane in 1960. He hit 132 in a match that produced in one five-day package everything that is fine in the game. It was not easy for Sobers; the West Indies at that time were not the traditional power they have become in recent times and they had had a rather painful journey around the States when they came to the first Test. On top of that they had a real bugbear about leg spin and their captain Frank Worrell had made it clear in this game that they had to triumph over the Australian captain Richie Benaud, or their summer was doomed. Sobers obliged. For technical perfection, cricket has offered little better than he did that day.

Some years later Sobers hit 254 for a World X1 in a match against Australia at the Melbourne Cricket Ground. For sheer brilliance this was better than his innings of the tied Test. The power and the timing were phenomenal and the more he threw the bat, the closer he came to the perfect innings. Many thought this the best he had ever played and some saw it as the finest innings the Melbourne ground had ever seen.

I lean to the Brisbane one, however, for the circumstances in which innings are played is important. The pressure was real in Brisbane. It was not so real in Melbourne. Batting, after all, is a team function and the innings which serve their team best are the innings which count the most in the long run.

It has been my experience to see so many fine players as I have toured the world and worked behind the microphone. The names roll out, a kaleidoscope of greatness that I feel truly privileged to have seen. Men like Denis Compton and Barry Richards, Len Hutton and Dennis Lillee, Alec Bedser and Everton Weekes, Graeme Pollock and John Snow, Maurice Tate and Stan McCabe, Richie Benaud and Ian Chappell, Peter May, Ray Lindwall, Keith Miller and Walter Hammond. On and on the list goes.

Suffice it to say that cricket is an enduring art and for every glorious innings that is written into the pages of the game's history, for every magnificent spell of bowling and every grand catch, thousands more are yet to be enjoyed. Cricket is a game of any era and no matter how much we all try to change it, its essential qualities remain unchangeable. Cricket will always be our summer game.

'Australia had erased England's lead for the loss of two wickets and . . . Australian bicentennial honour had been rescued.'

A wave for the Bicentennial

Jeff Wells

I first ran across the so-called Mexican wave, which was such a talking point at the 1988 Bicentennial Test, at Shea Stadium in New York a few years back.

Being a good Brooklyn resident I used to get along to the games and settle in with a big plastic cup of Budweiser and a couple of hot dogs with mustard and maybe some hot buttered popcorn and everything was fine. Fine, that is, until the accursed wave — just the plain wave then because nobody wanted to be unkind to our southern neighbours by accusing them of starting it — came along and disrupted things.

Baseball is a game with a lot more crises per hour than cricket, a crisis with almost every pitch if you are really into it, and some bum always seemed to start the wave at the wrong time.

Bottom of the seventh. Mets a run behind. Two outs, two men on base, pinch hitter at the plate, ace reliever for the Cardinals with the ball, a full count of three balls and two strikes. A hit or a bad pitch and the Mets take the lead, a swing and a miss and they are sunk. You are sitting on the edge of your seat, eyes popping like lotto balls as the pitcher winds up and . . . and at the crucial moment the guy next to you with his plastic cup of Millers Hi-Life and the woman in front of you with the hot buttered popcorn go up in the wave. By the time you recover your composure and calculate your dry cleaning bill the moment has been lost.

I hate the wave, and Bill O'Reilly, covering his last Test match after 41 years in the Sydney Cricket Ground press box, let the world know that he detested it too. But upon reflection it must be said that the wave was one of the more intriguing sociological aspects of this novelty affair.

In America, when the wave is on, it sweeps inexorably around the stadium without interruption, thereby demonstrating a good measure of good old Yankee egalitarianism. There are no preserves of privilege in baseball seating — the privilege of the best seats is earned with the price of the ticket.

At the SCG the wave usually begins somewhere in the belly of the Pat Hills Stand, or among the Lost Tribe of the Sunburned Poms on the hill, and moves through the Clive Churchill Stand. It is a great pagan sight, half naked bodies rising in exultation towards the sun god, spilling their brews, and stirring up snowstorms of paper pieces that momentarily turn the amphitheatre into one of those ornamental Christmas scenes in a glass bubble.

But then it hits the members' reserve where everybody reclines in fully-clothed dignity, some with whites chilled and others with good reds breathing, and peters out. It takes several attempts and a good deal of derisive hotting from the plebeians before the guilt-ridden patricians will cork their expensive vintages for safety and allow themselves to levitate towards the old green roof.

It was a grumbling gesture of goodwill, a salute to our own brand of equality at a most sensitive time, and to me it provided perhaps the best clue of all about why we were there.

I thought long and hard about this Bicentennial Test and found it rather confusing, a somewhat hybrid affair. Cricket had already had two centenary Tests and the time frame was wrong for another celebration of the history of the game.

The inescapable conclusion was that it is really no more than another special event in a crowded bicentennial calendar. I also came to the conclusion that rather than a celebration of the bicentennial it was, for many, a refuge from it.

Australia Day in Sydney had been magnificent with the stately parade of the tall and First Fleet ships on the harbour and the fireworks turning the sky over the city into a neon kaleidoscope and the bridge into a flaming, white-hot coat hanger. But that was only temporary relief from those agitators who, with the help of the obliging media, had come to spoil the party.

The litany of accusations had been relentless. The foreign media had spilled in to lap up the juice from the 'oppression of Aborigines' stories. The local media, as usual, gave biggest play to those who made the most noise. Left-wing journalists, pious historians and pro-

fessional stirrers were deluging us with so much guilt and gloom that the celebration of the enviable nation which Australia had made of itself in 200 years had almost been drowned out, and some people were actually beginning to believe that they were living in one of the most insecure, brutal and repressive societies ever spawned on barren ground.

At one stage at the SCG I actually muttered a prayer for the members. If they had continued to look down their noses at the wave, the proletariat, fired by one too many demonstrations of their inferiority, might have stormed the barricades, crushing wine coolers as they went, ripping designer polo shirts and old school ties from pale overfed bodies, and kicking them across Moore Parke into bloody defeat. But thank God the members got up and the angst brigade had one less atrocity to bleat about.

That having been settled Sydney hunkered down to enjoy cricket against England, an endeavour which I believe will still be going strong long after the last utopian socialist has gone to the wall.

But if this was not a celebration of the art or history of cricket, or a true bicentennial event, what was it? One thing it was was a joyous chance to see some old faces and relive some of the game's greatest memories. Beaurepaires had sponsored a 'computer Test' between teams of Australian and English 'Living Legends' and if you were lucky enough to be in the M. A. Noble Stand you could look at them and point them out to your children or grandchildren. 'That's Peter May, son. I was there when . . .'

The computer teams were: Australia: Bill Ponsford, Arthur Morris, Sir Donald Bradman (c), Greg Chappell, Neil Harvey, Keith Miller, Richie Benaud (vc), Ray Lindwall, Rod Marsh, Dennis Lillee, Bill O'Reilly, Lindsay Hassett (12). England: Sir Len Hutton (c), Geoff Boycott, Peter May (vc), Denis Compton, David Gower, Ian Botham, Alan Knott, Harold Larwood, Freddie Trueman, Bob Appleyard, Douglas Wright, Brian Statham (12).

The Australian team was an interesting contrast to

'The First Eleven: 1877–1988', an Australian best-ever selection from cricket writer Phil Derriman and ABC cricket statistician Ross Dundas. It read: Don Tallon, Fred Spofforth, Bill O'Reilly, Greg Chappell, Dennis Lillee, Alan Davidson, Clarrie Grimmett, Bob Simpson, Don Bradman (c), Neil Harvey, Sid Barnes.

Of the breathing legends all the Australians except Ponsford were there for the big parade. Unfortunately, only Boycott, May, Botham and Appleyard of England were there in the vintage cars which circled the ground at lunch on the second day, led by The Don himself in a 1911 Rolls-Royce.

Brian Statham could not make it because he is unwell and living on public assistance. Gower was off skiing. Larwood lives only a few miles from the ground but his wife apologised that his eyesight is too bad for him to enjoy such an occasion. But Alec Bedser, still as tough as polished old leather, Colin Cowdrey, still jolly after a heart bypass, Ted Dexter, still wearing the most swashbuckling jackets, John Edrich, Raman Subba Row, Bob Willis, and Tony Greig (who was given a compulsory booing) had made it and were in the cars and John Snow was seen prowling the grandstand.

You could look at their faces, down to their name tags, and back to their faces and tell yourself in some kind of fatuous delight that the tradition they have helped create was reason enough to celebrate. Unfortunately, out in the middle, there was little happening to challenge the memories of their deeds.

Most of those great men played in an era when the Test arena was unchallenged as the proving ground and each England-Australia confrontation, the clash of the great powers, was the stuff of legend.

And they came from a time when a Test was a battle and a series was the war. You might win glorious victory in one arena but at the next, with a change in the weather, you might find the enemy at your throat and your blood all over the sod. I doubt that any of those immaculately suited but flinty-eyed old warriors in the stand believed that much would be proved by this one-off novelty affair.

Gatting's Englishmen were courteously performing this chore as an addendum to an acrimonious and disappointing tour of Pakistan and as a prelude to a hard slog in New Zealand. Gatting himself seemed particularly world-weary, admitting that English professionalism would be put to a severe test.

The Australians meanwhile had cockily made themselves favourites, something which had proved fatal with monotonous regularity in recent years. It was something like being in England before another British heavyweight went to the slaughter in a world title fight.

Australia was coming off a close decision over New Zealand in a three-Test welter and some ego-boosting one-day victories in the World Cup and World Series Cup. Once again the selectors had been unable to divorce themselves from the one-day doings and had chosen a team stacked with would-be all-rounders and run-savers and had ignored the classic winning Test Match formula of three strong fast bowlers.

Even with two spinners there was room for them but Merv Hughes was made twelfth man and when Gatting won the toss Australia went to bowl England out twice with McDermott injured. Dodemaide, still not more than a useful change bowler, sharing the new ball, and the gentle but thoughtful medium-pacer Steve Waugh at first change.

It was a selection which showed faith in neither the incumbent batting nor the reserves of fast bowling. Both may have been thin but this was a unique affair in which only winning, and winning in good old Aussie ripsnorting fashion, really counted.

Australia may have looked favourites on paper but once Gatting won the toss and batted on a placid wicket, which didn't offer much to the quick men and didn't degenerate immediately into a spinning death trap, a draw, and a disappointment for a crowd which hungered for more fireworks, looked the likeliest result.

On the first day Australia put down three catches which would probably have been snatched up without a second thought during the one-day heroics. 'He's tipped it over the cross bar,' chortled one Fleet Street visitor when McDermott failed to hold a full toss spooned back by Chris Broad in the last over before lunch. Australia might have seen the last of Broad then but that didn't happen until the following day. At the end of the first day England was 2 for 221 with Broad not out 116 and any hope of an Australian victory was fading fast.

Broad's innings had been a fitful one but his great concentration had prevailed against mediocre bowling. It was his fourth hundred in six Tests against Australia and he moved into the select company of Jack Hobbs and John Edrich as the only Englishmen to have scored Test centuries on four different Australian grounds.

It should have been an occasion of unmitigated glory for the tall, elegant, blond opener but the next day it became a nightmare of his own making. At 139 he misjudged a ball from Waugh which hit him on the glove and dropped down on to his wicket. In his anger Broad turned and smashed the stumps with his bat before stalking off before an embarrassed and irate gathering of great players. England manager Peter Lush was waiting to slap him with a five hundred pound fine. The fine may have hurt but the realisation of his foolishness must have stung Broad more, especially after the stir he caused by failing to walk in Pakistan.

An out-of-sorts Gatting went for 13 after 53 tortured minutes but the English tail wagged mightily and after 672 minutes of grind the visitors were all out for 425 and a different type of bicentennial event was needed to raise the national spirits.

With McDermott suffering from two bad knees, off-spinner Peter Taylor, who had been ignored by captain Allan Border until more than an hour after lunch, finished with the best bowling figures of 4 for 84.

If Broad had brought dishonour to the game Border's men brought tragedy with their feeble battle efforts. In 384 reprehensible minutes they capitulated to ordinary bowling for 214 runs and were ordered to follow on. The chancy Dean Jones top-scored with 56 but honours went to leg-spinner Peter Sleep with a gritty 41. Batting at seven Sleep put his more fashionable team-mates to shame with his application and has now entered the genuine all-rounder class.

Chief culprit was the jaded Border himself. The Australian captain has shown a disturbing tendency not to give fresh bowlers a good sight in his latter years. This time he took an ungainly swipe down the leg side at rookie medium-pacer David Capel first ball, and just 14 balls later connected with the same shot from the same bowler and the catch was gratefully accepted by Broad at deep fine leg.

It was the toy bulldog David Boon who restored pride to the Australian game. The pugnacious little Tasmanian crafted an opening partnership of 162 with Geoff Marsh — a record for Australia at the SCG against England — and grew more resolute and dangerous as the fifth day wore on. He was unconquered on 184 when the match was abandoned half an hour before stumps. Australia had erased England's lead for the loss of two wickets and it might have been argued that, even though the points belonged to English professionalism, Australian bicentennial honour had been rescued.

With only a Test against Sri Lanka left on the summer calendar Australia was left to ponder the problems of balanced selection — especially in its attack — with the West Indians due for five Tests in November and an Ashes tour of England slated for 1989.

And the wave? It seemed to die along with Australia's chances and on the last two days only a ripple could have been raised at best. Maybe I wouldn't have minded a ripple. It doesn't have the same sociological significance, but the dry cleaning bills are a lot smaller.

'Bright took India's ninth wicket with the total at 344 and in came the turbaned Maninder, India needing four to win. Bob Simpson turned around to Alan Crompton and me and said, "How nervous do you reckon this bloke would be?".'

The finest cricket match I ever saw — the tied Test at Madras

Bob Radford

R. M. ('Bob') Radford, executive director of the NSW Cricket Association.

I was one of the few Australians who witnessed the second tied Test in cricket history which was played at Madras during September 1986. Apart from the Australian touring party itself there were three Australian tourists present at M. A. Chidambaram Stadium, seven Australian journalists covering the tour, and myself.

Scores and other details relating to the game have already been widely published and will remain part of cricket history forever. My intention is to record a few scenes and occurrences which I witnessed on the final day.

Apart from the Sheffield Shield finals of seasons 1984–85 and 1985–86 (both won by New South Wales against Queensland) which were great finishes indeed, this was the finest cricket match I ever saw. I spent the five days of the Test in the players' enclosure and during the fifth day, on which Australia fielded, I was sitting with team manager Alan Crompton, cricket manager Bob Simpson and, from time to time, the team's physiotherapist Errol Alcott. Those in the touring party but not playing were Davis, Dyer, Veletta and Gilbert.

It appeared at the start of the final day's play that Australia should win the Test, having mostly been in a commanding position throughout the previous four days. Border's courageous declaration overnight left India 348 to win from 87 overs. Australia needed all 10 Indian wickets on a pitch which was gradually taking more spin. Thus Australia's hopes rested on its spinners, Bright and Matthews. At 2 for 204 India looked a chance of taking a sensational victory. The way the match see-sawed from this point was extraordinary and, again, this has been well covered in the press.

In the last 20 minutes India's dominance increased and although they were losing wickets regularly in the chase, it seemed to me that they would get the required runs. I turned to Errol Alcott and said quietly 'we've had it' — he agreed. Two balls later India lost another wicket, breaking a 40-run partnership. Alan Crompton then said 'we can win it from here'. India was 7 for 331.

The atmosphere was now electric and I have never

known such tension at any sporting event. I estimate (and so did many local judges) that the crowd had built to some 25,000 from the 5000 odd in attendance at the start of the day's play. It is impossible in India to obtain what Australia (and most other cricketing nations) refer to as 'official attendance figures'. My estimate is made on the crowds who had attended over the previous four days of the game. I have mentioned, for the record, what I consider to be the attendance figure since some 500,000 now seem to have been present at the Gabba for the first tied Test in 1960–61 when in fact there were only a handful of spectators. Similarly, I have met many more thousands than the SCG could possibly have held in 1932–33 who claimed to have been there the day McCabe made his 187 not out in the bodyline series.

But back to the M. A. Chidambaram Stadium. On every occasion India scored, the crowd cheered, clapped, blew whistles and trumpets and generally went wild. If a four or six was scored they went absolutely crazy and the noise was deafening. Several had Indian flags which they ran about waving as the Indian score mounted. Many danced on one leg up and down the terraces to be turned back near the bottom, from which rose barbed wire fences, by the police who were there in their hundreds wielding lathis and batons with scant consideration for injury to the recipients of the blows. Overall though, I believe the crowd was excellently behaved. They were in a state of high excitement and they were enjoying every second of the cricket as only Indians (and West Indians) can.

Bright took India's ninth wicket with the total at 344 and in came the turbaned Maninder, India needing four to win. Bob Simpson turned around to Alan Crompton and me and said 'How nervous do you reckon this bloke would be?' I said 'Well, if he's as nervous as me then he's very nervous indeed!' I was chain smoking, and with a towel I brought from the hotel each day to mop myself in the intense humidity and 37°C temperatures which prevailed throughout the game, I continually wiped perspiring hands.

Several times Alan Crompton and I remarked on the unbelievable situation we saw before us. Indian vice-captain Ravi Shastri struck the run to tie the match and so there it was, two balls left of a five-day match and any of two results — a win to India or a tie — being possible. The noisiest crowd I have ever known at a cricket match was totally silent. It was 5.19 p.m. when Matthews ran in to bowl the fifth ball of the last over of the match. It hit Maninder on the pads right in front. Up went the umpire's finger.

The crowd went crazy in a mixture of excitement, despair, amazement, joy and disbelief. The Australian players jumped in the air and seemed to run everywhere. The four non-playing members together with Alan Crompton, Bob Simpson and Errol Alcott rushed onto the field. Embraces, which to me mar modern-day cricket, have never been so prevalent. Not being in the touring party I resisted the urge to run out too and this took some willpower. I had been following the team around India prior to this day: they were all friends and, further, the best bunch of tourists I had come across in my years accompanying Australian cricket teams throughout the world.

Hundreds of police appeared on the ground in an instant and attempts were made by the Tamil Nadu Cricket Association, the match authority, to cordon off with rope an area on the field in front of the main grandstand for the usual after-match presentations. As I observed the whole extraordinary scene an Indian official came to me conveying the request for drinks to be taken out to our enervated players. The moment had made me oblivious to what I should automatically have known.

As I went to the dressing room for the drinks, I was passed by an elated Alan Crompton running in from the field on the same mission. He was soon followed by Gilbert and Davis who, with Veletta and Dyer, had shared the 12th man duties throughout five most arduous days. Together, the four of us took soft drinks to the Australian players, most of whom were by now lying on the ground, absolutely exhausted. It was an opportunity for me to congratulate each of them on their participation in an extraordinary cricket match.

It occurred to me that the players were almost too tired to be jubilant, especially Border who was drained both physically and mentally. I patted each player in turn on the back and recall their soaking shirts. The exception was Zoehrer who had removed his completely. He had had a big day, all day, on a turning pitch in great heat and humidity wearing protective equipment which must have felt heavier with each passing over. Stephen Waugh came alongside me and I noticed he was carrying one of the stumps. I said 'Boy, are you lucky to have that — it will be worth a fortune in years to come'. Steve said 'Actually, I grabbed two but I gave one to Mo [Matthews] — he deserved it. And what about A.B.; he got the ball, that wasn't a bad score, was it?'

In the excitement the presentation ceremony was somewhat of a disaster. The organisation of it was haphazard to say the least; microphones were virtually inaudible and the Indian pressmen — especially photographers who seemed to number at least 50 — tended to spoil the official necessities. Our team was sad that Kapil Dev had been awarded Man of the Match jointly with Dean Jones. If you analyse the match scoresheets you will see why! This was a real hometown decision with two Indians and Alan Crompton as adjudicators. Naturally enough, Alan was outvoted. Mind you, in my opinion, a number of other individual performances merited an award in this fine match.

Basically though our players, on the point of expiry, were too tired to fuss about it and they trooped off the field to the Australian rooms. When inside, the Indian brass were calling for Greg Matthews to return to receive his prize as 'all-rounder' of the match. In the end Greg (who was prepared to return to the field) did not go, Alan Crompton explaining to the home officials that the whole presentation organisation had been a farce. Rightly so!

It was a curious scene in the room and I was the only 'outsider' there to witness it. The players slumped into cane chairs, consuming soft drinks and mineral water in large quantities. There was no talk or discussion at all — everyone just looked around the room at each other. Then Alan Crompton said 'Well, what a great game and what a fantastic performance you have all put up. I hope you realise you are the guys who participated in the second tied Test of all Tests ever played'. Allan Border said 'And I sincerely hope I never have to play in another one!'

Bob Simpson had been outside the room speaking with some of the Indian media and he returned at this point. He walked in with a big smile and said 'Well, there you are fellas, I told you before play today that India wouldn't get 348 to win this game. Right, wasn't I?' It was a marvellous line for Bob to come out with at that time and it really broke the room up. The tremendous tension dissipated immediately: and the team became human again.

Spontaneously, those not in the playing XI on the day stood and applauded those who were. It was the most extraordinary scene I have ever witnessed in a cricket dressing room. The eight of us (four players, Bob Simpson, Alan Crompton, Errol Alcott and myself) just stood there clapping for what seemed to be a very long time. Then Bob Simpson said 'And what about a round of applause for the skipper who handled the side so well today under such intense pressure — well done Allan!' And so we clapped again and this time the team joined in.

It had been arranged prior to the match that Air Indian would delay by one hour the scheduled flight to Hyderabad to allow both teams time to board the aircraft. So the players raced to the showers, porters arrived from everywhere and the team and baggage moved swiftly to the waiting bus. If it was thought that the crowd gathered outside the Australian room was large, then the one in the precincts of the bus departure driveway was huge. Hundreds of spectators had come to the rear of the pavilion and lined the balconies one and two floors up. Many hundreds more waited outside the ground and could be seen staring over the fence which encircles the M. A. Chidambaram Stadium.

They called 'Well played Australia', 'Thank you for a wonderful match Australia' and various other phrases expressing their happiness at seeing cricket history being made. When Border appeared from the tunnel beneath the grandstand to join the bus, they chanted 'Border, Border, Border'. I was standing next to Allan at the bus door — he looked up and waved to them all before disappearing into the bus. They loved it!

In the dressing room immediately after the game,

Bob Simpson had come to me and said 'I know you have some contacts in the Madras Cricket Club (which is situated within the ground). Is there any way you might be able to get some cold beer onto the team bus so the boys could have a beer on the way to the airport?' Not without some difficulty I was able to arrange it and the delight on the players' faces as they held the beers up when the bus ran out of the stadium will be another lasting memory from the finest finish to a Test match I was ever privileged to see.

The things they've said about cricket and cricketers

Selected by Leslie Frewin

Had Grace been born in Ancient Greece, the *Iliad* would have been a different book.'
> — *John Perceval, Bishop of Hereford*

I dunno. Maybe it's that 'Tally-ho lads' attitude — you know, 'There'll Always Be An England', all that Empire crap they dish out. But I never could cop Poms.
> — *Jeff Thomson*

Who writes your script?
> — *Graham Gooch to Ian Botham*

It seems everything I do people are going out of their way to knock down.
> — *Ian Botham*

We want the Ashes urn and its contents laboratory tested. Then you will see they will turn out to be the remains of the Aboriginal cricketer King Cole who toured England in 1868.
> — *Aboriginal spokesman Robbie Thorpe*

I don't care for cricket.
> — *The late Anthony Blunt, art historian and spy*

Cricket is a game which the British, not being a spiritual people, had to invent in order to have some concept of eternity.
> — *Lord Mancroft*

I became a bowler at school in the best of all possible ways — I used to bowl out the captain at the nets.
> — *A. A. Milne*

When we were children we asked my Uncle Charles what it was like to play cricket with W. G. Grace. 'The dirtiest neck I ever kept wicket behind', was his crisp reply.
> — *Lord Chandos*

There is one great similarity between music and cricket. There are slow movements in both.

— Sir Neville Cardus

There's more in bowling than just turning your arm over. There's such a thing as observation.

— Wilfred Rhodes

Batting is a major trial before an 11-man jury.

— Richie Benaud

Cricket is indescribable. How do you describe an orgasm?

— Greg Matthews

Douglas Jardine was a dour, remorseless Scot, 130 years after his time. He should have gone to Australia in charge of a convict hulk.

— Jack Fingleton

Playing against a team with Ian Chappell as captain turns a cricket match into gang warfare.

— Mike Brearley

I didn't get on with Bradman as a man. We had nothing in common.

— Keith Miller

Botham captains the side like a great big baby.

— Henry Blofeld

We have nothing against men cricketers. Some of them are quite nice people, even though they don't win as often as we do.

— Rachel Heyhoe Flint

The true spirit of cricket requires the bowler to aim at or near the stumps, rather than the batsman's head.

— Professor Aubrey Jenkins

We need to pray for all those concerned with cricket that worthy standards may be maintained.

The late Michael Ramsey, 100th Archbishop of Canterbury

England seem to have a fixation with so-called leadership qualities — and it usually means background.

— Geoffrey Boycott

Victor Trumper had the greatest charm and two strokes for every ball.

— C. B. Fry

Spofforth's no batsman, he's a conjuror.

— George Giffen

To hit O'Reilly for four would usually arouse a belligerent ferocity which made you sorry. It was almost like disturbing a hive of bees. . . .

— Sir Donald Bradman

If Arthur Mailey was not cricket's greatest bowler, he was its greatest philosopher.

— Ben Travers

Ray Lindwall was a great man at a party. He ensured that no English brewery went out of business through lack of patronage.

— Jim Laker

Botham? He couldn't bowl a hoop downhill.

— Fred Trueman

There's an enormous amount of mediocrity in English cricket.

— Richard Hadlee

Ashes to ashes, dust to dust, if Lillee don't get ya, Thomson must.

— *Sydney Telegraph* (cartoon caption)

I will never be accepted by a snob press.

— *Ray Illingworth*

It's 8.30 on a Friday night. What am I doing in Ahmedabad?

— *Graeme Fowler*

Did I find Test tours too strenuous? The very question is sacrilegious.

— *Arthur Mailey*

I don't think much of Australians' play but they're a wonderful crowd of drinking men.

— *Roger Iddison*

Cricket's a game, not a competition.

— *George Hirst*

Where the English language is unspoken there can be no real cricket.

— *Sir Neville Cardus*

Cricket? It civilises people and creates good gentlemen. I want everyone to play cricket in Zimbabwe. I want ours to be a nation of gentlemen.

— *Robert Mugabe, Prime Minister of Zimbabwe*

We've always set the trend. Remember, women cricketers were the first to bowl overarm.

— *Rachel Heyhoe Flint*

When we were living in Sydney a friend told me that one night, while she and her husband were making love, she suddenly noticed something sticking in his ear. When she asked him what it was he replied, 'Be quiet! I'm listening to the cricket'.

— *Vicky Rantzen in* The Observer

Through the lens of Patrick Eagar

Patrick Eagar, whose striking cricket photography is known and admired wherever cricket is played, was born in Cheltenham in 1944. His first cricket photograph (which he confesses didn't come out very well) was taken at Arundel, Sussex, in 1956. His first Test match was at Headingley in 1965; his first overseas Test at Bridgetown in 1973.

He has photographed every day (bar one) of every Test match in England since June 1972 and can boast a picture library of more than 250,000 images totalling 130 Test matches in all. Word has it that he has been seen recently photographing in a number of vineyards in Europe and Australasia.

Patrick Eagar.

The Australian team (minus Jeff Thomson) at Edgbaston in July 1975.

Kim Hughes.

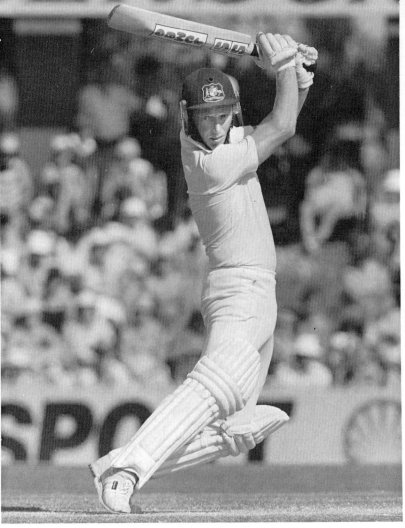

Greg Chappell.

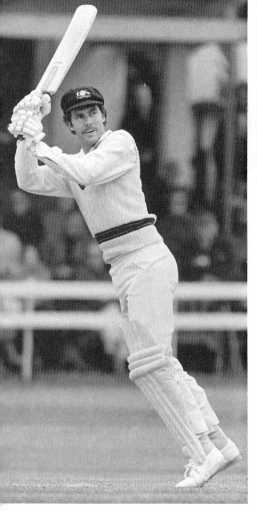

Jeff Thomson.

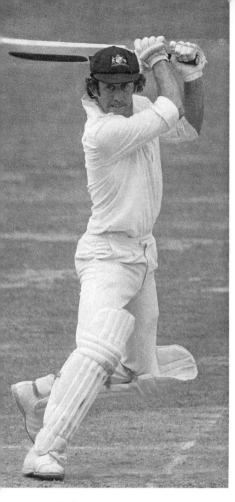

Ian Chappell.

Allan Border.

Dennis Lillee.

Dean Jones.

The last great innings of Victor Trumper

Jack Fingleton

Victor Thomas Trumper, 1877–1915, a classic right-hand opening batsman, a useful right-arm medium-pace bowler and a magnificent fieldsman. An artist with the bat, C. B. Fry said of him, 'he had no style and yet he was all style'. He died from Bright's disease, aged 37. Trumper remains one of the great legends of world cricket.

Trumper's last great innings was played in Christchurch, New Zealand, in February and March 1914, when he hit 293 in what was declared to be the outstanding innings ever played in New Zealand. He died almost within the year at the age of 37.

One would think Herbie Collins would be an acceptable authority on that innings, for he was in the team, but I read an article by him once that must be dubious, to say the least. He said that Trumper took a bat offered him by a schoolboy as he was going out to bat and made his 293 with that — and towards the end of his innings with only half of it, as the bat broke badly. I doubt this very much as, thanks to Walter Hadlee, who sought them out, I handled two bats of Trumper's in Christchurch and one of them, which had a bad split up one side of it but had been repaired, I believe to be the one that Trumper used in his 293 innings — at least up to when he had reached 130, when it split and Trumper changed it.

Another bat I saw was that used by Trumper in his preceding tour of New Zealand in 1904–05 season. It is now in the possession of Mr J. C. Saunders and, apart from bearing all the scores Trumper made in New Zealand on that tour, it carries all the autographs of the Australian team with the inscription, 'From J. J. Kelly to F. C. Raphael in remembrance of Victor Trumper. 11/3/05.' Mr F. C. Raphael was secretary of the New Zealand Cricket Council from 1901 to 1914.

The first bat, in which I was more interested, belongs to Mr O. A. Y. Johnston, a prominent Christchurch businessman and a leading golfer and golf administrator. It was given to him on the Sunday of the Canterbury match, the day after Trumper made his 293 — which included three sixes and 44 fours.

Mr Johnston's father, I was told, was one of several Christchurch men asked to provide car transport for a visit by the Australians to *Otohuna*, the home of Sir Heaton Rhodes. The party later went on to *Kinloch*, the Little River home of the Buchan family, to see Martian, the outstanding sire of the time. When the party returned to Christchurch, O. A. Y. Johnston, then aged

13, was asked by Trumper — with whom he had kept company on the trip — if he would like a bat because, Trumper said, he seemed to be keen on cricket. Trumper gave him the bat he had used and damaged the previous day, with advice on how to have it repaired. The bat was duly repaired and its proud new owner batted with it on several occasions later, when a member of the first eleven at Christ's College.

I think this story a more likely one than the one written by Collins, who does not appear to be a very reliable reporter. In the same story he says that Trumper began his innings by hitting the first ball from Bennett for six. Not so. The newspapers of that time used to give a batsman's name and follow with all his scoring strokes opposite his name, followed by the manner of his dismissal, and his total. This shows that Trumper started his big innings with a single.

The tour of New Zealand was due to the enterprise of Sir Arthur Sims, an old Canterbury boy, and in his day one of the best batsmen Canterbury turned out. For some years his wool business necessitated extensive travel between New Zealand, Australia and England, and his love of and enthusiasm for cricket enabled him to bring over to New Zealand the flower of Australian cricket. Trumper, Armstrong (who held the record score made in New Zealand of 335 for the Melbourne club against Southland in 1906), Ransford, Noble and young players such as Mailey, Waddy, Dr Dolling (later to be an Australian selector), the famous all-rounder J. N. Crawford, Les Cody and Bert Collins, with Sims himself, made up the Australian team. Reese captained the local side and the New Zealand *Referee* of the time enthused over the play:

Those who went to Lancaster Park on Saturday got the cricket feast of a lifetime. There were probably few in the big crowd who had ever seen anything like it, and doubtless the great majority will never see its equal again. There is only one Trumper in the world, and after watching him — for over three hours — execute his magic-like strokes all round the wicket one could subscribe enthusiastically to

the sentiment conveyed in his being styled 'The incomparable Victor'. Talk about the champagne of cricket! It was all that, with an electric sparkle running through it all the way. One might enthuse over it to the extent of columns and yet not be guilty of exaggeration.

It was a bit chilly towards the close, but neither the batsmen nor the fieldsmen noticed it. They were too busy. The wicket was in first-class order, Armstrong said, and he was in long enough to know. At any rate, Trumper liked it, and Sims had no fault to find with it, and he was there long enough for his acquaintance to ripen into intimacy. The outfield was accused on Friday of being on the slow side, but Trumper demonstrated on Saturday that this was only a rumour, for the lively manner in which the ball bumped and cleared the picket fence might almost have suggested that it was hard.

There was a big crowd to watch the play, probably nearly 5000, for the takings were £248. This assembly would include some two or three thousand who only get to cricket matches on great occasions, and they got their money's worth.

To return to the play. Canterbury had done well on the first day to get five of the opposition out for 105, but the champion batsmen were yet to come, and probably no one imagined that with Sims and Cody in, and with top-notchers like Trumper, Armstrong, Ransford and Crawford to come, this success would be maintained. And so it was quickly demonstrated — for though Cody did not stay long the next partnership between Armstrong and Sims put on nearly 100, and was the forerunner of what was to follow — a partnership that produced 433 runs in a little over three hours, and a display of batting that was an absolute revelation even to many who had seen the world's greatest batsmen.

The cricket scribe's vocabulary is quite inadequate to describe Trumper's innings. Much of the daring that electrified the cricket world a decade or more ago had departed. He is said to have mellowed with age, and strengthened his defence. It may be suggested that the mellowing process has left absolutely untarnished the superlativeness of his strokes. His defence may be sounder.

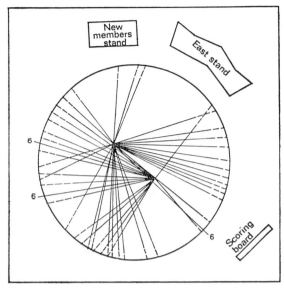

Australia versus England, first Test match, Birmingham, second day, May 1909. Armstrong (left) and Trumper go out to bat.

Diagram showing the direction of Trumper's chief strokes (44 fours and three sixes) in his huge score of 293, compiled in three hours and 10 minutes, against Canterbury in New Zealand in 1914.

One can easily believe it but that 'age has withered or custom staled' his remarkable powers as a batsman is unbelievable after Saturday's display. His driving? It was equal to that of great batsmen who have specialised in the stroke. More often than not the only description of its power would be the pace at which the ball would be seen travelling to the fence and the remarkably short space of time it took to get there.

His late cutting was a marvel. Bennett's perfect-length ball just outside the off stump — the most deadly ball in his repertoire — was flicked away anywhere between slip and point with the ease and precision of timing that was absolutely artistic. But probably the most astonishing feature of his batting was his play on the on-side. Balls just clear of the leg-stump, whether they kept low or bounced high, were unerringly despatched towards the on-fence, and the manner in which he kept the high-bouncing balls all along the sward and yet got the same power into the stroke

seemed nothing short of jugglery. Only cricketers could appreciate the difficulty of it. Altogether, it was a display of batting which for sound defence and purity of stroke with the maximum aggressiveness and minimum of risk has never been equalled in Christchurch.

The cricket gods, then, must have smiled on Trumper that day — and rightly so, for it was to be his last big innings of such a nature, although he was later to play another double-century innings at Invercargill. Bill Ferguson was the scorer at Christchurch and gave his scoring graph of Trumper's boundary strokes to the local newspaper. I reproduce it here, and it is to be noted that Trumper hit a six directly over point. Also noticeable is that from the scoreboard end he didn't hit a single boundary on the off or cover drive from that end, but the flow of on-side boundaries is truly staggering. I have seen a Test played at Christchurch between

The great stylist Victor Trumper in his prime.

England and New Zealand and I have never before heard such chirruping as the spectators indulged themselves in in the grandstand during the game.

I had mixed thoughts as I held the two Trumper bats in Christchurch. The one in my left hand was the bat used by Trumper in part of his 293 innings and which was subsequently given to the small lad, Johnston, whose father had it repaired. The borers have got into it and it is now badly marked by them. The other bat is in fairly good condition, considering its age.

I was most struck — apart from the thrill of just holding them — by their weight. They are much heavier than batsmen in my time would use, although moderns now go in for weighty bats. The handles are thick, unrubbered, and one could not imagine a prominent batsman, particularly a classical one, choosing such unpretentious bats. The point that impressed me about them was that Trumper must have had wrists of steel to wield them so dexterously and execute such delicate shots.

'I've been involved with my body for a fair while now and I can't come up with a better groove than that for polishing a cricket ball. Right? It's not just for women watching colour telly. It's for real.'

The gospel according to Max Walker

Max Walker

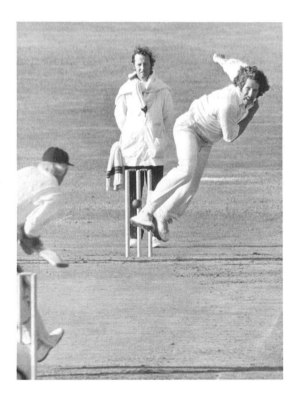

Max Walker bends his back in bowling to David Steele at Leeds, England versus Australia, 16 August 1975.

At the age of about 11 or 12 I was lucky enough to play cricket in the same team as my old man, Big Max, and being a Tasmanian we played in Tasmania in a Sunday afternoon competition on a concrete wicket.

I should tell you that the curators in Tasmania are not too flash. They turn up about every three months to cut the grass. And even though it was a grand final — Mathina versus Oatlands — I don't think anyone would have seen the match and it wasn't televised.

And even though it was a grand final, it had been two and a half months between visits. So the grass was about three feet high. It didn't worry me because I had the ability to hit the ball in the air, but some of our other players were a little bit inhibited by all this grass.

You can imagine the scene at the ground. Thirty-five of our relatives and their dogs have turned up, and the atmosphere is electric. The buzz; the barking, all the way around the ground, you can sense it. We want 17 runs to win. Normally we should romp in, but on this occasion, it's just a little bit tight, for there's only one ball left to get those 17 runs in. And worse than that, there's only one batsman left. And that's Big Max, my old man. Just how good a player is Big Max to bat number 11 behind me in a Sunday afternoon competition?

Worse than that, the previous batsman to be dismissed has chopped down so hard on a yorker that he's broken the handle of the only bat in the club. We used to drop the bat and run up and down between the wickets. There was no Kerry Packer in those days.

Now the opposition captain wasn't about to lend us their only bat, was he? No way. And the old man, very creative thinker that he is, walked out of the gate, grabbed a picket — lucky we were playing at Oatlands — went out and took block. Why he took block, I'm blowed if I know.

My old man is a dead-set imposter. He's got one shot and one shot only, and that is a slog straight down the ground. Normally when you play on concrete or malthoid there's a bit of chalk behind the middle stump. You mark your centre, don't you? There's no chalk in Tasmania. And the old man's got the Dunlop rubbers; made in India, size 11 and he's not having a lot of luck marking centre on the concrete.

Then he's had the audacity to look around the ground from third man to mid-off and way around to long leg, just like all the good players do. Fair dinkum, my old man would not be good enough to snick a ball to third man, really. He looks up, back beyond the umpire 30 or 40 yards back, and here he is, standing in the long grass; all you can see from the knee caps up is a mad quick.

No matter where you go in the world, every opposition side's got a mad quick, haven't they? The West Indies have got five of 'em. All they want to do is bounce the shitter out of the tailenders. Right? And this bloke's no different from the rest of 'em. He's got the ball and he is giving it heaps. He is polishing her up and down; really is giving it plenty, eh?

Now there's a lot of science involved in polishing a cricket ball: total maximum utilisation of one half of a cricket ball up and down your trousers, right? I've been involved with my body for a fair while now and I can't come up with a better groove than that for polishing a cricket ball. Right? It's not just for women watching colour telly. It's for real.

Every fast bowler worth his salt has been known to rub a cricket ball up and down his trousers. Apart from one — Jeffrey Thomson. 'Thommo' holds it in front of him and gives it the gyrating pelvic girdle. It does pay to advertise, doesn't it. Really? It never hurt 'Thommo'. Imagine the mad quick in the long grass polishing the cork composition ball. All the polishing in the world won't bring it up, will it?

In he comes, through the long grass. Up on the toe nails in the delivery stride — Tasmanians have got really long toe nails — he has let the ball go and the old man gives me the big Palmolive smile down the track. I'm nought not out up the other end, playing for the red inks. Now anyone that knows anything about the game of cricket realises you must not bowl a ball pitched middle or leg stump to a tailend batsman, okay? You'll end up being hit down the ground on the first bounce

The inimitable Max Walker gets into his stride!

for four or, depending on how much right hand is on the bat, whacked through mid-wicket for six.

So what's this bloke do? He bowls a big rank half-volley — didn't swing a lot 'cause not much paint on the ball — and like most number 11 batsmen, the old man plays straight down the track. Plonk. Almost trod on the ball which has got to be a bonus. Where do you think the ball's gone? Pitched middle and leg stump. The old man's hit through the most magnificent on-drive you've ever seen. We take off, run one, two, three, four, five . . . and there are five guys out at long-on — can't find the ball anywhere in the long grass.

As we crossed for six I said to the old man: 'Dad, that's it. You can only run six.' He said: 'Bullshit son, keep running, keep running.' Seven, eight, nine, 10 and there are now eight guys out there at long-on who can't find the ball anywhere . . . 11, 12, 13. The old man's got heartburn, dyspepsia, the whole lot. You just don't come in last ball in the grand final and chip 13 off the toes, do you? I mean, that is just not on.

We run . . . 14, 15, 16 . . . there are now 10 of 'em out there at long-on; can't find the ball anywhere. The wicketkeeper is the only bloke left — over the stumps for the run out. Rest of them are stamping down the long grass and a quarter of the ground is absolutely flat. Rest of it is two foot six, three foot high. Seventeen runs. What a fantastic performance. Get up, win the grand final, another flag for the dressing-sheds back home.

Great sportsman he was, the old man looked across to the opposition captain, who was a bloody long way away at long-on, and walked ácross, 'Do you really want to know where the ball is?' He turned over the picket, a nail in the end of the picket; *there* is the cricket ball.

For the love of the game

Here is a story of Horace,
That cricketer unknown to fame,
Who played as a cricketer ought to,
For nought but the love of the game.

They always put Horace at long-stop,
The least risky place in a match,
For there it was not very likely
He'd lose the game dropping a catch.

But life that is real, not invented
Is full of mishaps that arise;
And when such a mishap struck Horace
It should have caused no one surprise.

The match for the trophy was ending;
The visitors needed, to win,
No more than two runs (or two extras)
When number eleven came in.

Alas! when that rabbit endeavoured
To poke his first ball bouncing by
He tipped it, and up it went soaring
Behind him, towards the blue sky.

'Yours, Horace!' the home Captain shouted
As Horace stared up in the air.
But the ball disappeared — he saw nothing,
Made blind by the sinking sun's glare.

With the sun in his eyes it's no wonder
That Horace saw nothing at all;
While raising cupped hands, as if praying,
His head was well caught — by the ball.

Felled where he stood, his mates bore him
(On finding he wasn't quite dead)
Back to their hut, where they laid him
With cricket pads under his head.

'I think he's unconscious,' said someone,
'He certainly doesn't look well'
'Unconscious or not,' said another,
'With Horace you never can tell.'

Then, when the last over was over,
The Captain came stomping back, mad;
'Don't worry,' said somebody soothing,
'It's only a bump — it's not bad.'

'I don't mind his bump,' snarled the Captain,
'I *do* mind his missing that catch:
'As everyone knows, except Horace,
'His blundering's cost us the match.'

These words pierced through Horace's coma,
He sat up and opened his eyes,
And said, as he stared at his Captain
With something approaching surprise:

'It seems that it's you who've been smitten,
'You play cricket only for fame;
'I'm no catcher nor batter — what matter?
'I play for the love of the game.'

The Captain relinquished the trophy,
The visitors took it instead,
While Horace received for his efforts
A trophy-sized lump on the head.

And that is the story of Horace
Who won for himself the good name
Of someone who really 'played cricket' —
Just played for the love of the game.

— Donald D. Christie

'Now every man was round the bat, the sun had vanished and every sober soul on the ground was silent.'

Solace for Border as England go to Sleep

Matthew Engel

Matthew Engel.

The thing that will be remembered, and needs to be remembered, about Sydney 1986–87 is that it was one of the greatest of Test matches, perhaps a contender for the all-time top 10. The trivial bit is that it will be remembered most kindly in Australia because they won it. But what the heck? With an hour to go any result was still a possibility: England had every hope of saving it until the final delivery. All through the match there were the wonderful twists and turns of fortune that are the essence of Test cricket. In one-day cricket there are often equally tense finishes: this match hardly flagged for a moment through five days.

In a country where every second person you meet says they like cricket, but only the one-day game, and the pure form of the sport is in danger of being driven out of its habitat like a red squirrel faced with a grey one, it was a small miracle. It is a pity this could not have happened earlier in the series: grey squirrel cricket starts in earnest tomorrow.

Australia won by 55 runs when Peter Sleep sent a straight one through John Emburey's defence with six possible deliveries remaining. The Ashes were already settled and England had taken the series 2–1, though it could have been 4–0.

In several ways this has been a mirror image of 1982–83, when England were the team deprived of their rebels and Australia, vastly superior, only sneaked home by the same margin. All along Gatting has been just a little bit minimalist: too concerned with the Ashes, not quite concerned enough with winning each individual game. And future *Wisdens* will not reflect just how much better England were overall, and how desperately Australia needed this win.

At the start of play yesterday, an Australian win was the most likely result ('England's hopes are history', read one morning headline) but only narrowly, with England, needing a total of 320, on 1 for 39. The first one and three-quarter hours belonged wholly to England, with Athey and Gower holding out, getting the breaks, and scoring just enough runs to keep victory as an eventual option.

Then we saw what became a feature of the day: two wickets fell at the same score. One partner often becomes unsettled when his long-term mate disappears: it is as traumatic as any divorce. But it did seem as though this very fair pitch had an X-factor. It was fine to bat on once a batsman got in, but very tricky to understand at first. Thus England crumbled from 1 for 91 to 5 for 102, at which point defeat appeared a certainty.

This period began when Taylor, for the first time in the match, began to lose his nerve and Border was obliged to use his own little left-armers. Immediately Taylor, who had replaced Border at slip, put down a hard chance offered by Athey. Marsh made amends with a catch at silly point to get Gower and give Border his first Test wicket in almost four years. Then Sleep bowled Athey round his legs and in the first over after lunch Taylor returned and had Lamb caught at silly point — Lamb has had another wretched series, averaging less than 18. In came Botham. His first ball turned enough for him to miscue towards mid-wicket and apparent safety. But Wellham, making ground like a greyhound, got there in time. The weeping duck appeared on the big scoreboard and everyone contemplated an early finish.

Gatting and Richards, however, had a different idea. Over the next three hours they gave England what began as a glimmer of hope and turned, by the imperceptible degrees of a sunrise, into a genuine prospect of victory. They put on 101 knocking Hirst and Ranji out of the record books on the way as England's sixth-wicket record-holders on this ground.

Gatting is no Ranji, but he might now be the man you would choose to bat for your life if the spinners were on (he is good-hearted, too, and would charge less than most). He maintained his customary policy of counter-attacking rather than fiddling about, scored heaps of runs with leg-side heaves, and would have scored heaps more on the off if his square-cuts had not kept finding fielders.

Richards was less ambitious, but for the second time in the match he silenced the muttering about his uncertainties behind the stumps with a performance of immense character in front of them in the best tradition of English wicket-keeper/batsmen. They each survived the odd missed chance; they lasted past tea and the new ball and the start of the last 20 overs, when only 90 runs were needed. Would they? Could they?

Two overs later and just four short of his century, Gatting played too soon at Waugh and was caught and bowled. Emburey emerged and, in front of the lovely old Members' Stand, captain and vice-captain conferred. Gatting told him to get himself in, play normally, talk to Richards, and then see whether they felt like winning.

With 10 overs to go that was possible but no longer very likely: 64 runs wanted, four wickets left. 'Petered out into a tame draw,' said someone. Alas, no. Sleep produced a googly and bowled Richards off the inside edge. Next ball Edmonds, who has always liked to keep up with Botham, was leg before. Eight down, nine overs to go.

Taylor came back to the attack, and Emburey and Small settled into a pattern: block, pad, leave: block, pad, leave. With three overs to go Reid came back, he found Small's outside edge and Border just clung on to a ground-level slip catch. Dilley emerged as though to the gallows.

Now every man was round the bat, the sun had vanished and every sober soul on the ground was silent. The penultimate over was Sleep's. He even tried a bouncer to keep Emburey guessing: Block, leave, leave, block. The last ball of the over was dead straight. Emburey missed it. Eleven Australians clambered all over each other: one trusts the other 15 million did much the same.

Taylor was then named Man of the Match, which meant the wine goblets went to yet another teetotaller. But it was right dramatically as well as technically — this will be remembered as Taylor's match long after those of us who had a bit of fun after his selection are forgotten. He was embraced by his entire family —

mum, dad, three sisters and even an auntie — and fought back a few tears.

Broad was named Man of the Series, which was right too, despite his minimal impact on this match. He did not cry, nor did Gatting though after 14 weeks in Australia, he almost said something controversial when asked about the Australian close fielders' habit of appealing for everything: 'With the Aussies jumping up and down it reminded me of India,' he said. It got slightly excessive in the end. ''Slightly excessive'' is Gattingese for totally ridiculous. And less diplomatic souls would point their finger most directly at the wicket-keeper, Tim Zoehrer, who is no doubt a thoroughly nice chap but has his mouth open so often that in these climes there must be a statistical probability of him catching a funnelweb spider.

The standard of umpiring in this Test wavered for the first time in the series, but it was never an easy match to handle. A small part of Gatting was pleased for Border, who deserved some success and may now have the heart to keep going. The result halts Australia's winless sequence at 14 and maintains their eight-year unbeaten record on their one lucky ground of recent times.

But its immediate effect will only be to increase interest in the one-day World Series Cup, which is already hugely popular. That starts in Brisbane this weekend, with England playing the West Indies tomorrow and Australia on Sunday. There are a dozen preliminary matches before the top two meet in the best-of-three finals next month. For the first two matches Australia have kept Taylor in their 12 and brought back the one-day specialists Macleay, O'Donnell and Davis in place of Sleep, Hughes and Ritchie. Wellham is expected to open.

The grounds will be jammed solid, but I wager there will not be one match whose details will stick in the mind even 24 hours later. This Test will linger forever. The nearest parallel perhaps is Ritchie Benaud's triumph at Old Trafford in 1961 when the crucial stand between Davidson and Mackenzie put on 98, just as

A triumvirate of greats: Historic photograph of Australian Test cricketers, from left, Charles ('The Governor-General') Macartney, Hanson ('Sammy') Carter and John Morris Taylor, taken in April 1926

Three of the best: From left, Godfrey Evans, Keith Miller, Peter May during a Taverners' function in London.

Waugh and Taylor did. The margin was 54 runs instead of 55, and Peter May, like Athey, was famously bowled round his legs. But this contest was unique and a pleasure to everyone present. I hope some of the joy managed to cross the world and thaw you out just a little.

On the question of ball-rubbing

Sir Alan Herbert

Sir Alan Herbert

To the Editor of The Times

Sir, — 'Sam Cook,' I read, 'carefully rubbed the ball into a dusty ground to remove the shine. Then with his first two deliveries he proceeded to remove Dave Parsons and Dave Gibson.' But is this 'cricket'?

Then there is the inelegant and laughable rubbing of the ball on shirts and trousers by bowlers and fielders to maintain the 'shine'.

Sir, the ball, like the wicket, is for the use of both sides. The wicket may not be improved or tampered with by either side for its own advantage. Should the ball? Evidently not: for 'it is illegal for the bowler to lift the seam of the ball in order to obtain a better hold', and the use the resin by bowlers is also declared 'unfair'.

If the fielding side may alter the natural state of the ball, why should not the batsman capture it between the overs and rub some of the shine off on the soles of his boots? If the college of umpires have no mind in this matter, is there not a case for an amendment of the laws? But I feel rather a killjoy; for the spectacle of a fast bowler rubbing his way into the television screen is one of the funniest things in modern entertainment.

I am, Sir, yours respectfully,

A. P. Herbert, August 29, 1959

Sir, — In his letter in your issue of August 29 Sir Alan Herbert appears to regard the polishing of a new ball on shirt or trousers and the deliberate removal of its shine as equally open to criticism. But should not a distinction be drawn between attempts to maintain the original condition of the ball and an expedient that induces premature old age?

Yours faithfully,

A. W. Douglas, September 1, 1959

Sir, — Mr. A. W. Douglas asks if a distinction should not be drawn between trouser-rubbing, intended 'to maintain the original condition of the ball', and rubbing in the dust that 'induces premature old age'.

No, Sir, or not much: for each is an interference with the course of nature not provided for by the laws of cricket. In general the good cricketer must accept the natural hazards which affect the wicket or 'the implement used'. 'Under no circumstances shall a pitch be watered during a match': nor shall it be mown. The discontented batsmen may not send for a roller, or (it is presumed) pour their lemonades on the pitch. The bowler may not improve the ball with wax or resin, or 'lift the seam'.

But some exceptions are clearly made. After a certain period of wear and tear a new ball may be demanded. 'The batsman may beat the pitch with his bat' (I often wonder why). 'Players may secure their footholds by the use of sawdust'; and 'the bowler may dry the ball when wet on a towel or sawdust'. Nowhere do the laws say that he may rub the ball in the dust when dry to remove the shine, or on his abdomen or bosom to preserve or increase the shine.

The first, no doubt, is morally the worse (it is like deliberately damaging the wicket): but the second is unseemly and ridiculous, and if continued may lead to new excesses. If a shirt, why not a brush — or a velvet pad sewn into the trousers? The batsman, too, may wish to keep the shine on the ball, whether to assist in its passage to the boundary or to outwit the bowler who has rubbed it in the dust. If the umpires and captains have nothing to say, I hope that some aggrieved batsman will bring this question to a head, pick up a dead ball, produce his little polishing set — and see what happens.

Meanwhile, I suggest a simple amendment to law 46: 'The use of resin, wax, &c., by the bowler, *and any attempt by any player to alter the natural condition of the ball when dry, are forbidden*: but a bowler may dry the ball when wet, &c.'

I am, Sir, yours respectfully,

A. P. Herbert, September 4, 1959

The late Sir Alan Herbert's vastly-amusing piece was featured by me in the first *Boundary Book*. In my opinion it more than bears reprinting in this, the third of the trilogy, some 26 years later. I am sure it will delight the sons of the fathers!

— *Ed*

John McCallum, the distinguished actor and President of The Lord's Taverners Australia, chips in with a tale of tortuous deeds at the wicket during an austerity cricket match in England in that first, lean, post-war summer. It can only have happened in England!

Only one word for it — feudal

John McCallum

John McCallum.

I'd come across a few private golf courses in my time but never a private cricket ground — not one with a grandstand (a small one), a pavilion (a large one and residential; the opposing team could stay overnight), a picket fence, practice nets, sight screens, and a scoreboard large enough to display the batsmen's names. It was just as good a ground, in fact, as many a county ground and better than some. It was rather like Arundel, which was only about 50 miles away along the coast. And the address had a splendid ring to it: Pelsham, Peasmarsh, Romney Marsh, near Rye, Sussex, England.

I was told that the West Indies had played there — the team which had brought the great Constantine to England for the first time, as well as a great many other eminent players including the legendary Ranjitsinhji. It was all rather awe inspiring, particularly as the captain of the Pelsham team was himself a considerable crickter, Robert Scott, who had captained Sussex before the war.

It was the big match of the year — Pelsham, the manor house, versus Peasmarsh, the neighbouring village. The Pelsham team was made up of workers on the estate — the head gardener went in first wicket down and the assistant hop grower was the wicket-keeper — and, by co-optation, two far from eminent Australian players who happened to be staying at Pelsham at the time because Ealing Studios were making a film in the area called *The Loves of Joanna Godden* — Chips Rafferty and me. Incidentally, it was during the making of this film that I met my wife, later known to Taverners in England and Australia as the specialist spin bowler, Googly Withers.

It was the first summer after the war, 1946, and the first time the match had been played for seven years. Rationing of food, clothing and petrol was still in force, but people from surrounding villages had put on their pre-war Sunday best and somehow had found petrol to turn up in an extraordinary assortment of vehicles — tractors, any sort of farm machinery that moved, ancient Austins and Morrises, all of them at least eight years old, most of them many more. There were quite a few horse-drawn conveyances and here and there a smart pony and trap turnout.

Every player was in white flannels, waistbands let out, boots a bit cracked but carefully blancoed. Pads were somewhat moth-eaten, but bats had been oiled, gloves mended, and each team had somehow managed to get hold of a new ball.

I knew that Chips was a bit unhappy and sceptical about the whole thing. He hadn't played much cricket and he made no bones about the fact that he didn't like the game and would far rather have spent the day yarning in the pub with some of the locals over a few pints. If he thought he could have got away with it, he would have played the fool and sent the whole thing up, but he knew he couldn't do that, not with Robert Scott and all the others taking it so seriously. The only eccentricity he insisted on was to wear his wide-brimmed bushman's hat, which had become his trademark ever since his success in *The Overlanders*. He wore it everywhere, outdoors and indoors, just as Paul Hogan was to do 40 years later in *Crocodile Dundee*. In fact, Chips in those days played the same part, off and on screen.

Peasmarsh won the toss and decided to bat. It was a glorious English summer day (it would be when we weren't filming!) and the carefully prepared wicket looked a batsman's paradise. Robert Scott opened the bowling for Pelsham and it was obvious that he was still a good medium pacer in any company, able to swing the ball late towards the slips. He had their opening batsmen in all sorts of trouble and neither lasted very long. Their captain, a retired major who lived in Peasmarsh, got a thick edge to second slip and his partner, the local vicar, saw his stumps spread-eagled after comprehensively missing four consecutive balls on the offside. He had obviously been brought up, like many Englishmen, to think that a straight bat was more important than hitting the ball.

It was about then that I realised that this was a totally different type of cricket from any that I'd come across, particularly in Australia. There was only one word for it — feudal. Every member of the team, apart from Chips and myself, was an employee of Robert Scott's — he owned Pelsham and was therefore Lord of the Manor — and their attitude towards him both as a man and a cricketer can only be described as being one of such tremendous respect that it verged on servility. A great deal of 'sirring' went on, much touching of the forelock, and a misfield was followed by profuse apologies with the unfortunate miscreant almost prostrating himself on the ground. A dropped catch was a criminal offence and filled the wretched perpetrator with such gloom and foreboding that he obviously expected to be thrown into the dungeons as soon as the game was over. When a batsman was dismissed there was no outward show of jubilation, certainly nothing whatever like the modern habit of everyone rushing to the bowler or fieldsman responsible and throwing their arms around his neck and almost kissing him. All that happened was that a quiet hum of sympathy would emanate from the fieldsmen and the wicket-keeper would say, 'Bad luck, old boy', or 'Sir', according to the batsman's social status. Or a fieldsman whom the unfortunate fellow had to pass on his way back to the pavilion might say, 'That was a right nasty one, that was', and perhaps add 'sir'. I felt I had slipped back in time a century or two.

Two wickets were down for six runs. But now a complete change came over the game. First wicket down was a very large, ginger-haired, red-faced fellow with huge forearms, who was the local butcher. Second wicket down was an even larger man, certainly in girth if not quite as tall, whom Chips and I recognised as the local publican. The butcher was younger and fitter and by far the more aggressive and effective of the two. Unlike the departed vicar, he had obviously never had a classical grounding in the game but he did have a good eye and quick reflexes and his method of giving himself plenty of room to hit the ball by stepping a yard towards square leg resulted in several fours over cover point and one memorable six over third man.

Robert Scott's outswingers held no terrors for him

whatsoever. In fact they seemed meat and drink to him. He had made 50 in an astonishingly short time when Robert took himself and the other opening bowler out of the firing line. This increased the speed of scoring considerably because the rest of our bowling was palpably weak — a fiery left-hander who was more danger to silly point than the batsman and a leg spinner who served up long hops on the off at just the right height for square cutting.

In desperation, after the hundred was up, Robert threw the ball to me and said, 'Have a go'. The field was spread out like a turkey's tail but I suddenly found I had caught the feudal pecking order and thought that it might savour of *lese majeste* if I asked for any changes. As I looked down the wicket at the huge bulk of the butcher I was reminded of the story of the bowler waiting to bowl to Warwick Armstrong when he weighed 22 stone. 'Play!' said the umpire for the second time. Still the bowler didn't bowl. The umpire looked round at him. 'What's the matter with you?' he said. 'I can't see the stumps,' the bowler said. 'Oh, get on with it, man,' the umpire said, 'if you hit him in the guts he's lbw, if you hit him on the arse it's a wide.'

Neither happened in my case. The butcher advanced a yard down the pitch and clouted the ball for what looked like a certain six. It went so high in the air that I lost sight of it. When I looked at that part of the boundary to which I last saw it heading it was to see Chips nonchalantly watching it as he sat on the fence. I knew that his bushman's keen sense of sight would enable him to see the ball, but, if it came near him, whether or not he could catch it was another question. It looked, in fact, as though Chips was right underneath it because he hadn't moved an inch. Keeping his eyes on the ball the whole time, he slowly took off his hat and caught the ball in it.

The crowd loved it; lots of laughter and lots of applause. But I could see that Robert Scott was furious. He strode over to Chips and said, 'What the hell do you think you're doing?' 'It was the only way I could catch it, mate,' Chips replied. 'You're playing cricket, not a part in a farce!' Robert stormed.

Chips took the ball out of his hat and tossed it to him. 'They're still running,' he said laconically. 'It's a six!' Robert said. 'You were sitting on the fence. Pull yourself together man! And stand up!' Chips told me later he very nearly said 'Yes, sir' although an alternative reply did occur to him. However, he did stand up. He also told me later that he had never been spoken to like that before, not even by his *bete-noir* of a commanding officer during the war.

After taking 26 off my over the two beefy boys carried on in the same marauding style until tea, by which time they had taken the Peasmarsh total to 194, their remarkable partnership having yielded 190, of which the butcher had contributed an extraordinary 139. The Major magnanimously declared, leaving us just under three hours to get the runs — or get out. Stumps were to be drawn at seven o'clock.

'This is serious,' Robert Scott said, padding up. 'We've got to do it. They beat us last time, you know. McCallum, I hear you've played a bit; I hope your batting is better than your bowling, I've put you in number 7. Chips, you're number 11.'

And he went out and set about the bowling in fine style, 50 coming up in half an hour. Chips and I decided that we weren't likely to be wanted for some time, if ever, so we took off for a stroll around the ground. Frankly, even with Robert Scott batting as he was, I thought that Pelsham had no chance of getting the runs. So when we came across a spectator who had broached a five-gallon keg of beer he had brought along in the back of his truck, it took very little persuasion on his part to enlist Chips and me to help him dispose of the contents. He had half a dozen pals with him and in no time we were swapping tall stories about cricket.

One wicket had fallen but Robert Scott and the head gardener were batting steadily, not scoring as rapidly as the butcher and the publican but with far more orthodoxy. The chock of bat and ball would be followed by a flurry of flannel in the middle and a couple more runs would go up on the scoreboard. It was an idyllic scene to our eyes coming, as we did, from a wider, browner land, particularly so when enhanced by three pints of beer (I think Chips had had four). The trees were turning greener by the minute, the sky bluer, the peacefulness more perfect — when it was suddenly shattered by three wickets falling in one over.

'Better pad up,' someone said. The beer in my stomach churned over. I finished off what was left in my glass, told them I'd see them soon, and headed unsteadily for the pavilion. I was putting on some pads in the changing room when a shout from the ground told me that another wicket had fallen. I'd just sat down in the pavilion, accoutred with bat and pads, when another fell. This was disastrous. I was shakily going down the pavilion steps when I suddenly remembered that there was a distinct chance I might get married soon, so I hastily returned to the changing room and frantically rummaged around among the gear for a box. I found a very old one, *circa* 1932 by the look of it, rusting at the edges and without any straps, but I jammed it down the front of my flannels, making sure that my shirt insulated it, and hoping that my trousers were so tight that it would stay in place.

Robert, who, needless, to say, was the surviving batsman, was waiting for me impatiently halfway to the wicket. 'This is serious,' he said. 'This fellow ducks in late from the off. Keep your head down and watch him right onto the bat.'

I would have said 'I'll do my best, sir,' to those confidence-inspiring remarks if I hadn't been speechless with fright. As I took block I tried to stop the bat trembling. The bowler started his run, arms and legs jutting out at all angles. I had noticed that the wicketkeeper was standing back so I was aware that he might be quite nippy. Which he was, and for all I knew he might well have ducked in from the off as well, but fortunately the first ball went down the leg side. And so did the next one, which gave me a chance to focus and to get some sort of locomotion into my limbs. The third ball was an attempted bouncer and I was able to sway back out of its way, which came to me quite nat-

urally, and I watched it go by in what seemed like slow motion. I knew I had to hit the next one because it was well up and on the stumps. I stretched forward in the general direction of where I thought it would pitch. There was an impact, and to my utter astonishment I saw the ball go between point and cover to the boundary. That went a long way towards giving me some sort of confidence that I could actually see the ball, and even hit it if necessary. By dint of some clever running by Robert to keep me away from the bowling he made another 50 while I made three. Six for 141 and the pavilion clock showed 6.26.

Robert walked down the wicket to me. 'It's getting late,' he said. 'We'll have to quicken up. Have a go.' He certainly had a go himself, two fours and a six off the next three balls. But then he attempted another six and was caught on the boundary for a splendidly made 116. Thirty-nine to make in 23 minutes with three wickets in hand. I didn't fancy our chances and I don't think anybody sitting around the ground did. Pelsham supporters were very quiet, while the Peasmarsh ones, sensing victory and stimulated by a generous sampling of the local beer, were becoming increasingly vocal.

Alas, we were down to the rabbits now. The show-off spinner and the fiery young left-hander (batting right-handed) were out in quick time, contributing only five runs between them, paving the way for Chips's entrance. I knew that it was likely to be an erratic one so I went towards the pavilion to meet him. Sure enough he came out of the gate zig-zagging towards the wrong end. I looked at the scoreboard, 161 for 9. And then I looked at the pavilion clock, 6.44. Sixteen minutes to get 34 runs — or to get out.

'That bugger Scott says we've got to do it,' Chips said. 'Well, it's possible,' I said. 'Like bloody hell it is,' he said. 'Where do I go?' I pointed him towards his end. He didn't ask the umpire for a block, just plonked his bat down in front of the stumps. His bat was so small and he was so tall that he had to bend down double to get it on the ground. Chips at the wicket was an extraordinary sight — like a praying mantis, all thin legs and

345

arms, with his bottom stuck out about a yard towards square leg. Although the sun had gone down he still had his bushman's hat on. The bowler, the one who ducked in from the off, was on a hat-trick and he came in for the kill, elbows and knees pumping with adrenalin. It was a good ball, just short of a length and got up sharply. To my astonishment, Chips didn't move a muscle. He just stood there, stock still, as the ball went within an inch of his off stump. Then I realised that not only had he not seen the ball but he still didn't know that it had gone past him.

I walked down the wicket. 'Are you all right?' I asked him. 'Of course I'm all right', he said, 'I'm leaving the wide stuff alone. Getting a sighter or two.' 'That one was bloody close,' I said. 'Oh, not really,' he said, and took up his praying mantis position again.

The bowler came thundering up, furious that he'd missed his hat-trick by a whisker. This one was even closer to the stumps. Again Chips remained absolutely immobile. The ball hit him in the stomach. A huge shout went all around the ground for lbw. Chips slowly unwound himself and stood up, massaging the spot where the ball had hit him, which now, of course, was about three feet above the stumps. The umpire shook his head.

I walked down to Chips. 'Bodyline,' he said, 'I know how to deal with that.' The next ball was short, a sort of slow bouncer. This time Chips did move. He didn't duck, didn't move the upper part of his body at all, he simply bent his knees and lowered himself towards the ground, which gave him the appearance of sinking into the wicket — but not far enough, because his hat disappeared. Whether it had been knocked off by the ball or whether it had ballooned off his head as a result of Chips's perpendicular descent no one ever discovered, but when next seen it had made a perfect landing on top of the stumps. There was no sign of a bail on the ground. The fieldsmen gathered round to look at the phenomenon. The square leg umpire tentatively took hold of the hat, one hand on either side of the brim.

'Hold it, mate!' Chips said. 'That's my hat.' And with

one hand he grabbed it by the dent in the top and swiftly lifted it off like a waiter whisking the lid off a dish as though it were a great surprise. Both bails were intact. 'Play on fellers,' Chips said.

For the next ball Chips went back to his *rigor mortis* technique. I thought that this time it had to be the end, because the ball was absolutely straight and must hit his stumps. Instead it hit the inside of his bat, went between his legs, and streaked down to the boundary for four. Pelsham supporters applauded loudly; it had looked like a consummate French cut.

The bowler came tearing in for the last ball of the over. It was a wild one fully a yard outside the off stump and very short. Chips languidly waved his bat in its general direction, contemptuously dismissing it. The ball got a thick edge and went over the wicket-keeper's head for the most extraordinary six I had ever seen.

'Over', called the umpire. Pelsham supporters were really coming to life now. I noticed that the bowler I had to face, a new one, only took a six step run, so he must be slow. Probably off-break. But he wasn't a bit slow, or off-break. He had a sort of slinging action, rather reminiscent of Eddie Gilbert, the Aboriginal fast bowler who had got Don Bradman for a duck and who was very quick indeed, probably the fastest in the world in his time. They said he threw the ball. Well, if he didn't, this fellow certainly did. But I felt that it was hardly the time to appeal against that: I probably would have been lynched. Fortunately he didn't seem to be able to bowl straight. The first two balls went down the leg side. But it was precious time wasted. The clock said 6.56. The next one was fairly straight and all I could do was go forward and smother it. Suddenly I heard Chips yell 'Come on!' and looked up to see him charging down the wicket. It was madness of course, but there was nothing to do but to set off for the other end. I was fully 10 yards out when the bowler got to the ball, turned round and hurled it at the stumps. It missed and went on to the boundary. Five runs to me, and suddenly we were 175.

Chips gave me a big grin and a thumbs-up sign and

whacked his bat into the blockhole as though he couldn't wait for the next ball. Long before it left the bowler's hand it was obvious that Chips had abandoned his immobile method and was intent on aggression. Two steps took him halfway down the wicket. When the ball arrived on the full he took a wild swing at it. He missed it by at least two feet, it missed the stumps by a whisker, the wicket-keeper missed it altogether and it went to the boundary for four.

The clock showed two minutes to seven. Fifteen runs to win. We just had to get another over. It was fortunate that the slinging bowler only took six steps. I quickly walked down to Chips. 'Let the next two go or just keep 'em out,' I said. 'Why?' he asked incredulously. I pointed to the clock. 'We must get another over,' I said and hurried back.

The next one he did let go, although it was very near the off stump. The next one was straight, Chips managed to block it and it trickled out towards cover point. 'Come on!' Chips yelled. It was the last thing I wanted, but there was nothing for it but to go. I had to stretch full length to make the crease. Chin on the ground I looked up at the clock. One minute to seven. The square leg umpire was coming in for another over. Fourteen runs to win.

It was the tearaway bowler who ducked in from the off. The field closed in. 'Run for anything,' Chips called out. I saw the wicket-keeper sneak up to the stumps. It had to be a slower ball. I walked up to warn Chips.

I walked back, hoping that it would be a long hop on the leg and that Chips could somehow loft it over the square leg fieldsman. And, marvellous to behold, it was a long hop on the leg. Chips was superb. He simply turned on his axis, pirouetting like an elongated ballet dancer, and looking exactly like Russell Drysdale's batsman in 'The Cricketers'. The ball hit the meat of the bat and sailed over square leg for six. Robert Scott caught it on the pavilion steps. Pelsham supporters were delirious with delight, jumping up and down and clapping like mad. 'Perhaps I'll be given dinner tonight,' Chips said. 'He might even buy me a drink.'

The next three balls were an anti-climax. Chips certainly did his best to hit them for four but missed comprehensively every time. Each time a groan came from the pavilion. Two balls to go, eight to make. Chips went for another big hit, and succeeded in snicking the ball through slips for four. Tremendous applause from the pavilion. Four runs to make, one ball to go.

There was a deadly hush all around the ground as the bowler came in for the last ball. I said a little prayer for another long hop on the leg. It was short but straight. Chips shaped up for his pirouette hook shot. But this time all he managed to do was somehow to turn it into a catch to cover-point. The fieldsman was so surprised that he dropped it.

'Run!' yelled Chips. To this day I'm not sure what happened next. What I think happened is that cover-point threw at the stumps and missed — one run — square leg threw at the stumps and missed — two runs — but hit the umpire. The umpire fell over — three runs — we had just turned for our fourth and winning run when mid-off dashed up to the umpire, rolled him over, retrieved the ball and threw it to the other end.

'Dive!' I yelled at Chips. He was only halfway up the wicket but he launched himself into the air in what must have been, from the tip of his bat to the soles of his feet, a twelve-foot missile. At the same time the wicket-keeper projected himself at the stumps, ball in outstretched hand, not trusting himself to any more throwing. There was a great cloud of dust. It was impossible to see what had happened. The square leg umpire came running in. I ran up the pitch. The fieldsmen came running in. The stumps were shattered all right but Chips by now was a length and a half past them. 'Not out,' the umpire ruled. We had won by one run!

Robert Scott was first on the scene. 'Wonderful! Wonderful!' he said. We picked Chips up and dusted him down. 'Are you OK?' Robert asked, pumping his hand. 'Yes, I'm all right,' Chips drawled, putting his hat on, 'but I'm never going to play this mad bloody game again.' And to my knowledge, he never did.

Acknowledgements

Acknowledgements and grateful thanks are due to the following for their interest, contributions, suggestions and help: His Royal Highness The Prince Philip, Duke of Edinburgh, KG, KT, for graciously consenting to write the Preface. His Serene Highness Prince Rainier of Monaco.

Sir Donald Bradman, AC. Sir John Leahy, KCMG, British High Commissioner in Canberra. Brigadier Clive Robertson of Prince Philip's staff. Monsieur M. Jean-Pierre Dieter of Prince Rainier's staff. Mr John McCallum, President of The Lord's Taverners Australia. Mr John Darling, Chairman of The Lord's Taverners Australia. Mr John Varley, Founder and Chief Executive of The Lord's Taverners Australia. The Rt. Hon. The Lord Boardman, Chairman, National Westminster Bank PLC; Mr David Noble and Mr Lyall Menz.

Air Vice Marshal Desmond Hall, CB, Chairman ACT branch; Mr Andrew Buckle, Chairman Victorian branch; Mr Ken Piesse, Editor of the Australian Cricketer; Mr Richie Benaud; Mr Clive W. Porter, Editor of The Cricket Society Journal, London. Dr Richard Cashman; Mr Donald Trelford, Editor of the London Observer; The Lord Callaghan, KG; Mr Henry Blofeld; Mr James Fraser of NSW; and Miss Christina Barnes of Century Hutchinson, London. Mr Patrick Collins, Mr Donald Short, Ms Sian Jones and Solo Syndication and Literary Agency, and The Mail on Sunday, London. Professor R. W. V. Elliott, Emeritus Professor of English at Australian National University, Canberra, and Member of the Australian Academy of Humanities. Mr Mike Coward, chief cricket writer of the Sydney Morning Herald.

Mr Ric Smith, Mr Jimmy Edwards, Mr Frank Tyson, Mr Desmond H. Jackson of Tasmania; Mr E. W. Swanton; Mr Michael Davie; Mr Ian Johnson; Mr Ray Jordon; Mr G. B. Martin; Mr Michael Melford; Mr Colin Webb, Managing Director of Pavilion Books, London. Mr Michael Parkinson; the directors of John Farquharson Limited, London; and Mrs Vivienne Schuster; the directors of Norman Gilier Publications, London; the Executors of the late Mr Raymond Robertson Glasgow; Ms Julie Ivelaw-Chapman of International Management Group; Mr Ralph Nodder, Syndications Manager of the London Times; Mr Simon Barnes; the directors of Michael Joseph Limited, London; The Lord Chalfont, PC.

Mr Robert Spence; Mr Martin J. Tobin; Mr Jack Pollard; Mr W. J. Woodfull; Mr Greg Burns, Treasurer of the Canberra Branch of The Lord's Taverners, Australia; Mr Dennis Castle; Ms Ann Mitchell, Captain 1967 Australian Ladies Cricket Tour; Ms Marlene Matthews; Ms Sheila Scotter; Mr Paul Sheehan; Mr David Frith, Editor, Wisden Cricket Monthly; Mr D. F. Whatmore; Rabbi David J. Goldberg of the Liberal Jewish Synagogue, St John's Wood, London; Mr Dick Brittenden; Mr Fred Trueman; Mr Brian Johnston, Dr Donald Beard, AM, QHS. The family of the late Mr Les Favell; Mr Sam Loxton; Mr Michael Muschamp; Mr Harold ('Dickie') Bird; Mr Steve Randell; Mr Ernie Wise; Mr Allan Border; the directors of Methuen Publishers, Australia; Mr Garry Lightfoot and Fairfax Publications, Australia; Mr Peter McFarline; the Executors of the late Mr Ray Robinson; Mr Greg Chappell; Sir Brian Rix; Mr Dennis Lillee; Mr Leslie Crowther; Mr W. J. ('Bill') O'Reilly; Mr C. L. R. James; Miss Grace Garlick; and the editor Sunday Mail magazine; Mr Pat Mullins; Mr Ian Ferguson; the editor, the Australian. Rothmans of Pall Mall; the editor, Daily Mirror, Australia; Mr Robin Letts; Mr Ewan ('Mick') Letts; Mr Alec V. Bedser; the directors of William Collins and Co. Ltd.; Mr Patrick Murphy; Mr John Cleese and Ms Sophie Clarke-Jervoise; Miss Margaret Hughes, Literary Executor to the estate of the late Sir Neville Cardus.

The directors of W. H. Allen PLC and Ms Yvonne Weaver of that firm; Mr Lou Rowan; Dr Richard Gordon and Mr D. Colley of Harrap, London; Mr Colin Cowdrey; Mr William Rushton; Mr Alan Davidson; Mr Frederick M. Bennett; Mr Robin Bailache; Ms Kate Fitzpatrick; Mr Frank Keating and Guardian Newspapers Ltd, London; Mr Imran Khan; Mr Andrew Neill and the editorial staff of the Sunday Times, London; Mr Christopher Martin-Jenkins, editor of The Cricketer (GB); Mr Alan McGilvray; Mr Bob Radford. Mr John Alexander, editor, and Mr Peter Allen, Ms Crystal Condus, Ms Joan Parker, Mr John Pinfold and Ms Mary McDermott, all of the Sydney Morning Herald.

The editor, Daily Telegraph, London; Mr Graham Wilkinson; Mr Austin Robertson of Austin Robertson Associates Pty. Ltd.; Mr Warwick Hadfield of the Australian; Mr Max Walker; Ms Sonia Smirnow of the Regent Hotel, Sydney; Mr Philip Derriman; the directors of Eyre and Spottiswood Ltd.; The Australian Cricket Board; New South Wales Cricket Association; Advertiser Newspapers Ltd, Adelaide, and Mr John Satterley, Editorial Manager; Ms Francesca Hobart and the directors of Collins Publishers, London; Mr Matthew Engel; Mr Jeff Wells; Mr Jack Wood; the directors of J. and K. Dent and Sons Ltd.; Mr Ian McLachlan; Mr Patrick Eagar; Mr Derek Nimmo; the editor, West Australian Newspapers Ltd.; Mr Donald D. Christie and Miss Amanda Ripley of The Cricketer (GB); Mr Robert Spence; the directors of Unwin Hyman Publishers, London; the directors of Angus & Robertson, Australia; the directors of Oxford University Press, Melbourne.

There are, of course, many others who helped me in the compilation and editing of this book — to them all, I offer my gratitude and respects. These must include Sir Frank Callaway, CMG, Emeritus Professor of Music at Western Australia University and President, The Lord's Taverners, W.A. Branch; Dr John Lill (Secretary), Mr Rex Harcourt (Librarian), Mr Bryce Thomas (Assistant Secretary) of the Melbourne Cricket Club; Ms Kerry Humphries of PBL Marketing Pty. Ltd.; Ms Liz Peddie of Weldon Trannies Library, NSW; the editor, Sydney Daily Mirror; the editor, Sydney Morning Herald; Mr Phil Wilkins of the Australian; and the trustees of the Australian National Library; the staff of the Sydney Library; Mr Harry Sorenson; Mrs Charleen Ragazzo; Mr Grahame Monaghan (WA); Mr Ken Kelly; Mr Frank Bohlsen; the Picture Editor, Central News Service, London; the editor, the Bulletin, Australia; the Chief Librarian, The Hulton Press Picture Library, London; the Governors of the BBC, London; Mr Ion Trewin, Editorial Director, Hodder and Stoughton, London; Mr Donald Sinden. Mr Adam Sisman, Mr Martin Neild, Miss Jo Stanfield of Macmillan London; the directors of The Australian Cricketer; Mrs Nina Catterns. Mr Jack Dunkley; Mr Garry Lightfoot; Mr Gary Webb; Hargreaves; Belsky; Mr Jack Broome; Mr David Langdon; Mr Willy Rushton.

Lastly, my grateful thanks go to Mr Richard Smart and Mr Michael Hast of the Macmillan Company of Australia. I offer warm thanks for their unstinted enthusiasm and guidance.

If I have inadvertently omitted thanks to others who should have been acknowledged, I tender my regrets and apologies. I should, perhaps, end by excusing myself for largely omitting honours and awards which ought to figure as deserved suffixes to the names of those who have been granted signal honours. For reasons of space, I have had to discipline myself by quoting only those in the 'highest echelons' — I feared that I might do less than justice to distinguished men and women who have been given more than I was capable of citing, especially having regard also to my ignorance of Australian governmental awards. I settled to include only KGs, KTs and ACs, with the odd PC and KCVO thrown in for good measure! I hope I shall be forgiven by those whose chests are bared by my assailable incompetence.

'Can I be a Taverner, Mister?'